A Handbook of
Play Therapy with
Aggressive Children

A Handbook of
Play Therapy with
Aggressive Children

David A. Crenshaw, Ph.D.
John B. Mordock, Ph.D.

JASON ARONSON
Lanham • Boulder • New York • Toronto • Oxford

Published in the United States of America
by Jason Aronson
An imprint of Rowman & Littlefield Publishers, Inc.

A wholly owned subsidary of
The Rowman & Littlefield Publishing Group, Inc.
4501 Forbes Boulevard, Suite 200, Lanham, Maryland 20706
www.rowmanlittlefield.com

PO Box 317
Oxford
OX2 9RU, UK

British Library Cataloguing in Publication Information Available

Library of Congress Cataloging-in-Publication Data

Crenshaw, David A.
  A handbook of play therapy with aggressive children / David A. Crenshaw, John B.
Mordock.
    p. cm.
  Includes bibliographical references and index.
  ISBN 0-7657-0031-X (cloth : alk. paper)
  1. Play therapy.   2. Aggressiveness in children—Treatment.   I. Mordock, John B.,
1938- II. Title.

  RJ505.P6C74 2005
  615.8'5153—dc22   2004019131

Printed in the United States of America

♾™   The paper used in this publication meets the minimum requirements of American
National Standard for Information Sciences—Permanence of Paper for Printed Library
Materials, ANSI/NISO Z39.48-1992.

This book is dedicated to Charles E. Schaefer, Ph.D., RPT-S, whose encouragement and support of this project are very much appreciated. Dr. Schaefer is cofounder and director emeritus of the Association for Play Therapy. He stands alone in his prolific writings on play therapy and has done groundbreaking work on the prescriptive (directive) approach to play therapy.

Contents

Figures   xv

Preface   xvii

1   Play Therapy, the Child's Expectations and Psychodynamics,
    and the Therapeutic Alliance   1

    Play Therapy   2

    The Child's Initial Expectations of Therapy   2

    The Contribution of Play Therapy   4

    Efforts to Facilitate Verbalization in Play Therapy   5

    The Psychodynamics of Gorilla-Suit Wearers   6

    The Therapeutic Alliance   10

    Difficult Alliances: Children in Gorilla Suits   12

    Three Efforts That Aid in the Formation of the Alliance   13

        Attend to Their Visible and Invisible Wounds   13

        Convey Profound Respect   15

        Highlight Their Strengths   15

    Signs of a Developing Alliance   16

    A Case Example   18

2   Aims of Play Therapy with Fawns in Gorilla Suits   21

    Increased Capacity for Sound Judgment Making   22

    Clarifying Intention and Motivation   26

    Reduction of Excessive and Unrealistic Self-Preoccupation
        and Increased Understanding of Self   27

    Developing New Perspectives   30

    Increased Understanding of the World of Feelings   31

Increased Understanding of Choices and Consequences   32

Fortification of Weak Defenses and Easing of Rigid Defenses   33

Stronger Relationships with Caregivers   33

Finding Meaning and Coherence   33

Facilitating a Vision of a More Hopeful Future   34

Countertransference Feeling Can Aid Treatment   34

3   Setting Limits on Destructive and Controlling Behaviors   36

Limit Therapy to the Therapy Room   36

Limit Destructive Behaviors   37

Silent Limits   41

Humorous Limits   41

Limit Controlling Behaviors   42

Limit Physical Involvement   45

What Limits Achieve   48

4   Setting Limits on Other Obtrusive Behavior   49

Limit Efforts to Anger   49

Limit Seductiveness   50

Limit Projections   51

Limit Unproductive Play   51

Limit Dilution of the Therapy Relationship   52

Limit Undisciplined Behavior outside Therapy   53

Limit Comparisons with Other Therapists   55

Limiting Perseveration   56

Limiting Institutional Practices That Distract from
the Total Treatment Program   57

Limits Are Not Forever   58

Limits Set in Later Phases of Therapy   59

Limit Defiance, Both Obvious and Disguised   59

Limit Adoption Fantasies   60

5   A Decision Grid for Play Therapy   62

The Invitational Approach   65

The Coping Approach   70

Differential Decision Making   75

Switching Approaches in Midstream   75

Therapeutic Expectations   77

Orientation to a Positive Future   78

6   Typical Play Themes of Fawns in Gorilla Suits   79

    Control, Dominance, and Power   79

    Threat   81

    Abandonment and Rejection   82

    Separation and Loss   84

    Guilt and Shame: The Need for Punishment   85

    Deprivation   86

    Need for Nurturance   88

    Symbols of Healing: Caring for the Wounded
      and Fixing Broken Things   89

7   Developing Distancing and Displacement through Playful Actions   91

    Clay   93

    Harmless Destruction!   94

    Reaming Them Out!   95

    Knocking Down the Walls of Anger!   95

    The Mad Game   96

    The Anger Bucket!   96

    Having a Field Day with Magic Markers!   97

    The Anger Balloon   97

    Drawing Strategies   98

        Volcano Pictures   99

        Storm Pictures   103

        Fire-Breathing Dragons   103

        Anger Thermometer   105

    Encouraging Communication of Violent Fantasies   107

    Conclusion   109

8   Developing Displacement and Distancing by Teaching, Modeling,
    and Structuring Action Play   111

    Getting at Preverbal Concepts   115

    Structuring Memory   115

    Development of Displacement and Distancing   117

    Playroom Toys   121

        The Fair Trial   123

        Rage toward Others and toward Victims   124

9   Creating More Mature Defenses and Calming Strategies   126

    Developing and Supporting Defenses   127

	Splitting	128
	Binding and Compartmentalization	129
	Dissociation	131
	Grandiosity	131
	Negativism	131
	Development of the More Mature Defenses	132
	Encouraging Sublimation and Reaction Formation	134
	Calming Activities	135
	Rewarding Mature Defenses	138
	When to Begin to Interpret Defenses	139
	Conclusion	139
10	The Role of Interpretation: Elementary Concepts	141
	Empathetic Interpretations	143
	Dynamic Interpretations	144
	Preparation	145
	Attention Statements	145
	Reductive Statements	146
	Situational Statements	147
	Interpretation of Defenses	148
	Step-by-Step Progression	150
	Interpretation within the Metaphor	151
	Wording the Interpretation	152
	Conclusion	155
11	Making Interpretations: Advanced Concepts	156
	Seven Stages	156
	Session 23: Interpretation and Response	157
	Sessions 24 and 25: Working Through	158
	Session 26: Insight	159
	Generalization, Externalization, and Projective Identification	160
	Transference Interpretations	163
	Interpretation of Wishes	166
	Conclusion	168
12	Windows into the Inner World: Spontaneous Drawings as a Bridge to Fantasy Play	169
13	Windows into the Inner World: Specific Drawing Techniques	176
	Boat in the Storm	177
	Family Doing Something Together	183
	A Safe Place	187

Color Your Life   189

The Magic Key   193

Your Place   196

Draw the Problem   198

Draw the Worst Experience of Your Life   200

14 Teaching and Modeling Pro-Social Skills with
    Special Emphasis on Empathy   204

Becoming More "Likable"   205

Appropriate Self-Assertion   205

The Importance of Empathy   207

The Empathy Picture and Story Series   207

Film Clips   211

Empathy Practice Scenarios   211

Empathy for the Healer   215

15 Teaching the Language of Feelings   217

Basket of Feelings   218

Gingerbread Person/Feelings Map   221

Affect Recognition Pictures and Stories   223

Feelings Charades   229

16 Facilitating Affect Expression and Modulation   230

Empowerment Play   231

Psychodrama   233

Garbage Bag Technique   233

A Cautionary Note about Timing and Pacing   234

17 Facilitating Contained Reenactment of Trauma   236

Why Undertake Trauma Work?   237

The Meaning Given to the Experience   238

Secondary Trauma: The Silent Bond   239

Intervening in Posttraumatic Play   240

Crucial Cues from the Child   241

Reflections of Affect and Motives   245

An Illustrative Case   246

Enactment of Trauma as a Result
of Unpredictable Triggering   252

Dynamic Flexibility and Titrating the Approach   254

18 Helping Children to Mourn Tangible Losses   255

Children Grieve in Steps   256

Treatment over Time   257

Acknowledged Losses   258

Dramatic Play and Tangible Losses   261

Structured Activities to Help Express Tangible Losses   262

  Memory Book or Album   262

  Poems, Songs, and Journal Writing   263

  Photographs and "Linking Objects"   263

  Reliving Funerals and Memorial Services   264

  Family Therapy Sessions   265

19 Helping Children to Grieve Unacknowledged, Intangible,
    and Invisible Losses   267

  Denial of Loss   267

    Conflicted Relationships and Loss   270

    Insecure Attachments   272

    Divorce and Loss   273

    Finding New Meaning and Shaping a Narrative Memory   275

    Shaping a New Perspective   275

  Structured Activities to Access Feelings Associated with
  Intangible Losses   275

    Structured Drawings   275

    Re-Create the World   277

    Two Memory Books   277

    Evocative Aids: Color-Coded Time Line   278

    Evocative Aids: Selected Video Clips   281

  Conclusion   282

20 The Process   283

  The First Stage: Anxiety Management   284

    Session 1   284

    Sessions 2 and 3   285

    Session 4   285

    Later Sessions   286

    Revelations in the First Session   286

    Violent Play and Identification with the Aggressor   287

  The Second Stage: Conflict Resolution   289

  Increased Negativism   290

  The Third Stage: Productive Play   293

    The Reemergence of Anger and Chaos   296

    The Struggle with Confusing Parental Ties   297

The Fourth Phase: Counseling about Present Concerns   297

The Last Phase: Termination   298

21   Ending Therapy   299

The Process of Ending Therapy   302

Prior Losses Revisited   303

Rehearsals for Ending   304

Specific Techniques for Preparing the Child for Termination   305

The Talk Show Interview   306

The Year Book   306

Jose and Pete on the Mountain   307

Expanding the Circle of Trust   307

The Countdown to Termination   308

Planning Together the Final Sessions   309

One Final Conversation about Words Unspoken   309

Some Concluding Remarks   309

Jose and Pete on the Mountain   310

Bibliography   315

Index   327

About the Authors   337

Figures

5.1   Decision Grid   64

7.1   Volcano Picture   100

7.2   Volcano Picture   102

7.3   Storm Picture   104

7.4   Dragon Picture   106

9.1   The Strong Container Drawing   130

9.2   Grandparents' Farm: Calming Scene   137

13.1, 13.2, and 13.3   Boat in Storm Serial Drawings   178, 179, 180

13.4   Boat in Storm Drawing   181

13.5   Family Doing Something Drawing   185

13.6   Safe Place Drawing   188

13.7   Color Your Life Drawing   191

13.8   The Magic Key Drawing   195

13.9   Your Place Drawing   197

13.10   Draw the Problem   199

13.11   Worst Experience Drawing   201

14.1, 14.2, and 14.3   Empathy Picture and

                       Drawing Series   208, 209, 210

15.1   Gingerbread Person   222

15.2   Gingerbread Person   224

15.3   Gingerbread Person [related to father's drinking]   225

15.4   Feelings Map [reflecting split down middle]   226

15.5 and 15.6   Affect Recognition and Story Series   227, 228

19.1   Color-Coded Time Line   279

Preface

$\mathcal{A}$lthough beginning play therapists will find this handbook helpful, it was not written with this audience in mind. This handbook does not discuss the basic principles of play therapy or review the major theoretical notions of child development and personality theory on which play therapies rest. Readers unfamiliar with goals of interviewing, empathic focusing, principles of communication, the functions of children's play, the purposes of specific play materials, or how to structure initial interviews should read a basic book on play therapy or one on interviewing children. Two books by Dr. Mordock present these fundamentals—*Crisis Counseling of Children and Adolescents: A Guide for the Nonprofessional* (expanded edition) (2002), written with William Van Ornum, and *Counseling the Defiant Child: A Basic Guide to Helping Troubled and Aggressive Youth* (1998); some of the more complex topics related to play therapy in both books have been updated, revised, and included in this handbook.

Readers may wish to consult our companion volume, *Understanding and Treating the Aggression of Children: Fawns in Gorilla Suits*, if they are unfamiliar with the roots of aggressive behavior; special problems in treating traumatized children, especially the sexually abused; treatment of children in foster families; development of defenses; ways of strengthening relationships with natural parents, educators, and direct-care staff; methods of creating therapeutic milieus; new directions in treating aggressive children; and ways to foster hope and facilitate resilience.

Because a major focus of therapy with fawns in gorilla suits is helping them to deal with loss, readers unfamiliar with the concepts of grief and mourning can read sections of Dr. Crenshaw's book, *Bereavement: Counseling the Grieving throughout the Life Cycle* (2002). Those unfamiliar with treatment planning can read Dr. Mordock's book, *Selecting Treatment Interventions* (1999a). Those needing more background in developmental concepts are encouraged to read the references we have cited related to the topics in both volumes. Additional practical techniques are described in Dr. Crenshaw's *Guidebook to Engaging Resistant Children in Therapy: A Projective Drawing and Storytelling Series* (2004).

Most treatment handbooks are edited works by many authors. Nevertheless, we chose to call this book a "handbook" because we believe that each chapter stands alone. For example, the reader familiar with the aims of therapy for children wearing gorilla suits can read any chapter in the book without having to read chapter 3, which is devoted to that topic. To avoid duplication, references are listed alphabetically at the end of the book rather than at the end of each chapter.

Earlier versions of some of the material, including case material, appeared in the following professional journals and books: *Journal of Clinical Psychiatry and Human Development, The International Journal of Play Therapy, Residential Treatment for Children and Youth, Children in Residential Care: Clinical Issues in Treatment, Counseling the Defiant Child, Crisis Counseling of Children and Adolescents,* and *The Counselor's Source Book.*

Play Therapy, the Child's Expectations and Psychodynamics, and the Therapeutic Alliance

The reasons are presented for selecting play therapy as the initial treatment modality to employ with aggressive children. The child's initial expectations of therapy are contrasted with others' expectations. Verbal versus nonverbal approaches to play therapy are compared. The child's developmental difficulties are anchored in Erik Erikson's stages in the life cycle. The chapter concludes with a discussion of the therapeutic alliance.

*I*n *Understanding and Treating the Aggression of Children*, we present our rationale for the metaphor of children in gorilla suits. The children, under certain conditions, behave aggressively and, in extreme cases, violently, sometimes inflicting serious bodily harm on others. The children's aggression protects a vulnerable sense of self. The gorilla suits mask their fears and emotional scars. The suit comes off and the true essence of the child is revealed only after patient and persistent efforts by caring adults to earn the child's trust and thereby connect with the disconnected.

The gorilla suits will not be taken off even partially unless the children become convinced that they are safe and can no longer be hurt. To convince children who have been betrayed by adults, who never established a sense of security, or whose security has been badly shattered is an extraordinary task—a task that takes place only with considerable testing and retesting of the adult's sincerity, trustworthiness, and commitment. Along the way are discouraging setbacks. Many would-be helpers and caregivers fail to pass the relentless tests because, in order to protect what's left of their wounded spirits and dignity, the children set the bar extremely high. Nevertheless, a part of each child secretly hopes the adults persist and ultimately succeed in their efforts to navigate the obstacle course created to discourage those very efforts. This ongoing conflict goes hand in hand with bonds of trust that have been established, and therefore the bonds are subject to being severed abruptly on even the slightest perceived breach of trust. Frequently, the fragile bonds are threatened by cognitive distortions resulting from the children's hypervigilant perceptual states. The children are always on guard, constantly scanning their environment for cues of threat, and frequently misperceiving the intentions and well-meaning actions of adults.

PLAY THERAPY

Play therapy is often the initial treatment of choice for chronically maltreated children, a choice we review in *Understanding and Treating the Aggression of Children*. In summary, play therapy is used initially because the family sees the child as the problem. To insist initially that the family redefine the child's problem as a family problem is to confront the family before groundwork has been laid for the family to accept this notion. The result will be withdrawal from treatment. Many children in gorilla suits live with single parents. Seeing the single parent and child together is often unproductive because the tension between the two cannot be diluted by the therapist's asking for opinions of other family members. The children cannot get enough distance between themselves and their problems to handle the anxiety that joint discussion with a single parent often produces.

Whenever possible, natural parents should be involved in their child's treatment. Typically the parents are controlled or manipulated by the child, which aggravates already strained relationships. A child can control adults by making them exert controls. Children have been known to say, "If I can't be the best, I might as well be the worst!" The parents need help to cope with their child's disruptive and defiant behavior. Parents who display immature behavior because of their own unmet needs, which characterizes the parents of many gorilla-suit wearers, may require an individual relationship with the therapist before they can learn to appropriately respond to their children. We present our approach to treating parents in *Understanding and Treating the Aggression of Children*.

THE CHILD'S INITIAL EXPECTATIONS OF THERAPY

The prepubertal child, on whom this handbook focuses, is unwilling to experience conflict as coming from within. Most children never express their worries to parents or other adults, but gorilla-suit wearers, although they may complain about others, are more silent about themselves than is typical of any other group. Adult caregivers complain, "Maybe you can find out what's troubling him; goodness knows I've tried," failing to appreciate that even well-adjusted children rarely observe their own behavior, moreover the happenings in their own minds. The latency-age child's natural inquisitiveness is directed away from the inner world to the outer world. Only at puberty do self-examination and introspection become possible, and then they are both carried to the absurd. The child tends to externalize internal conflicts. Only after identifying with caregivers who are reflective and self-examining, as well as capable of accepting blame, will the child develop the same traits. Not only are the gorilla-suit wearers unable to identify with reflective and thoughtful adults, but their hostile feelings experienced after parental rebukes are displaced, externalized, and projected onto others in the external world, including the therapist. These others then become the persecutors or seducers with whom the suit wearer must forever do battle.

This tendency to externalize internal conflicts influences the children's expectations of treatment. None expect to be working toward the goals set by the therapist. Bonime (1985) notes that clients typically enter treatment seeking relief from the consequences of their unhealthy personality traits rather than a change in their personality functioning. The child hopes the therapist, through superior powers, will change the environment for the better. The girl who hates and fears her teacher expects help by a change in class. The girl does not expect or want the therapist to help her realize that she wants to change teachers to obtain relief from guilt feelings. The boy who expects the therapist to remove him from bullying classmates does not expect to receive help to realize his own passive, self-punitive inclinations. In short, the therapist is expected to approve of and to aid the child to gratify infantile demands. When the therapist refuses to accept this role, he or she soon becomes, in the child's view, an adversary rather than a helper. Children are not alone in their unrealistic expectations of treatment. As Mitchel (1993) observes:

> The hope that the patient brings to the analysis and the hope that drives the motion of the work (including the analyst's hope) are always partially "hope for the wrong thing." The patient's initial hopes are always a complex blend of wishes and needs, hopes fashioned from pain, frustration, longing, laced with restoration, magical transformation, and retribution. According to the Greek myth, Zeus put hope in the very bottom of Pandora's box, beneath greed, vanity, slander, envy, and the other dark realms of human experience. Sometimes, hope for the right thing can be reached only through an immersion in prolonged and harrowing dread. (p. 228)

The lack of introspection that characterizes childhood is employed as a protection against mental suffering. Only when the child can identify with a trusted adult and, therefore, form an alliance with the adult can the denial of conflicts be given up and replaced by more honest views of internal discomforts. When children do speak, they speak primarily of the present. They don't expect to speak of past or even of present thoughts that have been kept secret for a long time. They have little interest in gaining insight into cumulative patterns of behavior or into their precursors. In the therapist's favor, however, is unconscious pressure to reveal preoccupations through actions, play, or playful acts. But many gorilla-suit wearers do not reveal their preoccupations through make-believe play. Fantasy behavior is play-action, and many children's play has never developed to that level. At best, they discharge their feelings through action-play or, at worst, through action only. Instead of banging two toy trucks together, they bang themselves into other children, and fights ensue. If they have escaped traumatic situations by running, they don't create a play scene of an escaping child; instead they run all over the place when experiencing screen memories of the traumatic event.

Play therapy with such children involves a long preparation period, during which the children are taught to play after first limiting their impulse to action. Play therapists who take children outside or to a gym and let them shoot baskets or play gross motor games (and both of us have known many therapists who do so) are actually encouraging action rather than discouraging it. The children need to replace action, first with action play, later with play actions, and finally with structured fantasy.

THE CONTRIBUTION OF PLAY THERAPY

Most gorilla-suit wearers are candidates for play therapy because they suffer from firmly entrenched intrapsychic conflicts and poorly integrated responses to trauma. Usually they display repetitive patterns of maladaptive responses to stress that transcend the specifics of the current family situation. The children need to develop trust in their good impulses and the ability to control or mitigate their bad or aggressive impulses. They also need to learn that prohibitions can be protective rather than punitive or humiliating. Some parents are unable to perform this function when continually faced with their child's misbehavior.

While children initially resist the idea of therapy, play therapy can be disarming because play is the child's natural mode of expression and communication. The play material selected allows healing through the metaphoric images of play or drawings. Direct verbalization is more difficult, if not impossible, especially about painful events. In addition, the pace and tempo of the play can be set by the child. Play empowers children to gradually risk disclosure of threatening and anxiety-laden issues. Traumatized children can regulate the distance needed to feel safe in their play scenarios. Their distance from painful issues varies not only from session to session but within a given session. The variability is driven by the child's anxiety level and the triggering of memories that produce affects at different levels of intensity. Children can explore their repressed reactions to horrific past experiences, provided their present isn't equally horrific. Play therapy is of little value if the child remains in a hostile, abusive environment. But if the child is not still in that environment, play therapy plays an important role in the child's initial treatment plan. Topics can be addressed that children dare not mention at home for fear of angering, and perhaps even losing, the only caregivers they know. Many children need a period of charitable, sensitive, and sophisticated listening that only play therapy can provide.

Children also use the therapeutic relationship to test out and, we hope, discard old, internalized images of self and self in relation to others. The play therapy relationship is used to build new and positive images of self and of intimate relationships that will enable more adaptive and constructive behavior. A skilled play therapist is comfortable with a wide range of affect yet stands ready to intervene when a child begins to feel overwhelmed. The therapist's interventions help to modulate the child's expression of emotions. The child grows confident when boundaries necessary for safe expression of emotions have been established, including a restriction, not only on aggressive and dangerous behavior, but also on attempts to eroticize the therapeutic context, a topic discussed in chapter 6 of *Understanding and Treating the Aggression of Children* and in connection with limit setting in chapter 4 of this volume. As the therapeutic relationship grows, as therapy progresses from expression of diffuse anxiety to expression of more specific anxiety, and as anxiety-laden topics and scenarios surface, the child begins to face the "really hard stuff" related to early traumas.

EFFORTS TO FACILITATE VERBALIZATION IN PLAY THERAPY

A number of play therapists stress efforts to get reluctant talkers to verbalize. They employ play materials to occupy the defensive child while efforts are made to increase the child's verbalizations. The therapist talks casually with the child as play proceeds, asking about favorite movies, foods, sports heroes, and similar topics, and when the child becomes comfortable taking with the therapist, topics distantly related to the core problem are introduced with comments such as "I understand you have some problems sleeping at night" (a question that can be used to get children to relate or draw dreams or to act them out in play). Some play therapists introduce specific toys designed to stimulate the child to talk about problems, such as a small playhouse with a large bathroom, introduced to help the child talk about bed-wetting. Bed-wetting is not just a problem of the neurotic child. Bed-wetting occurred in about 80 percent of the children in the residential center in which both of us worked. In most cases, it was a symptom of missing home. Nevertheless, the topic was rarely addressed in therapy because the symptom disappeared when the children made progress in treatment.

While we often talk while the children play, we rarely expect the voiceless gorilla-suit wearer to respond in kind. Children whose inner and outer realities are confused, who are impulse-ridden, and who are seriously disorganized by their own strong feelings are unable to respond to problem-focused discussions. Their therapy is designed to help them gain self-control and control over their immediate environment. The child's talking about worries may contribute to gaining control, but other behaviors can be just as helpful. While the play therapist may engage in numerous monologues during the course of treatment, the monologues are efforts to clarify the child's feelings, explain the feelings of others, including the therapist's, or correct perceptual or cognitive distortions. The child isn't necessarily expected to reply verbally. Often, responses to the therapist's efforts are revealed in actions or in play displayed a number of sessions later. (Dr. Crenshaw [2004] has developed, however, an original projective drawing and storytelling series to facilitate meaningful verbal dialogue with resistant children. Before we discuss the specific aims of therapy with gorilla-suit wearers (see the next chapter), the concept of the therapeutic alliance needs to be understood.

THE PSYCHODYNAMICS OF GORILLA-SUIT WEARERS

In *Understanding and Treating the Aggression of Children*, we review the basic psychodynamics of children who habitually respond to frustration with aggression, and we include empirical evidence in support of our therapeutic approach. Most gorilla-suit wearers have been poorly socialized. Many have been neglected by parents consumed with meeting basic survival needs. Others have been neglected because their parents are physically ill, depressed, or consumed by substance abuse. Still others have been neglected and abused because they were rejected by their natural parents. As a result, few have been able to master the developmental tasks of early childhood. An encapsulated view of their problems, embedded in Erik Erikson's notions (1963) of human development, follows:

Children neglected from birth never master Erikson's first nuclear conflict of *trust versus mistrust*. Children who move forward with a basic sense of trust in others do so with a sense of solid identity that evolves into a sense of being "all right," right with oneself. Already weakened by distrustfulness and disconnectedness, the child is denied the gradual and well-guided experience of making choices. As a child learns to "stand on his own two feet," protection from experiences of shame and self-doubt need to be provided. If not, then the child never resolves Erikson's second major developmental stage of *autonomy versus shame and doubt*. As a result, the child gains power by stubborn control over minute portions of life. Too much shaming leads to, at best, a determination to get away with things or, at worst, defiant shamelessness. Doubt is the brother of shame. Doubt comes from the pervasive feeling that nothing can ever be accomplished: "I can never do anything right" or "I can't do that."

During the stage of *autonomy versus shame and doubt*, the child unconsciously decides how much to cooperate and how much to resist, as well as how much to express and how much to repress. The child who feels control over life develops feelings of goodwill and pride. The child who feels controlled develops a propensity for doubt and shame. When a child moves into the stage of *initiative versus guilt* without having mastered the earlier two stages, failures cannot be forgotten quickly. True initiative does not develop. Problems cannot be attacked playfully with zest and enthusiasm. Lacking initiative, many fail the early grades in school or, if physically larger than their peers, are socially promoted or referred for special education. The child arrested at this stage of development feels the need for aggressive powers to cope with his sense of unsafety, pseudoautonomy, and sense of aloneness. The longing for a reunion with caregivers is now blunted by a need to save face. This need leads to overt defiance of external directions and control and, even worse, to efforts at revenge. Because of repeated humiliations in a dependency relationship, the child becomes entrenched in a state of pseudoindependence, which includes a self-image as a bad child. In reaction to anxiety about the self-image, self-willed protests of independence and defiance occur. Because wishes remain like those of a younger child, a primitive sense of guilt develops over the wishes.

Erikson's next stage is *industry versus inferiority*. Nevertheless, Blatt and Blass (1990), based on Bowlby's work (1969–1973) on attachment and on the British school of object relations (Fairbairn 1963; Winnicott 1958), have interposed, between *initiative versus guilt* and *industry versus inferiority*, a stage they call *mutuality versus alienation*. In this stage, because of the human capacity to form stable, enduring, and mutually satisfying interpersonal relationships, the child normally bonds with others. If mutually satisfying relationships have not developed, then the child becomes alienated from others; in other words, instead of experiencing gratifying involvement, the child experiences isolating alienation. The bonded child expands the self system to include a "we" dimension: the self is experienced with the other or the "we," and empathy becomes highly developed. Feelings about the self that arise within relationships gradually become internalized aspects of the self, and "relatedness" becomes a major dimension by which developmental process is measured. Gorilla-suit wearers almost never master this stage, and their alienation underlies much of their rage.

In the stage of *industry versus inferiority*, the child begins to experiment with the utensils, tools, and even the weapons utilized by big people. The child's anger at this stage lies in feeling inadequate and inferior. If the child loses hope of participating in the "industrial" world, he or she will remain fixed in earlier worlds, feeling doomed to mediocrity or inadequacy. "What's the use. No matter what I do, it's never right." Failure in school escalates as the academic tasks become more challenging, and special education becomes a "holding tank" rather than a place for progress. Several sentences written by Demos (1983) serve as a summary to this section.

> If the self is understood as an organizing structure, then it too probably consists of a combination of affective and cognitive components that have formed on the basis of at least the following three aspects of experience: judgments of one's competence versus incompetence; trust in one's inner states versus mistrust; and judgments of one's relatedness to others versus one's isolation. . . . To the extent that the self is experienced as relatively competent, trustworthy, and related, positive self-esteem can be maintained. (p. 47)

Many of the early books on play therapy present vignettes of play behaviors that can be easily understood by the reader. A bed-wetter spanks a doll for wetting her pants. An anxious, fearful child hides toys in the playroom. A child spoon-feeds a baby doll so roughly that the baby chokes. In contrast, the play of many gorilla-suit wearers, when they can play, is usually disorganized and interrupted. Therapist confusion and the child's increased anxiety are all that usually result when it is first attempted.

Because the child's development was chaotic, play therapy will also appear chaotic. The therapist who is not confused by the child's behavior is practicing self-deception. Such therapists are likely to be those who make wild interpretations. When in doubt, silence is best. We like to think of the initial stages of play therapy as similar to two records playing at two different speeds. The therapist plays at one speed, and the child plays at another. Eventually, the therapist recognizes the song that the child's record is playing (although the child often switches records) and modifies the speed of his or her record to accommodate the child's. Gradually, they play parts of the same record, and finally they both listen to the same record at a speed at which the song is easily recognized. Witness the following verbalizations of one child:

> CHILD: Bang it, it still works, beetle juice [*puts his hand over his mouth*] stop it [*in clipped speech*] damn, damn, damn, bad word today, hope you're not mad at me. Okay, now read a book [*babbles*].

The therapist can speculate that the child has gone from anxiety to anger, but that is about all that is revealed. With time, the therapist may figure out what the contents of this communication mean, but in the meantime the therapist is as confused as the child is anxious. Witness the rapid changes in the next child, a seven-year-old boy:

> CHILD: [*Writes "doll" on colored paper to make stop signs. He then starts to cut his hair with the scissors and then stops.*] I don't know what to make, I'm finished. [*Gets a stick, stops, and asks for scissors to cut the hair on the doll.*]
> THERAPIST: The doll's hair is not for cutting.
> CHILD: [*Gets the alligator puppet.*] This is the alligator that bites kids who do things bad. The alligator is going to attack you.
> THERAPIST: The alligator can attack the dummy and pretend it's me.
> CHILD: No, I'll throw sand at you.
> THERAPIST: You sure are sharing all the bad things you feel today.
> CHILD: I'll erase the blackboard for you.
> THERAPIST: Thank you.
> CHILD: Oh, shut up, or I'll throw this at you.

The therapist speculates that the child feels inner pressure to express an unacceptable impulse. The boy starts to make a stop sign in an effort to "stop" the impulse's expression. But the thought seems as bad as the action, so the child attempts to punish himself by cutting the doll's hair (Are there sexual thoughts and corresponding guilt?). But the thought of self-punishment also raises his anxiety. Does he express his punishment symbolically by cutting his hair? When forbidden, he now gets the alligator who "bites bad kids" (Is this another sign of guilt or fear of bodily harm?). This, too, causes anxiety, so he regresses to attacking the therapist (Children typically hold adults responsible for their troubles), or he attacks the therapist in hopes of getting punished and thereby avoiding self-criticism. He then attempts to undo this attack by doing a good deed—cleaning the blackboard.

While all this was taking place, the therapist was not sure what was happening. Only by reflecting on the sequence, in the quiet of an office, can a therapist make a possible reconstruction of what might have been going on. This reconstruction is kept in mind for the next time the therapist witnesses similar behavior. If the child again wants to cut his or the doll's hair, the therapist can respond by giving the child an acceptable substitute and commenting, "For some reason you seem to want to punish yourself for some bad thoughts you may have."

On other occasions, the child's fantasy makes sense only when it is related to some recent environmental event. For example, a child reports a daydream of "a rich man who has lots of things. A boy takes them and hides them in a tree. The man bumps into the tree, and his stolen items fall out at his feet." While this approximates a punishment fantasy that suggests underlying guilt, the story is immediately understood when the therapist discovers that the boy had taken a toy from the therapy room at the end of the preceding session.

When children gain an awareness of and tolerance for their inner emotional needs, they feel better about themselves.

> THERAPIST: The voice telling you to do things is really the anger you feel that you often hate feeling. If it comes from outside you, you can own it. Remember when we talked about "Mr. Angry?" Now Mr. Angry has become so strong that you've put him outside of yourself and have him actually talking to you. I'll bet that's really scary.

When helping a child develop play actions or when exploring primitive fantasies, the therapist is always walking a thin line. Talking about feelings or exploring action fantasies can lead to action. It is no easy task to help the action-oriented child develop delay mechanisms. Although a therapist's comment to an upset child expresses a wish to understand, the child immersed in upsetness is struggling to become free of discomfort. Like an animal that has been hurt, the child is apt to bite the helping hand. Dr. Crenshaw (the first-listed author of this book) remembers when he was a boy and tried with his grandfather to free a fawn whose hind legs were caught in a fence on his grandparents' farm. "We finally freed the fawn, but not before the two of us were severely bloodied by the razor-sharp hooves of the panic-stricken fawn." At the height of distress, the fawn or the child in a gorilla suit doesn't recognize the good intentions of helpers. As with most children in gorilla suits, the fawn's aggression was driven by abject fear, if not terror. The experience was an early lesson in how challenging it can be to help a fawn in a gorilla suit (Crenshaw 2004).

THE THERAPEUTIC ALLIANCE

A chief task of psychotherapy with a client of any age is to help the client form an alliance with the therapist. The concept of the therapeutic alliance is not just a vague concept but a theoretical construct that has been made operational and subjected to numerous investigations (Ackerman and Hilsenroth 2003). In fact, some therapists believe, in the present quick-fix environment of managed care, that therapists who display its chief component, empathy, may be an endangered species (Bennett 2001). In any case, both clinical experience and empirical research have demonstrated that establishing a therapeutic alliance with aggressive and distant clients is a difficult task (Saunders 2001). Only after an alliance has been formed, however, can a client engage in meaningful therapy in which feelings are thought about and talked about, or in the case of children, played out, and emotions are experienced and worked through.

The term *alliance* designates a state of functioning in which one part of the client's self is able to look at, listen to, feel, and even analyze another part of the self. The therapist becomes an ally of the client's observing, "split-off" self. The client's observing part is the more autonomous, adaptive part of the self whereas the observed portion contains the painful, conflicted parts.

The therapist first helps the client to handle the strong feelings that are elicited by treatment, to synthesize data received from within and from outside the self, and to perceive the therapist as a helper. This is not easy when treating a child, primarily because of the child's propensity for action rather than reflection. But the playful context of child therapy, accompanied by the benevolent strength of the therapist, helps the child to form a therapeutic alliance. Forming an alliance with a gorilla-suit wearer, who rarely, if ever, engages in self-reflection and who rarely enjoys play, can be difficult, but it can be done. It cannot, however, be hurried. Although this handbook contains numerous examples of a therapist's putting a child's worries into words (defined in chapter 10 as clarifications and interpretations), such actions by themselves do not produce change. In fact, in the zeal for helping a child, a therapist may put a child's worries into words before the child can handle such awareness. If this happens only on occasion, the alliance will take longer to form. If it happens regularly, the alliance will never form. Fortunately, the initial play behavior of gorilla-suit wearers is so confusing that it rarely lends itself to interpretation. *Attention statements* are about all that can be made (see chapter 10).

The alliance forms as the therapist accepts whatever material the child brings into each treatment session. Tactfully, the therapist interprets the defenses the child displays when he or she is anxious and verbalizes the affects contained in words and behavior (see chapter 10). The wishes and needs the child reveals through actions, play, or dreams are left untouched until an alliance is securely formed. For example, a thirteen-year-old boy, whose emotional age was about five, told his therapist the following dream:

> CHILD: Last night—you know the star of *Ghostbusters*, Bill Murray?—in my dream my mother was mad at Murray, and he challenged her to a race

in his car, except he is a tricky guy, and he drove his car along a road that led to a cliff, except that Murray knew that his car was on the side of the road where, when he went over, he would land in the water. My mother's car was on the side that would land on the rocks. When I went down to the rocks, my mother's head was missing, and it was weird. Her body was like it had been zipped down the middle, but there were no blood or guts, only veins, like in a biology book.

THERAPIST: That was a scary dream, but remember, it was only a dream.

The boy acted like a buffoon, displaying clowning, clumsy, passive-aggressive behavior. Yet the therapist felt the boy was not yet ready to accept either his identification with Bill Murray, who plays inept characters in his movie roles, or with his thinly veiled hostility toward his mother. If the boy interprets his own dream along this line, with no apparent anxiety, then that is fine, but beneath his hostility is an even deeper concern. From other material, the therapist is aware that the boy is cut off from his feelings. He thinks (he is "heady") rather than feels and has denied sexual interests. In the dream, his mother is headless, and her dead body is without substance, without sexual parts. But he was not ready to deal with his sexual feelings until a solid alliance had been formed. Later, after an alliance has been formed, the boy will be asked about his dreams. In fact, it is rare for children to bring up their dreams; most need to be asked about them directly (Ablon and Mack 1980).

DIFFICULT ALLIANCES: CHILDREN IN GORILLA SUITS

Children with severe behavior disorders stemming from marked parental-child conflict, conflict that has existed from the child's first "no," are the most difficult children with whom to form an alliance. Their disruptive behavior is a vital extension of their self-concept. Their lying, stealing, extreme noncompliance, and other antisocial acts are their way of handling both their anxiety and their emerging impulses. Overwhelming stresses are mastered by doing to others what has been done to them (identification with the perceived power and the tactics of the aggressor). Antisocial behaviors have been adopted to combat overwhelming feelings of helplessness and rejection.

These antisocial behavior patterns prevent the split in the self necessary for self-observation. To observe their own helplessness and despair, to become painfully self-aware, is avoided at all costs. Action and gross motor activities are the only outlets for feelings. Rarely are they in touch with their positive feelings for others. They may like adults when the adults meet their needs but hate those adults when they frustrate the children's needs. For a child to remain in touch with affectionate feelings for another person when that person frustrates the child requires a bond with a loving adult or the memory of such a bond. Many of these children never had such a bond, or if they did, it is long forgotten.

Gorilla-suit wearers constantly bombard the therapist with their hostile, attacking defenses, often eliciting urges to retaliate. The child ignores comments by the therapist such as "You attack me because you have been repeatedly attacked" or "Underneath the rough exterior, your gorilla suit, you actually crave love and attention." Sometimes such comments actually escalate anger. But the observing part of the therapist's self, and the failure to counterattack, presents a consistent model for the child to observe and with which to identify. Suit wearers who are narcissistic and who use grandiosity as their chief defense can quickly tire therapists who resent having to continually admire the child's empty achievements. But if countertransference feelings are managed properly, and the therapist can remain patient in the midst of either bombardment or boredom, the alliance will progress. When the child wants to be like the therapist, he or she will form an alliance and examine self-defeating behavior. A firm stance, illustrated in chapters 3 and 4, on limit setting serves as the turning point in the child's therapy. Considerable work with aggressive children involves preparing them for what others would call therapy. It takes a long time for such children to become aware of their problems, much less to talk to someone about them.

THREE EFFORTS THAT AID IN THE FORMATION OF THE ALLIANCE

Since gorilla-suit wearers receive so little recognition of their invisible wounds, discussed in chapter 2 of *Understanding and Treating the Aggression of Children*, these wounds need to be approached with care, respect, and sensitivity. Their repeated experiences with devaluation make them suspicious of treatment. Hardy (2003) emphasizes three factors that are especially important in the early stages of treating aggressive children: (1) attend to their invisible wounds, (2) convey profound respect, and (3) highlight their strengths. If these factors are addressed, the child will gradually form an alliance with the therapist.

Attend to Their Visible and Invisible Wounds

If a severely abused child takes off his shirt to reveal the scars on his back or rolls up his sleeve to reveal the burn marks on his upper arm, adults are deeply moved. But if a child has lost hope and feels deeply shamed and humiliated, no one may notice. The child may be viewed simply as an aggressive child who needs punishment. We have been confronted innumerable times by adults who state, "That child needs a good spanking," yet the records of almost all aggressive children reflect the harsh physical punishment they received from parents. In fact, the more they were aggressive, the more severe the punishments they received, but they responded to these punishments with even higher levels of aggression. Their lives became a kind of war based on the principle that "the harder the enemy fights, the harder we will fight." Underneath each gorilla suit is a deeply hurt and wounded child with a crushed spirit. Looking beyond the child's ugly aggression, however, is a difficult task. Those who dare to do so will see a child with a wounded spirit. An entry into the child's invisible pains often occurs after the child realizes that the therapist cares about the visible pains.

Forming an alliance with gorilla-suit wearers can sometimes be hastened by attending to their physical complaints. Many of them suffer from chronic pains; headaches; sleep disturbances, including nocturnal panic attacks often preceded by frightening dreams (often dreams loaded with trauma flashbacks), insomnia resulting from fear of anticipated nightmares or of simply losing their tight reins on life, and sleepiness during the day as a result of sleep loss; skin eruptions; digestive upsets; respiratory problems; hysterical seizures; and obsessions or rituals, all of which are symptoms displayed by trauma victims (Goodwin, Simma, and Bergman 1979; Schredl et al. 2001; Sharp and Harvey 2001; Weil 1989; Clum, Nishith, and Resick 2001; Sharp and Harvey 2001). In fact, trauma-related sleep disturbances contribute to the physical symptoms seen in post-traumatic stress disorder (PTSD) victims (Clum, Nishith, and Resick 2001). Self-injurious behavior also leads to cuts and bruises (de Young 1982). Some victims of physical abuse also display symptoms of chronic brain syndrome, sometimes inflicted by chronic shaking at birth, ongoing disciplinary blows to the head, or mishaps resulting from neglect, all of which can result in learning disabilities that contribute to school failure.

The physical problems either restrict the children from doing what other children do or place them at the mercy of unknown and compelling forces. Therapeutic attention to their physical suffering helps the children more quickly form a therapeutic alliance. All children are more likely to verbalize physical concerns than emotional sufferings, and gorilla-suit wearers are no exception, particularly if the therapist shows sympathetic attention to the minor injuries that often result from their reckless behavior: "Let me see that bruise. Boy, I bet it hurts." King (1975), working with especially violent teenagers, remarks that, in spite of their tough exteriors, administering to their wounds, as would the mother of a young child, is a chief way of developing a relationship with them.

Those with compulsive behaviors, often reenactments of partial memories of early traumas, may express their helplessness when the therapist witnesses their ritualistic behavior. "Now you can see what my worries force me to do." Some children also make conscious efforts, especially at night, to suppress unwanted thoughts or images. Unfortunately, their efforts often have a paradoxical effect, and the thoughts and images become even stronger. Tentatively and sympathetically expressed queries by the therapist about these fruitless struggles may prove productive.

Children with academic anxieties often relate that "I want to go to school. Each night I say, 'Tomorrow I'm going.' And then in the morning I feel so sick I could throw up." When openly depressed, some will express, "Mom says I get hurt because I misbehave. Why am I so bad?" revealing the gulf between their ideal self and their real self and their frustration at being unable to change either.

Convey Profound Respect

Therapists addressing the invisible wounds of children should engage in dialogue that demonstrates their sensitivity to the child's need for respect and dignity. Children suffering from repeated blows to their dignity need to feel respected by potential healers (Crenshaw 1990b). With younger children, respect can be conveyed by positive comments following home visits, such as, "I visited your old school and was surprised that all the students entered the building through one door manned by a security guard. Man, I don't know if I could have survived in your neighborhood!" Or, "I talked with your older brother, who told me how you and he always get into fights, but I could tell from the tone of his voice that he respected your refusal to back down." But respect can't be merely a matter of words; it has to be felt. To develop genuine feelings of respect for a child, a therapist may need a significant amount of knowledge about the child's everyday life. If that life can't be observed, then interviews with parents, teachers, and other caregivers should focus on identifying the child's strengths and the obstacles the child has overcome.

With children approaching adolescence, the therapist can say to the child, after setting a limit, "Look, I treat you with respect, and I expect to be treated with respect. If I ever do anything you consider disrespectful, tell me right away, and I will sincerely apologize, because I would never intentionally disrespect you. And I expect the same from you." Putting this issue directly on the table can lay the groundwork for later dialogues with healing potential.

Highlight Their Strengths

The negative self-concept that develops following humiliating and demoralizing encounters needs to change. To help with this process, the therapist needs to highlight each child's strengths, talents, and redeeming personal qualities, referred to by Brooks (1993) as "islands of competence." When a gorilla-suit wearer is asked to list his or her positive qualities, the list created is very short. In fact, it is so short that a therapist can add a strength to the list even after meeting the child for the first time. The list can be kept in a safe place, with the therapist commenting along these lines:

> THERAPIST: The list will become longer when I get to know you better. It will never become shorter. No one can ever take your strengths away. They will always be part of you.

Over time, the therapist helps each child to identify strengths and add them to the list.

SIGNS OF A DEVELOPING ALLIANCE

A therapeutic alliance isn't something that just happens—there today, but not yesterday. It results from accumulation of experiences in therapy, and it can be subject to periodic setbacks, particularly when treating gorilla-suit wearers. Often a child reveals the developing alliance by progression in play. Dorothy Block (1968) describes the process:

> During this period of her fantasy, like her, I remained vague and shadowy. I had no clearly defined form, but was merely there. I waited for cues, however, and as I picked up the first one and then another, the fantasy began to evolve, and with it, both our identities. . . . Her fantasy was to progress through three different phases and a coda, each one representing an advance on the way back to health, and each requiring a different set of identities for both of us. . . . As long as she indicated that she needed a particular response, I provided it. When it served its purpose—to strengthen her ego—she automatically abandoned it herself and through her own decision moved on to the next stage. (p. 312)

Block presents a child who pretended to be a bad dog that bit the therapist or destroyed the furniture. The therapist, in play, had to make a show of beating her, muzzling her, putting her in a cage and starving her, shouting at her, and denouncing her wickedness. Sometimes the child had to be "beaten" so hard that a doctor was called. In that role, the therapist was solicitous and tender, commiserated with her, and expressed the hope that she would change and make such punishment unnecessary. After several months, a gradual shift in the fantasy took place. The wicked behavior was reduced and the punishment expanded. The roles were reversed. From having been a bad dog with the good but necessarily punitive owner, the child became the good dog with the wicked owner. The therapist now was directed to engage in erratic, irrational cruelty. A third character was introduced, one that evolved from the healing "doctor." The therapist was to play two owners, a wicked one and a good one. The child was so bad with the wicked owner that she was sold to the good owner, under whose care she blossomed and became a wonderful dog.

Block's work illustrates one of the chief tasks of play therapy: to meet the child's emotional and maturational requirements during each phase of a developing fantasy until the real child emerges. The therapist fulfills those needs by taking direction from the child and praising, punishing, scolding, caring for, or loving the fantasized characters.

In addition to more revealing play, a sign that an alliance is forming may simply be a slight pause for silent reflection or a question: "Why do you think that?" A child may offer an interpretation of his or her own behavior:

> CHILD: I know why I keep coming to see you when I'm always angry at you. It's so I can be angry at you and not at my family.

An eight-year-old spent the early months of treatment attacking the male therapist and complaining that she would rather be somewhere else. The therapist kept commenting that she attacked him because others attacked her (identification with the aggressor) and that these attacks kept them from working together on her real worries. The angry defense gradually subsided. One day she paused in surprise and commented, "I just had a thought about my anger, but I can't remember it now. Maybe I can later."

Oftentimes an alliance is formed when the child gives a name to the unacceptable part of the self. "Tough Joe made me do that." The therapist and the child can attempt to figure out, understand, and tame this "Tough Joe." Other children will project the unacceptable parts of themselves onto an imaginary character in the therapy room. The therapist can then talk to this "other person." Still others will make the therapist a partner in their dramatic play and direct, but not demand, the partner to play various roles while they play others. Sometimes play in early sessions is an effort to appease a therapist rather than to genuinely relate.

> THERAPIST: I wonder if the drawings you always make of smiling, neat little girls are your way of telling me that you want me to think of you as a nice girl who never gets into trouble.

When efforts are made to reflect possible feelings held but not directly expressed, acknowledgment should not be expected. It will take many such communications before a child will feel comfortable enough to express feelings more directly to the therapist. The child will wax and wane in becoming more direct, and indirect expressions will vary in style. Anger toward the therapist may be revealed by making a violent drawing, knocking over blocks, punching a doll, hiding in a corner, displaying mock anger, or playing catch and throwing the ball poorly to the therapist. When feelings change to positive ones, the child might do things for the therapist, make the therapist things, or brag about the therapist to others. Rarely will the therapist hear the words, "I like you!" In fact, those children who repeatedly make this statement usually make it to all staff. They are the most difficult to like and to treat because they are so empty.

A CASE EXAMPLE

Antonio, a Latino boy, was nine years old when therapy with Dr. Crenshaw began. He had been in a series of failed foster care placements after removal from his mother at age six for extreme abuse and neglect. He was so aggressive and sexually preoccupied that he was shuffled from foster home to foster home in a desperate search for someone to safely manage him. In his last home, he set fires and abused animals. Antonio had dehumanized his losses, and when his defensive layers were peeled away, a deeply hurting and profoundly scared child appeared.

In all settings, Antonio wore his gorilla suit, displaying belligerence toward both children and staff. After testing the limits in therapy, he hid behind a figurative brick wall of detachment. Throughout the first year of once-a-week treatment, he insisted on playing board games and demanding strict adherence to the rules and conventions of the games. This highly structured activity allowed for virtually no self-disclosure or sharing of personal information.

At the end of the year, Antonio displayed no outward signs of progress. The author thought that his therapy plan should be revised. Nevertheless, after Dr. Crenshaw consulted with the second-listed author of this book, Dr. Mordock, the original plan remained in force. During the second year of therapy, Antonio gradually began to "regain his voice" and told his story through puppet play, first reenacting fragments of his traumas and, later, large sequences that made the play more understandable. Eventually, because the therapist was neither repelled nor disgusted by his revelations, he talked, whenever he found the right words, about what he had revealed in his play. What a horror story it was! Between the ages of four and six, he had been prostituted by his mother in return for money and drugs. He was forced to dress up in various costumes and to perform sexual acts with numerous men. If he resisted, he was beaten by his mother or the male perpetrators. The police arrested his mother on a tip from a neighbor, and Antonio was placed in foster care at age six, but the information about his mother's behavior toward him was never shared with authorities, so it never appeared in his clinical record. The omission may have been just as well, however, because it prevented him from being pressured to work on these problems before he was ready.

When Antonio began telling his story, the degree of rage he expressed frightened everyone in the program, as well as Antonio. During that period, he would claw, bite, scratch, and strike out at anyone who approached. Often he had to be placed in the crisis room with a one-to-one aide, where he crouched in the corner and uttered primitive, guttural sounds. Staff meetings focused on whether he should be referred to a psychiatric hospital, where his safety, and that of others, could be assured. Although safety is always a paramount concern, clinical staff felt Antonio would view his placement in a hospital not only as abandonment but as rejection of his painful and agonizing struggle to reveal himself. He would never feel safe enough to do so again. The risk was taken, and he was not placed. Such agonizing and heart-rending decisions are often made over the course of a child's residential treatment. We are convinced that without the professional caregivers' willingness to take risks, after carefully weighing both the pitfalls and the benefits, few seriously troubled children would be helped.

As a part of the agreement to keep Antonio at the center during this critical period, he was seen in therapy five times a week. Most of the sessions took place in the crisis room because it was not safe to escort him to the therapy room. Although it was difficult to weather the storm of his primitive behavior, after about three weeks the worst of his violence and rage began to subside. What followed was even more disturbing. Antonio became dramatically depressed. He would not eat, resisted taking fluids, and would not communicate felt sorrows and pain. Keeping him from dehydration and malnourishment was a major challenge. Gradually, however, he became more clinically accessible, but only in small, incremental steps. In therapy he shared his sense of hopelessness about his future. He said he would never get well enough to leave the treatment center, and even if he did, he had no place to go. Empathy and silent companionship were all therapy could offer him in the throes of his profound pain and sorrow. The authors would maintain, however, that this is an instance of "less being more."

When abused and traumatized children confront their early traumas, they must accept that the longed-for, ideal, and nurturing parent has been lost. This knowledge is devastating, ushering in a period of intense grieving. By our joining Antonio in this deeply painful state, he realized that his hopelessness, sorrow, and pain could be heard, that they were bearable, and that they could be transcended. Witnessing and sitting with children when they are going through such deep suffering are difficult tasks. Nevertheless, unless such emotional processing and working through is undertaken, the cycle of violence cannot be broken. As Hardy (2003) points out, anger management training, the most popular approach to working with angry clients, does not reach the labyrinth of emotionality that underlies the violence.

Antonio gradually began to trust others as well as his therapist. With selected staff, he began to share parts of the nightmare that had inhabited his inner life and blocked his emotional development since he was four years old. He particularly liked, and came to trust, two of the child-care workers in his living group and a teaching assistant in his classroom. Like many who don gorilla suits, Antonio also had distinct talents and strengths. He was quite bright, and after his emotional turmoil subsided, he made dramatic progress in school. He was also athletic and enjoyed success in the basketball and baseball programs in the community leagues in which he was now able to participate. He was liked by peers, and his good looks and recently found charm made him popular with girls. At the end of his third year in placement, he was well enough to move on and was discharged to an aunt and uncle who lived in a distant state. They had shown an interest in him and were able to provide a stable home. He continued to live with this family until he graduated from high school.

Antonio showed amazing courage and perseverance of heroic proportions in learning to trust others and then facing the horror of his life. Bonime (1989) emphasizes the healing impact of a collaborative therapeutic relationship. Antonio's painful catharsis, while necessary to work through his deep emotional pain, was not as crucial to his healing as was the "active declaration of trust" that resulted from the collaborative relationship between him and his empathetic therapist. For Antonio to trust enough to share the story of his terror-filled early years took a leap of faith beyond imagining.

Aims of Play Therapy with Fawns in Gorilla Suits

The aims of therapy include increasing the capacity for sound judgment; reducing excessive and unrealistic self-preoccupation; increasing the understanding of self, the feeling world, and choices and consequences; fortifying weak defenses and easing rigid defenses; and strengthening relationships with caregivers. Additional goals are finding meaning and coherence and facilitating a vision of a more hopeful future. Countertransference feelings can aid rather than hinder reaching these aims.

Although the specific goals of treatment are individualized on the basis of each child's unique needs, the broad attachment-oriented play therapy goals we seek to reach include the following.

1. Increased capacity for sound judgment making (primarily through efforts to improve reality testing by empathetic focusing, clarification, and interpretation).
2. Reduction of excessive and unrealistic self-preoccupations, increased understanding and acceptance of self and self in relation to others, and the development of a new perspective about the past (primarily through the transference relationship and through efforts to help the children redefine themselves from their positive life experiences).
3. Increased understanding of the feeling world (by bringing early traumas to the play experience and ultimately to consciousness so that they can be worked through rather than acted out, often called *reenactment* play).
4. Increased understanding of choices and consequences (by reeducation, clarification, role-playing, and practice).

5. Fortification of defenses that are weak and easing of others that are rigid (by modeling, teaching, and interpreting defenses).
6. Stronger relationships with caregivers (through working with caregivers and also through the transference relationship).
7. Meaning and coherence to one's life (primarily through efforts to relate past to present experiences).
8. A vision of a more hopeful future (primarily through finding hidden resources within the child and the child's immediate environment).

In the chapters that follow, we introduce specific techniques designed to meet the first five goals. In our companion volume, *Understanding and Treating the Aggression of Children*, we address developing stronger relationships with caregivers. In this chapter we discuss the first four goals and illustrate some general efforts to meet them in selected play therapy sessions.

INCREASED CAPACITY FOR SOUND JUDGMENT MAKING

The therapist's task is to stir the children to think about their response to others. The therapist demonstrates, concretely and empathetically, how the children unwittingly hold distorted views of others; misperceive their own emotions, intentions, and capacities; and misconstrue those of others. The therapist provides a model by which the children can make new judgments about their inner reality and particularly about their own contributions to the difficulties that have beset them.

The therapist helps children to move from displaying massive anxiety of unknown dangers to articulating specific fears. Therapists strive to reduce the extreme hyperarousal displayed by the children (and discussed in chapter 4 of *Understanding and Treating the Aggression of Children*) and to help them identify specific dangers. With developmental advancement in cognitive growth, the child's anxiety patterns change. As the child grows from an undifferentiated to a differentiated being, anxiety changes (1) from a global conception of one's destruction, disappearance, and helplessness to more limited possibilities of injury, pain, or loss; (2) from an implicit, diffusely experienced dread to a more delineated experience of signal anxiety; (3) from a relative absence of temporal and spatial causality, in which anything is possible, to reality testing and distinction between probable and improbable.

Most gorilla-suit wearers fail to show this progression, while others regress to earlier developmental levels when under stress. The therapist helps anxiety to move its attachment from global fear to specific fears. To help a child distinguish reality from the child's distorted constructions of it, one must first understand that distortion is an inevitable consequence of conflict. The child comes about his or her beliefs honestly. What the child believes is what the child thinks is true. Encouraging children to examine conflicts and related beliefs helps them distinguish what is real from what is not real.

An important point to remember is that fantasy unfolds in response to play materials. The fantasy is not in the child's head in a planned fashion and the toys merely used to express it. Rather, the toys stimulate the expression of thoughts that are there but are not consciously organized. Teaching the child to play and providing the "right toys" for the child bring the child's concerns to the surface. A toy wheelchair can help a child express feelings about his mother's or his own illness; a toy ambulance can help a child bring out feelings about bodily harm. The therapist can help the child expand upon the ambulance play so that it becomes more elaborate and thematic. Unlike adults, who remember by thinking, children think by remembering. Getting children to think is akin to getting them to remember. But, of course, to remember painful events is to reexperience painful affects. Consequently, the child will resist this effort.

We will illustrate throughout this handbook how a child comes to terms with the compulsion to recall painful experiences by distorting memory with masking symbols. Uncomfortable affect is masked, modified, encapsulated, and even isolated. Such efforts protect the child from being overwhelmed by anxiety and make extended periods of calm possible, but they also distort reality. The therapist's job is to help the child remember in manageable doses, and in so doing, distortions can be examined and corrected.

Tad, a seven-year-old, who was hated by his mother because he looked like his real father, was left with a number of sitters during the first four years of his life. When his mother considered divorcing his stepfather, Tad began soiling again. He had a long history of impacted bowels and of taking enemas. In the waiting room of the female therapist's office, he was very anxious, tense, teary-eyed, and in a hurry to get to the playroom. On entering the playroom, he immediately drew a picture of the "Six-Million-Dollar Dummy."

> CHILD: Plastic face—it's a stupid she. She-dummy has a dumb peanut on her shirt. She-dummy has a plastic face, plastic shirt, dumb pants, dumb colored teeth, pointed head, dumb hair, girl's hair. She-dummy has a she-dummy heart. She-dummy has green pants and black boots. She's a real "Six-Million-Dollar Dummy."
>
> THERAPIST: [*Silence*]
>
> TAD: [*Discovers clay, starts to roll it around and pound it; looks nervously at the therapist.*]
>
> THERAPIST: In here, you can play with clay and get messy without getting scolded.

TAD: What you need is a good slap in the face. How would you like a good slap in the face—you need that. [*He starts to throw the clay at the counselor, who restrains him.*]

THERAPIST: I can't let you throw things at me, but you can draw me and do what you want to the drawing.

Tad started to draw a picture of the female therapist and then "messed her up" with clay "cow pies" before he completed it. He covered the eyes and then the mouth. He liked the "sticky splat" it made. He then went about slapping the clay-embellished drawing against the floor, peeling the clay off, and then slapping it again. With lots of nervous laughter, he told the therapist that "she'd better 'watch it' or she'll get a slap in the face." He continued to mix the clay with water, rub it, and stick his fingers in the mound he made, remarking how sticky and neat it was. He then washed up and decided he wanted to paint more on the large paper provided. He said that he had to paint a ship. First he painted the ship's base. Then he made lots of churning water and said that the ship was bouncing all around.

TAD: My mother's afraid of water. She can't swim. Once she had to be carried like a baby from the dock to a boat because she was so scared.

THERAPIST: [*Silence*]

TAD: [*Continues to paint with great zeal. Before his referral for therapy, he had smashed a ship model that his mother liked a great deal.*] The ship needs to be tied up to a dock. It is still choppy. I'll draw an anchor. The anchor would help keep it docked.

Tad then made dark waves rising higher and moving faster. He drew a sailor and said the sailor was dumb. He tried to catch a fish but the fish swam right past him. "I should throw clay at the dumb sailor." He began throwing clay with the intent of covering the whole ship. He said that he just had to cut the line, to keep throwing clay until he wiped out the whole ship. Tad is typical of impulse-ridden children. But he had some controls. He agreed to display his anger in make-believe, although he was never far from expressing it directly, and he often halted his own regressed behavior by switching activities when he got too anxious. Tad's behavior illustrates the confused feelings of many troubled children. His anger at his mother and stepfather is confused with his own self-hate. His desire to slap the therapist is a reflection of his own experience of being slapped. But he does not know what compels him to want to slap and mess up the therapist, nor does he know why he holds back his stools and then soils.

The therapist refrains from responding because Tad's communications, while revealing, are not fully understood. Who is the sailor fisherman? His stepfather? Himself? Is the ship he draws and destroys the one prized by his cold, indifferent (plastic-faced) mother? But then why does he try to anchor the ship against the waves he created? To save the ship from his own destructive urges? There are too many unanswered questions to respond appropriately to Tad's productions, productions made rapidly in a compulsive manner. And remember, Tad's play is not just his compulsion to master his rejecting home life but also his fear that the therapist will treat him similarly.

Because the therapist will, in an accepting yet limiting manner, let Tad play, Tad's play will become less driven, less diffuse, and more organized. When it does, the therapist can comment on and attempt to clarify the child's confusions. Tad can then begin to understand his behavior and its role in reinforcing his mother's view that he is just like his father, further solidifying her rejection of him.

A less extreme example is Troy, an articulate eleven-year-old who was troubled by extreme restlessness that resulted in school failure and angered his parents, and he, in turn, responded in kind. He could sit in therapy only when drawing spaceships and space platforms. Encouragement to play with less structured material proved fruitless. He had no explanations for his hyperactivity except that a neurologist had put him on a medication that didn't help. He spent numerous sessions drawing and describing his fictional ideas about traveling and living in outer space. At the beginning of each session, he stated that everything was fine in his life. (All reports continued to emphasize his hyperactivity.) He would draw and relate his fantasies while he moved nervously around the therapy room. All efforts to get him to examine his preference to spend so much time in an unreal space world rather than in the real world of peers, family, and school met with resistance. He would simply reply that his space world was more fun.

Considerable conflict existed between Troy's divorced parents, and the therapist feared that Troy got caught up in their battles. By staying in his space world, he could avoid problems in the real world. With continual reassuring comments from the therapist, such as "Most boys worry about family problems," Troy moved tentatively from discussing space to discussing his family.

> THERAPIST: Troy, staying in a space world is like the ostrich with his head in the sand, who, because of his position, is more vulnerable to a surprise kick in the rear than he would be if his head was up and looking around. While you are out in space, things are happening over which you have no control.

Troy began to examine his frozen view of his parents; neither was seen realistically. He began to appreciate both parents independently from their views about each other. The therapist gave him "homework" assignments to find out what other adults thought about his dad. He began to refuse to pass along messages to Dad from Mother about visiting arrangements. And he tolerated the notion that part of him accepted the divorce because he now had his mother all to himself—a thought that also caused him great anxiety but which was "normalized" by the therapist's comments. Troy's flights into space also represented a retreat from sexual feelings toward his mother, as well as banishment for replacing his father. His restlessness was not only a motor discharge of his anxiety; it was also connected with sexual fantasies.

When his mother started to date again, Troy's hostility toward her dates was interpreted as rivalrous jealousy. At the same time, the therapist stressed that Troy would no longer have to be so disturbed by his fantasies about his mother because she now had a boyfriend. Troy began to concentrate on his schoolwork, and teacher feedback indicated less hyperactive behavior.

CLARIFYING INTENTION AND MOTIVATION

Gorilla-suit wearers never learned to understand their own mental states or the mental states of others. Nor can they view the minds of others as having less aggression than their own. Mayes and Cohen (1993) remark,

> Relationships with important others that are marred by explicit violence and abuse may bring the child face to face with the mind of another that is too frightening and dangerous to try and understand. In such cases, despite maturational readiness, the capacity to understand others' minds and different states of aggressive intention may be seriously impaired. (p. 164)

Consequently, suit wearers, regardless of age, are prone to eruptions of hostility that seem irrational or even incomprehensible. Often they perceive an accident as a personal affront or hostile attack, even when someone bumps into them by accident. They respond to ambiguous situations with aggression, not because they simply don't understand another's motives, but because they attribute hostile reactions to others: "Because I'm always angry, others are always angry at me." Nonaggressive youth typically judge accidental events as "accidents."

Jackie, a five-year-old girl enrolled in a Head Start program, erupted into a temper tantrum when three-year-old Lillian collided with her while they rode their tricycles on the playground. She screamed at Lillian, scared her off the trike, and chased her up the monkey bars. Upon catching up with Jackie, her teacher explained that Lillian was a little girl who did not yet know how to ride her trike as well as Jackie did. The collision was an accident. Lillian did not mean to bump into her. She was sorry. After hearing this explanation several times, Jackie settled down and returned to her group.

Therapy should include a thorough discussion of the difference between an accidental and a deliberate act, with reference to the child's own pervasive anger:

> THERAPIST: David, just because you're angry at other kids doesn't mean they're always angry at you. I happened to see you today when you hit Sam in the hallway. Sam wasn't even thinking about you when he ran into you in the hallway. He was looking at Jose and didn't even see you.

REDUCTION OF EXCESSIVE AND UNREALISTIC SELF-PREOCCUPATION AND INCREASED UNDERSTANDING OF SELF

Because many disturbed children feel rejected and unloved, they never develop a genuine self-love. They like themselves only after successfully manipulating others to meet their needs. Their whole life becomes centered around having their needs met. Their narcissistic self-love is injured by excessive worries that they cannot meet their needs. Troy's preoccupation with his space world kept him from achieving in the real world, and part of him knew that and felt guilty about it.

When children like Troy learn that they are inwardly compelled to act and feel in certain ways, their disturbance becomes understandable—some healing is provided for their injured self-love. Therapeutic explanations provide relief from painful self-accusations that have been keeping self-esteem low. Sometimes they help even when they are wrong! When children learn that the behavior of others has reasonable meanings and can be responded to reasonably, their unhealthy self-absorption decreases. They begin to see that some of their wishes are worth gratifying and that appropriate ways exist to gratify them. This knowledge increases the feeling of authenticity.

Most gorilla-suit wearers are absorbed in compensation fantasies of self-importance, sometimes referred to as "grandiosity" and classified by some as a defense (Kernberg 1975) and by others as a character fixation (Masterson 1975). The therapeutic task of replacing self-preoccupation with a true self-love is extremely difficult. The children's compensation fantasies create unrealistically high ideals. Consequently, any praise they receive or accomplishments they achieve are never enough. "To love myself, I must be a world champion. Anything less is failure." In school they are often heard to say, "I won't do that baby stuff." In athletics, they want to hit home runs instead of practicing basic baseball skills.

The therapist must spend hours attending to the children's fantasized exploits at the same time that special gestures are made toward them (e.g., helping with specific tasks, advising how to handle specific situations, showing interest in achievements, negotiating with others on the children's behalf). While listening to their fantasized exploits, the therapist tries to discover what the children might be able to do, encourages adults in their lives to expose them to these activities (bowling, pool, table games, weight lifting, magic, fishing, camping, music, mystery writing, storytelling, cooking, tailoring, etc.), and then makes an effort to learn about the children's real, rather than their fantasized, achievements so that a strength-oriented treatment plan can be developed (Mordock 1999a).

Cognitive distortions, particularly of self-blame and self-contempt, need to be addressed in order to repair the sense of self. Intense feelings of self-blame and self-condemnation, partially resulting from stigmatization by others, should be confronted to fashion a more positive self-concept. Children will cling to these distorted views of self to protect their fantasy of an ideal parent who someday will come and rescue them. To confront the reality that their parents were unable to provide for them, whatever the reasons, may require them to confront this major loss in their life, and they may be unprepared to do so. They would much prefer to continue to view themselves as "bad" or defective in some way than to face the intense grief that emerges when reevaluating their self-concept. The child's cognitive distortions are often rooted in powerful emotional dynamics. These distorted beliefs also give a child a sense of control; if the child is to blame for all the bad things that have happened, then the child has some power to prevent future occurrences.

When children experience being liked and attended to, and particularly the experience of giving pleasure to the therapist, they begin to like themselves better. At that time, achievements will become more meaningful. Many adults believe that when children master concrete tasks and develop specific skills, their problems will disappear. Yet many bright and creative people fail to appreciate their own self-worth. It is difficult to love ourselves (and appreciate our own accomplishments, which are extensions of ourselves) without having been loved by another. While acceptance and understanding are not love, they are the best substitutes. Out of such acceptance, self-acceptance may grow.

Parents of aggressive children often refer to them as monsters, viewing their aggressive reactions as willful assaults. In addition, parents both externalize and project their own unacceptable behaviors onto their children, who accept them to avoid rejection. During the first stage of therapy, the children typically intensify the manifestation of their "gorilla" identity, putting themselves in the same role with the therapist as they experienced with their parents—repeating their maladaptive, but familiar, experiences. Each child's negative self-image must be brought into the open so it can be seen as a purposeful fantasy rather than as the reality both the child and the parents believe it to be. The therapist also shows the child how he or she uses behavior to arouse anxiety in others and to maintain distance from them.

> One day, eleven-year-old Valerie, a streetwise, pseudosophisticated girl, made clay cookies, put them on a plate, and put the plate on the floor. She then got down on her hands and knees, crawled around on the floor, growled like a dog, and started to eat the clay. The therapist took the plate from the floor, saying, "You're not a dog, but you're trying to show me how sometimes you feel like one."

Lora Tessman and Irving Kaufman (1967) present the case of a nine-year-old girl who often thought of herself as a pig. She would say, "At home I'm always a pig. People don't invite pigs into their houses; they let them stand in the street." This child had been seen at the same clinic six years earlier, at which time she endlessly dipped toilet paper into the toilet bowl and retrieved it. Her first complete sentence was about toilet activity. She seemed identified with feces, suggesting that the self-image can change its literal form but retain its dynamic meaning—from feces to pig. Her mother was simultaneously attracted and repelled by the idea of smearing. She unconsciously needed the child to portray her concrete symbolism of this messy component of herself. Thus, the girl's self-image was a reflection of her mother's unconscious view of her.

The therapist conveys an effort to understand, remaining unfrightened by the child's display of angry feelings, steadfastly conveying that the child's images of destruction and of the self as both the destroyed and the destroyer have symbolic meaning. The case of Gerald (from Tessman and Kaufman 1967) reveals how a child's angry behaviors are often communications about the child's self-image rather than communications about facts.

> Five-year-old Gerald was seen in a hospital, where he had been sent after attempting to cut off his sister's arm with a saw. He was destructive to himself and to others, seemingly unaware of the consequences of his behavior. Early in therapy he filled a glass with red paint, yelled that it was blood, and started to throw it. The therapist stopped him, telling him that no blood would be spilled here, that in here she would keep him safe. He then showed her a scratch on his finger. She replied that he must have lots of hurts. He replied, "They used to kick the football bloody." In later sessions, he conveyed his concept of himself as the football between his parents, who had both used him in some perverse sexual practices. Still later, Gerald tried to break the limbs of a baby doll, saying, "I'll break it so I can use it for a

ball." The therapist stopped him, saying she knew how he felt like a broken baby, but that he was a real boy.

Rudolph Ekstein (1966) writes of forming a working alliance with the monstrous self-image. The therapist points out that the child's monsters seem to serve a positive function despite their cruel sadistic methods. Later, we present a drawing strategy, discussed by Crenshaw (2001) and Boyd-Webb (2001), which is used to transform into helping agents the monsters and other scary inhabitants of the children's internal worlds.

> THERAPIST: I wonder if the monsters can be helped to become more reasonable so that they can give reasons for what they do.

When appropriate, the therapist directs remarks to the monsters. Each monster becomes someone with whom the child and the therapist can negotiate. Through this process, each monster becomes more reasonable. The child now sways each monster to help him or her to be less punitive, less destructive, and more adaptive. Eventually the monsters fuse, become more benevolent, and recede into the background as the real child emerges.

The children's self-esteem is further damaged by their reactions to their abuse. Many abused children suffer, not only from the effects of the actual abuse, but also from the belief that they should have been able to prevent it or escape from it. A young boy in a foster home confided that he had been sodomized by a much bigger child while in a prior placement. He told his male therapist when visited at the home, "I never told you or anyone else, not so much because I was ashamed about the act itself, but more because I wasn't man enough to prevent it." This boy, who had an excellent relationship with his therapist, felt that he would be judged as harshly by other men as he judged himself for his passive compliance. It wasn't until after he told his foster mother that he felt strong enough to tell his former therapist. If his therapist had been female, perhaps he would have revealed the trauma sooner.

DEVELOPING NEW PERSPECTIVES

Once they shed their gorilla suits, the children need help to view themselves differently. They need a new perspective on life, and they need to find meaning and coherence within past chaotic events. Later in treatment, after the children have faced some of the traumatic issues in their young lives, the Time Line, presented in chapter 13 of our companion volume, *Understanding and Treating the Aggression of Children,* can be used to assist children to develop a different life view, one counteracting the tendency to define themselves by their problems, the aggressive behaviors that caused them, or the traumatic blows they received. The therapist emphasizes that the time frame of traumatic events actually encompassed a relatively brief period in each child's life span, helping children to learn that they are more than the problems others focus on. Seeing themselves in a more balanced way and appreciating their unique qualities and humanness help to shift their self-image to a more positive one.

INCREASED UNDERSTANDING OF THE WORLD OF FEELINGS

Considerable effort is devoted to helping the child learn that people can experience many different feelings and that people can have different feelings about the same situation. The therapeutic task is to help the child learn that people can have similar feelings but that they may differ in strength. Perhaps the most important thing to learn is that feelings are not "right or wrong." The child will often hear people say that he or she has no "right" to feel that way— that he or she "should" feel differently. The child must be helped to disregard these beliefs and taught that feelings are not subject to rational analysis; that when one is hurt, one is simply hurt. People will be angry at the child for having certain feelings, but the feelings should not be hidden simply because others do not like how the feelings are displayed. The child will learn that behavior, and not feelings, get one into trouble and that behaviors can change. The child will learn different ways to handle disappointment and frustration and different ways to behave when angry or upset. And, more important, the child will learn to differentiate real fear from imaginary fear.

Children who have been abused early in life, particularly before age five, develop significantly more dissociative problems (as well as difficulties modulating anger, in addition to self-destructive and suicidal behaviors) than older victims of interpersonal trauma do (van der Kolk et al. 1996; Bowman, Blix, and Coons, 1985). As a result, many of these children's feelings are far removed from their causes. It took Dr. Mordock two years to realize that a girl's preoccupation with witches with sharp claws was the child's distorted memory of her mother's long fingernails, which scratched the little girl when she was an infant. It took an equally long time to learn that a boy's preoccupation with doorknobs resulted from his being locked in the closet. In addition, it took two years to uncover his unconscious belief that he should have been able to escape from the closet, a belief that compelled him to display escape behavior in situations where none was needed, which got him into considerable trouble with adults.

Ricky, age eight, a child in residential treatment, reacted catastrophically to his teacher's not believing him when he insisted (correctly) that he was not the one who threw the eraser. His extreme self-righteousness about being correct was cut off from his early insistence that his "mother was not his mother." Ricky had been given to his mother's friend to raise when he was a young baby. One day his biological mother showed up at school, with all the proper legal papers, and took him in spite of his protests that she was not his mother. He never saw his "psychological mother" again.

INCREASED UNDERSTANDING OF
CHOICES AND CONSEQUENCES

Another aim is to help the child to think about actions in light of motives—to ask, "Why did I do that?" The child should become able to respond with options to questions such as "Hitting is one thing you can do. Is that a good idea?" The child comes to appreciate how his or her actions might make another person feel. Alternative solutions will be learned, as will anticipation of alternative consequences of various behaviors displayed following experiences that arouse feelings. In short, the child will learn planned responses to frustrations, in contrast to being overwhelmed by them.

Abused children also need to realize that their parents could have made different choices and that the choices they made didn't always relate to the children's behavior but rather to their own separate needs as adults. The children also need to learn that some of the choices their caregivers made left them with limited choices about their behavior. Salvador Minuchin and his colleagues (1967) believe that the powerful sense of entitlement aggressive children display comes from internalizing their parents' feelings that whatever they gave to their children was never enough. Consequently, the children come to expect more. We think the feelings are more basic than that. We think they come from the feeling that they were actually cheated in life and that they deserve more. In the long run, these children need help to forgive a world that basically wasn't very good to them. Bonime (1989) sees the core dynamic of depression as consisting of rage and sorrow at not receiving what every person needs in early life: "Non-obligating solicitude." Furthermore, Bonime believes that when one doesn't receive this solicitude, it can never be made up. Unless this huge loss is faced and mourned, the child goes through life with a sense of destructive entitlement, and whatever is received is experienced as one more increment of "not enough."

> THERAPIST: It really stinks having to be in the middle of fights between Mom and Dad.
> THERAPIST: It really hurts that your parents never came to see your school or to see you play in the ball games.

The child also needs to learn that some of his behavior was, and perhaps still is, in response to inconsistent and erratic parental behavior.

> THERAPIST: I don't know what made your mother so mad. You either never know where you stand, or sometimes something you do is "naughty" and another time it isn't.
> or
> THERAPIST: Because your parents' rules seem unfair, the only rule you follow is to do what you think is best for you.

FORTIFICATION OF WEAK DEFENSES AND EASING OF RIGID DEFENSES

Chapters 9 is devoted to achieving the aim of fortifying and building defenses. Chapters 10 and 11, on the interpretive process, focus on helping the child to understand the defenses he or she uses and how they are both self-reinforcing and self-defeating. The child is encouraged to give up rigid defenses and to utilize those that will enable others to get in touch with their fondness for the child. Once fond of the child, they can provide the love and attention the child desperately craves, provided he or she has done the work of mourning as described above. At the same time, the child will be helped to master age-appropriate developmental challenges.

STRONGER RELATIONSHIPS WITH CAREGIVERS

In *Understanding and Treating the Aggression of Children*, we devote a full chapter to working with the child's natural parents, part of a chapter to working with foster parents, and a complete chapter to working with teachers and other direct-care workers (such as child care workers and recreational staff). We also devote a chapter to creating a therapeutic milieu that would strengthen each child's relationship with caregivers.

FINDING MEANING AND COHERENCE

Children in gorilla suits need to attribute new meanings to the horrific events that have influenced their sense of who they are. The lyrics from a Neil Diamond song, "I'm lost and don't even know why," denote their state. The children need a meaningful narrative memory—a story that makes sense to them about what happened in their lives. In some cases, the narrative will be constructed from disconnected pieces because much of their early life has been forgotten. In fact, some children fill in the banks with lies, which the therapist must accept until they can be replaced by truths (Wilkinson and Hough 1996). Children often create fiction when the realities of their lives are too horrible to comprehend.

FACILITATING A VISION OF A MORE HOPEFUL FUTURE

Finally, the children need to develop hope for a more viable future. The hope, however, needs to be built on the basis of realistic plans to improve their life circumstances. Children can dare to hope only after their invisible wounds have been shared with an empathetic listener courageous enough to accompany them into their "deep pit of rage and sorrow" and to emerge from it with a healthier child. The hope has to be based on resources available to the child both internally and externally and cannot be based on "empty reassurance." Bonime (1983) observed that empty reassurance is of little or no help because it keeps the recipient dependent on the strength of the helper. Real help, and a more solid basis for hope, is built on locating resources within the child and family and connecting them to external resources within their extended family, friends, and community. In *Understanding and Treating the Aggression of Children* we discuss specific strategies to facilitate hope.

COUNTERTRANSFERENCE FEELINGS CAN AID TREATMENT

Neither of us agrees with the assertion of early psychoanalytic writers that countertransference refers only to the therapist's inappropriate responses to the patient. In the early psychoanalytic literature, countertransference reactions are viewed as the private preoccupations of the therapist stimulated by the client but not related to the client's problems. Such reactions need to be constantly examined within oneself and in supervision and consultation. We highly recommend the in-depth self-examination that results from the child therapist's own extensive personal therapy. Based on the work of the Tavistock Clinic (Boston and Szur 1983), Winnicott, Bion, and Anna Freud, we believe that many reactions to aggressive children's behaviors are the result of *projective communications*. In other words, not all personal reactions are unhealthy contaminants contributed by the therapist's own issues. By the creative use of self as a healing instrument, the reactions that arise in the therapist during the course of therapeutic interactions can provide a window into the child's inner world and past experience. When the therapist feels impotent, hopeless, or defeated, the question should be asked, "Is this how the child feels, only much more intensely? During his psychoanalytic supervision with Walter Bonime, Dr. Crenshaw was constantly reminded, "No matter how frustrated, hopeless, impotent, or miserable the therapist may feel in the midst of a therapy process that is fraught with obstacles and setbacks, these feelings cannot begin to match the intensity of feelings experienced by the client" (Bonime 1982).

Setting Limits on Destructive and Controlling Behaviors

Limit setting is presented as a four-step series of therapist behaviors: acknowledging the child's feelings, wants, and wishes; communicating the limit; targeting acceptable alternatives; and when a limit is broken, stating the final choice. Discussion in this chapter focuses on limiting behaviors that obviously ruin the therapeutic process. They are destructive behaviors, controlling behaviors, and behaviors that require the therapist's physical involvement. Not all limits are verbal; many limits can be set silently.

$\mathscr{M}$ost children seen in outpatient psychotherapy quickly learn what can and cannot be done in the playroom, and "rule enforcement," or *limit setting*, is rarely necessary. Not so with gorilla-suit wearers! Limit testing and rule breaking are their way of life, and their behavior in the playroom is no exception. But limit testing is usually at its worst in the play therapy setting because the children are given a choice about how they wish to proceed. As we discuss in chapter 1, most gorilla-suit wearers have never mastered the *initiative versus guilt* stage of development and become extremely anxious when expected to show initiative. Because they are uncomfortable both with making choices and with playing imaginatively, the first rule they test is staying in the play therapy room.

LIMIT THERAPY TO THE THERAPY ROOM

Gorilla-suit wearers, preferring actions to play actions, will request, if not demand, to be taken outside to play catch, shoot baskets, or take walks. Many therapists accede to these requests, especially with latency-aged children, claiming they are too old to play with toys and will talk better when engaged in more age-appropriate activities. These therapists fail to appreciate that such activities are not appropriate therapy activities for developmentally arrested children. The children need to move from actions to play actions and eventually to fantasy play. When children talk outside, they relate everyday concerns. Mostly they complain and express dissatisfactions. Their expectations of the therapist, those discussed in chapter 1, dominate the sessions. Ablon (1990) describes a latency-aged boy's reaction to this limit.

> Craig then became furious with me for not going outside and playing baseball with him during the hours. If I were really a "friend," I would do whatever Craig wanted and would be Craig's buddy the way he wished his father would be. (p. 344)

LIMIT DESTRUCTIVE BEHAVIORS

Children should not be allowed to destroy objects in a playroom. They should be prevented from breaking crayons or pencils, from taking the clothes off dolls when the clothes are supposed to be permanent, and from damaging playroom toys. They should be prohibited from mixing up all the finger paints or continually pouring water into the sandbox until the sand is soaking wet. They are not inhibited and constricted neurotic children who need finger paints or sand play to become more expressive. Their mixture of paints or wet sandbox play easily reminds them of fecal matter, and regressed play follows. They continually ask for more paper because obtaining paper is more important than drawing on it.

> THERAPIST: Every time I see you, you order me about, try to break toys, and hope to get me angry. When I tell you to draw your angry thoughts or to express your feelings with the miniature dolls, you laugh and run around the playroom. Nevertheless, you're in therapy to get help with your worries. You need to either play or talk to me about what bothers you. If you continue to try to be the boss and break the rules, then I will have to prevent you from behaving this way until you can play out or talk about your angry feelings.

In many cases, the children may need to be seen in a sterile setting equipped with minimal toys (Magic Markers and paper, clay, human and animal puppets, and a cloth punching bag kept behind a puppet stage). Antonio, presented in chapter 1, was seen in an empty room during one stage in his treatment. If the therapist conceives of gorilla-suit wearers as infants emotionally, limit setting becomes immediately understandable. No mother of an eighteen-month-old would let her child do any of the inappropriate actions mentioned above; neither should a therapist. We once read a published case in which the therapist suggested using natural consequence as a limit setter. We quote from this paper:

> THERAPIST: You can break the crayons, but you will have to use the broken crayons for drawing.

Absolutely not! Would a mother of a two-year-old respond in such a fashion? No! She would say:

> MOTHER: I'm taking these crayons from you before you break them all. When you can play with them correctly, I will give you one or two to use. If I let you break them now, you'll be upset that there will be none to play with later.

The limit tester breaks the crayons or other toys to see what the therapist will do. To allow the child to break the crayons is bad enough. The adult's allowing disruptive behavior (or being so easily manipulated as to let rules slip) not only frightens the child; "broken crayons" have always been the gorilla-suit wearer's way of life—"So what's different about this place?" Subtle disrespect is conveyed in the above limit testing, and to take a permissive stance devalues the competence of the therapist. On the other hand, if a child is breaking the crayons because of an "imperfect" drawing and self-hate is being displaced onto the crayons, the response can be as follows:

> THERAPIST: [*Quietly rescues the remaining crayons.*] I can't let you break the crayons because you're not happy with your drawing. Part of you sure gets angry at another part when that part can't do something right. Can I talk to the angry part, the part that says to you, "That drawing stinks"?
> CHILD: No.
> THERAPIST: Well, someday maybe I can speak to the critical part. I will call him "Mr. Critical."
> CHILD: Oh, shut up.
> THERAPIST: Okay. When you silence me, you also silence Mr. Critical. I guess he's a very powerful guy. I sure would like Ralph, who's a fairly good drawer, to be able to stand up more to Mr. Critical.
> CHILD: [*Begins to play checkers with the therapist but sees that he is losing and knocks the checkers on the floor.*]
> THERAPIST: A guy can feel mad about losing a game, but it's more grown-up to say so than to scatter checkers all over the room. I have been playing this game much longer than you. Let's play again, and I will start with fewer checkers.

We agree with the steps elucidated by Gary Landreth (2002), namely acknowledging the child's feelings, wishes, and wants; communicating the limit; targeting acceptable alternatives; and stating the final choice when the child continues to break the limit. We disagree, however, with the amount of latitude he gives children when they continue to break limits, at least in the example he presents. From page 4 of his article we have reproduced verbatim his example of presenting an appropriate ultimate choice.

> *David*: [*Throws sand out of the sandbox onto toy shelves, no feelings evident*].
> *Therapist*: David, I know you would like to throw the sand on the shelves, but the sand is for staying in the sandbox.
> *David*: [*Throws the sand on the shelves again*].
> *Therapist*: You just wanted to see how that felt to throw the sand again, David, but the sand is not for throwing out of the sandbox.
> *David*: [*Throws sand on the shelves again*].
> *Therapist*: David, sand is for staying in the sandbox. If you choose to throw the sand on the shelves, you choose not to play in the sandbox for the rest of the play time.
> *David*: [*Throws sand on the shelves again*].
> *Therapist*: David, I see you have chosen not to play in the sandbox for the rest of our time in the playroom today.
> *David*: [*Sticks his tongue out at the therapist and looks angry*].
> *Therapist*: You are angry at me. You really don't want to stop playing in the sand, but when you chose to throw the sand again, you chose not to play in the sandbox for the rest of our time today.
> *David*: [*Gets out of sandbox and begins hitting the Bobo*].
> *Therapist*: You have decided to hit the Bobo.

If therapists let five-year-old gorilla-suit wearers throw sand four times before stating the final choice, not only will they be seen as weak, but they will also be cleaning the playroom for the next half hour and will miss their next appointment. The limit should be set as follows:

> CHILD: [*Throws sand out of sandbox.*]
> THERAPIST: [*Blocks child from sandbox.*] Sand is not for throwing. It must stay in the sandbox. Here are some darts. Throw them at that target on the wall. If you want to play in the sand later, you can, but only if you don't throw the sand.

The child's destructive behaviors are interrupted immediately, an alternative action is provided, and the clarification is delivered that if the child can play with the sand appropriately, he or she may do so at another time. Landreth (2002) cautions that therapists often become caught up in enforcing limits and move too quickly to implement the final step, but that has not been our experience. Too often, the therapist presents the limit tentatively, trying to cajole the child into compliance rather than stating the limit firmly but not angrily. Then, when the child doesn't comply, the therapist becomes angry, the limit is set too forcefully, and the child wins the "anger game" he or she is so good at.

A major purpose of limit setting is to block nonproductive interactions. For children with severely arrested development, therapy is a corrective emotional experience. The children are provided, in the "here and now," with a reaction that is different from their previous experiences—one that does not perpetuate the malignant interactions to which the children have grown accustomed. With most children, reflections, clarifications, and corrections of misconceptions create an environment different from the lectures, admonishments, and scoldings they get elsewhere. But the aggressive child's goal is to create familiarity. Relationships will be initiated with thinly veiled anger.

The taming process begins with blocking the child's aggressive behavior. It also includes verbalizing what the child feels when actions are limited.

> THERAPIST: I want to help you to control yourself, and I also realize that you feel helpless and weak when I won't let you do something.

Any attempt at self-control is acknowledged and praised. To improve the child's reality testing, the therapist needs to verbalize continually what could happen following the child's dangerous or reckless behavior.

> THERAPIST: I know you climb on that cabinet to show me how strong you are, but the cabinet's not stable, and I can't let you hurt yourself should it fall.

Verbalizing the difference between reality and fantasy is also needed— "Wishing won't make it so." With limits, the child will initially escalate aggressive behavior. If the therapist withdraws under the child's provocations, the child intuitively reacts to this withdrawal with new provocations, which can increase the therapist's withdrawal. The child interprets this withdrawal as either a lack of interest or moral condemnation. Therapists who fail to anticipate that they will lose their temper with gorilla-suit wearers are headed for trouble. Those who also fail to appreciate countertransference, or the projection of the therapist's feelings onto the child, will also hinder the therapy process (Hayes and Gelso 2001; Kiesler 2001).

When a child destroys drawings displayed by another child or spits in the therapist's face, anger is inevitable. Dr. Mordock angrily removed a girl from his office when she tore up several pictures that were hung on his wall by a proud child after the child had struggled for hours to produce recognizable images.

He later sought out the girl and apologized for his loss of control. When the child said she deserved it, the issue of appropriate and inappropriate discipline was discussed with her. To help maintain self-control, the therapist has to continually verbalize his or her feelings.

> THERAPIST: If you continue to do that, I'm going to get angry. I'm not angry yet, just annoyed, but you need to stop that.
> CHILD: And what will you do to me?
> THERAPIST: I will have to take it from you.
> CHILD: [*Runs around the room breaking legs off a doll.*] See, you can't catch me!
> THERAPIST: Next time I will remove those toys from the room until I learn to trust that you will use them properly.

Silent Limits

If therapists followed all four limiting-setting steps every time a gorilla-suit wearer tested a limit, children would be bombarded with communications. More often children are limited, especially later in therapy, by quiet actions. When ripping up paper, the pile of remaining paper is simply removed, and the child is handed a puppet. If all the finger paints are being mixed together and the result is a brown mess, the paints are quietly gathered up and put away, and the child is handed a crayon. If too much water is being poured in the sandbox, the water faucet is shut off, the pitcher returned to the cupboard, and the child given play dough. Nothing else needs to be said.

By and large, American parents and American therapists overly rely on verbal communications. Children are spoken to harshly, yelled at, cajoled, scolded, lectured, quietly reprimanded, or given explanations for rules placed on them. In contrast, other cultures more often use actions instead of words to both instruct and limit children. For example, on a playground in China, a young boy squirmed his way into the head of a line of older children waiting their turn to climb up a ladder and slide down an aluminum slide. A caregiver gently picked up the boy, lifted him up onto the slide, held his hand while he slid down, and then led him to a sandbox where children his age were playing. She never said a word, and the child was never again seen entering a line of older children. The implicit message she conveyed, and one the child learned, was "You can experience what the slide is like, but the activity is for older children and you need to engage in another instead."

Humorous Limits

Not all limits are set in a firm, serious tone. Limits sometimes can be set in a humorous manner. For example, one time an angry day-treatment student threatened to call his mother. She was a big, strapping woman who could have knocked the therapist for a loop, but had the boy actually called his mother, she would have knocked him around for embarrassing her by his behavior, something the therapist felt the child was not ready to face. The boy still hoped his neglectful mother would come to his rescue, and he was not ready to face the unreality of this sustaining fiction. When he got in trouble in public school, she often came to school, grabbed him roughly by the collar, dragged him kicking out of the building, threw him into her car, and took him home. After several days at home, he would return to school with even more pent-up anger, and the cycle would begin again. The public school practice of calling parents when their children display disruptive behavior is often the reason some children get referred to treatment settings. The schools aggravate already difficult situations. Normally the therapist would have responded to the boy's seemingly ridiculous demand as follows:

> THERAPIST: [*Handing the child the play phone.*] Here, call your mother and pretend to talk to her on the phone.

Instead he told the child that he could call his mother on the pay phone down the hall from the play therapy room. The child looked surprised but then replied that he didn't have any money for a pay phone. At the same time, the therapist revealed his empty pockets, and the child said, with a slight chuckle, "I guess I can't call her, then!" Such limit-setting tactics can help therapists maintain their sanity when repeatedly faced with limit-testing behavior.

LIMIT CONTROLLING BEHAVIORS

Needy children will repeatedly request objects from the therapist. These children, while often deprived, typically ask for these objects, or even take them, not because they want the objects (they are usually quite good at stealing from stores when they want something) but because they want to control the therapist. (Later, they may take objects to feel attached to the therapist.) Acquiring things from others feeds fantasies of power and omnipotence, fantasies that compensate for feelings of helplessness and despair. Other children ask for things because they know they will be refused, turning kind adults into rejecting adults and thereby justifying the children's aggressive actions toward the adults.

> CHILD: Can I have this car?
> THERAPIST: The toys are all for use only in the playroom.

> CHILD: But it's only one car. There are lots more here.
> THERAPIST: All the toys stay in the playroom for use here.

While it is very tempting to explain to the child why toys cannot be removed ("If every child took a car, all the cars would be gone in a day, and there would be no cars left for anyone to play with" or "Next time you'd want another car"), the child would vehemently deny the explanation ("I only want this one"). It is important to limit the child's actions clearly and leave no perceived avenue of getting around the rule. "The toys are not for taking" is the clearest message. The child's disappointment, anger, and manipulative efforts can be responded to later.

> THERAPIST: Jim, you've asked me for everything in my office, and now you're asking me for a paper clip you found on the floor that you know I don't really need. You're sure trying hard to make me look like a "meany" because I'm going to say no to this request also.
> CHILD: But it's only a paper clip, and you don't even need it!
> THERAPIST: I know, Jim. It's like you're saying, "You don't even like me enough to give me one lousy paper clip!"
> CHILD: Yeah, give it to me!
> THERAPIST: Whenever you feel really bad about yourself, you want something; it doesn't matter what it is, and if you don't get it, then you can replace your bad feelings with anger at the stingy world and at stingy me.
> CHILD: I can borrow the car! I'll return it! I will! Don't you trust me?
> THERAPIST: All the toys in the playroom stay in the playroom. You still want me to give or lend you things you know you can't have. You want to see if I value things more than I value you—and you think that I won't lend or give you things because I value possessions more.

Children will also demand food, the demand stemming from needs to control, from oral cravings, or from a need for anxiety management or a concrete sign of caring, but the therapist's job is not to meet such needs concretely. The children need to learn that the therapist's job is to help them learn to gratify emotional needs in more mature ways. Futile attempts to gratify them by requesting material goods, including food, from others is not one of those ways. Although some excellent therapists believe that rock candy helps very young children to be less anxious in therapy, both of us have treated and tested children between one and three years of age without needing to use this "adjunctive" tool. Classroom teachers don't feed children in their classrooms, except at scheduled snack times, nor do gym or speech therapists use candies or cookies to bribe children to cooperate or to win them over. They expect cooperation and they eventually get it.

Richard Epstein's report (2003) of his therapy of Alice, an eight-year-old girl in residential treatment, illustrates the difficulties encountered when a therapist meets a need concretely.

> Alice asked me if I would get her a special candy jar for her to keep in my session room so that she could have a sweet during our sessions. The next day I purchased a small blue ceramic candy jar and some "treats" with which to stock it. I also told Alice, who was overweight, that there were a couple of conditions to this arrangement. The first was that she could only have a modest amount of candy at each session. The second was that she could not make the other children jealous by returning to her classroom after our sessions and gloating to the other children about the candy. Initially, this worked out well. Alice soon began to try, however, to bargain different arrangements that would allow her to eat as much as possible. (p. 62)

Alice's demands illustrate the truth of the old saying about needy individuals: "Give them an inch and they will take a mile." Epstein was eventually able to limit Alice's candy demands. Nevertheless, the constant bargaining for control of the candy jar, until she accepted his limits, not only slowed down therapeutic progress but may have produced a fantasy of Epstein as a "rescuing angel" (Benjamin 1994) or even the "golden fantasy" —the need to have her needs met through no work of her own (Cohen 1988). The behaviors Alice displayed following this segment in her treatment suggest that, for a while, she viewed Epstein more as a rescuing parent, or even as a boyfriend, than as a therapist. She placed her hand on his shoulder when following him downstairs from the therapy room to the classroom, and when this action passed without comment for several weeks, she asked him if he liked it when she did so. She ran away from the crisis counselor to his office. She ran to him when she was upset, giving him big hugs while complaining about unfair treatment from child-care staff. She searched for him when upset by other children and used him to intervene in her conflicts with other staff.

Epstein explains her behavior as the result of his becoming a "new object" in her internal object world (Altman 1995)—a goal of therapy that we discuss elsewhere. Later, Epstein confesses that his own rescue fantasies, his countertransference feelings, may have contributed to these behaviors and temporarily set back her treatment. We commend him for his honest presentation of this interesting case—one illustrating the dilemmas therapists face when treating children in gorilla suits.

Silence can also be controlling, particularly if the therapist feels pressured to respond to it in a certain way. For example, Christopher Bonovitz (2003) states of being faced with a silent child,

I found myself desperately trying anything that might spark his curiosity, inviting him to take notice of the world around him. Zachary drifted further away, and my zealous invitations seemed to crowd him out even more and thwart any morsel of will on his part."

The child controlled the therapist by his silence and refusal to interact. In this instance, limit setting is in order, but the process is more difficult. The child can't simply be told that "therapy is a place for talking or playing," followed by an explanation of the consequences for failing to do so. Bonovitz hit on the tactic of mirroring the child's every action, stating that he surrendered to the child's control and domination, something that he felt was required to "pass his test," a concept articulated by others (Weis, Sampson, and the Mount Zion Psychotherapy Research Group 1986).

Instead of mirroring the child's actions, a client-centered therapist might reflect the child's fears of interacting or efforts to control:

> THERAPIST: It seems like you don't want to be here today. I wonder if you're not a little scared to play with the toys in the room, thinking that if you play you might have to stay here a long time. But your mother is out in the waiting room and will come and get you when the big hand of the clock is on the three.

When faced with silence, both of us engage in some play activity while the child sits silently. Rarely do we respond to the child's silence in kind because the child will experience the therapist's quietness as distance, disinterest, or disengagement, which are the reasons for the child's silence in the first place. We draw or have puppets talk to one another about the child's possible feelings. Sometimes we whisper into a tape recorder and play it back.

A substantial amount of literature exists on treating children referred for silent behavior, called selective or elective mutism, because they usually talk at home, often a "blue streak," but we do not discuss this disorder here since most gorilla-suit wearers are silent resisters only on occasion.

LIMIT PHYSICAL INVOLVEMENT

Some children want the therapist to restrain them physically because restraint fulfills a wish to be hurt and attacked. With such children, the therapist may need to terminate particular sessions.

Restraints often follow other limits placed on behavior. When toys are taken from the child to prevent them from being destroyed, the child often becomes disruptive and needs to be held by the therapist until calm. Often when children are restrained by the therapist, they respond along these lines:

> CHILD: I'm not afraid of you! Let me go! You're hurting me!
> THERAPIST: All I'm going to do is hold you until you calm down and agree to stop breaking the toys in the playroom.

Typically children promise they won't continue the prohibited behavior, only to do so when given the opportunity. While they know what a promise is, few have ever experienced promises being kept. Parents don't keep them; why should they? Often when restraining a child, the inexperienced therapist will accede to seemingly desperate pleas for freedom. The response of a more experienced therapist follows:

> CHILD: Let me go. I'm calm. I won't break any more toys. You don't trust me!
> THERAPIST: That's true, I don't. You have betrayed my trust on several occasions. Just last week, you promised that if I let you go, you wouldn't break a toy, and when I did, you broke it anyway. No, I will hold you until I can feel that you are physically relaxed.

With some children, the response should be as follows:

> THERAPIST: I will not become a policeman and hold you when you misbehave because this would fulfill your old wish to be hurt and attacked. We will have to stop therapy for today, and your wish to attack me can be worked on in our next session when you are able to play about it or talk about it.

Therapists working in school systems will experience considerable difficulty terminating such sessions early because the child will refuse to leave the room, often yelling, "You can't make me!" When the therapist attempts to escort the child back to class, the child will either run away or display behavior that results in being physically restrained by an adult. This behavior feeds the need to be attacked and disrupts the class when the child returns. Often the child will refuse to leave therapy, even when the session is terminated at the usual time. If the therapist leaves the room instead of trying to escort the child, the child may attempt to destroy the room or may disrupt others by running through the hallways. This behavior makes the therapist feel and look helpless and ineffective to others; the child has done to the therapist what has been done to the child. It also makes the therapist late for the next appointment, angering both the waiting child, who tries to wait patiently, and the child's teacher, who has to deal with the student's anxious anticipation. No professional can handle such children without supports, even when the therapist is big enough to restrain the child.

> THERAPIST: See, you win. You got me to physically restrain you. You left me no choice. Now you can yell and scream that I, like all adults, am mean and rotten. You really want me to care about you and play with you, but your anger at me is so strong that it gets in your way! You want me to feel as helpless as you have felt.

The therapist will need a secure place to take the child so that the child can calm down and return to class without venting anger at the teacher. If the child is stronger than the therapist, as can be the case with large latency-aged children, then the program in which the child is enrolled will need a crisis counselor to assist in the child's removal. After the children get used to the crisis counselor's presence, they will often leave the therapy room on their own when requested to do so.

> THERAPIST: Bill, you have a choice: either you leave on your own or I'll get Mr. Brown to escort you out. I'm not going to get into a scuffle with you. That's how you handle all your differences with me and other adults.
> CHILD: You can't make me, so you get someone else. Big deal! I don't care.
> THERAPIST: You're right, I can't physically make you leave. In fact, I can't make you do anything you don't want to do, and you can go through life challenging me, and all other adults who could care about you, and I can't do anything about it. I will feel as helpless as you do. Now please leave on your own, or Mr. Brown will come and escort you.

Whenever a therapist works with children who may have to be physically restrained to limit their destructive behavior, parents, other caretakers, and adults servicing the children in other settings should be forewarned that physically restraining actions may be taken with the children. Parents should sign a written consent that allows the staff working with their child to use physical restraint when necessary. The type of restraints that may be used should be demonstrated so that parents will be familiar with what their child may have to experience, particularly when the child's versions of what happened can vary considerably from what actually happened.

At times, the children's anger is triggered unpredictably, they lash out, and they must be held by adults to prevent injury. High-quality residential and day treatment programs, which typically serve the most aggressive children, train all staff to apply state-approved physical holding techniques that minimize the risk of injury. They also monitor regularly the number of such holding incidents in order to keep them to an absolute minimum, ensuring that holds are used only when absolutely necessary to prevent harm to oneself or others. Often children's angry outbursts can be defused when the adult in charge remains calm and employs verbal techniques that reduce threat, ensure safety, and redirect or distract the child from his or her rage. We discuss these techniques in *Understanding and Treating the Aggression of Children* and elsewhere (Mordock 1999a). Humor and distraction, if well timed and contextually appropriate, are included among the techniques. Verbal de-escalation of anger is not always possible, however. Consequently, professionals working with aggressive children and with their families need to be well versed in the application of therapeutic holds to prevent unnecessary harm. Therapeutic holds should never be used as a punishment or a correctional measure.

WHAT LIMITS ACHIEVE

Two seemingly disparate images of the therapist need to occur for therapy to be effective with gorilla-suit wearers. First, a strong, firm attitude needs to be displayed. This attitude will help the child feel protected from feared emotions. Nevertheless, the attitude also arouses rebellious feelings because the child loses control and, in turn, self-respect. Second, the therapist must display a comradely parental attitude with which the child can identify. The child hopes to be as strong as the therapist so that feared emotions can be managed. The therapist also has to be perceived as kind but not weak. Gorilla-suit wearers often respond to kindness with distrustful contempt. This link must be broken before they can be helped to curb their impulses. And efforts to break the link will be resisted because the child experiences an identity crisis when identification with the aggressor weakens.

Setting Limits on Other Obtrusive Behavior

Less obvious, but equally ruinous, behaviors also need to be limited. We discuss limiting efforts to elicit anger, seductiveness, defiance (both obvious and disguised), projections, unproductive play, efforts to dilute the therapy relationship, behavior outside the session, comparisons with other therapists, perseveration, and institutional practices that distract from the therapy process. Limit setting, while it can take up considerable time in the beginning of therapy, contributes to the therapy process and diminishes as therapy progresses.

A corrective emotional experience is created by the therapist's constant non-critical objectivity and by the therapist's not responding in kind to the child's intense anxiety and hostility. Some children will attempt to anger the therapist, others to seduce the therapist, and still others to defy the therapist. Particularly needy children will try to get the therapist to play any role but the role of therapist. All these behaviors must be limited.

LIMIT EFFORTS TO ANGER

Because children in gorilla suits are chock full of anger, they expect others to be in the same state. When the therapist doesn't appear angry, the children do their best to provoke the therapist's anger in order to protect their world view. And often they are successful at doing so. But eventually the children learn that the therapist uses power only for the children's benefit. The child experiences this power when facing the therapist's steadfast commitment to the child. After a series of efforts to anger the therapist, a child remarks:

> CHILD: What does it take to get you angry?
> THERAPIST: You've made me angry often.
> CHILD: No, you just raise your voice.
> THERAPIST: You mean what will it take to see me lose control and act wildly and run around like a crazy man, screaming and yelling?
> CHILD: Yeah.
> THERAPIST: I may yell at you someday and I will restrain you, but I will never punch you in the face, call you awful names, or deliberately deceive you.
> CHILD: [*Silence*]
> THERAPIST: I understand how you feel. You don't trust anyone who tries to stop you from doing something you want to do, but my job is to help you explore why you feel and act as you do. While I won't try to put anything over on you, I'm sure you will do so to me since that's a serious problem of yours.
> CHILD: What do you mean?
> THERAPIST: You will try to get me to do things for you that you can do for yourself, and you will try to get me upset to prove that I neglect you and don't do things for you.
> CHILD: I want to leave now. You can't make me stay here.
> THERAPIST: [*Places himself at the door.*] I will stay here until the time is up. I could let you go and be unconcerned about you, but this is not what I'm going to do. I will help you not to run from your problems all your life.
> CHILD: I've got no problems.
> THERAPIST: But lots of adults and kids have problems with you. Your mother reports that she can't get you up for school in the morning, you're not working in class, you hit other children. It would seem to me that you're not very happy.
> CHILD: Well, that's what you think.

LIMIT SEDUCTIVENESS

Children who have been sexually abused can become easily excited or aroused in the playroom. Others display seductive behavior because it has become a significant component of their personality makeup. They have identified not only with the aggressor but also with his or her controlling sexuality. Putting limits on such behavior can be as simple as the following:

> THERAPIST: Alice, you don't have to do that in here.

Corrective efforts can be included:

THERAPIST: Lisa, please pull your skirt down over your knees and sit up straight—that's how girls are supposed to sit.

LIMIT PROJECTIONS

Sometimes children are frightened by their own projections. The child who picks up the scissors and then flees, saying "You're going to hurt me," reveals confusion between attacker and victim. The child who wants to make swords will quickly want to duel. He or she is closer to tearing the room apart than is the child who draws swords or spins fantasies about sword-wielding warriors. Encouraging fantasy development sometimes alternates with discouraging grandiose fantasies that feed omnipotence.

CHILD: [*Picks up a large piece of paper and says it's a sword.*]
THERAPIST: You wish it were a sword.
CHILD: I once had a sword.
THERAPIST: It was not a real one.
CHILD: It was plastic but it had a real pearl handle!

LIMIT UNPRODUCTIVE PLAY

When the child remains defensively silent (by silent, we mean engaged in un-revealing solitary play, endless drawing, model building, or game playing) in or-der to avoid revealing the self, information obtained from parents or teachers must be used to confront the defenses of denial and isolation. Richard Gard-ner (1986) uses the term *ignorant interrogator* to refer to the style of questioning put to the child. With younger children, therapists can use a wizard puppet to ask questions, and on some occasions the therapist can be a television news re-porter interviewing the child.

Many angry children will not draw or play out their feelings. Neverthe-less, the goal is to convert action into fantasy. Often the progression is first from action to action fantasy. For example, the therapist uses a cylindrical cloth punching bag on which drawings can be made in chalk to encourage play ac-tion. The child can be given a Nerf ball and told to throw it at a fantasy target on the wall. The child can be asked who the target is, why he is mad at the target, etc. These outlets are initially used to block destructive interaction and to encourage movement toward symbolic and verbalized aggression. Getting the child to talk while engaged in play action is a step toward delaying the direct expression of impulses.

LIMIT DILUTION OF THE THERAPY RELATIONSHIP

Clinicians in schools or in other group settings may be pressured by the children to let a peer accompany them to their individual sessions. Acquiescing to this pressure is a bad idea for several reasons. First, the child may be testing the therapist's commitment to him or her as an individual. Second, the child may be attempting to avoid dealing with his or her own issues. In one day treatment program, inexperienced clinicians, following pressure from children to be seen in therapy together, allowed children to pick a peer they wanted to be seen with for an extra "socialization" session. The extra session was added not because the clinicians had considered the "real" reasons the children might have made the requests, but because the Individualized Educational Plans developed by the referring public school required that all the children be seen individually. The extra session would avoid the legal problem. Nevertheless, if the clinicians had extra time for service delivery, the vast majority of children would have been better served if they were scheduled for more sessions of individual play therapy. The result was children switching selections at a whim, vying with one another for selection, or even plotting with one another for selections that would get them out of class during a particular period. Needless to say, this practice was stopped not because the clinicians realized they had been duped, but because the teachers found the practice disruptive and complained to the principal. It should never have been allowed in the first place.

In some intensive treatment centers, duo therapy, formerly called peer therapy, has been employed as a bridge to peer relationships in the ego-impaired child (Applestein 1993; Lieberman and Smith 1991; Mitchel and Levine 1982). Nevertheless, gorilla-suit wearers rarely meet the criteria for this treatment modality (listed in Bar, Karcher, and Selman 1998, and Mordock 1999b) early in placement.

Although gorilla-suit wearers express the desire for friendships, their strong need for adult attention makes them rivals and interferes with friendship development. In addition, their need to be "first in everything," their distrustfulness and refusal to share, and their misperception of intention destroy friendship efforts.

In some institutional or special educational settings, particularly those in which the children earn small sums of money, either through chore performance or a behavior modification program, the therapists escort the children to a neighborhood store where they can spend their money. Therapists, especially those with a behavioral bent, justify these trips by claiming they are socialization experiences that help the children to be appropriately assertive or to make choices. Others say that teaching and child-care staffs are busy with groups of children and have no time to escort individual children to town. If that is truly the case, and some children's treatment plans call for trips to town following improved behavior, then perhaps therapists should escort children who are not on their own caseload. If the children act up when in the company of someone other than their therapist, then they are not really ready for trips to town, and the practice should be abandoned or postponed. By engaging in such practices, the therapist not only dilutes but also blurs and confuses, in the mind of the child, the role of the therapist.

LIMIT UNDISCIPLINED BEHAVIOR OUTSIDE THERAPY

Every antisocial act that the child displays needs to be explored, both in terms of its appropriateness and in terms of identifying the ideas in the child's head that led to it. Because the therapist does not punish or scold the child for these disclosures, the child learns that disclosure is not traumatic. Introducing confrontations in the role of the ignorant interrogator usually provokes the child to tell his side of the story. Sometimes parents, and even teachers, are unwilling to share information about a child's behaviors. If a teacher is reluctant to be observed, the child can be watched on the playground, and his or her difficulties will be easy to see. In a child-care setting, not only will the staff tell the child's therapist about the child's transgressions, but they will expect them to be addressed in therapy.

We will never forget witnessing a session in which a boy played aimlessly, in silence, throughout a fifty-minute session. The therapist knew that the child had injured his favorite staff member following a loss of control. Everybody in the center knew it! Even the casual observer could see the child was distraught and was willing to reveal these feelings in therapy. Yet the therapist said nothing. When questioned after the session, the therapist defended his actions by stating that his introduction of the topic would destroy the transference relationship. Not so! An empathetic therapist could remark, "You look very troubled today—how come?" or "You seem lost in thought today—how come?" Others would be even more direct: "I heard that you hurt your favorite staff member today. That must make you feel guilty and worry that you have lost her as a friend." Even if the boy doesn't feel bad—even if he lacks empathy—he needs to learn that empathetic feelings exist and that others have them. But in the case mentioned above, the boy's guilt was written all over his face!

The therapist needs to "think out loud" in the presence of the "silent" child. The therapist talks about various problems currently troubling the child's caretakers and explores past and present reasons for their occurrence.

THERAPIST: I understand that you hit your best friend today. You must feel bad.

CHILD: No, I didn't—I don't feel anything.

THERAPIST: No, it's not true that you don't feel anything. You just don't feel bad or guilty. Perhaps you feel defiant—a defiant feeling: "I don't care!" Maybe you feel righteous—he deserved it because he treated you unfairly. Maybe you feel indifferent or numbed.

Because the child initially responded with a "feeling" instead of an excuse, the therapist took the opportunity to help the child to label possible feelings. Labeling is an affective-educational approach used with aggressive children when anger is their only response to frustration. We discuss its use further in chapter 15. The children cannot label feelings of disgust, embarrassment, discouragement, shame, jealousy, worry, etc. Helping them to do so also helps them to realize that there are other ways to deal with feelings besides simply striking out.

When reality is brought into sessions, children in gorilla suits are masters at excusing their behavior, avoiding effort, playing the victim, refusing to accept obligations, and refusing to acknowledge fear. They feel entitled to display unrealistic expectations and false pride, fail to plan ahead, and make irresponsible decisions. All these behaviors are part of their power tactics as well as their defenses. They are efforts to dominate others in struggles and to avoid shame and helplessness. They are used in efforts to fool not only others but also the self. These behaviors are also manipulative. We use this word with caution because so much of children's anxious and symptomatic behavior is described by parents and educators as manipulative. We use the word here to mean the child's efforts to discredit the therapist's trustworthiness. If the child's stories are believed, the believer is weak and not worth identifying with. Moreover, the child cannot be truly liked because the real child remains a mystery. A person strong enough to resist the child's manipulations provides the child with the security the child so desperately needs. At the same time, one part of the child believes the stories (assumptive realities). Confrontations, put in the form of gentle puzzlement, are required to chip away at the child's "reasons" for inappropriate behavior.

THERAPIST: Did you bring your point sheet to show me?

CHILD: I forgot.

THERAPIST: Gee, last week you remembered that I said I'd help you build a model. Suppose I forgot to bring the model? Probably you didn't bring your point sheet because you didn't earn many points. You must have been disappointed.

CHILD: [*Changes the subject.*] My mom's going to give me a race-car set.

THERAPIST: [*The therapist could point out that the child's failure to "win the therapist's approval" for a favorable point sheet is followed by fantasies of getting some-*

thing. Instead the response, on this occasion, was a limit-setting statement.] I think Mom is too upset with you to give you that, particularly since you order her to buy it like you order me to give you things. You're going to be disappointed.

Many caregivers are angered by the aggressive child's chronic lying in an attempt to avoid responsibility for actions. But lying should not be confused with denial or feelings of entitlement. These children, not unlike other children whose "facts" become truths, quickly believe their own lies, a quick fix for their inability to tolerate the shame or primitive guilt they feel. They are masters at distorting situations, and the lie is part of this distortion. Direct confrontation of the lie is useless. They also feel entitled, as in the following example:

> A child-care worker heard a noise in the kitchen, went downstairs, and turned on the lights. The room was empty, but when he opened the door to the small pantry, a nine-year-old with cookie crumbs on his face immediately cried out, "I didn't take the cookies!" When this incident was discussed in the next therapy session, the child insisted that he felt entitled to the cookies because he felt he had been unfairly deprived of his dessert at the evening meal.

Confronting children with their behavior in therapy is different from confronting them elsewhere. The children are usually engaged in an activity with the therapist. Sometimes the therapist is making something or doing something for them, timing symbolic giving with "taking away."

LIMIT COMPARISONS WITH OTHER THERAPISTS

When working where a number of therapists provide services, such as in a child-care institution, residential treatment center, psychiatric hospital, day treatment center, special education complex, or public school, therapists should stick to limit setting regardless of other therapists' actions. Both of us have worked in settings in which other therapists gave their child clients candy, cookies, or donuts at every session. Not everyone understands the limits most children need.

> CHILD: Dr. Bonopart lets his children have donuts in therapy!
> THERAPIST: I'm not Dr. Bonopart!
> CHILD: But why can't I have a donut?
> THERAPIST: With me, therapy time is not eating time.
> CHILD: But how come? Dr. Bonopart's kids get donuts [*get to go uptown/to the gym/to build more models/to call their parents, etc.*]!

THERAPIST: I guess you think Dr. Bonopart likes the kids he sees in therapy better than I like you.
CHILD: Yes.
THERAPIST: Then you probably wonder why you got me for a therapist instead of Dr. Bonopart, who likes children better.

Although therapy could continue in this vein, with reflections of the child's feelings about being denied wanted goodies, such efforts are usually unnecessary. Most children respect both the limit and the individual differences between adults, and they move on. In addition, children in group settings almost always compare notes. After they learn that all the children seen by Dr. Crenshaw or Dr. Mordock are treated equally, the topic is rarely broached again. In fact, for clinical reasons, we have seen children in places other than in the playroom. When confronted about our behavior by children who want similar "privileges," we respond, "Different children have different needs, and your need is to be seen in the playroom," and we are rarely challenged.

Therapists should refrain from explaining why they don't do what other adults do. In the dialogue above, the therapist responded, "With me, therapy time is not eating time." The "with me" prefaced the response in order not to belittle Dr. Bonopart or to imply that children seen by him get inferior treatment. In fact, Dr. Bonopart may not actually give his clients donuts! The child may have lied! But if the good doctor does and he is under the supervision of a trained child therapist, then his need to give or to bribe will soon disappear. If he is not, and he continues to feed his clients, then the less said about him the better. To squelch the impulse to criticize the Dr. Bonoparts of the world, therapists should contemplate getting sick and having their clients reassigned to one.

LIMITING PERSEVERATION

A number of children in gorilla suits suffer from developmental deficits, mostly from subtle injuries to their brain following physical abuse, that result in a variety of symptoms that used to be subsumed under the informal labels "minimal brain damage" or "minimal cerebral dysfunction," but which are now subsumed under the diagnostic label, "learning disabled." One symptom sometimes seen in children with this label is perseveration, the inability to immediately stop a motor action once it has been initiated.

The classic example is the child who draws a circle and then keeps going around and around the completed circle so that when the child is distracted by something and stops drawing, he or she is surprised to see that what has actually been created is either a series of overlapping circles or a thick, dark circle. But other perseverative behavior is not so easy to recognize. Children repeat themselves verbally, tap their fingers or stamp their feet longer than usual, cut food repeatedly, run around longer, or count to twenty instead of ten. Any motor act, including verbal acts, can be repeated, and often adults perceive the repetitions as noncompliance. And aggressive children may bluster longer, punch longer, and display longer temper tantrums. We have seen some children so exhausted by prolonged temper tantrums that they fall asleep immediately afterwards, and the neurologist working with them suspects seizures aggravated by the arousal of strong emotion.

When a therapist suspects that a child, in sort of a trance, endlessly repeats an act for no apparent purpose, the activity should be gently interrupted. If it is endless scribbling, the crayon is gently taken from the child and an alternative activity suggested. Endless swearing is also interrupted by some planned distraction. Although a long-range goal may be to help the child recognize that he or she suffers from this difficulty, early in therapy the less said the better.

LIMITING INSTITUTIONAL PRACTICES THAT DISTRACT FROM THE TOTAL TREATMENT PROGRAM

Therapists working in institutional, day treatment, or special education settings should schedule children for therapy sessions not when the child wants to go, but when the child's treatment team, or the staff working with the child, decides the child should be scheduled. For example, if the child is a poor reader, then the child should not be scheduled for therapy during the reading period. In fact, because of the serious academic deficiencies of gorilla-suit wearers, none should be taken for therapy during academic subjects unless the staff feels that a particular child can be reached academically first through art, music, or shop, but this decision should be evaluated regularly and the therapy schedule changed accordingly.

Some children have been known to make rapid academic advancement after a major breakthrough in therapy, but such events cannot be predicted. While play therapy holds an honored place in the comprehensive treatment of children, the research suggests that children who are closest to grade level when discharged from treatment facilities make better adjustments in the community. Therapists should have faith in teachers—most can find ways to help children to learn. Counting on a breakthrough in therapy to accomplish this task demeans the role of special education.

To facilitate a flexible therapy schedule, clinicians working with gorilla-suit wearers should work late afternoons and evenings. A number of well-known treatment centers employ therapists who work from 9:00 a.m. to 5:00 p.m. and who take children away from academic classes for therapy, primarily because the therapy staff believes the children would resist therapy if taken out of art, music, or afternoon and evening recreational activities. If teachers are consulted in such settings, the consultant will find that therapy scheduling is often a source of unspoken friction between the educational and clinical staffs.

If a child refuses to come to therapy, for example during art class, and the treatment team has decided that the child should be scheduled for therapy during art class, then plans need to be developed to set limits—to find nonpunitive ways to get the child to come. But such "institutional resistance" by children has not been encountered in settings where the adults in charge decide when the children should receive therapy. Just like children should not rule the therapist, they should not rule the institution. There have been several studies that suggest adolescents can get worse in intensive treatment settings; we wonder if the culture of these settings was not a contributing factor. Professionals often leave programs designed to treat adolescents who still wear gorilla suits, complaining that "the kids actually ran the institution."

LIMITS ARE NOT FOREVER

When children in gorilla suits discover they are consistently unsuccessful in inducing the therapist to react to them as have others in their past—that they have failed to produce the expected outcome—they alter their behavior in the therapy room. Later, much later, if treatment has been successful, they will change their behavior elsewhere.

In chapter 1, we talk about the therapeutic alliance. All therapist actions, including limit-setting ones, are directed toward building and maintaining this alliance. The children need to develop positive ties with the therapist. They cannot be interpreted out of anger any more than they can be talked out of it. The therapist's goal is to create feelings that will tame anger. All children, no matter how tough, are looking for a redeeming relationship. There is a chink in their armor, and that chink is the need for love—the need to fill that "vast empty space," for which their "anger" is a substitute, with feelings of self-worth. Limits on their behavior, or control by a significant other, contribute to the development of self-control, and self-control is followed by the possibility of meaningful attachments.

The goal of initial sessions is to make a connection. Focusing early in treatment on understanding reasons for children's anger can impede that task. Reasons for rage cannot be understood until the children have built up a reservoir of positive images of the therapist and of the self. Helping children to build a therapeutic alliance is in keeping with the goal of strengthening relationships with caretakers. The therapist is a caretaker, and the aim applies to him or her as well.

> THERAPIST: I realize how upset you are with me. And I'm pleased that you have kept control of yourself and your feelings. Can you draw a picture of how you feel?

Limit setting also helps to shift feelings acted out to feelings verbalized, a major goal of therapy. Limit setting often results in the children's communicating the violent diffuse fantasies kept hidden in their heads, and fantasies revealed are less frightening than those hidden. And once revealed, they are less likely to be acted upon. Limit setting also brings reality into the treatment sessions, and reality is something else gorilla-suit wearers need.

LIMITS SET IN LATER PHASES OF THERAPY

While limits are most often set in the initial stages of therapy, there are times when the child regresses and long-obeyed rules are broken. There are also limits that need to be set because of the relationship that has developed.

Limit Defiance, Both Obvious and Disguised

Often, and particularly after a session the therapist thinks was especially productive, children will refuse to do anything. Some therapists let them sit and do nothing, responding with statements such as "It seems like you want to do nothing today. If that's the case, I'll just sit here and do nothing with you!" While both of us have responded similarly at times, usually the child's anxiety in such a situation gets unbearable, and he or she asks to terminate therapy. This request puts the therapist in a quandary. Should the child be given permission to leave, or should he or she be required to stay? If the child is required to stay, anxiety can escalate to physical aggression. More often, especially if the behavior followed a productive session, the therapist can say something along these lines:

> THERAPIST: I wonder if you were troubled by what took place in our last session and you don't want to be troubled again? Perhaps I made a mistake when I let you play in the sandbox and you angrily buried several adults in the sand. Perhaps the anger you showed bothered you.

It can also be helpful, when a sensitive issue has surfaced in a therapy session, for the therapist to predict future resistance:

THERAPIST: I think that telling me about your mother was very up-setting to you. Next time, you might not even feel like coming to therapy, or you may refuse to talk about anything that matters to you.

Sometimes the defiance is more subtle and the reason for it unknown. Usually this type of defiance occurs early in therapy. The therapist should make neutral remarks when it does, such as the following:

CHILD: I can't do that.
THERAPIST: Lots of times you didn't feel like doing something you're capable of doing, particularly when you know I want you to do it—you hate feeling controlled by me. Sometimes just doing what you think I want feels like I held you down and sat on you—that's what "feeling controlled" can feel like to you.
CHILD: I'm too tired to do that.
THERAPIST: Gee, you have lots of energy for those things you want to do.

It is crucial to help children to distinguish between "I can't" and "I won't." The latter is a form of pseudohelplessness that the therapist should not accept. Bonime (1989) calls this *angry unwillingness*. The child actively resists using his or her own capabilities and personal resources. The price of winning this battle of resistance is chronic underachievement and stunted personal growth. This pattern, rooted in feeling exploited and overcontrolled in child-hood, can lead to a lifetime practice of low productivity in order to thwart the expectations of others.

Limit Adoption Fantasies

Adoption fantasies occur in all children when angry at parents or disillusioned by them. Children from rejecting homes or those living away from home fre-quently fantasize that the therapist will adopt them or become their foster par-ent. These fantasies need to be addressed.

THERAPIST: Sometimes I think that you'd like to come and live with me.
CHILD: Yeah, could I?
THERAPIST: It's only natural that you'd want to live with someone you trust and feel kindly toward. I like you very much, too. But I will never re-place your parents. It's not my job to do so. Some children do live in foster homes, but I'm a therapist and not a foster parent.
CHILD: But you could just take me.
THERAPIST: It would be wonderful if I liked you best of all the kids I had in therapy and made an exception for you.

CHILD: Yeah, could you?

THERAPIST: I know it's very painful not to feel special when you're not sure who loves you—my taking you home would help ease that pain. But I can't help you that way. I can only help you to work at how your pain sometimes keeps you from getting affection from other adults in your life.

CHILD: [*Sulks for a while, and just before the end of the session asks for something on the therapist's desk.*] Can I have this pen?

THERAPIST: You'd like to have something of mine to keep me with you even though I can't take you home to live with me.

CHILD: [Silence]

THERAPIST: You can't have my pen, but next time you come, I will make you something that you can keep.

CHILD: [*Storms out of the room.*]

Unlike the child who requests objects to control the therapist, this child requested the therapist's pen for solace. The request is still denied, but the therapist's response differs.

Therapists also need to limit their own adoption fantasies because attachments to grossly neglected children can easily create the desire to make up for the poor parenting the children received. Marianne Parsons, a therapist on the staff of the Anna Freud Center, in London, describes her feelings about one of her clients.

> During Peggy's treatment, I have often been severely tested in the countertransference by feelings of helplessness, hopelessness, and irritation, and at such moments I was sometimes tempted to give up on her. On other occasions, I felt so bad about her, and so angry toward her parents for their past and present contributions to her difficulties, that I was tempted to offer myself as a more reliable and caring figure than either her father or mother seemed to be. (1990, pp. 452–453)

In fact, helpless feelings often trigger the therapist's need to make visible changes in the child's life—to parent the child rather than to continue treatment they perceive as unsuccessful. The therapist may display physical affection toward the child, bend the rules a little here and there, and if the child is in a treatment center, seek out the child more often between therapy hours or take the child home on holidays. Therapists with strong rescue fantasies and who take pride in being good parents are especially prone to this countertransference problem. For example, therapists who work in residential treatment or day treatment centers and who find themselves drawn to some of their cases are experiencing countertransference feelings that can hinder treatment, and they need to discuss these feelings in supervision.

· 5 ·

A Decision Grid for Play Therapy

This chapter discusses making a major decision when starting therapy. The clinician needs to decide whether to explore the child's troubled past, called the invitational approach, or whether to shore up the child's defenses, help the child to develop new defenses and better skills to cope with strong affects, and leave the child's past traumas alone, called the coping approach. The decision is usually not an either-or one but rather a question of which approach to select first. The selection should be based on a number of factors. They include a careful assessment of the strengths of the child, the involvement and support of the family, the level of ego functioning at any given point in therapy, the presence or absence of additional stressors in the child's life at the time, and the presence or absence of external supports. Often the child's entering behavior dictates the coping approach, such as when the child presents as too weak and disorganized or too well defended. Other children require the coping approach when they regress under the invitational approach. Both need a period of ego strengthening before tackling strong affects. Consequently, in actual practice, the therapist switches back and forth between the two general approaches.

$\mathscr{I}$deally, all traumatized clients would display better mental health if they faced and worked through the painful or traumatic life events they repressed. Unfortunately, such work involves considerable emotional unburdening. Those with insufficient resources to cope with strong affects and those whose intense feelings would seriously interfere with their daily functioning should not focus on their past traumas. When exploring traumas, clients can experience emotions so disorganizing that their concentration is significantly impaired, and regression occurs. In children, the regression can put them at risk for school suspension, foster home expulsion, or placement in more restrictive environments. In such situations, the improvement the child might make as therapy progresses and the child regains composure would be offset by further disruptions in life.

In contrast, if the same child is enrolled in a day treatment program, residential treatment center, or psychiatric hospital, where staff can make accommodations for regressed behavior and create a "holding" environment where other demands are minimized, then the benefits may outweigh the risks. Soldiers can't grieve the loss of fallen comrades or deal emotionally with the horrors of war until the war is over, nor can children mourn their losses or face their past traumas when actively struggling with a demanding environment.

Repression, or selective forgetting of traumatic experiences, has been demonstrated outside clinical situations. Interviews of adults known to have been physically abused as children reveal that some report never having been abused (Femina, Yeager, and Lewis 1990). In addition, clients who terminate treatment without making substantial inner changes and who return for treatment later often repress earlier experiences. For example, a girl who had been repeatedly sexually abused by her cousin and who attended a highly structured therapy group for sexually abused girls was referred again for treatment five years after her first treatment. When she began her second treatment, she wore a locket around her neck with a picture of her cousin in it. She denied ever having been abused by him and insisted that she was treated earlier only for her angry "behavior." At no time was she willing to examine her past, and ego-supportive therapy was used with her (Mordock 1998). Dr. Mordock knows a young man who has been in and out of mental hospitals most of his life and who, in a casual conversation about fathers, stated, "My old man never once laid a hand on me!" His sister was repeatedly raped by their father, and her subsequent aberrations were mistaken by psychiatrists for hallucinations, leading to a diagnosis of schizophrenia, her psychiatric hospitalization for eighteen months, and a defeating image of herself as mentally ill. She related in private that her brother had been beaten unmercifully for years by their father and that both of them were regularly taken to the backyard chicken coop to witness the bloody beheading of a chicken, with their father threatening to do the same to the children if they didn't "mind him at all times." She felt that her brother's denial was the only way he could keep his sanity. His ego had been so damaged by his father's rejecting and abusive behavior that denial and repression kept him from being overwhelmed by terrifying memories. He will probably never be a candidate for an uncovering therapy.

Not only do some clients deny their abuse, but their parents deny it as well, even years later. Wives will deny that their husbands abused their children long after the husband's death and the children's entry into adulthood. To admit to the abuse means that they failed to protect their children, so they repress the abusive episodes.

Adults who function quite well in spite of earlier unresolved traumas can decide if they want to face their past traumas. For example, a young woman who raised herself out of poverty, who survived a traumatic divorce, and who put herself through college while raising two young children entered treatment for several problems, one of which was her inability to enjoy sexual relations in intimate circumstances. When it became obvious that her sexual difficulties resulted from incest with her father when she was a child, she made a decision to drop out of therapy and forgo her sexual adjustment. She knew that if she got in touch with her real feelings about the incest, she would become so distraught that she wouldn't be able to function at her job or even as a mother. She felt traumatized just by flashbacks of the experience. As a teenage runaway, she had received therapy while in a psychiatric hospital, and when she dealt with other significant traumas in her early life, such as chronic physical abuse and ongoing threats to her life, all she did between therapy sessions was take her medication, stay in the bed in her hospital room, and sob herself to sleep.

Children receiving therapy, however, aren't mature enough to make such decisions and need help from the therapist to do so. When encouraged to face traumas, then the invitational approach, called the *mastery approach* by Beverly James (1993), is the treatment offered. When treatment is needed but the children are not strong enough for an invitational approach, the coping approach is offered. The Play Therapy Decision Grid presented below was developed to delineate the key components of the invitational and coping approaches to therapy. We use the term *invitational*, rather than *mastery* or even *uncovering*, because the child is "invited" to go as far as he or she can at any point in therapy or at any stage of development.

A Decision Grid for Play Therapy

Child with Weak Ego Resources   **Child with Strong Ego Resources**

↕   ⇨   ⇦   ↕
Coping Approach   **Invitational Approach**

↕   ↕

**Psychoeducation   ⇨   ⇦   Relationship Building
Focusing on Developing   Focusing on Resources
Coping Skills   and Safety**

↕   ↕

**Building Defenses and   ⇨   ⇦   Gradually Confronting
Teaching Pro-Social   Trauma**
Skills

↕

Orientation to a Positive Future

Figure 5.1.   Decision Grid

THE INVITATIONAL APPROACH

In the invitational approach, the child is encouraged, one step at a time, to approach each trauma, abuse experience, or other painful life event and to re-experience and work through the powerful affects and cognitive distortions associated with each, thereby mastering the experience and integrating it into the personality, from which it was split off. While the child can be asked directly about early traumatic experiences, encouragement usually involves the therapist's introducing materials and activities that stimulate memories of aspects of the early abusive experience. A dollhouse can be set up with miniature people arranged in a scenario similar to something the child may have experienced. The therapist may put on a puppet play, create scenes distantly related to the traumatic experience, and ask the child to follow suit. The child can be asked to draw pictures of scenes depicting some of the events suspected, or known, to surround an earlier trauma. Storybooks can be read about other children who have experienced similar traumas, such as abandonment, loss, or death, and the child asked to relate to them. We discuss a number of structured techniques in later chapters.

The invitational approach gets its name from the guiding principle that the child is *invited* to uncover as much as can be uncovered at any point in therapy or at any stage of ego development. Before confronting traumatic experiences, however, the therapist focuses on building the therapeutic relationship, delineating and highlighting ego resources, and making the therapeutic context a safe place (Havens 1989). All of the above entail laying the groundwork for the highly taxing, emotionally focused work of uncovering traumatic memories. When the working-through stage of the therapy is reached, it can last a long time, six to nine months in some cases, especially with children who have been severely abused and traumatized. During this period the child will not make much progress in school or have much energy to learn new skills. Most children, however, will need to do further work at a later stage in their development. And those lacking adequate psychological resources to undertake uncovering work may be able to do so at a later point in their development, when they are more emotionally mature.

Even well-adjusted children with considerable family support will experience an exacerbation of symptoms when working on trauma issues. Gaensbauer's writings (1994, 1995; Drell, Siegel, and Gaensbauer 1993) suggest that he uses an invitational approach with most traumatized children. Nevertheless, he works with very young children in relatively intact families whose parents can support them through the process. In one publication, he presents his treatment of five children traumatized before their development of speech (Gaensbauer 1995). We will present two of them, Beth and Audrey, as examples of the general pattern of heightened symptoms as trauma issues are reexperienced.

Beth was involved in a dramatic auto accident at nine months of age and carried out an accurate enactment of the accident thirteen months later. Gaensbauer saw her for two sessions when she was twenty-two months old.

> In the first session, Beth was presented with miniature people, a toy automobile, a toy truck, and some flat pieces of plastic to represent the river bed into which the car had rolled. She was then asked to demonstrate the accident. She responded with an accurate representation. Toward the end of the session, some toy ambulances were introduced and the family was taken to the hospital.
>
> Immediately following the session, Beth showed an upsurge in symptoms. She woke up screaming twice during the night and at least once each night for the next three weeks. She also repeatedly uttered a word she used when hurt. Her appetite diminished, and she became withdrawn and aggressive, hitting her mother on several occasions. Beth was seen again three weeks later.
>
> Beth sought out the previous play materials and recreated the accident again, but also activating the play siren on the toy ambulance. She and the therapist put play bandages on the doll's injuries, after which she spontaneously turned to her mother and put bandages on her body.

A follow-up after these two sessions suggested that the child was less symptomatic.

Audrey, the second patient, was twelve and a half months old when she witnessed her mother mutilated and killed by a letter bomb, sent by the mother's ex-boyfriend, that exploded in the dining room. The explosion also injured a female family friend, who later died of her wounds. Audrey was found close to her mother's body, unhurt except for minor abrasions on her leg. Since her natural father had abandoned her at birth, she was placed in a foster home and later adopted by a family friend. She displayed numerous symptoms over the next two years that did not abate when treated by a behavior therapist when Audrey was three and a half. When four, she was treated by Gaensbauer. He set up a situation similar to the trauma scene.

> Audrey initially played an affectionate scenario between the baby and the mother, but when holding the baby figure, she violently knocked over the play furniture and the two female doll figures. Her adoptive mother, who was watching, burst into tears. When asked what happened, she held the baby doll close to the prone mother doll and then put it into bed. Shortly thereafter, she showed the therapist a scratch on her arm, explaining that she hurt herself. She then returned to the play items, and following her comment that "the police came," the therapist introduced a policeman into the scene. Shortly thereafter,

while holding the policeman in her hand, she knocked down all the remaining furniture.

After Audrey left the session, she told her adoptive mother that "the doctor hurt me bad" and described having a pain in her chest, a headache, and a stomachache. Nonetheless, two days after the session, she said that she wanted to return to "the doctor where she played with the toys to make [*her*] feel better." Her adoptive mother reported that for the next two days after the first meeting, she had been noticeably calmer and better behaved.

During the second session she was visibly sad and hid behind her adoptive mother, but toward the end of the session, she initiated play and again violently knocked over the dolls. This time, however, she placed the two female dolls in beds in a very nurturing manner, but, as she was leaving, she sent the beds flying. She then received two weeks of intensive therapy directed at helping her to grieve. Audrey was seen again at age six. She presented the therapist with a number of drawings she said were of bombs [*splashes of color on paper*]. She said that one bomb was a picture of herself, suggesting a connection between the violent image of the bomb and her bad behavior. She also knocked over a sewing set in the same manner as she knocked over the dolls when younger.

While less symptomatic, the aftereffect of the trauma, and her new interpretations of its meaning, had affected her self-concept—there was a "Good Audrey" and a "Bad Audrey," one preoccupied with violent images and the other that felt loved and loving. Gaensbauer, worried that she might develop disassociative problems in the future, did not give her a favorable prognosis.

In-depth uncovering of repressed emotions is crucial since correcting cognitive distortions and faulty beliefs, such as self-blame, cannot usually be done until the emotional work is completed. Audrey's status at follow-up revealed how the self-concept can be affected by meanings given to the trauma. In Audrey's case, her negative self-concept developed well after the trauma, suggesting that she attributed new meanings to the trauma long after it occurred. If the emotions connected to the trauma, and perhaps to the later meanings given to it, are not successfully unveiled, the details of the abusive experiences, in which some of the cognitive distortions are rooted, may never surface.

After the children have worked through their intense feelings about their abuse, they often express, reluctantly, that in the terror of the moment, they passively submitted to the abuse, adding with intense emotion, "And I hated myself for it!" Shame is a significant by-product of abuse, especially sexual abuse, and a signal for repression and other defenses to ward off feeling helpless and humiliated. In all shame, an observer is present, either in reality, memory, or fantasy (York

1990). And in the case of abused children, the observers of the abuse-related shame include the abuser and earlier socializing agents identified with shame (Abrams 1990), making it hard to uncover the shameful feelings. The abuser can be around the next corner and can retaliate. Abused children's parents know about their shameful behavior. Children helped to remember their abuse and to integrate the associated experience into their personalities then have to face the self-blame, which was also repressed but which contributed to their symptoms. They can do so only if it is clear that the "observing abuser" can no longer hurt them.

> THERAPIST: It must have been very scary to be driven around in the trunk of a car with your hands tied.
> DARLEEN: I thought I was going to die. It was dark and smelly and hot in there. I thought I was going to suffocate. It seems like hours, but I guess it wasn't.
> THERAPIST: So your mother's boyfriend finally stopped the car and let you out.
> DARLEEN: Yes, but he let me out only after I promised to suck his penis. I will never forgive myself for that! It was disgusting. I thought I was going to gag or vomit. How could I have gone along with it?
> THERAPIST: You are a child, and when this happened, you were a much younger child, and you were scared to death. You did what you did because you were afraid that if you didn't, you would never get out of that dark, suffocating, and smelly trunk.
> DARLEEN: Nothing any therapist could ever say would make me believe that it is not my fault. I should have been stronger. I didn't have to give in. I hate myself for it!
> THERAPIST: Children believe that when something bad like this happens, it is their fault. It's okay to believe that, but it is not true. When there is an adult who performs a sexual act on a child, it is always the adult's fault. You are older now, and you know some other things that you can do to protect yourself, but you were younger then and terrified, and I'm here to tell you that it was not your fault!

The interchanges above illustrate how the self-blame experienced by many abused children is rooted in the conviction that they should have prevented their abuse. Even under the traumatic conditions described, Darleen believed she should have successfully resisted her mother's boyfriend's demands for fellatio. She knew her self-blame was not logical, but it did not yield to reason or logic. She was able to relinquish it only after recalling her terror during therapy, an emotionally charged experience in and of itself, after which she could gradually develop empathy and compassion for the little girl who was scared, confused, and as van der Kolk (2003) explains, the victim of "frozen inaction," believed by some to be at the core of traumatic experiences.

Even if the child is not tormented by self-blame, shame is a universal response to sexual abuse because early shame, necessary to socialize the child, is rooted in exposure of the body, of body parts, and of body products (York et al. 1990). Victims relate that they no longer feel their body is theirs, that there is nothing private because the abuser has taken over the privacy of the body, and that they are constantly being watched (Shengold 1989). If not treated before adolescence, they often feel, when masturbating or in a sexual relationship with another, that the seducer is always there, watching or sharing in the sexual gratification.

Children also give idiosyncratic meanings to shameful experiences. In order to make sense out of an experience—to explain why a particular event happened to them—children interpret experience. From that moment forward, the interpretation, and the unconscious fantasies related to it, provide a set of complex derivatives that lead to feelings of painful shame or to defensive maneuvers (signal shame) to ward them off.

Gaensbauer's work with traumatized children over time reveals how internal representations of trauma can expand in the direction of increased organization and narrative coherence and simultaneously in the direction of distortion and disorganization. Gaensbauer (1995) writes, "One could also see illustrations of how early experiences are reworked at each developmental level and how subsequently gained knowledge can result in new anxieties." For example, Audrey's anxiety increased when she came to understand the nature of the relationship between her birth mother and the mother's ex-boyfriend (the bomber), and she developed the fantasy that the ex-boyfriend was her father. Gaensbauer comments (1995) as follows:

> It was my impression that the reenactments and verbalizations of the younger children had more direct connections in affect and content to the original experiences. As the children became older, their advanced cognitive development and increased defensiveness, and the influence of what they had been told made it difficult to know the extent to which they remained in touch with their original memories. (p. 145)

Gaensbauer (1995) goes on to say that regardless of the fate of the actual memories, the traumatic experiences had a significant and enduring impact on the children's development, not just in the form of posttraumatic symptoms, but in the ways they interfered with the resolution of important developmental issues, including the establishment of basic trust, the development of a sense of autonomy, the regulation of aggression, and physiological regulation, a point we have made throughout this and the companion volume. Michelle's mother died when Michelle was four years old. Her treatment by Dr. Crenshaw is another example in which the invitational approach was used rather quickly.

Michelle's father was troubled at the time of his wife's death because Michelle displayed little overt reaction to the loss, and he, therefore, assumed she just didn't understand. Years later, on a Sunday morning, a frantic call was received from her father, who described how he had been awakened by uncontrolled sobbing from her room. She was unable to explain or talk with her father about what was troubling her. Her father had remarried about three years earlier. After meeting with Michelle, [Dr. Crenshaw realized] that she now understood and was able to appreciate, in more complex and meaningful ways, what the loss of her mother actually meant to her, something she could not appreciate when she was four. She now felt a desperate need for her mother. She longed to know more about her, but was hesitant to ask for fear of upsetting her father and her stepmother. She was invited to bring pictures of her mother to therapy sessions and, with encouragement from the therapist, began to ask more questions of her father about her mother. She needed answers to help solidify her own sense of identity.

In meetings with her father and stepmother, the therapist emphasized the importance of Michelle's learning more about her mother and how such information could contribute to her own development. Her father began to share stories with Michelle about how kind her mother was and how she volunteered for a number of charities. Later in her life, Michelle also volunteered at the local hospital to carry on the unfinished work of her mother, and the work gave her great satisfaction. It also strengthened her identification with her mother as a good person.

Michelle needed a year of once-weekly treatment to come to terms with her devastating loss. Yet in spite of her mother's tragic death, Michelle grew up under relatively favorable circumstances, as did most of the children treated by Theodore Gaensbauer. Michelle's father and stepmother, her grandparents, and other extended family members loved and cared about her. If children with good supports require a lengthy and developmentally sequenced approach to treatment, then only therapeutic narcissism can lead one to think that relatively brief and one-time interventions can help traumatized children who lack the family supports and favorable socioeconomic conditions that Michelle and Gaensbauer's cases enjoyed. Yet shockingly few children exposed to multiple loss and trauma receive in-depth, developmentally sequenced treatment.

THE COPING APPROACH

Not all children have sufficient ego strengths to undertake uncovering work. James (1989, 1994) discusses the need for a developmentally sequenced approach when working with some traumatized children. Within the sequence are therapeutic activities designed to strengthen the child's internal resources so an invitational approach can eventually be offered. In the coping approach (James 1993), a judgment is made, subject to revision, that the child lacks sufficient ego strengths and coping resources to confront the trauma *without significant risk of re-traumatization.* Indicators of inadequate ego resources include extremely blunted affect, rigid use of isolating and avoiding defenses, extremely poor impulse control, inability to tolerate even minimal frustrations, limited ability to regulate affect (becomes overwhelmed with feeling when emotional), identity confusion, thought disorder, or tendency to lose reality contact under stress. We will see examples of these weaknesses in some of the cases presented.

In the coping approach, the therapist deliberately stays away from material or activities that might remind the child of early traumas and does not actively encourage the child to play imaginatively when reluctance is demonstrated. If the child becomes highly anxious during fantasy play, the anxiety is usually masked immediately by primitive defense. (Defenses against feeling anxious are listed in chapters 8 and 9 of this volume and are defined in *Understanding and Treating the Aggression of Children*). Following a significant disruption, the therapist does not encourage the child to return to activities that immediately preceded the anxiety. The therapist redirects the child to more neutral activities, such as structured games or drawings of pleasant events.

In the coping approach, the goal is to expand the use of defenses; increase coping strategies; teach, model, and reinforce pro-social and problem-solving skills; and find hidden strengths. Many of the chapters in this book describe strategies to highlight and reinforce existing strengths as well as model and teach defensive and coping mechanisms that the children can summon when needed. Chapters also are included that discuss approaches to enhance the therapeutic alliance and to structure communication and play so that children, even those who are relatively nonverbal, can learn a language with which to later express their underlying sorrow and rage.

Helping children to cope is not considered inferior to the invitational approach, but one necessary to move the child's development forward. In addition, research has demonstrated that the more that interpretative-expressive psychotherapies are modified in a supportive direction, the more clients change (Wallerstein 1994). In actual practice, therapy is a mixture of supportive and expressive techniques designed to fit the needs of specific patients. The coping approach differs from social skills training, such as assertive training, anger management training, and concrete skill building—common practices in children's treatment—in one significant way. We have emphasized the fragmented, rather than integrated, nature of the personalities of gorilla-suit wearers. Fragmentation is probably adaptive for children raised by highly erratic parents, who are sometimes violent, often neglectful, and occasionally caring. The children learn to treat both themselves and their parents as if they were actually many differ-ent people (Herman 1992). Fischer and Pipp (1984) introduce the phrase "growing up strangely" to explain fractionated personalities. They postulate that development is characterized not only by increasing differentiation, as well as increasing synthesis, but, in some individuals, also by *fractionation*, which de-velops in parallel with integration. In the process of fractionation, certain ideas, feelings, and behaviors are formed in relation to specific situations and, because of heightened anxiety, are never generalized across contexts.

This context-bound disconnectedness increases over time and leads to "strange developments," which are atypically organized but sophisticated lines of psychological growth—a multiple self system, a complicated achievement that cannot be explained by the defense of splitting alone. Unlike defensive splitting, which results from the inability to contain complexity, the basic force behind fractionation is movement toward increasing complexity. Gilligan (1991) uses the term *dissociation* to describe the process of hiding aspects of oneself from oneself and from others, the goal being to "take oneself out of the relationship for the sake of the relationship" (p. 26). We speak of looking for "is-lands of strength" in gorilla-suit wearers. Some of these islands can be found submerged in their hidden selves.

Often the child's behavior in the initial session dictates the coping ap-proach. Dr. Crenshaw once entered a waiting room to greet a child for a first visit, and the six-year-old boy, Charlie, sprang off the sofa with a knife in his hands, leaped through the air, and lunged at the therapist. Fortunately, the knife was rubber, and no one was hurt, but it was a stormy beginning in the treat-ment of a youngster who displayed almost no internal controls with which to regulate his impulse or emotional life. A child at such an early level of ego de-velopment needs considerable work on the coping track until ready for un-covering work on the invitational track.

Another example is the case of Jenny, a seven-year-old placed in resi-dential treatment after a series of placements elsewhere. Jenny was first placed in a child-care institution along with her three siblings after the drug addic-tion of her parents had resulted in homelessness and exposure to violence and abuse. Before the children were placed in foster care, the family had wandered from one abandoned building to another for shelter and would beg and steal food and eat out of garbage cans. After a series of foster homes, where the children were not managed successfully, all four were placed in a child-care institution. Jenny, however, the oldest of the children, was too dangerous to be safely managed in that center and was sent to the residential treatment center where both of us worked for many years. The social service agency was re-luctant to separate the siblings but felt that Jenny needed intensive clinical ser-vices to address her extensive and repeated traumas. She had been repeatedly raped and beaten by her father and other men when the family lived on the streets.

> Jenny saw her therapist twice a week, but during the early stages of therapy, she was too phobic to be alone with her female therapist in the therapy room. The center's therapy rooms are extremely attractive and well equipped with materials needed to help the children to play out their life dramas, including a sandbox, puppet theater, puppets, all kinds of art and drawing materials, dolls, and playhouses. Most children eagerly enter the playrooms since they are so inviting and designed as "a child's place." It was terrifying, however, for Jenny, because of her nightmarish life history, to be left alone even with a warm and friendly adult, such as her therapist, Linda.
>
> To begin the process of creating "a safe place" for Jenny and building a relationship with her, Linda took Jenny to the gym. Linda would stand at one end of the gym and Jenny at the other, and they would throw a ball back and forth. The only communication that took place was related to their game of catch. The initial stage of Jenny's play therapy was an exception to our rule of "staying in the therapy room." Jenny's extreme anxiety in the confines of the therapy room necessitated this approach. She needed a safe place to begin to develop a trusting relationship, the foundation of all meaningful therapeutic work, and she felt safe in the gym.
>
> After a month, Jenny was willing to enter the therapy room, but only if Linda sat in an adjoining room equipped with a one-way mirror such that she could watch Jenny but be unable to communicate with her. Gradually, Jenny's phobic anxiety lessened. After a series of sessions, in which Jenny engaged in solitary play while Linda observed through the one-way mirror, Jenny began asking Linda to come into the room briefly to help her locate play materials. As the sessions continued, Linda was permitted to stay in the room longer and longer and, after three months of therapy, Jenny allowed Linda to be present for complete sessions. The trust and attachment with Linda continued to grow.

Jenny's treatment demonstrates the power of the therapeutic relationship and the pivotal importance of creating a "safe place." It also illustrates the role of supporting the child's defenses and coping skills at whatever level they present, even at the primitive level of flight, to enable the child to gradually gather the strength to face intensely painful material. In the beginning of treatment, Jenny needed more space and distance than most traumatized children in order to safely begin the therapeutic process. Had her supervisor insisted on having therapy take place in the playroom, as is the practice with most children who test limits, Jenny might not have made any therapeutic progress. Research on outcomes in psychotherapy suggests that 30 percent of the variance is accounted for by the quality of the therapeutic alliance (Hubble, Duncan, and Miller 1999). To develop one, exceptions, such as beginning Jenny's therapy in a gym, sometimes have to be made. In Jenny's case, however, it was the therapist's idea to begin treatment elsewhere, not the child's conscious demand to do so. As Havens (1989) states, "The work of psychological healing begins in a safe place, to be compared with the best of hospital experience or, from an earlier time, a church sanctuary" (p. vii).

Children working within the coping model may develop sufficient re-sources and inner strengths to work on reexperiencing trauma as therapy pro-gresses. For example, after nine months of therapy, Jenny's therapist, Linda, switched to an invitational approach, helping Jenny to begin to use the dolls and puppets to enact traumatic events. Likewise, a child working within the in-vitational model may become overwhelmed, and the therapist accommodates to the child's need and shifts to a coping model. Thus the arrows in the Deci-sion Grid go in both directions, allowing for shifts back and forth between the invitational and coping tracks as needed. Shifts may be required in response to the buildup of external stressors, such as a home visit, placement in a new school or classroom, or a mother's new boyfriend.

In *Understanding and Treating the Aggression of Children*, we present a boy whose Rorschach responses revealed considerable turmoil over an upcoming parental visit. Had the boy been in treatment, the therapist would have needed to stay with neutral topics during this period. Or if major upheaval in the fam-ily prevents a child's home visit, the taxing demands of therapeutic exploration may need to be shelved until a future time. If the therapist fails to make these adjustments, unnecessary crises and even psychiatric hospitalizations of the child can follow. Such shifts may be only temporary while the child regroups and rebuilds strengths and inner resources.

Even children with highly developed fantasy play can reveal frightening, or perhaps embarrassing, material too early in treatment. Dr. Mordock treated nine-year-old Barbara, who put on a puppet play during her first therapy ses-sion. The child-puppet was severely scolded and then beaten by an adult pup-pet for wetting the bed. Although Barbara crouched behind the puppet theater and never showed her face, even that distance wasn't enough: she re-fused to come to her next scheduled therapy session. The therapist visited her in her living group and told her, "When you come again, we will draw and color together rather than play with puppets." Barbara came to her next sched-uled session and later, after an alliance was formed, was able to work rapidly through her early abuse experiences at the hands of her substance-abusing mother. She was not, however, able to forgive her mother and refused to live with her when both were ready for her discharge, which occurred after only eight months in treatment. The mother had successfully completed her own treatment for substance abuse and seemed like a good resource. Consequently, in spite of her protests, Barbara was discharged to her. Shortly after returning home, however, Barbara deliberately acted up and was placed in a group home, where she remained, happily, throughout her youth.

The arrows in the Decision Grid go both horizontally and vertically. This multidirectionality indicates that, regardless of the approach, therapy is fluid. In some cases, after working on traumatic issues within the invitational approach, the therapist may have to help the child to reintegrate by means of a period of ego strengthening and relationship building.

DIFFERENTIAL DECISION MAKING

The presenting behaviors of Charlie, who wielded the rubber knife in his first session, of Jenny, who couldn't tolerate interpersonal closeness, and of Barbara, who revealed her trauma too early, dictated a coping approach, but in other cases the decision about which approach to take is not so simple. Well-defended children can play structured table games or draw neutral themes in therapy indefinitely, and the therapist must decide if their rigid defenses are needed to prevent serious regression when they are faced with emotional arousal or whether they can be gently challenged to face their repressed feelings.

A five-year-old boy hid under a table while his mother knifed to death his older siblings. While he occasionally displayed marked temper outbursts, he was referred for residential treatment primarily for his failure to learn in school. He was ten years old at the time of placement but was virtually a non-reader and able to do only first grade math problems. In play therapy, he would play only simple table games and wanted to modify the rules so that he would always win.

Because the boy was so out of touch with his own emotions, he was not considered ready to deal with the killings he witnessed, with his narrow escape from them, or with other traumatic experiences his mentally ill mother un-doubtedly exposed him to. His therapy concentrated on developing his coping skills and the use of defenses other than repression and isolation of affect. He eventfully demonstrated some academic progress, suggesting that his avoidance defenses were not rigidly applied, and he tolerated frustrations without losing his temper. He was discharged to a special education center, where he contin-ued to remain behind his age peers. Then, at age nineteen, he walked into a bar and picked a fight with a known knife wielder and was stabbed to death. Did this enactment reveal survivor guilt or a twisted effort to work through the horrific ordeal he experienced as a child?

SWITCHING APPROACHES IN MIDSTREAM

Willie, to be presented below, is an example of a child who required a change from the invitational to the coping track for a period of regrouping and shoring up of defenses. In therapy, Willie spontaneously played out trauma-related material. Initially the therapist followed his lead, but eventually the emotions uncovered could not be contained within the therapy sessions and began to intrude into his daily activities. Evidently he had not developed sufficient defensive resources to handle this material. He began to display difficulty making the transition back to class after the therapy session and had difficulty leaving at the end of the session. The therapist's actions described below illustrate that redirecting the child to less emotional material is not necessarily a sudden switch of activities but rather a transition that also conveys a message of safety.

> WILLIE: [*Takes the crocodile puppet and begins to attack the other puppets and eat them one by one.*]
>
> THERAPIST: I'm worried about the crocodile. It seems he doesn't know how to make a friend. I'm afraid he is going to be very lonely.
>
> WILLIE: He wants to eat everybody.
>
> THERAPIST: When he eats everyone, who will be there to keep him from getting lonely, to play and be a friend to him? Maybe you could pick a puppet who could show him how to make a friend.
>
> WILLIE: [*Chooses the porcupine puppet, takes Crocodile and begins to attack Porcupine, but gets quills in his mouth and starts screaming.*] Ow! Ouch! That hurts! [*Crocodile attacks the porcupine again but gets more quills in his mouth and yells even louder.*]
>
> THERAPIST: Maybe Mr. Crocodile attacks everyone, even Mr. Porcupine, who is trying to help him, because he is afraid. Maybe he doesn't realize that the reason no one wants to be his friend is because he believes he has to attack first or they will attack him. Why don't you choose two other puppets. Maybe the porcupine is not the best one to teach crocodile how to be a friend. Good, you chose Rabbit and Monkey. Now, bring them over into the far corner of the room. Let's keep them a safe distance away from Mr. Crocodile but where he can still see them. Now, have Monkey and Rabbit play together in a friendly way and show Mr. Crocodile how much fun it can be to have a friend.

Willie's choice of Porcupine to be Crocodile's teacher reveals the vulnerability he feels when letting down his guard and risking being hurt. When identified with the aggressor in the role of Crocodile, he (like children putting on the gorilla suit) took the stance that "I will hurt you before you can hurt me." Even when asked to take on the role of the helper and friend, he went in well protected, armored with sharp quills, taking the stance, "If you get too close, one or both of us are going to get hurt."

Many of the empirically supported cognitive-behavioral-based problem-solving treatments and social-skills-based treatments are useful in developing coping skills (Shure 1996; Goldstein 1989; Kendall 2002), as are some of the specific programs addressing aggression in children (Goldstein 1989; Goldstein, Glick, Reiner et al. 1987; Kendall, Ronan, and Epps 1991; Larson and Lochman 2002).

A major component of the coping approach is psychoeducation that includes not only expanding the use of existing coping skills but also helping the child to get in touch with hidden skills as well as with the role the child plays within the family.

Social skills programs that are narrowly focused fail to address the emotional underpinnings of aggression. For example, anger management training, the most popular approach to working with angry clients, does not reach the volatile emotions that underlie the violence (Hardy 2003). Children requiring a coping approach benefit most from social skills training programs that are broad based rather than narrowly focused. Marcia Stern (2002), in her excellent book, *Child-Friendly Therapy*, describes many useful tools and strategies to improve coping skills, but she also underscores the need to demystify both the child's and the family's dysfunction so they can develop a common language with which to understand and talk about their difficulties. She also stresses the importance of developing empathy. She calls her broad-based approach "Biopsychosocial Innovations for Children and Families."

Another useful resource is Martha Strauss's book, *No-Talk Therapy for Children and Adolescents* (1999). The work contains an appendix, which lists and describes useful games and activities to increase coping and mastery. Beverly James (1989) also presents many useful strategies. Although most of these activities are useful within a coping approach, some can be employed as lead-ins in the invitational approach.

Garritt and Crenshaw (1997) developed an *Ego-Supportive Drawing Series* that focuses children on their strengths and internal resources as well as on external supports.

The remaining chapters of this book, especially chapter 14, feature other practical strategies to use within the coping approach and also for laying the groundwork for later use of the invitational approach.

THERAPEUTIC EXPECTATIONS

The therapist may feel compelled to deliver the invitational approach because it conforms to notions of what is good therapy. Or under a managed care organization's limits on therapy sessions, pressure may be felt for quick results. Expectations of parents, schools, or other referring agencies can also create a desire to plunge into grief work. A hurried approach to therapy ignores the developmental constraints impacting on the child's ability to understand and to tolerate intense and distressing affect. It also ignores the need for ego strengthening and defense building before undertaking intensive affective work. The unintended result may be serious decompensation; dramatic increases in acting-out behavior; and self-destructive, dangerous, or runaway behavior.

At the other end of the spectrum are therapists who are "affect phobic" and miss repeated cues from children that they are ready to confront the trauma of the loss. Both of us have encountered children and adolescents who have received therapy in the past from therapists who ignored the clues that they were ready to talk about the really "hard stuff."

We have also encountered therapists whose therapeutic approach was a combination of client-centered techniques and social skills training. These "therapists" took children to the gym, outside to play gross motor games, on trips uptown, and elsewhere, making no efforts to get them in touch with their early losses or traumas. In one case, an elderly, experienced female therapist urged a young male psychologist to address a child's past sexual abuse, seeing signs of sexual preoccupations in videotaped presentations of his therapy sessions. In frustration, the staff member predicted that, because of the boy's sadistic behavior and blunted affect, he would sexually abuse others if this area were not addressed. The young psychologist, several years out of a graduate school and armed with a variety of "cook-book" techniques, claimed the staff member was "too psychoanalytic" and continued to play basketball with the boy in gym, confusing the role of "Big Brother" or "Adult Companion" with the role of therapist. Several years after the boy was discharged, he was arrested for raping an eighty-year-old woman in his apartment building.

Invariably children feel abandoned by therapists who won't accompany them into the depths of pain, sorrow, rage, and despair. This "rejection" replicates earlier abandonments, when caregivers failed to read the signals or to pursue aggressively the children's hidden hurts. Their invisible wounds remain invisible!

ORIENTATION TO A POSITIVE FUTURE

Finally, in the closing phase of therapy, in both the coping and the invitational approaches, efforts are needed to help the child create an orientation to a positive future. This stage of therapy focuses on restoring hope and helping the child to separate, psychologically, from the past in such a manner that the next phase of life is entered with more energy. Strategies to accomplish this task are detailed in *Understanding and Treating the Aggression of Children*. Restoring connections to important attachment figures is a pivotal component of this phase of treatment. Consequently, ways to strengthen ties to parents, caregivers, and teachers are described in several chapters in *Understanding and Treating the Aggression of Children*.

· *6* ·

Typical Play Themes
of Fawns in Gorilla Suits

Children wearing gorilla suits are preoccupied with needs for control, dominance, and power; with feeling threatened; with feelings of rejection, abandonment, separation, and loss; with a need for punishment; with feelings of deprivation; and with needs for nurturance. While the themes often unfold in therapy in the sequence presented in this chapter, they overlap and wax and wane over the course of treatment.

*C*hildren in gorilla suits, victims of abuse and traumatized by family or neighborhood violence, exhibit redundant themes when they play in the therapy room. The themes discussed in this chapter have been observed by therapists in the course of their work in residential treatment, day treatment, and outpatient treatment centers that serve children wearing gorilla suits. The list is not exhaustive but covers the most frequent and emotionally powerful themes. Knowledge of the themes can serve as a useful map or guide for the play therapist working with this clinical population. We present the themes in the order in which most children display them in treatment although themes appear simultaneously and each waxes and wanes over the course of treatment.

CONTROL, DOMINANCE, AND POWER

Because the lives of children wearing gorilla suits have been terror filled, causing them constant anxiety, if not fear, it comes as no surprise that suit wearers manifest a strong need for control, dominance, and power. When a man tells his friend that his wife is too controlling, he hasn't the foggiest notion about what real efforts to control look like. The children first display their need for control in their relationship with the therapist by ordering the therapist about, shouting instructions to be quiet, or demanding that he or she behave in some specific way or engage in some specific, and often undesirable, activity. Control issues will be particularly pronounced in the early stages of treatment, before trust in the therapeutic alliance has been established. When the children move from directing the therapist to directing the actions of dolls, puppets, or "miniature people" (tiny wooden or plastic figures, typically consisting of family members), their directives will also reflect a strong need for control.

The therapist honors the child's needs to exercise control by allowing the child to choose play materials. The content of play can be largely determined by the child who is capable of playacting or fantasy play. If the child acts directly on the environment in dangerous or destructive ways or interferes with the ongoing conduct of therapy (e.g., wants to leave the room before the end of the session), then, of course, the therapist will need to intervene by setting limits or redirecting the child. Often the child's demands to leave the therapy room reflect fears that control will be lost, and the therapist can reframe the demand by stating, "You don't need to leave the room just because you feel angry. We can find ways for your anger to be safely expressed. I have helped many children to do so." (Or, "You have done so before and you can do so again.") If the child is fairly well controlled, he or she is given wide latitude in making choices, reinforcing the sense that therapy is a safe place to orchestrate the drama and tell the story the child feels both afraid and compelled to share.

In the early stages of therapy, some children play out scenes in which a powerful creature or force completely dominates and destroys weaker creatures. Typically, the child adopts a powerful character, such as a dinosaur, usually Tyrannosaurus rex, who wipes out all the other dinosaurs and sometimes even more helpless jungle animals or farm animals who "don't stand a chance against the far more powerful, giant dinosaur." Control is almost as essential as food in the lives of children repeatedly subjected to terror. The children, through play characters, terrorize the weaker and more vulnerable characters, reflecting how they were terrorized in the past. This play serves a compensatory function, allowing the children to exercise power that counteracts feelings of powerlessness and helplessness—feelings they have experienced throughout their young lives. If a child gets stuck in endless repetitions of this theme, the therapist should introduce variations or intervene and redirect. Domination, control, and forcefulness are the perceived behaviors of the abuser, and the child should not become overgratified in this role.

THREAT

As mentioned earlier, gorilla-suit wearers, primarily to deal with constantly feeling threatened, strongly identify with those who wielded power over them. Through the defense called *identification with the aggressor*, they mask their fears in counterphobic behavior and dispense severe and punitive treatment to those who object to the aggressor's tyranny. But the expression of such raw aggression creates additional stress because intense anger produces not only mental and behavioral chaos and confusion in those expressing it but also chaos and confusion in those receiving and witnessing it. When the therapist feels threatened by the child, as well as helpless and inept because nothing seems to work, the child's threatened and helpless feelings can be easily appreciated. And when the therapist feels angry in return and thinks about terminating the therapy, the child's identification with the aggressor and his or her abandonment feeling can also be experienced.

Early in treatment, repressed anger toward abusers is displaced onto innocent parties and also onto the self. Initially, it is displaced onto the therapist, who disappoints the child when demands are not met. Later, after limits have been set, children with masking symbols will displace their anger onto playroom toys, usually in the midst of chaos and confusion. A common scenario is one in which the child destroys whole towns and villages, and the police, firemen, and doctors are unable to help because the roads and bridges also have been blown up and destroyed. The scenes of chaos reflect the disorganization and out-of-control lives these children have experienced.

> A boy played out a scene in which two men beat up each other's wife. Then one guy beats up the other unmercifully. He also kills off all would-be helpers, such as doctors and policemen, and he then kills his family. In other play scenarios, animals ram their heads into walls to prove they are strong. The boy also drew "musclemen" who never felt much pain. Outside of therapy, he displayed considerable self-injurious behavior, not only through "accidents," but also directly. His therapy room play revealed his longing for money—lots of it—and his strong preoccupation with food and with babies rescuing parents.

The last theme in this boy's play made the others more understandable, even without having details of the boy's history. "Babies rescuing parents" suggests that the generational boundaries were dramatically blurred in his family and that his parents expected care from him instead of providing care. Such expectations are not unusual for parents whose own needs for nurturance were never met. Often they have a baby so they will have someone to love them. When the baby cries or "doesn't comply," they feel unloved and depressed, and they neglect, or even abuse, the child.

The boy's search for food and money (symbolic of his needs for nurture) and for hidden strengths, revealed by the animals ramming their heads into walls to prove their strength and the musclemen feeling no pain, highlighted his need to be self-sufficient, and his self-injurious behavior was motivated by the need to prove he "feels no pain" and cannot be hurt by threats. Finally, the violent themes reflected his underlying rage at never having his needs met. Eventually he revealed that, when he was four years old, he was locked in a basement for long periods and fed morsels passed under the door by his psychiatrically disturbed mother.

ABANDONMENT AND REJECTION

Because so many gorilla-suit wearers are rejected, if not outright deserted, themes of abandonment dominate their play. Families drive off in (toy) cars and leave (doll) children behind. Children (dolls) are buried in the sandbox and never found. Adult dolls take trips to faraway places, and children are lost. Children live alone in the dollhouse, in caves, and in deserts. Child dolls try to feed and cloth themselves, and some starve to death. Unlike other themes, the anxiety over abandonment is kept alive by ongoing parental contact.

Rarely, however, are the abandonment themes clearly articulated early in therapy. The diffuse, undifferentiated expressions of anxiety over rejection displayed by most troubled children when beginning therapy are illustrated by the behavior of Carol, a seven-year-old who fell asleep in school, cried a lot, appeared sad, and played tricks on other children, the beginning of aggressive displays. Her mother admitted not caring enough and being too tired to spend time with Carol but says Carol is such "a good little girl" and loves her little brother—usually a sign that the child manages jealous anger at the little brother through the defense called *reaction formation*. The defense, her solicitous behavior, keeps her from acting on her impulses. But if her mother were observant, she would probably find that Carol plays tricks on the baby, perhaps pinching or twisting his arm or leg when the mother is not looking.

Such knowledge often puts the therapist in a bind. If the mother is told to watch out for the baby, the older child can be rejected even more. But if the mother is not told, the baby may be seriously injured. We usually handle such situations by normalizing the behavior. We tell the mother that most children, in spite of how they may present, resent the attention directed at younger siblings. We suggest that if she can't give the older child more attention, she let that child help care for the baby in the mother's presence, if the child wants to, but not in her absence since children are not very responsible; even though they may appear to be so, their minds become preoccupied with other things, they are easily distracted, and their attention wanders. Below is a vignette from Carol's first session of play therapy.

I never do anything fun. I'm not happy. [*She looked sad and scooped sand end-lessly for no apparent purpose. She then noticed the stuffed bears.*] The bear is un-happy, too. This is Winnie Gentle Pooh, Small Bear, Honey Bear, and I am "Carol Sunshine" because I like that name better than mine. Your name is "Bracelet Mouth" [*The therapist wore braces.*] or "Mousie." [*She then gave Pooh Bear a spanking.*] He should "Ssh." He was a naughty bear. [*She built a house out of blocks and put Pooh Bear in a room with no way out.*] He had to stay there cause he said naughty words—the "f" words. His parents could say them, but he couldn't. I don't like Small Bear. Pooh Bear swore at Small Bear and needs to go to bed.

[*She then made a "tea party" and brought some friends.*] There's only Raggedy Ann, Andy, and me. Pooh Bear, Pooh Bear, Pooh Bear. There is the quiet box. He's got to go in the quiet box. Pooh—you're too fat. Too much honey. You take the slide and squish him, squish him, squish him. Nobody can look in and he's not going to look. Pooh would be screaming if they came in and didn't let him out of there. [*She then stacked four big blocks to block Pooh Bear in there.*] I don't care—somebody cares, but not me. I don't care.

In this first treatment session, the child, almost parrotlike, reports that she is unhappy. It is not clear whether she identifies with Winnie Gentle Pooh or if she hopes that the therapist will be gentle. Then she punished Pooh for bad behavior and locked him in the quiet box. Pooh Bear is too fat because he eats too much honey (too needy?) and needs to be squished (punished for efforts at need satisfaction or for the need to be thinner?). Is the bad behavior calling the therapist "bracelet mouth?" She told Pooh to "ssh" and gave him a spank-ing. Most likely, it is a mixture of punishment for present and past behavior, all blurred and confusing to her at this point. In the chapter on the therapy process, we will show how Carol's play progressed from this diffuse, undiffer-entiated expression of anxiety to the more focused anxiety needed for further progress.

Eight-year-old Albert's fascination with the maps of New York City il-lustrates a child's efforts to master abandonment fears.

Albert had been placed in residential treatment following removal from his home in New York City. He became so obsessed with studying maps of New York City that his teacher used it to motivate him to complete other academic activities. For example, if he did ten math problems, he could have the map for five minutes. Af-ter about a month of study, he put the map away and anxiously challenged his teacher to name any street in New York City. When his teacher did so, he verbal-ized all the streets he would need to take to reach home from the street the teacher selected. Of interest is that he showed no interest in the New York state map—one he could study to learn how to get home from the treatment center if need be. Ev-idently, he feared being abandoned in the city, perhaps in response to threats made by his parents when he acted badly or perhaps to threats carried out in the past. It is quite common in our culture for parents to threaten to leave children when they disobey.

Some staff doubted that Albert's map obsession reflected abandonment anxiety because his diagnosis included autistic tendencies. While most autistic children display massive anxiety, some of it can be traced to specific experiences. They, too, can follow trauma experiences with futile efforts at mastery. The fascination with and repetitive twisting of doorknobs by a ten-year-old autistic boy no longer seemed bizarre when staff learned that he was locked in a closet for hours. In fact, many, if not all, of the bizarre behaviors displayed by autistic children could be their efforts to master situations that made them anxious. Because of their limited cognitive abilities and their inability to manage anxiety, they are prone to conditioned fear reactions. The inability to make sense out of the world can make mild events traumatic.

As the children get older and better able to take care of themselves, the theme weakens in strength, but the anxiety is still there, a part of their personality makeup for the rest of their lives. They are the adults who can't bear to be alone, protest when their partners plan a trip, and have considerable difficulty taking trips themselves. Not only do they display a strong need to control their mates, as well as their children, but they also suffer from mild symptoms of post-traumatic stress disorder and are prone to panic attacks. Their dreams reflect abandonment anxieties, as do some of their everyday concerns. Their inability to separate from their partners and children and their reluctance to accept the privacy needs of family members contribute to ongoing interpersonal conflicts. They respond poorly to divorce and experience difficultly passing through the "empty nest" stage of adult life.

SEPARATION AND LOSS

One pervasive and powerful theme in the play of children in gorilla suits is separation and profound and repeated loss. Death scenes, people and animals disappearing and then reappearing, people and animals losing their way and unable to find their way back home, people who have lost their homeland and want to return all reflect the intense and pervasive sense of loss these children have experienced. The game of hide-and-seek played by children around the world is an attempt to master the anxiety associated with separation and loss.

Separation and loss are a part of life, but children in gorilla suits have been exposed to an extreme and unusual degree of loss, particularly the loss of feeling safe. Stabbings, shootings, suicides, homicidal deaths, and other violent acts in their neighborhoods are dramatically enacted in the playroom. These events are defining moments in their emotional lives that they failed to assimilate, and the accommodations they made to them stunted their emotional growth. The play of Roberto, a six-year-old suit wearer, serves as an example.

> Roberto's play reveals redundant themes of loss, abandonment, and separation. He has one powerful creature, usually a T. rex, kill off the weaker dinosaurs and jungle animals. Then each of the animals receives a proper burial. Sometimes they magically spring back to life, reflecting his inability to comprehend the finality of death. In other scenes an animal has disappeared, and a search party is sent out but to no avail. In still other play scenarios, two animals who knew each other in a faraway land are reunited but then get separated again and are unable to find each other.

Anthony, seen by Dr. Crenshaw when the boy was five years old, was constantly blown off course in a puppet play where Frog (Anthony) and Turtle (Therapist) were riding a hot air balloon. They often found themselves on some faraway island, lost and frightened. A variation on the theme was Anthony's scenes of Frog and Turtle visiting the alien planet Bird. Their space capsule always broke down, and they were unable to return to Earth. The themes of separation and loss were prominent for Anthony, a child adopted from a foreign country.

GUILT AND SHAME: THE NEED FOR PUNISHMENT

Because of the primitive guilt and shame gorilla-suit wearers experience, their play often reflects a need to be punished. Melanie Klein's (1948) treatment of Peter, an inhibited and extremely apprehensive child who resisted educational efforts, is illustrative. In the initial stages of therapy, Peter was incapable of playing; he could do nothing with his toys but break them. His inhibition of play, as well as his anxiety, was closely connected with his oral-sadistic and anal-sadistic fixations. Sadistic wishes toward his mother, coupled with his desire for her, led to his withdrawal from her and to rather bad relations with her. He directed his energies toward his father, but since he was also frightened of his father, his only real relationship was with his little brother, but it was an ambivalent one. Peter's expectation of punishment was revealed when he did begin to play.

> He once played, presenting himself and his little brother by two tiny dolls, that they were expecting punishment for their naughtiness to the mother; she comes, finds them dirty, punishes them, and goes away. The two children repeat their dirty acts again, are again punished, and so on. At last, the

dread of punishment becomes so strong that the two children determine to kill the mother, and he executes a little doll. They then cut and eat the body. But the father appears to help the mother, and is killed too in a very cruel manner and also cut up and eaten. Now the two children seem to be happy. They can do what they like. But after a very short time great anxiety sets in, and it appears that the killed parents are again alive and come back. When the anxiety started, the little boy had hidden the two dolls under the sofa, so that the parents should not find them, and then happened what the boy called "becoming educated." The father and mother find the two dolls, the father cuts his head off, the mother that of the brother, and then they, too, get cooked and eaten. (Klein 1948, p. 193)

Klein (1948, p. 193) points out that "after a short time the bad acts are again repeated, it may be even in different performances; the aggression against the parents starts again" and stresses that self-punishment will follow. Gorilla-suit wearers who act out in the autosphere (the realm of the body in Erikson's 1963 classification of play development) inflict punishments on themselves, resulting in observers' calling them "accident prone," but when the children get really upset and start banging their heads against the wall until they have to be restrained to avoid serious damage, staff see the accidents as minor versions of these more obvious self-punishments. The therapist's job is to move these direct actions into play actions and then into playacting so that the actions can be worked on in therapy.

DEPRIVATION

Along with the expressed and often poignant longings for nurture, children in gorilla suits often play out scenes of stark deprivation. One frequent scenario is to set up a storefront that sells food and invite the therapist in to buy food. When the therapist, in the role of customer, arrives at the store, he or she is turned away and told to come back tomorrow because the store is closed. The next day the customer (therapist) shows up only to have the door slammed in his or her face again. The degree of affect expressed or symbolized in such scenes is important to monitor. The affect may be overtly expressed when the storekeeper angrily sends the customer away. When the customer pleads with the store owner that he or she is hungry and needs food, the store owner mocks the plea and laughs. Or the affect may be symbolized in other ways. The door may be slammed in the therapist's face, the windows closed up, or a sign posted that says "Store closed for a week." The child communicates, through role reversal and in symbolic form, that his or her legitimate and essential needs for nurture and sustenance were met with rejection and angry refusal (slamming the door shut!).

Children who create the above drama are letting the therapist experience, via *projective communication* (Boston and Szur 1983), just how bitterly they have been "shut out" from satisfaction of basic needs. After all, the store is not selling luxury goods; it is selling food, and the hungry are harshly turned away. The metaphor, however, is not always used to mask blame of a parent. It can reflect how poor and economically depressed individuals are devalued by society. Those living on the margins of society experience, in a dramatic way, what it is like to be excluded from the "goodies of life"—and often from the basics needed just to sustain life. Sometimes a sibling has died, and the children have witnessed the parents' pain, accompanied by anger at not receiving adequate medical care. Going back each day to the store and finding it closed may symbolize the feelings of children who grow up in families where the struggle to survive is paramount.

Less distant masking symbols are revealed in children who serve the therapist make-believe food. One boy created the following scene repeatedly. In the role of parent, he served breakfast to a child (played by the therapist) that was supposed to be cereal, but the child turned it into dog shit! When the therapist found the food repulsive, the child would laugh in a mocking and almost sadistic manner. Other children, losing distance, often try to force-feed the therapist wet sand from the sandbox, and when the therapist refuses by turning his or her head away (and remarking, "I'll pretend to eat your food, but I won't eat sand."), significant anger follows, perhaps reflecting the anger expressed by the parent when the child turned his or her head away from offerings of food. These scenes reflect the betrayal, deprivation, and rage the children have experienced. Instead of cereal, they received what they perceived as the equivalent of feces! To add further to the humiliating sense of devaluation, the parent thought it was uproariously funny!

We would like to add, however, that some children were force-fed as infants by well-meaning but ill-informed or overly concerned parents who feared that if their children didn't eat enough, sickness or even death would follow. In a custody evaluation performed by Dr. Mordock, a man complained that his wife had been obsessed with their boy's health since his birth and that conflicts between the boy and his mother resulted from her overzealous child-rearing tactics. In contrast, the mother complained that the father was uncaring and paid scant attention to the child's health needs. In this case, unlike many custody evaluations, there was little doubt about whose complaints were valid. The mother's responses to the Rorschach cards revealed intense preoccupation with body parts, bleeding and damaged organs, and missing limbs. What a shame! Perhaps their marriage could have been saved had the mother sought treatment for her own phobias. Perhaps she had been severely traumatized by either injury or abuse before her marriage and kept her own fears in check by obsessing over the health of her son.

"The Story of the Jolly Green Giant and the Baby" was told by Jimmy, an eight-year-old boy in residential treatment. Jimmy, like Dr. Crenshaw, loved food. Just before Thanksgiving, he anticipated in therapy what his Thanksgiving Day feast was going to be like, describing with tremendous enthusiasm the turkey and all the trimmings in such imaginative detail that both he and Dr. Crenshaw "licked their chops." Nevertheless, when Jimmy returned the following Monday, he was noticeably downcast. He related that after his mother picked him up at the bus stop, she took him to a shelter for battered women and their children. She and his stepfather had been involved in a violent episode. She had been badly bruised and shaken and had sought refuge at the shelter for protection. On Thanksgiving Day a special meal was served by the center's volunteers, but it fell far short of Jimmy's expectations, probably because his mom didn't prepare it and he couldn't enjoy it at home with his family.

> When Jimmy entered the therapy room, he immediately went to the cupboard, took out the toy pots and pans, and began cooking a "Thanksgiving Feast." He was the Jolly Green Giant and didn't need help because he wanted to do it himself, although he allowed the therapist to set the table. He greatly enjoyed the preparations. When finally ready to serve the dinner, he brought the food to the table and was just about to put it down when his gaze froze on a baby [*doll*] in a high chair in the corner! He stood speechless for a moment, and then he blurted out, "Oh, my God! We forgot to feed the baby!" The forgotten baby in the corner was, of course, him. He was no longer the giant.

It was the story of his life! His parents, although well intentioned, were beset and overwhelmed by their own problems. Going from crisis to crisis, they forgot, or were unable, to feed the baby—to provide the nurture, caring, and protection Jimmy so badly needed! In an instinctively strong voice, the therapist said, "It is not too late! Bring that baby over here; there is plenty of food!" Jimmy immediately ran with the idea, not only bringing the baby to the table, but also all the puppets in the room because, as he repeated over and over, "It's not too late; there is plenty of food!" There was even enough for the Jolly Green Giant, and he was invited to the table as well. Jimmy seemed very pleased with this adaptation of his story because it offered hope—it introduced the possibility that things wouldn't always be bleak.

NEED FOR NURTURANCE

Children overcome by anger and pent-up rages have suffered major losses. They long for love, often demanding it, but believe it will never be received. And if it is received, it will be fleeting and stripped from them. Some are not even sure what love is, but they have witnessed other children getting it. This conflict is played out in the therapy room when the child adopts the role of nurturer. By assuming this role, the child maintains control. The child feeds the dolls and sometimes the therapist. Feeding is a metaphor for or a symbol of hope. The child has not given up—caring and nurturing can be envisioned, even if the child is the one doing it. Vicarious satisfaction of needs is at least a start. The child's unfolding play often reveals past experiences. If the child treats the babies gently, kindly, and soothingly, the play suggests the child has been exposed to caregivers who, at one time, were caring and attentive. Such signs are hopeful, not only in terms of prognosis, but also because the therapist can help the child get in touch with positive introjects and pave the way for future attachments, a topic discussed in the last chapter. The child recognizes love and caring and knows how to give them to others. In contrast, if the feeding is harsh and rough, and the care of children punitive and rejecting, these scenes suggest a less hopeful prognosis because they suggest that the child has not experienced love, kindness, caring, and nurture and does not know how to give it. Yet the child is still alive. Someone must have cared for it and fed it when it was a baby. The child will need help to identify that person, or at least to appreciate that some unknown adult provided care, and grow from the knowledge that he or she was once cared for and was not the unlovable child that underlies the negative self-image.

Hopefully, the child will relinquish the rigid controls as trust builds in the therapeutic relationship. The child may gradually allow the therapist to feed the babies or heal the wounded. The ultimate achievement would be allowing the therapist to nurture and heal the character's wounds within the metaphor of the symbolic play. The betrayal such children have experienced is sometimes played out by the mother offering the babies "sour milk" or even "poisoned milk." These betrayals are powerful metaphors, not only of unmet basic needs, but also of the caregivers as "frauds." They also symbolize the dramatic rupture of basic trust.

Nevertheless, it is rare for placed children to maintain the role of harsh feeders throughout a stay in a treatment center because they begin to identify with the care and concern provided by staff as well as the therapist. If, however, a child is abruptly removed from treatment by a county looking to save money or by a pleading parent whose hidden motive is an increase in her monthly welfare check, then the child will quickly regress and will be placed again, but not necessarily in the same setting. Every time a child is placed in a new setting, successful treatment becomes more difficult.

SYMBOLS OF HEALING: CARING FOR THE WOUNDED AND FIXING BROKEN THINGS

Along with feeding, healing metaphors symbolize hope. The child takes care of wounded animals or plays doctor and administers to the illness of the therapist. As trust develops, the child allows the therapist to take care of the wounded creatures. If care of wounded and sick animals, or babies, is offered in a kind and gentle way, the play scenarios suggest an optimistic prognosis since the child has internalized benign, loving, or protective adult figures from the past. In contrast, if the child is unsympathetic, harsh, rejecting, or punitive in response to vulnerable creatures, this behavior suggests a less hopeful prognosis and treatment that will take a longer time. It is always encouraging to see metaphors of hope and healing emerge in the course of therapy, especially if they were absent in the early stages of therapy or were manifested in a hostile, rejecting form.

In addition to healing play (a doctor's kit and toy hospital should be available in every playroom), this theme is expressed through a wish to repair and fix broken things. Sometimes the toys in the playroom get accidentally broken (occasionally deliberately), and the child insists on fixing them. The intensity with which this goal is pursued is often striking and reflects an equally intense longing for the child "to be fixed" and healed. This theme is so compelling that when toys are not broken, the child will want to pretend something is broken so he or she can fix it. Again, this is a metaphor of hope and optimism that one can be repaired and healed.

· 7 ·

Developing Distancing and Displacement through Playful Actions

A number of techniques are presented to facilitate appropriate expression of aggression, directly, symbolically, and verbally. Children unable to engage in make-believe play are initially encouraged in games that make use of clay, easily replaceable materials, absurd and amusing actions, cardboard bricks, magic markers, buckets, and balloons to express their pent-up anger. Drawing techniques include volcano pictures, storm pictures, fire-breathing dragons, and the anger thermometer. Discussion of the inhibiting role played by the revelation of hostile fantasies concludes the chapter.

*I*n the next chapter, we present a boy who entered the therapy room and threatened to wreck everything. The therapist quickly built a tower of blocks and told the boy he could wreck the "tall building." The boy promptly knocked down the tower of blocks while the therapist simultaneously arranged the wooden toy furniture on the floor, saying, "You can knock these around, too." For a number of sessions, the boy began therapy with the Wreck Everything Game, with the objects to be wrecked initially selected by the therapist. Within a short time, the boy was building his own towers and knocking them down. Eventually, the boy's anger subsided, probably because his mother was also in treatment and had relaxed some of her extremely punitive behaviors, allowing him to slowly move from playing the Wreck Everything Game to play activities that expressed his underlying sadness.

We have emphasized that many gorilla-suit wearers fail to play imaginatively with playroom materials, instead pressuring the therapist to take them outside or to a gym, and when this fails, pressuring them to play outdoor games in the small playroom, such as catch, handball, or basketball. Those who are undisciplined may climb on the furniture, throw sand from the sandbox or pour water into it, or express disorganized destructive impulses, such as "wrecking everything," breaking toys, or hitting the therapist. Limiting such behavior and helping children to engage in imaginative activities is a key to moving forward in treatment.

Many aggressive children reenact their earlier traumatic experiences in either the *autosphere* or the *macrosphere* instead of in the *microsphere*. For example, some children reenact their early abusive experiences by hurling their own bodies, or pieces of furniture, against a real wall instead of throwing toy people at a dollhouse wall. These children employ direct actions rather than play-actions or playacting to express anger and to relieve anxiety (Ekstein 1966). Most gorilla-suit wearers do not play imaginatively because they grew up in stressful environments where they were bombarded with stimuli so intense that assimilation and accommodation were prohibited. Therefore, they could not effectively organize their experiences because they had been repeatedly overwhelmed, even traumatized by them (Cohen 1981; Krystal 1978; Pynoos and Nader 1989; Roseby and Johnston 1995; Schwartz and Kowalski 1991; Shengold 1979; Terr 1979, 1981, 1988, 1990; Westen 1990). The children were unable to reenact these experiences in their play or to play out their fears and anxieties and, as a result, lack imaginative play.

Most children in gorilla suits need to express their anger in more controlled and structured ways than trying to wreck everything in the playroom and being constantly prevented from doing so by the therapist. While the Wreck Everything Game was "invented" by the boy, it has been used on numerous occasions with other children.

In chapter 9, we discuss the defenses children use against feeling anxious and then illustrate how to model, teach, and support these defenses so that children can move from the primitive defenses of "fight or flight," typically displayed in all settings, including the therapy room, to more mature defenses. In this and the next chapter, we lay the groundwork for that discussion by presenting efforts to make more adaptive two major defenses used by children wearing gorilla suits. The two defenses are displacement and distancing. The children displace their anger onto others or retreat behind brick walls of detachment.

Yet both these defenses can be used adaptively. The techniques to be presented are the first step in an effort to get children in gorilla suits to distance and displace feelings into the world of make-believe play. Unlike other defenses, which have a strong repressive element, displacement places anxiety-laden conflicts where ego mastery over them can be obtained. The very fact that certain sensations or happenings can be assigned to another place, or displaced, creates the distinction between inner and outer (Freud and Sandler 1985).

In this chapter, we present activities designed to help children displace their anger and distance themselves from it by using playful actions. In the next chapter, we present techniques to get children to use these two defenses in fantasy play. The techniques can also be used with children capable of fantasy play because they contribute to emotional development beyond their use as distancing and displacement activities.

Landreth (2002) writes that "every playroom should have some inexpensive items that are for smashing, breaking, or throwing. Egg cartons seem to fit this purpose quite well. They can be stacked and kicked over, jumped on and smashed, broken apart, thrown, and painted" (p. 530). Nevertheless, we rely more on the techniques to be discussed in this chapter because they lend themselves more to fantasy elaborations than do smashing egg cartons, breaking popsicle sticks, or pinching play dough to pieces. The goal with children in gorilla suits is to channel their aggression into acceptable substitutes, moving them from direct actions to action play, to playacting, and finally to expressive fantasy. We list below, in order of increasing sophistication, some useful techniques.

CLAY

Children who cannot express feelings through playacting or drawing can be encouraged to do so initially through action play. Clay is a good medium with which to develop this skill, and it appeals to gorilla-suit wearers, many of whom psychoanalysts would place at the anal-sadistic stage of psychosexual development. In a totally safe manner, the children create, in clay, fantasy figures that they pound with a wooden hammer. If they wish, they can smash them repeatedly or create new figures on whom to vent their anger.

Another option is to make "Clay Bombs" (James 1989). The children make a life-size drawing of the person they are angry at, who, early in treatment, is often the therapist, and then they throw clay bombs at the drawing laid out on the floor. It helps if the child says or yells something at the hated person as the clay bombs are hurled toward it. The child might say, "I hate you, Doctor Dave, for not taking me outside."

Later in treatment the child can be encouraged to express anger that has surfaced at past abusers. While throwing bombs, the child is encouraged to yell, "I hate you for what you did to me." "I hope you rot in hell for what you did." The therapist can join in and yell at the perpetrator such things as the following: "What you did to Jenny was wrong!" "No adult should ever do that to a child!" "She is a sweet girl and she didn't deserve to be treated that way!" "Shame on you!" This evocative technique helps children get in touch with their anger, displaced onto others over the years, and to express it toward the actual abuser in a safe manner. The technique, because it involves body movement, may help victims to get past their "frozen inaction."

Some children may prefer using sand-filled stress balls (which can be very soothing to children, who love to squeeze them in their hands) instead of clay. A playroom should be equipped with several of these balls; they wear out quickly because children also use them to relieve tension and anxiety.

HARMLESS DESTRUCTION!

A second safe and empowering technique that allows children to freely express anger is ripping up newspapers. The therapist sets a timer for several minutes and asks the child to see how many newspapers can be ripped up within the time limit. Sometimes a child allows the therapist to participate. Together they can create a rather impressive mess on the floor. This evocative exercise can include verbalization of anger during the task and reflection after task completion. While the room will look ransacked, it doesn't take long to clean up, especially when child and therapist clean up together.

The therapist can suggest that they roll a certain number of the shredded newspapers into balls and shoot the balls into an improvised hoop (waste basket) from a spot across the room. This action symbolizes a transformation of anger into a collaborative activity; things are put back together after the discharge of feelings, and a fun activity is made from the derivatives of the ripping and shredding. This activity moves therapy in another direction and, if completed late in a session, helps create a positive mood. Very defiant children, who are unlikely to help the therapist clean up, can be told to use rolled up newspapers to hit the dummy. Later, they can be guided to use the rolls for more constructive purposes.

Children in gorilla suits find it difficult to transition from intense emotional ventilation to activities of daily living. Consequently, it is crucial that therapists "wind down" the child toward the end of each session. Some pleasant and relaxing activity should occur. If it does not, children may be returned to parents or teachers in a turbocharged emotional state, one unlikely to enhance the therapist's reputation.

Some children arrive for therapy in a souped-up emotional state and, after using one or more of the rechanneling techniques, will need help to calm down and self-soothe before moving beyond their entering anger. Children exposed to endless violence can be in a constant state of physiologically heightened arousal, leading to hypervigilance. When children feel unsafe, they have difficulty applying themselves or profiting from therapy. Pelcovitz (1999) states, "It is like trying to treat [post-traumatic stress disorder] in the midst of a hurricane." In chapter 9, we discuss techniques to help children calm themselves.

REAMING THEM OUT!

One technique that children enjoy is called Reaming Them Out! The technique seems absurd, but most children get a good laugh out of it. Since humor can be helpful, a significant bonus is added. Early in treatment, the child is asked to name an offending person. Often it is the therapist, but sometimes it's someone who has recently offended or humiliated the child. The therapist and child take turns reaming out the person or the life event (school failure, a physical ailment, etc.) by yelling at it in the wastepaper basket. Because the children see the task as silly, the therapist usually takes the lead, willing to look the fool, and sticks his or her head in the wastebasket and screams at the identified person or life event. At this point, the children usually double over in laughter and can't wait for their turn.

If the family is present, each member can take a turn. Sometimes the child beckons them from the waiting room, and when the task is explained to them, they evince a mortified look and undoubtedly think, "My goodness, what kind of therapist did I pick for my child?" After they take a turn, however, they usually can't wait to do so again. The playful strategy becomes contagious, and everyone gets into the act.

Just so the technique doesn't get stale, the child is asked to yell into the toilet whenever he or she gets mad at home. We leave the decision to the child about whether family members are recruited to do the same. Families have been heard from months after termination of therapy, asserting that they still get a good laugh when reminiscing about yelling into the wastebasket. Some even feel that exposure to this exercise was a turning point in their child's therapy. One child requested a follow-up visit one year later to have one more chance to give the offender a piece of her mind by yelling into the waste basket. She brought her entire family with her, and they each took a turn for one final venting of their anger toward the perpetrator. If a play therapist worries about looking foolish, he or she should pick a different profession.

When children reach the stage at which anger at abusers surfaces, or where sadness over a loss materializes, the same technique can be used to vent angry feelings at the abuser or at having had to experience such a devastating loss.

KNOCKING DOWN THE WALLS OF ANGER!

Virginia McGrory introduced us to a procedure used by a fellow graduate student, Jennifer Leonetti. The materials required are a soft ball, like a Nerf ball or soft rubber ball, and cardboard bricks (sold by Childcraft). The child makes a wall of the cardboard bricks and is encouraged to kick the ball into the bricks and knock the wall down, a sophisticated variation of the Wreck Everything

Game. The rules of the game, however, require that before the child can force-fully kick the ball, the child has to name one thing he or she is angry about. At a later stage in therapy, the therapist identifies the wall as a particular feel-ing, such as anger related to abuse, and asks the child to destroy that wall of anger. It is important, however, that the child be ready to "let go" of long-held anger before focusing on this objective. When the child is finally ready to give up the suppressed anger, the game can symbolize the child's readiness to both "let go" and to "take down the walls."

THE MAD GAME

A fifth technique, one which makes use of cardboard, wood, or plastic boxes, is the Mad Game (Davidson 1997). The therapist divides the blocks evenly between himself or herself and the child. The two take turns placing blocks on top of the previous one. Each time a box is stacked, each expresses some-thing that makes him or her angry or something that is unfair. All statements, no matter how foolish or freakish, are accepted. Davidson suggests that ther-apists begin by bringing up minor annoyances and then progress to sensitive issues.

THE ANGER BUCKET!

This technique, a modification of the Anger Box, was first used in groups (Kaduson 2001). The child writes angry words on construction paper that is used to wrap the outside of the bucket. The bucket is then filled with twenty to fifty three-by-five-inch index cards, on which are written sentences such as "I get angry every time _____" or "When I get angry, my face _____." (Kaduson lists her favorites in her publication.) The child gets one chip for each sentence completed. The game can be expanded by introduc-ing provocative scenarios on the cards. The child is awarded three chips when a nonviolent solution is proposed for a scenario. For example, one scenario is a boy who is teased at school by a bully and who returns home and dis-covers that his little brother turned his room into a big mess. The therapist also draws cards from the bucket and, first, models the expression of a feel-ing and, second, introduces a nonviolent solution to the provocative situa-tion. Whoever ends up with the most chips at the end wins the game. While kids can get caught up in the competitive chase for chips, the therapist uses his or her turn to express a feeling and to model nonviolent solutions to frustrations. These exercises provide opportunities for the therapist to coach, guide, model, and reinforce the efforts of children to express anger in more constructive and modulated forms. The modeling helps expand each child's range of responses as most children in gorilla suits have a limited repertoire. Before they learn more and better ways to respond, they typically either attack or withdraw.

HAVING A FIELD DAY WITH MAGIC MARKERS!

A strategy that doesn't trash a room or require much time to clean up involves taking an old newspaper, giving the children an assortment of magic markers, and letting them scribble, in bright colors, with vigorous strokes, all over the newspaper to demonstrate how angry they feel. They are encouraged to verbalize their anger at the same time. If they cannot, they are encouraged to reflect on it while admiring their completed colorful work. The emphasis is on redirecting and rechanneling anger and rage. The message the child receives is that anger is legitimate but that its expression must occur in ways that do not inflict harm on oneself or on others. Children love the freedom of expression the markers allow, as well as the fact that the witnessing adult shows no concern about how their "artistic" productions turn out. In addition, the bright colors epitomize the power of emotive ventilation.

THE ANGER BALLOON

This technique also was introduced to us by Virginia McGrory. It facilitates the safe expression of anger and allows practice at modulating anger expression. The materials required are colored, punch-size balloons with elastic cords; colored markers; and paper. The child is given the paper and markers and asked to create an "angry list" by listing all the things that make him or her angry. Children with adequate language skills may spontaneously verbalize their anger as they list each item. The balloons are then introduced, and the therapist asks the child, "When you fill the balloon with air, pretend that the air is your anger." The child then selects a balloon whose color is equated with anger. Most commonly, a red one is picked.

Next the child is instructed to select an item from the "angry list." After the item is picked, the child blows the anger about that item into the balloon. The child can blow until the balloon is partially filled or can blow "really hard" and fill the balloon completely with anger. The amount of air blown depends on how angry the child is made by the item on the list. This procedure is repeated for each item on the list. The therapist coaches the child on items that make the child really angry by saying, "Now take the anger about that item and blow it into the balloon. Take all that anger from your toes all the way up your body, and blow it into the balloon." When the balloon is filled, and the child has exhausted the list, the balloon is tied off. The child then chooses what is to be done with the balloon (e.g., pop it, keep it, discard it). Some children label the balloon as their "anger balloon" and write their name on it. Every time a child can make a choice, feelings of powerlessness diminish.

Horn (1997) expands the technique. She tells children that the balloon represents the body and the air inside the balloon represents anger. She asks them, "What would happen if this anger (air) was stuck inside of you? Would there be room to think clearly?" She then instructs children to stomp on the balloon until it explodes, after which they discuss the possible actions taken by individuals who explode in this way (e.g., hitting a person, kicking someone). Children are then asked to reflect on whether this seems like a safe way to release anger (Horn 1997). Horn's next phase requires children to blow up another balloon, but instead of tying it, they pinch the end closed. Children are instructed to slowly release some of the air and then pinch it closed again. They are then asked, "Did the balloon and the people around the balloon stay safe when the anger was released? Does this seem like a safer way to let the anger out?" (Horn 1997, pp. 250–53).

DRAWING STRATEGIES

Children who cannot engage in make-believe play with toys can be encouraged to both contain and express their anger through imaginative drawings. Imagination also improves coping skill (Oaklander 1988; Singer 1976). The drawing techniques that follow are used to manage the pent-up anger that children reveal when they enter therapy—anger they typically displace onto the therapist until they learn to displace it elsewhere. Therapists are encouraged to invent their own drawing techniques because the ones we describe will become routine after a time. Drawings are also used to help children work through their angry feelings about their abuse, but we discuss using play and art for this purpose in chapter 17.

Putting feelings down on paper allows them to be managed in creative and symbolized ways. It also allows for greater objectification and distance from raw feeling. Drawing activities also provide opportunities for collaborative problem solving, so valuable in building a child's internal resources. The best opportunity to defuse anger, and then to "problem-solve" about it through negotiation and compromise, is at the anger's "front end." Once the child, and the family, get to the "back end," or "meltdown phase," the best options have evaporated, leaving only explosive anger.

Children as young as five can be taught the meaning of words like *compromise*, *negotiation*, and *problem solving* and can practice these skills by role-playing. The drawing exercises we describe help children to generate solutions at milder levels of eruption or storminess, solutions that can be utilized before the child faces turbulence. When children erupt in rage, the ability to cognitively process the eliciting event, to reason and apply logic, decreases dramatically. Children need to think, reflect, communicate, and problem-solve when mildly angry. Otherwise, destructive levels of anger and rage follow as a situation escalates. No one wins the power struggles that often characterize adult–child disciplinary interactions.

Volcano Pictures

A natural-world metaphor that can symbolize various levels of anger and rage is an erupting volcano. If drawn enthusiastically, volcano drawings are a step toward sublimation. The drawings also serve as a barometer that provides regular readings of the child's struggle with anger and rage. Volcano drawings can be used alone or in a serial drawing sequence to get readings at different points in the therapy process. Children can be instructed to draw them at home to redirect their anger and rage. The degree of the child's anger can be strikingly revealed in the drawings. The children are encouraged to color each volcano drawing after it's finished, as the use of bright colors, red and orange especially, allow for symbolized affective expression. If the red-hot lava overflows and destroys towns and villages, and all the people in them, there is little doubt about the anger the child is trying to manage.

Volcano drawings also can be used for problem solving. The child is instructed to draw volcanos at various stages of eruption and overflow. At each stage, the child engages in collaborative problem solving about available options to manage anger at that stage. If the volcano is experiencing some unrest and rumbling turbulence, the child has far more options available than when the volcano starts to overflow. At the "meltdown" point, it is usually too late, and damage control by others is the only alternative (Greene 1998). The child can also be asked how each stage in the eruption might be handled differently the next time it occurs.

Figure 7.1.   Volcano Picture

THERAPIST: If that volcano could talk, what do you think it would be saying. Is it okay if I write what you tell me right on the picture?

CHILD: Okay. I think it is saying "F— you! I hate you!"

THERAPIST: It looks very mad; it looks like pure red-hot lava. I wonder what could get it that mad?

CHILD: Maybe it is really tired of people walking up it and stepping all over it.

THERAPIST: That could do it. No one likes to be stepped on and dissed [*street language for disrespected*] all the time.

THERAPIST: What if the volcano were to talk when it was just beginning to get stirred up, long before it erupts? What would it have to say at that early point?

CHILD: You better watch it! I am starting to get really mad. I think you better leave me alone, if you don't want to get hurt!

THERAPIST: Let's say the volcano doesn't want to hurt anyone. What could he do to keep from erupting?

CHILD: Maybe he could slow things down, like you always tell me to take a deep breath, count to ten, or think of something that makes me feel calmer, like going fishing with my dad.

THERAPIST: So being alert to the anger building up and heading it off before it reaches the eruption or meltdown stage seems to be the key.

The eight-year-old boy whose volcano drawing appears below has manifested uncontrollable rages since nursery school, alienating him from peers and adults alike. His sadness and masking rage resulted from multiple losses compounded by his restless temperament. In the therapist-child interchanges that followed the drawing, despair reared its ugly head in the final interchange, but the therapist refused to be engulfed in the hopeless mood.

THERAPIST: If this volcano could talk, what do you think it might say?

CHILD: I hate everybody in the world! That's why I am exploding—so some people can die!

THERAPIST: Wow! That's what I'd called red-hot, overflowing lava anger! What did it take to get the volcano that angry!

CHILD: I don't know.

THERAPIST: What if you knew the volcano didn't really want to hurt anyone? What could you do that might help the volcano avoid these red-hot burning eruptions?

CHILD: I guess I . . . would tell him to get his mind off it.

THERAPIST: Get his mind off of what?

CHILD: The way he is treated.

THERAPIST: How is he treated?

Figure 7.2. Volcano Picture

CHILD: Everybody teases him and laughs at him, and they all think it is a big joke. He'll show them! He can't take it anymore.
THERAPIST: Sounds like the volcano needs a friend.
CHILD: Yeah, but it's too late!
THERAPIST: It's only too late if he decides it's too late!

Storm Pictures

Another colorful metaphor from the natural world is pictures of storms of varying degrees of intensity and threat. The child may choose a thunderstorm or a hailstorm or, if the child is really furious, a cyclone or a tornado to pictorially represent the degree of rage felt. As previously stated, when feelings are expressed in symbolic form, such as putting an image on paper, the intensity of the suppressed feelings is defused.

THERAPIST: If the storm could talk, what would it say about how angry it is?
CHILD: That I am so mad I want to destroy the whole world!
THERAPIST: Is there any way to calm the storm?
CHILD: Only momentarily, but it will come back fiercer than ever!

This eight-year-old child expresses, through the metaphor of the angry storm, that "Band-Aids" will help only temporarily. Until the conditions creating the storm are addressed, it will not subside and fade away. When inquiring about the drawings, the therapist plays the role of the ignorant interrogator, trying to create more complex understandings so the child will eventually see himself or herself in a new light.

Fire-Breathing Dragons

A third metaphor for raw anger and rage is drawings of dragons or other aggressive creatures, especially dinosaurs (notably T. rex), that commonly devour and dominate other creatures. The degree of anger is reflected in the drawing, from faint roars to increasingly fierce and loud bellows of anger, and finally to fire-breathing, red-hot rage. Depending on the stage of the symbolized rage, the child is asked, "What could the dragon or dinosaur do to stop such destruction before reaching the 'fire-breathing' point?" Again, collaborative problem-solving skills are exercised and reinforced. Options are generated and reflected on. If a child is unable to generate alternatives, the therapist can call on a strong, but calm and reflective, dragon puppet or other puppet to coach the dinosaur and dragon to be more in control. The control can be framed as strength. No dinosaur, dragon, or lion roars all the time. At times,

That I am so mad I want to destroy the world!

Figure 7.3.   Storm Picture

they express their strength by restraining themselves in a calm and confident manner.

Initial attempts to collaboratively problem-solve with a child don't usually get very far. It takes a number of attempts. Repeated dialogues, like the one below, help children to consider alternative actions. The fourteen-year-old immature adolescent whose dragon drawing and interchanges with his therapist appear below displayed odd and socially inappropriate gestures and mannerisms since birth. As a result, he experienced constant humiliation and ridicule. When he entered middle school, he threatened to burn the school down and to blow up a bomb on a bus.

> THERAPIST: Tell me about your picture.
>
> CHILD: It's the dragon that everyone hates. No one likes this dragon, and it has always been that way. Now he wants his revenge.
>
> THERAPIST: Do they hate him because they fear him?
>
> CHILD: Everyone is afraid of him now. But when he was small, everyone made fun of him and picked on him. They thought he was weird and wanted nothing to do with him.
>
> THERAPIST: Suppose the wise old owl [*puppet*] was consulted by the dragon? Do you think he might be able to help him find other choices? It sounds like the only choice the dragon sees right now is to kill or be killed!
>
> CHILD: How would you feel if you had been shit on your whole life? Wouldn't you want to even the score?
>
> THERAPIST: I would be mad, all right. Very enraged! But I might be so mad that I couldn't see any other choice but to kill or be killed. I think I would want to hear what the wise old owl might have to say.
>
> CHILD: Screw the wise old owl! This dragon is going into battle!
>
> THERAPIST: How will we know when he has achieved victory?
>
> CHILD: When no one else but him is alive.
>
> THERAPIST: Then who will he have left to celebrate with? He will truly be all alone.

Anger Thermometer

An anger thermometer is a useful tool to help children learn self-control options available at different degrees of anger. When describing a frustrating incident, the child indicates, by a check mark, the level the anger reached. At each level of anger, the child is taught words to express feelings at that level (see chapter 15). At lower levels of anger, words taught could include *bothered*, *annoyed*, *aggravated*, *irritated*, *irked*, *needled*, *peeved*, or *stung*. For the boiling point, the words taught could be *bang*, *blow up*, *burst*, *explode*, *rage*, *roar*, or *seethe*. For points in between, the words *abhor*, *detest*, *despise*, *hate*, or *loathe* could be taught. The focus is on finding ways to self-calm and self-soothe when the child becomes

Figure 7.4.   Dragon Picture

aware of his or her annoyances but hasn't reached the burst levels that can shut down the higher cortical areas so that thoughts become confused and jumbled. In chapter 9, we describe calming techniques that children can use when upset.

Plans and strategies can be developed to help both the child and the family to defuse the child's anger when it reaches the "peeved" level, a level when planned interventions are most effective. These strategies can be rehearsed, in both individual and family therapy sessions, using role-playing to simulate the situations that provoke various levels of anger. If the family is involved in planning and rehearsing suggested strategies, the therapist underlines the concept of teamwork, reinforcing parents as members of the child's team and reducing the adversarial struggle that often develops in families of gorilla-suit wearers.

ENCOURAGING COMMUNICATION OF VIOLENT FANTASIES

Some years ago, John Leon, of the Violence Clinic in Baltimore, found that when he encouraged clients to express to him in detail the fantasies of their anticipated violent behavior, it reduced their acting out. The development of the fantasy seemed to produce anxiety, and this anxiety inhibited action. All of us want to deny that children have sadistic fantasies. While Melanie Klein discussed children's sadistic fantasies in 1927, we still like to believe children incapable of such thoughts. Klein (1948, 1932) believed that fantasies are the motivating power behind play and that children with cruel and sadistic fantasies will not play when beginning therapy because they keep these fantasies repressed. Nevertheless, when they trust their therapist, who is not shocked by angry fantasies, sometimes they reveal the hostile and violent fantasies that accompany their anger. Maxwell Gitelson (1973) presents the case of a young adult who had the following fantasies throughout his life, sometimes when he masturbated and other times during daydreaming.

> He is commanding a powerful air fleet which is executing a bombing mission. He is in an underground country where people cannibalize each other, especially eating each other's genitals, which preferably are torn from the living person. He is a ten-year-old boy and an older girl is about to do this to him. Another boy kills the girl by stabbing her in the rectum or vagina. (p. 267)

Leon Shenken (1964) presents the case of a sixteen-year-old who killed his two younger sisters, one six and the other three, as part of a plan to kill his father. After the child turned himself over to the police, a large volume of prose and poetry was discovered in his room. Many of his stories involved multiple murders, mutilation, and dismemberment. The culprits were always apprehended and given the death penalty. There was a story in which he visualized his own death, and there were many others liberally illustrated with drawings of men being hanged or lying dismembered. One drawing in particular was captioned with his own name as "preacher and gunman."

Although the boy had idle thoughts about killing his father, his literary efforts were never at any stage concerned with intrafamily violence. The characters, both killers and victims, were strangers. If he was depicted, he was the victim. Evidently, the child lost the distance these fantasies provided him and could no longer contain his murderous rage. After his rage was discharged against his sisters, his sense of reality returned, and he turned himself over to the authorities. He killed his sisters painlessly because he reasoned that they would have no one to care for them after he killed his father and mother. He killed his mother because she would be lonely without a husband. By writing down his sadistic fantasies, perhaps he kept them from being acted upon earlier, or maybe they needed to be told to someone else to prevent their actual occurrence—and they never were.

An example of a confrontation that led to a discussion of fantasy appears below:

> THERAPIST: Your mother tells me you can't get to sleep at night.
> CHILD: I like staying up.
> THERAPIST: And you and your mother argue endlessly about your bedtime.
> CHILD: So.
> THERAPIST: I wonder if you're actually unwilling to fall asleep because you think you might die in your sleep.
> CHILD: [*Silence*]
> THERAPIST: Or maybe you have bad dreams. Children who are angry a lot usually dream of scary things—monsters, evil men, or vicious criminals.
> CHILD: Sometimes.
> THERAPIST: I could help you to stop having these dreams.
> CHILD: How?
> THERAPIST: By helping you to understand why you're always so angry at everybody. But first you need to tell me about your daydreams and what you think about each time you get angry at someone.
> CHILD: What do you mean?
> THERAPIST: Like when your dad hits you and sends you to your room. How do you plan to get even with him?

When these fantasies are explored in detail or when the child presents a violent dream, the idea is not to trace their origins to anger at parents but to keep the boundaries between fantasy and reality clear. The task is not to bury the hostility, but neither is it to deal with the feelings explicitly. The goal is to strengthen the child's feeling that emotions are manageable and that they will not run wild.

> THERAPIST: Lots of kids who are upset have some of the feelings you reveal in the drawing of your dream. But remember it was only a dream. Your mother didn't really die in that accident. Part of you must have felt frightened by your dream.

This statement helps the child to avoid the repressive process that results in explosive behavior and supports control over the underlying feelings. Even when death wishes toward parents are barely concealed in an aggressive child's dreams or play, the need for connectedness far outweighs the need for awareness. Only when children gain control over anger can they begin to examine its sources. If a child is openly hostile toward parents, the response becomes,

> THERAPIST: Often kids get angry at their parents, and this anger stirs up all kinds of confusing feelings. We will be talking about these feelings often in therapy.

Sometimes children experience their anger as "voices telling them what to do." These voices frighten not only them but also others whom they tell about the voices.

> CHILD: Only crazy people hear voices.
> THERAPIST: The voice telling you to do things is really the anger you feel and that you often hate feeling. If it comes from outside you, you can own it. Remember when we talked about "Mr. Angry?" Now Mr. Angry has become so strong that you've put him outside of yourself and have him actually talking to you. I'll bet that's really scary.

When helping children develop play actions or when exploring primitive fantasy, the therapist is always walking a thin line. Talking about feelings or developing action fantasy can lead to action. It is no easy task to help the action-oriented child develop delay mechanisms.

CONCLUSION

Gorilla-suit wearers need acceptable alternatives to their destructive display of anger at the same time that they need their anger validated. Their rage is usually the result of horrific experiences and frequently associated with a series of profound losses. Young children do not easily verbalize such feelings. Consequently, they need tools to redirect and rechannel rage into safe venues. They also need freedom to express their feelings without fear of repercussion. The activities described in this chapter offer opportunities for ventilation and emotive expression using playful actions. They also involve close collaboration between the child and the therapist, a chief ingredient of healing therapy. Some of the activities also offer the bonus of being playful, if not funny.

Trauma victims need to reset the frozen body state associated with the trauma to a position of safety and control. Verbal processing alone may be inadequate to accomplish this task. Therapeutic approaches that emphasize body movement, massage, and exercise may be more helpful (van der Kolk 2003). The action-oriented techniques described in this chapter may help address the helplessness that results from inhibition of effective actions when faced with overwhelming terror.

Although the suggested activities encourage safe and constructive redirection of anger, the activities by themselves do not address the sorrow and pain underlying the rage of children in gorilla suits. Anger management tools, such as those we have described, while valuable for self-containment, need to be followed by efforts to uncover trauma. In later chapters, particularly those addressing trauma reenactment and profound loss, we illustrate efforts to address the complex emotional issues presented by children wearing gorilla suits.

Developing Displacement and Distancing by Teaching, Modeling, and Structuring Action Play

The importance of masking symbols in latency to distance children from unacceptable thoughts, impulses, and actions is emphasized, and the oscillating nature of children's play is stressed. Many children in gorilla suits never developed the ability to use masking symbols to manage frightening experiences, and they reenact those experiences through behavioral acts instead of through fantasy play. Many must be taught to play to get at distorted preverbal concepts and to help them structure their memory. The development of two defenses, displacement and distancing, to help children develop masking symbols in action play is illustrated through a series of brief vignettes.

$\mathcal{I}$n the preceding chapter, we presented techniques to help children rechannel their anger and rage. The techniques encourage children to displace their anger in symbolic actions, some of which involve gross motor actions, such as "knocking down the walls of anger," while others involve more fanciful actions, such as drawing volcanoes and storms. Still others, such as drawing cards from the anger bucket and discussing alternative courses of action in frustrating situations, bring coping skills into play. The use of fantasy drawings helps children to develop masking symbols for their rage, symbols needed to work through turbid emotions while maintaining distance from them.

In normal development, latency-age children use masking symbols to assist in maintaining the state of calmness that characterizes this stage and results in its name. Nevertheless, a child's latency state can be overwhelmed if overstimulated. The child who has developed symbolization can quell the humiliation of trauma, the excitement of overstimulation, and the latent fantasies they stir up by actually reorganizing and resynthesizing these experiences into highly symbolized and displaced stories. By reliving the events couched in the symbols and stories of latency play, the child finds an outlet for heightened drives.

This ability to employ fantasy to mitigate drive expression depends heavily on the capacity to form masking symbols, which in turn requires abstract thinking, delay, and repression. The child who can use masking symbols can manage conflicts or feelings that cannot be experienced consciously because of the strong fears or intense feelings they arouse. The child who, angry at a parent, develops a fantasy of "consuming flames that burn down a house and kill a mean mother" is able to transform anger into a symbolic story.

With the recent interest in identifying victims of abuse, therapists need to remember the role of masking symbols in normal development. Adults who believe there is a direct correspondence between a child's play and reality are mistaken. If the child plays out a scene with a "mean, cruel mommy doll" beating a baby doll, investigators can wrongly assume that the child has experienced similar beatings, failing to appreciate the nature of children's moral development. During one phase of development, children are harsh punishers, who punish more for the consequences of an action than for the intentions of the actor. Children believe that a child who breaks five teacups should be punished more than one who breaks only one cup, even when the five were broken accidentally and the one purposefully. The child at this stage has internalized the harsh and judgmental aspects of his parents' personalities rather than their protective, loving aspects, and only later, with increasing maturity, does the child fuse these disparate images. Terence Moore (1964), after observing the play of normal four- to six-year-olds, made this remark: "Parents are commonly made far more punitive than any real parent would be, and many children take obvious pleasure in portraying them thus." For example:

> CHILD: She's got to stay in the bath all night and sleep there.
> CHILD: [*Makes father doll smack child doll hard.*] She won't have a bath, and no jelly, and she's got to go to bed. Then mother comes and smacks her. [*Batters and squeezes a child doll with a mother doll in a violent assault.*]
> CHILD: The father—he's going to fight with Mother—and then with the children. He kills them and eats them up, and they are all dead.

Young children think of the characters in their play at any given moment as either good or bad. And without comment, the child's play will reveal a sudden change of heart. "Now he's good," "Now he's naughty." Such children have difficulty answering the question, "Is Daddy mostly good or mostly bad?" Only the very mature preschooler can answer with, "A little bit bad and a little bit good." The normal child's play typically reveals clear alternations of positive with negative feelings. The play is oscillating in nature. A child initiates play by spanking a doll in a mild and playful fashion. Slightly later the play becomes more aggressive. The play then meets with parental retaliation, which becomes increasingly more violent. But the sequence of play is interrupted again and again by harmonious family life, in which children are fed, clothed, and put to bed. Paralleling this oscillation of affect, the play swings back and forth between realistic and unrealistic fantasy as a result of fluctuating certainty. As fantasy becomes freer, aggression is released; this aggression produces anxiety that some children moderate by momentarily turning back toward reality. When made anxious by their play, they can (1) make it more realistic and derive reassurance from the knowledge that reality has limits that fantasy lacks; (2) make explicit references to real life; or (3) step back and view the play as nothing but play (e.g., "These are just toys."). Another option is to distance themselves from frightening fantasies by making the play less realistic. The healthy child uses distance to make the play so obviously impossible that it looks ridiculous. It becomes a slapstick farce. Because this play is so unreal, the player can laugh at fears. The pleasure in such humor lies in the child's realization that he or she is strong enough to master dangers, that the clown will survive its outrageous misfortunes. But for truly traumatized children, there is no such knowledge. They cannot use distance in this fashion but instead create a never-never land where, deadly serious, they spend as much time as possible.

Children who have not achieved these developmental advancements because of constant exposure to traumatic stress do not engage in make-believe play. Some of the rechanneling techniques we presented in the last chapter help them to employ playful actions to move past this primitive stage. Children who can playact, however, don't usually need these techniques. They can express their anger through puppets and other playroom toys. Other children are too young for the rechanneling techniques and need to learn to play. We teach them to do so. We were stimulated to move in this direction by the success of both Jernberg (1979) and Smilansky (1968), who taught children to play imaginatively.

In *Understanding and Treating the Aggression of Children,* we stress that the environment surrounding gorilla-suit wearers is a jumble of stress-producing images that bombard their immature nervous system. Only when children interact with novel stimuli within their capacity for mastery will they continue to show interest, alertness, and positive emotional responses to them. When material is presented too rapidly, or too chaotically, without the opportunity for the children to assimilate it effectively, children will be startled and become frightened. If confronted for an excessive period of time with a high rate of "unassimilable" material, children will both act out and shut down. If children's past experiences are stressful and disorganizing, the children will resist reorganizing them. The experiences are too painful or too difficult to manage and to recall. Consequently, the emotional concomitants of these experiences persist as increasingly incongruous parts of the self and compromise the children's ability to play and also to mature.

Children who find it difficult to play out the immediate past cannot put these experiences outside the self to see them more clearly. They cannot transcend the actual situation in which they find themselves. They will not use play to imitate what goes on around them and, therefore, cannot reassure themselves as to the purpose and meaning of the adult world. They cannot use play to express feelings because the initiation of playful behavior is associated with painful affects. There are no pleasurable experiences to repeat, only painful ones, and these tend to get repeated in action rather than in play because play development is disrupted by high anxiety levels. Play helps normal children to master anxiety. Play in seriously traumatized children produces anxiety.

In the mother's absence, a baby hallucinates the mother's reassuring and loving face in order to mitigate the anxiety that accompanies her short absences. But what if the mother's face produces anxiety? What if the mother is an angry, disturbed woman whose baby is a source of frustration to her or a reminder of her mistakes, a woman who is angry at the child every time she has to feed it? What if she angrily props the baby in a chair and shoves the bottle in its mouth? What if she never soothes or comforts the baby, and her only contact with it is to feed it when it is hungry and change it when it is wet, tasks that she actively resents? The answer to these questions is the following: the baby will experience extremely ambivalent feelings about the mother. Hallucinating her image will produce anxiety and rage. A baby who is left unattended not only cries when in need but also angrily protests when needs go unmet for long periods. Eventually, these unanswered protests turn to despair and then to apathy. Such a child will not hallucinate an image that is not need-satisfying. The child's very first play behavior, the prototype for later play, never fully develops. If the infant does hallucinate his mother's face, the image will quickly fade, establishing early the prototype for play interrupted by anxiety.

Action is an attempt to master reality immediately, to make it subservient to the needs of the individual. In contrast, play-action delays action in reality. The "play" of traumatized children is sometimes closer to action than to play-action. Since posttraumatic play is observed in children who are capable of ordinary play in other situations, no wonder we see an absence of symbolic play altogether in severely and repeatedly traumatized children.

Jo Ann Fineman's observations (1962) of mother–infant interactions suggest that some children do not play because their mothers exert an inhibiting influence on their imaginative play. Children who constantly feel threatened by the loss of their mother's approval and affection express this fear by being unable to relinquish what cannot be handled or touched. They simply play with objects in ways dictated by the objects themselves; they do not make use of the objects to represent or animate a fantasy.

GETTING AT PREVERBAL CONCEPTS

In addition to helping children to assimilate experiences by managing them through symbolization, there are two other reasons to teach acting-out children to play. First, the limited nature of the young child's experience leads the child to group together events, feelings, and sensations that have occurred at different times and have the same quality. They may or may not "belong" together in the way an adult would group them. These concepts are aggregations of sensations, emotions, and images grouped together in highly individual configurations long before the child develops speech. They result from the child's needs to make sense of and to introduce order into experiences. Once these concepts are formed, the child acts as if they are true when in actual fact they may be false. For healthy later development, the child must have an opportunity to externalize these concepts in play. Lacking such an opportunity, the concepts become "stuck" and become the source of later pathology.

For example, the child who has been force-fed as an infant may mentally group a spoon with painful objects because of strong nonverbal associations with a spoon (Feldman and Mordock 1969; Mordock and Feldman 1969). Similarly, the child does not realize why he or she is particularly anxious around adults who want all the food on a plate to be eaten. The child never gets to test his or her highly personalized symbols against reality because high anxiety levels bring into play defenses that retard further cognitive growth.

STRUCTURING MEMORY

A second reason for teaching play is that trauma disrupts even the verbal child's organizational abilities. A child exposed repeatedly to traumatic experiences fails to perceive and to register these experiences adequately. Even mild anxiety restricts and distorts perception. Such experiences, when repressed, are registered in the unconscious as poorly structured images, such as somatic memories or cognitive distortions, or (as has been repeatedly stated) as the need to act or to be acted upon (repetition compulsions). Traumatic experiences are imbued with painful feelings and are, therefore, different from normal memory traces. Jonathan Cohen (1981) uses the term *deviant mental organization* to describe one's response to trauma. The disorganization following trauma results not only in the formation of defensive wishes (wishes to avoid the trauma's repetition or wishes to control the experience by fantasies of active mastery) but also in the failure to develop normal wishes.

The child who can play out traumas can be helped to understand the play as forms of memory and defensive wishes and to transform the feelings connected with them into forms that can be verbally expressed. The therapeutic task with many children is to uncover memories and wishes that were structured to begin with. With the repeatedly traumatized child, the task is to construct memories. The former task is an uncovering process while the latter is a structuring one.

> ADULT: [*To a child who has repeatedly force-fed dolls in the playroom.*] You want to hit me with the spoon because the spoon makes you anxious. You also get anxious around mealtimes, particularly with adults who want you to eat everything on your plate.

Added to the task of interpreting active defenses against the expression of unacceptable wishes (discussed in chapter 9) is the task of transforming pathological forms of memory into normal memories. For example, a girl's preoccupation with claws in her drawings and her nightmares was traced to her mother's abuse of her as an infant (see chapter 12). The child resists efforts at transformation, partly because the feelings associated with the traumas are experienced as overwhelming and "crazy." The child actively avoids reexperiencing the frightening physical sensations that accompanied the trauma and also resists efforts to understand the fantasy elaborations that accompany efforts to master the traumatic experience. These elaborations become part of the deviant mental organization, making it hard for the child to distinguish fantasy from reality. The therapist will need to help the child to make such distinctions.

> THERAPIST: The monster in your nightmares can't really hurt you anymore. You are too big for the daddy-people to smother you with a pillow like they did when you were little. You can run and call for help. Besides, the daddy-people couldn't stand your screaming when you were little—you don't scream like that any more. Only babies scream like that. Now your dad hits you when you talk back and it hurts, but he has never hit you hard enough to kill you. Your big brother is still alive, and I'll bet Dad hit him a lot.

Keep in mind that children remember by playing. Our first task is to introduce toys that stimulate a child's memory. Our second task is to expand and elaborate on the child's play in order to stimulate associations to the memory. By doing so, we help the child to transform traumatic registrations into normal memories. Play therapy with traumatized children involves modeling a different way to play with the materials selected. All normal latency-age children, because they cannot express unacceptable feelings directly, play them out in fantasy. Our task is to help children who lack fantasy play to develop the symbolization needed to construct need–fulfilling distant fantasies. The child without adequate symbolization skill will continue acting out conflicts.

Dorothy Block (1968) introduces specific play materials into sessions to assist her and the child in playing out different roles. For example, when treating a child who assumed the identity of Mighty Mouse, she introduced two appealing little woolly mice, one white and the other gray. The child immediately named the white one Mighty Mouse and ordered a tiny red cape for him. The gray one he named after himself. The use of these mice, and of other play materials, reveals how themes that gradually evolve in play contribute to a child's recall of traumatic events. The child angrily banged together a mother and father doll, proclaiming their wickedness. He then picked up the boy doll and charged, "They don't love their son!" He then confided for the first time that he remembered that day Mighty Mouse arrived. It was a terrible day. The man was put in jail and finally died because they did not give him any food. "He was worse than a pirate." He added, "It was twenty years ago." Thus, in response to his discovery that mice, and he, could be lovable, he could recall the traumatic battle between his parents the night they separated, when he was three.

DEVELOPMENT OF DISPLACEMENT AND DISTANCING

The vignette below illustrates the child who, other than the most primitive defenses of "fight or flight," has not developed any defenses against the expression of forbidden impulses.

A boy of six immediately begins to toss around the toys in the playroom, accompanying these efforts with the following chatter:

CHILD: I'm playing a game called "wreck everything." I'll wreck everything, then I'll be even stronger. It will make me even stronger; lifting weights makes me feel strong, too. I like doing dangerous things. If I fall, that wouldn't hurt me. I'm wrecking the house. Bare naked, eee, eee, ha ha ha, make me angry [*baby talk*]; me wreck it, hee, hee.

The boy proceeds to tell "playground jokes" about urination, defecation, and sexuality. The boy's play [*crashing cars together, dropping dolls off cliffs, burning down houses with people trapped inside*] is chaotic and continually interrupted by thoughts and by flights into action or new play. While these behaviors can reflect the boy's chaotic home environment, his maladaptive response to the chaos reflects his inability to assimilate and accommodate these experiences.

The next vignette illustrates a child who employs some play action to displace feelings, but the defensive play contains anxiety for only short periods.

In the playroom, a young girl immediately hit a baby doll with a drumstick, saying,

CHILD: The baby is not going to bed; she needs a whipping.

Then, dissatisfied with the drumstick, she asked the play therapist for his belt so she could beat the bad baby.

THERAPIST: My belt stays on me, but babies aren't bad just because they won't go to bed [*educative statement*]!

Then she wanted to leave the room and take the doll with her. She hit the therapist when he went to retrieve it from her.

THERAPIST: [*Restraining the child*] The doll belongs in the playroom. It will be here when you come again.

The first effort with both children is to help them to displace. For displacement to be successful, the child must move from action-oriented displacement to symbolic displacement. Once symbolic displacement occurs, distancing naturally follows. For some children, a situation-specific transition from direct action to symbolic displacement can take place in several sessions. For others, particularly for more disturbed children, even a situation-specific transition can take many sessions. Discouraging expression of anger toward the therapist and redirecting it elsewhere is an example of a situation-specific transition from direct action to play action, from direct expression to displacement. Children who attack the therapist are encouraged to hit a dummy instead, after which the therapist draws a picture of himself or herself or of others and tapes it onto the dummy.

Some years ago, social learning theorists criticized therapeutic efforts to get children to hit a dummy, demonstrating that hitting dummies only increased the behavior and contributed to more hitting by the children outside the playroom. Neither of us would dispute these findings, nor Singer's finding (1966, 1976) that expression of aggression increases arousal rather than decreases it. Nevertheless, the dummy is not hit for cathartic purposes. The children have plenty of opportunities for emotional release. They do it all the time. The intent is to get them to displace anger onto the dummy. They are encouraged to draw a face, name it, and stick it onto the dummy. Then they are encouraged to draw a figure on paper, name it, and tell it why it is hateful while scribbling their hate. Then they are instructed to draw an imaginary scene to which anger is displaced, all while in communication with the therapist.

To help a child learn these actions, the therapist can draw angry scenes or make puppets hit one another. The therapist can then draw a specific individual who arouses the child's anger and draw the child verbally confronting the individual. Again, the child is encouraged to draw similarly, and in this situation he or she may eventually perform these actions independently. For some time, however, the child might not transfer this "learning" to situations outside the therapy room. While the child may hit a toy or draw angry scenes when mad at the therapist, he or she may still hit another child until this response, too, is modified by therapeutic efforts. When the child can spontaneously perform symbolic actions, movement has been made from experiencing diffuse anxiety and diffuse displacement to experiencing signal anxiety. As a consequence, a more adaptive response to the signal anxiety can be made.

Children who anxiously demand to play gross motor games in the small playroom can be encouraged in graded steps to play small motor games. The therapist can add fantasy elaborations to the games, and the child can be encouraged to emulate this behavior. For example, a small ball basket can be hung on the playroom wall and the child encouraged to sit and shoot baskets. While he is doing so, the therapist can verbalize that an actual contest is taking place, that the boy is the star shooter, it's the last second of the game, and so forth. This can be followed by playing the table game where a ping-pong ball is lofted into a small basket. Again, the therapist verbalizes fantasy elaborations on the game and encourages the child to do likewise. Such efforts can help the child to develop the symbolism needed for imaginative play. Our approach differs from Hudak (2000), who uses ball play to facilitate talk therapy. We use it to facilitate symbol formation.

The play therapist can select representative hand puppets and have them talk angrily to one another or can engage miniature figures in other sociodramatic situations. The therapist can draw soldiers fighting (stick figures for the less skilled). The therapist can build forts from blocks and employ toy soldiers to defend them. For the child mentioned in the first vignette, who seemed preoccupied with feces, the therapist could select toy toilets from the dollhouse and model miniature dolls bathing and toileting. Sixty years ago, Levy (1937, 1939), perhaps the first to use structured play therapy techniques, preselected toys and set up play situations that replicated an area of real-life conflict for the child. In the present approach, toys are similarly selected, but the therapist first models imaginative play and encourages the child to follow suit, the reverse of Gardner's mutual storytelling technique (1971), in which the child tells a story and the therapist retells it, adding a therapeutic message.

Distancing can be encouraged by the therapist's playing with dolls he or she labels as kings, witches, sorcerers, or robots and then labeling himself or herself as the barbarian warrior or knight who slays the sorcerer. The child is then encouraged to play similarly. By encouraging the child to displace and distance anger from actions into play actions, the play therapist also is encouraging split-ting (the division of self and other representations into contradictory ego states of "all good" or "all bad"). While splitting is a primitive defense, its use is more adaptive than "flight" or "fight." By verbalizing that the "lion has a right to be angry because the tiger attacked first," the child can split in the play and feel less overwhelmed by anxiety.

> THERAPIST: Let's make the little boy into Superman so he can capture his enemies and put them in jail. Here, put this little cape on the boy doll and fly him around.
> or
> THERAPIST: The little boy can pretend to be a lion, and he can growl ferociously at his enemy.

Some traumatized children rely too much on distancing and must be helped to employ other defenses, the topic of the next chapter. Their make-believe play is restricted to scenes of faraway battles, space monsters, evil emperors, and brave warriors. They seem to have stayed in those faraway places they sought when first disillusioned by their parents. The children use the monsters as the personification and receptacle of all their bad impulses, which enables them to establish distance from them and deny them as their own. The children also put the monster out in some distant space, far away from them. The undesirable, unconscious, forbidden, and repressed are sent far away. Anxiety is defended against by distance.

> CHILD: Here's a witch killing people, cowboys eating people up! [*Child becomes anxious, loses distance, remarks*] It's just a story.
> and
> CHILD: [*An anxious child, asked to tell a story, introduces her task by immedi-ately distancing.*] I don't know any stories, but I'll tell one that isn't true.

Dragons and monsters have always characterized early conscience develop-ment; the small child experiences the parent as both threatening and punitive, on the one hand, and magically omnipotent and giving, on the other. Normally the child's early images become modified and synthesized into developing moral structures. As the internalization of values and identification with parents pro-ceed, the archaic, distorted features recede. In contrast, the disturbed child is un-able to synthesize the good and bad parental images and, thus remains with only the primitive precursors of a conscience, derived from a period in development in which loving and hating are fused rather than synthesized. The child's fantasies reflect this integrative failure. Such children suffer from certain integrative deficits. Their personalities are composed of disconnected and fragmented parts (split off and compartmentalized parts of themselves). Some children achieve distance from their problems by maintaining a strong, although not total, commitment to a self-centered, illusory world of pleasure. Yet even these fantasies, upon close inspection, reflect terrors being denied.

> Martha, a nine-year-old girl, spent most of her waking life daydreaming about life on another planet, where a cyclops and his wolf were her guardians. There was an abundance of food, beautiful scenery, and a temperate climate. In art class, Martha would draw aspects of this world, and each drawing would be accompanied by gleeful laughter and much pleasure. These were the only times she showed pleasurable emotions. She involved another girl in this fantasy, with both of them planning to live in such a place when they got older.
>
> One of the major functions of her fantasies was to fully separate pleasure from pain and to keep the pleasure world intact. Martha's fantasy life filled each play therapy session and tolerated little interference. Any references to her daily life experiences were viewed as irrelevant intrusions. In fact, if her life became more troubling, her fantasies would intensify. Denial was used extensively to split off the intrusive reality. Unlike less disturbed children, who can allow painful themes to be elaborated upon and dealt with during therapy, Martha resurrected and intensified these stereotypical fantasies in the presence of even mild anxiety. On one occasion when her therapist [Dr. Mordock] became frustrated with both her grandiose insistence that she was as powerful as any Planet X person and her denial of fearful feelings, he challenged her to arm wrestle [a rather untherapeutic procedure, since defenses can't be confronted directly, and a sign of his increasing frustration].
>
> She of course lost, but explained that her right hand was her weakest. When she again lost using her left hand, she responded that her left hand was more tired than usual and that she would win on another day. She then became agitated and left the session. When her grandiosity weakened, she regressed to escape. Needless to say, confrontation resulted in her use of an even more primitive defense. Martha's development was followed over a ten-year period. While distance remained her primary defense against anxiety, its use became more adaptive. She developed an interest in the occult and in ancient Egyptian artworks. She went on to a local junior college to study archaeology.

PLAYROOM TOYS

Playrooms needn't contain every conceivable toy to help children play out conflicts. Children will find ways to make use of items in the playroom or office and will display far more imagination and fantasy when doing so than when plopped in front of a computer or television screen playing aggressive video games. Landreth (2002) feels that every playroom should have what he labels "acting out or aggressive release toys." He lists the following:

> Handcuffs (spring-release type without key), toy gun, 4-ft. (1.2m) length of rope, toy soldiers (30-count size with two different colors of soldiers is

sufficient), aggressive puppets (e.g., alligator or dragon), pounding bench, and rubber knife. A Bop Bag (Bobo) is an important item if space permits. Items in this category facilitate the expression of anger, hostility, and frustration, among other feelings and needs, and thus may necessitate the need for limit setting. (p. 530)

Nevertheless, we mentioned earlier that controversy exists over whether play therapy rooms should include items such as a Bop Bag or Bobo, toy guns, handcuffs, ropes, masks, plastic knives, and swords to facilitate expression of anger (Rapier 2000; Stone 2000; Whited 2000). We concur with Drewes (2001a) that children struggling with aggressive impulses are easily overstimulated by toy guns, knives, ropes, masks, or handcuffs and can be rapidly lured into the very behavior they need help to contain and master. We prefer puppets, including alligator, dinosaur, hawk, and lion puppets; dolls and dollhouses; schoolhouses; and miniature toy animals, all of which create the emotional distance needed to explore these issues in symbolized form until reliable self-control is developed.

Drewes (2001) notes that the residential treatment center where she and both of us worked remodeled its playrooms in 2001, and a deliberate decision was made, after extensive discussion by clinical staff, to remove the Bobo punching bags and other punching items. Had Dr. Mordock been there during the discussion, however, he would have suggested keeping the Bobo available in a nearby supply closet because he would rather have the extremely aggressive child punch Bobo than the therapist. One time, in order to be less intimidating to a five-year-old boy, Dr. Mordock got down on his knees to talk to the child. Seeing the author at eye level, the boy quickly smashed him in the face. It was the first and only time Dr. Mordock was hit by an angry child, including the years he spent intervening in crisis situations (Mordock 1999b). The authors use aggressive toys to channel raw aggression into more suitable outlets—to convert actions to action-play, then to playacting, and finally to fantasy. Others also have made a strong case for Bobo to remain in the playroom (Trotter, Eshelman, and Landreth 2003).

Children stop playing with the Bop Bag rather quickly (Rapier 2000). After developing a sufficient sense of personal power, children rarely play with the Bop Bag again, except when they reach a stage in trauma work in which they are encouraged to make the bag the perpetrator and to punch and yell at it and later to write it a letter.

The battles we encourage children to create in the playroom take place between ferocious dinosaurs and their prey or between tigers and lions and timid animals. Children wanting to wage more realistic wars can use the plastic or rubber miniature soldiers, tanks, planes, and various vehicles. They also are encouraged to use the ambulances and rescue trucks when someone is injured and needs to be transported to a field hospital for emergency surgery. Sometimes battles take place in cities: battles between the police and the "bad guys." The dual forces of good and evil represent the child's internal conflict between destructive urges and the guilt that follows, which is the function of a healthy conscience. By observing the outcome of duels between "good" and "evil" forces, the therapist learns something about the child's internal struggles.

The Fair Trial

In *Understanding and Treating the Aggression of Children*, we emphasize the role guilt and shame play in aggressive behavior. To review quickly, guilt is self-condemnation for a specific behavioral act or thought and is typically constructive. Its existence does not produce psychological symptoms unless it is primitive, retributive guilt. Shame, on the other hand, is constant self-condemnation. It is a destructive emotion, inextricably linked to rage, which leads to a wide range of psychological symptoms (Tangney and Dearing 2002). Observing the child's aggressive play can help therapists distinguish between these two phenomena. If the punishments the child dishes out during play fit, more or less, "the crime," then constructive guilt predominates. In contrast, if the evildoer is remanded to prison for eternity, with no visitors, the punishment usually reflects contempt and rage closely linked to a painful sense of shame.

In such cases, the therapist can intervene by insisting that the "bad guy" have a fair trial. In the mock trial, the therapist makes the case that the prisoner has some redeeming features and waits to see if the child shows any empathy or forgiveness. Sometimes a program of restitution is proposed when a child shows no mercy. In this manner, the depth of shame can be tested. If the child allows no form of restitution and insists, in the role of judge, on dispensing unforgiving and harsh sentences, the therapist learns how unmerciful the child is when judging peers and the self. Since empathizing with the pain of others is required to break the cycle of violence, often transmitted from one generation to the next, ways must be found to develop each gorilla-suit wearer's capacity for empathy.

Empathizing with the pain of others can be modeled by the play characters the child assigns to the therapist. While the capacity for empathy evolves slowly, it's never too early to model, facilitate, and encourage this vital link to human connection. Children as young as three years will comfort each other, with both the injured child and the comforting one in tears after an incident on the playground. The capacity to put oneself fully in the shoes of another, and to appreciate what the other is feeling, doesn't develop until late adolescence. Nevertheless, the process needs "seeding," and therapists are encouraged to model empathy at every opportunity because its absence is associated with violence and dehumanized loss.

In the beginning of treatment, when the therapist is often the object of displaced anger, battle scenes can be furious and violent. As time goes on, and the child has had ample opportunity to express anger in a safe and controlled environment, the battles become less intense. At that point, the child becomes absorbed in setting up the opposing armies in a variety of clever ways. Some children demonstrate ingenuity and cleverness in the strategies displayed and in the planning and thought that goes into arranging the opposing armies. The battles often take a backseat to the artistic elements. The child has moved from struggling with raw aggression to controlled expressions of anger.

Rage toward Others and toward Victims

O'Connor (1995) proposes that, regardless of the degree of fantasy involved, the expression of rage toward perpetrators is allowable, but its expression toward victims should be discouraged and redirected. When a child rages at a victim, O'Connor redirects the child to a superhero role. He hands the child a puppet, whom O'Connor labels as a helper or rescuer, and stops all actions at the end of the rescue operation to keep the child from returning to the aggressor role. O'Connor believes this strategy allows the child to feel the power of the superhero role and also to feel relieved by the help offered the victim, with whom part of the child identifies. The boy who plays superhero in the autosphere and who crashes into walls is also the victim of his own reckless abandon! Rescue behaviors allow the boy to practice the defense of undoing (discussed in chapter 9) as well as to practice helping others—a key feature of resilient children. Through helping others, children obtain the validation needed to counter profound feelings of devaluation. To help, to give to others, and to contribute all elevate the spirit. To feel that one has nothing to give or nothing to offer punctures the spirit (Hardy 2003). Affiliation with powerful play characters also serves a secondary function. It helps to allay feelings of devaluation that children of color and of poverty, gay children, and girls often experience. Not having equal access to society's goods and services, these children experience humiliation and shame by virtue of their low status. These coercive, yet sometimes subtle, forces of domination related to class, race, gender, and sexual orientation are formidable barriers to those wishing to create a better life. Very young children receive messages from the wider community about how they are perceived—whether they are valued or devalued. Marginal members of our society become aware of their status early in life.

O'Connor's rationale (1995) for limiting aggression is based on the assumption that the child is overidentified with the aggressor, even if the child aggresses against masking symbols of the perpetrator. We take a somewhat different view. Children can get stuck in aggressive play in much the same manner that Terr (1990) describes in posttraumatic play. When the child becomes overgratified in the aggressor role, the behavior should be redirected, not only because the gratification makes it difficult to relinquish this role, but also because it suggests that losses have become dehumanized. Often the child has not grieved unrecognized losses because he or she has *lost the capacity to feel*. A child engaged in repetitive violent play, regardless of whom the aggression is displaced upon, needs help to acknowledge and work through these losses before the cycle of violence can be broken and the most crucial of all pro-social skills—*empathy for others*—develops.

We would not discourage aggression against the victim if we thought the play were a trauma reenactment. Reenactment play is the child's way of telling the story of his or her abuse. If the therapist immediately intervenes to redirect the play, the child may receive the unintended message that "I can't bear the painful story you are revealing." Alice Miller (1997) emphasizes that trauma victims have a great need for their pain to be witnessed by someone they trust. If the play is considered a trauma reenactment, but it becomes repetitive in therapy, we would redirect the child's play or model other activities, as would other therapists (Terr 1990; Gil 1991).

Play in the dollhouse often reveals overwhelming fears stemming from parental abuse and tyranny. May Nilsson (2000) presents a case of a four-year-old foster child whose dollhouse play moved from playing on the outside of the house, to playing in part of the inside, to using the whole house and how this play paralleled the girl's relationship with the therapist.

The play of some children suggests that they have repeatedly witnessed destructive interchanges between their parents. When children verbally attack one of the puppet characters or dolls, the affect pervading the playroom is unmistakable. Their play replicates their painful experiences. When the therapist experiences his or her stomach wrenching and churning, the therapist is in touch with the strong feelings the children are reenacting in an infectious and somber manner—actual life events that left an indelible and emotionally charged mark. Children can yell at the dolls or puppets in such angry and vicious tones that, momentarily, the therapist is "frozen in inaction." Such experiences enable the therapist to appreciate the strong emotions behind the children's surface behaviors.

· *9* ·

Creating More Mature Defenses
and Calming Strategies

This chapter illustrates techniques to develop and enhance the functioning of defense mechanisms in children who lack adequate defenses against anxiety and who lack imaginative play. Selecting play materials, modeling imaginative and defensive play, encouraging and reinforcing the child's play and defensive use of play, verbalizing alternative defenses, developing mechanisms of restraint, teaching calming activities, and acknowledging progress are all illustrated through brief clinical vignettes.

$\mathcal{E}$rik Erikson (1940, 1963) described children whose imaginative play was interrupted by the anxiety evoked by their own associations to their play. In contrast, the rudimentary play displayed by children wearing gorilla suits reflects not only the extreme anxiety their play elicits but, more important, their inability to think imaginatively. They cannot really play "war" because they cannot construct a cast of characters in their minds and then have the characters create a sequence of war activities. In Erikson's terms (1963), these children cannot play in the microsphere, and their play in the macrosphere is primitive and undeveloped. Often they mimic the behavior of a superhero or supervillain who runs around stabbing and shooting everybody. They are still playing in the autosphere, where the supervillains are merely extensions of their own small selves.

We have also seen that children lacking imaginative play also lack mature defenses against anxiety. The primitive defenses they employ when anxious typically break down when anxiety becomes more intense. As a result, interpretations cannot be used to help them understand their defenses because the anxiety aroused when a defense is interpreted causes regression. Simple reflection of feelings also can cause the children to regress. The psychoanalytic approach with children lacking adequate defenses typically involves quiet reassurance and instructions not to talk about certain topics when "they get you excited." Yet psychoanalytic therapists often accompany these instructions with interpretations of the primitive defenses the children do display. These interpretations often result in more anxiety than the children can tolerate, and temporary therapeutic impasses occur (see, for example, the cases presented in Chethik 1987, 2000; Ekstein 1966; Furman 1956). Fenichel's observation (1953) that it makes no sense to make interpretations when there is no ego capable of digesting them applies equally to children.

The approach described in this chapter expands upon the material presented in the last chapter, where we focused on teaching children to displace and distance their feelings to play materials, and illustrates helping children make better use of existing defenses and developing more mature defenses against anxiety. The approach includes modeling, encouraging and reinforcing play behavior, modeling the use of defenses in play, and developing mechanisms of restraint. While the examples of therapists' actions include verbalizations to the child, these verbalizations are attempts to identify or to clarify what the child might be feeling; they are not efforts to interpret to the child how the child uses a particular defense when upset.

More than sixty years ago, Anna Freud (1936) described the defenses used by children. Since then, more has been learned about how defenses are revealed in play and fantasy (Adams-Tucker 1985; Chethik 1987; Ekstein 1966; A. Freud and Sandler 1985; Gould 1972; Mordock 1994, 1997; Rosenthal 1987; Terr 1981). The play therapist who understands the defenses a child uses ineffectively can encourage the child to use defenses more effectively and to develop more mature defenses. For children on the coping track, this effort is a must.

DEVELOPING AND SUPPORTING DEFENSES

Table 9.1 below lists the major defenses used by children, categorized for both developmental and heuristic purposes into *primitive* and *mature*. The defenses listed in the left-hand column of table 9.1 typically get a child into trouble with others. Denial, blaming, externalization, and so forth, while helpful to the child in containing anxiety, not only are socially unacceptable behaviors but often lead to displays of aggression, particularly when these defenses are confronted by others. The child who employs the defenses in the right-hand column in table 9.1 gets into less trouble with others. The "mature" defenses can be employed to fend off anxiety without adversely affecting others. Overuse of mature defenses, however, can be just as damaging to the self as can the overuse of repression.

Table 9.1   Ego Defenses of Children

Primitive	Mature
Introjection	Somatization
Denial	Avoidance
Minimizing	Inhibition
Blaming	Restriction
Negation	Distancing (Autistic Fantasy)
Splitting	Reversal
Binding and Compartmentalization	Isolation of Affect
Dissociation	Turning Feelings Inward
Grandiosity or Omnipotence	Self-Hate, Self-Love
Externalization	Undoing
Projective Identification	Overcompensation
Projection	Reaction Formation
Identification with the Aggressor	Sublimation
Provocative Behavior	Rationalization
Displacement	Devaluation
Regression	Anticipation
Negativism	

A precise definition of some of the defenses and their developmental manifestations appears in the latest edition of the American Psychiatric Association's *Diagnostic and Statistical Manual of Mental Disorders* (1994). The defenses used by children are also listed and defined in chapter 8 of *Understanding and Treating the Aggression of Children*. Repression, or the active suppression of thoughts, unacceptable wishes, or impulses, is not listed in table 9.1 because it accompanies use of all the defenses except displacement.

Because of the strong role they play in helping children in gorilla suits ward off their anxiety, splitting, binding and compartmentalization, dissociation, and grandiosity will be defined here. Negativism, used so frequently by gorilla-suit wearers that it can become a character trait, will also be defined.

Splitting

The anxiety-arousing aspect of what is repressed becomes "split off" from the child's conscious image of self. But when repression fails and anxiety is generated, the child's feeling is not "I feel this emotion" but "something alien to me operates within me!" or "the bad me made me do it." Splitting also applies to the play actions the child displays. The play figure who kills or messes is not the child; as a result, the child is freed from guilt or shame since the child does not feel responsible for the action of the play figure. Extreme splitting has been linked to multiple personality disorder and has been called *dissociation*. Extreme splitting combined with the defense of turning feelings inward can produce grandiosity or omnipotence.

Binding and Compartmentalization

Children made anxious by a specific stimulus tightly restrict their behavior to master the feared stimulus—put another way, they "bind the anxiety" associated with that stimulus. They also split the stimulus off, or separate it, into a detached "compartment." Children who momentarily close their eyes, tighten their muscles, and continue ongoing activities when faced with fear, rather than fleeing from it, are using binding to manage anxiety. But once it is bound, they split off the images associated with the trauma, "file" them in a "drawer in their personality," and continue functioning, minus the psychic energy it takes to keep the drawer closed and the frightening images safely inside. When they do this, they are compartmentalizing the images associated with a traumatic experience. They function reasonably well as long as they can avoid situations that might evoke the frightening images.

In the "Ego Supportive Drawing Series" (Garritt and Crenshaw 1997), one of the drawings, "The Strong Container," facilitates the use of binding and compartmentalization. A "strong container" drawing created by a twelve-year-old boy appears in figure 9.1.

The drawing depicts an elaborate network of locks and chains, high-tech, digital eye and palm recognition security devices, and a key pad, all of which guard the security of this strong container. The drawing, a graphic, symbolic representation of the boy's desperate need to compartmentalize his anxiety, signals in a dramatic way that he is not ready for uncovering therapy.

A child incest victim might store the images connected with her incest experience until she is faced, in her adolescence, with a date who tries to fondle her. With considerable energy, however, she might be able to bind her anxiety and continue dating the boy, even becoming sexually involved with him. But when the relationship becomes close and intimate, as was the traumatic bonding of her incest experience, or when the boy puts on weight and begins to look or act like her father, she might flee from the relationship. A child raped by an alcoholic might function reasonably well until around people overindulging in alcohol. If too many traumatic experiences are compartmentalized, the individual has little energy left to function well. Each compartmentalized experience must be faced and integrated into the personality in order for the person to feel whole again and to function normally.

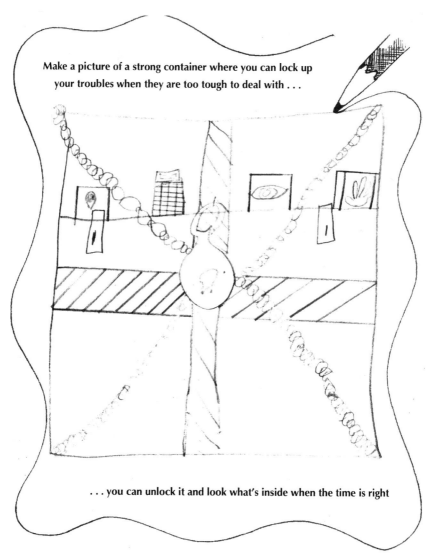

Figure 9.1.   The Strong Container Drawing

Dissociation

Dissociation entails a disturbance or disruption in the normally integrative functions of identity, memory, and consciousness (Gil 1991). Children may dissociate experiences, disowned parts of their identity and consciousness that were too overwhelming to be integrated due to extreme stressors often related to trauma (James 1989). As Gil (1991) explains, dissociation occurs along a continuum that includes depersonalization, psychogenic amnesia, and fugue states. At the most extreme end of the dissociative continuum is dissociative identity disorder, or what was commonly referred to in the past as multiple personality disorder. Dissociation is considered a primary defense in the face of exposure to trauma. A young girl, for example, who is being molested by her older brother in the backseat of a station wagon might view the experience from a detached, almost out-of-body vantage point, as if it were happening to someone else and she is an onlooker, as a way of coping with what would otherwise be a totally overwhelming emotional experience. These defenses, however, can become a liability to the extent that they become employed automatically, and repeatedly, long after the traumatic events have ceased.

Grandiosity

The child attributes to the self strengths that enable the domination of enemies and the protection of those worthy of rescue. The child fabricates an exaggerated sense of self and self-attributes, believing the self to possess superior traits, such as cunning, secret knowledge, deceit, artful craftiness, hidden physical strength, and so on. Grandiosity can shield the child from feeling helpless and abandoned. The defense masks the impotence that results from feeling alone and unwanted. The defense is also employed to mask feeling depreciated and worthless. Grandiosity is activated to increase the sense of self-value. The child devalues others, especially the therapist, since self-worth is measured only in comparison with another (see Cohen 1981). Although grandiosity is a defense against anxiety, some of the superior traits the child attributes to the self can be better developed than other traits. The child may actually be stronger or more cunning than others his age. And the child may actually cultivate these traits. Sometimes the traits can be the hidden strengths that the therapist looks for when attempting to foster a more realistic self-concept. Keep this in mind during the treatment process.

Negativism

To ward off anxiety (either present or anticipated), fears of passive surrender, loss of identity, or fear of merging, the child becomes actively defiant and oppositional. Remember, however, that some negativism is necessary for self-differentiation, so phase-appropriate negativism must be differentiated from negativism as a defensive maneuver.

DEVELOPMENT OF THE MORE MATURE DEFENSES

Ekstein (1966) described the development of impulse control as progressing through the following stages: action without play; play action, in which acts of others are reproduced; visualization, whereby a child may visualize performing some concrete action; action-fantasy, or playacting; elaborative fantasy, such as creating stories; and reality-oriented thought. Those children whose development of impulse control is arrested at action without play typically employ the most primitive defenses of "flight" or "fight." In the last two chapters we discussed helping such children to develop distancing and displacement. Those whose development is somewhat further along the continuum, at play action, and who display variable controls, use denial (with lots of blaming, externalization, negativism, and provocative behavior), but they also continue to employ splitting and its related mechanisms (Gould 1972; Mordock 1988).

With children who display some defenses, the therapeutic effort is directed at reinforcing defenses used and introducing new ones for possible use. The child who already displaces his anger at the therapist by smashing together toys can be helped to project his feelings onto the toys by the therapist's modeling such play behavior. The child who regresses by wrapping up in a doll blanket and hiding in the therapy room closet can be encouraged to wrap up a doll and hide it in the cupboard. This play should be accompanied by the therapist's verbalizing feelings that the doll might have. Children who externalize their self-hate and accuse the therapist of being stupid or crazy can be encouraged to name a doll after the therapist and to talk to the doll in a similar fashion.

Children who repeatedly destroy parental figures in their play and then anxiously interrupt the play can be taught the defense of undoing. Efforts can include using a toy ambulance to rescue injured victims of the child's displaced aggression. Toy fire engines can rescue the people from the child's pretend fires. Army medical corps personnel or Red Cross dolls can rush injured soldiers to medical stations. Injured dolls can be fixed with the doctor kit, hugged, and given tender loving care. For example, in the three cases to follow, each child needs help in making more effective use of undoing.

> CHILD: Once there was a witch who killed everyone in town, and a burglar came and killed the witch. And a policeman came and killed the burglar.

Then another burglar took the policeman to jail. Then one man, the chief of police, that was me, I killed them all. And I ate them all—meat and blood and guts. [*Child leaves play area to run around the room.*]

Here the child attempts to use both distancing and undoing, but they break down. The policeman is not strong enough to overcome the burglars, and the child, identified with both the burglars and the police, loses distance and is made anxious by his or her own oral-aggressive fantasies. The therapist responds as follows:

> THERAPIST: It must be really scary to live in this town where all the good people are killed. Let's give the police chief some more deputies, and together the chief and his deputies can round up all the burglars and witches and put them in jail.

In the second case, a boy repeatedly played "air raid," bombing and destroying most of his potential supports, including his own family. He reacted to each of his bombings by running around and asking to leave the room. In response to this play, the therapist took control of the airport.

> CHILD: I'm the pilot loaded with bombs, and I'm coming to bomb you.
> THERAPIST: Airport to pilot. You're about to bomb a friendly airport. Please divert mission and drop bombs into the sea.
> CHILD: [*Ignores airport controller and bombs town anyway.*]
> THERAPIST: Attention, the Airport Medical Corps is needed. Alert antiaircraft guns not to fire, repeat, do not fire. Pilot temporarily confused and mistakenly bombed airport as a result of angry confusion. Repeat, pilot is not an enemy.

The third case concerns a three-year-old girl referred for nighttime terrors of seeing "monsters with different-colored hair." When she was encouraged to play with the dollhouse people, it became apparent that the "monsters" were all the different men her mother had been entertaining in her house, the majority of whom yelled at her or put her angrily in her room. The child was then asked what she would like to do with these "daddy-people" who kept visiting her. She proceeded to bury them in the sandbox. She was also asked what she would like to do with the "mommy-people." She selected one mother doll, angrily buried her in the sand, simultaneously telling her to "go to her room and stay there." The girl's mother was made aware of her daughter's feelings and became more discreet with her boyfriends. The girl was helped to deal with the anxiety raised by her murderous anger at her mother (Killing her mother would leave her without a caretaker). The play therapist helped her "undo" her anger at her mother by modeling play where "the mother doll was rescued from the burial grounds." With some children, the therapist can verbalize the defense of rationalization.

> THERAPIST: When the Mary doll gets angry, do you know what she does? [*Therapist has played a scene in which the Mary doll has gotten angry.*]
> CHILD: What?
> THERAPIST: She decides, "Who needs that stupid old ribbon anyway!"
> or
> THERAPIST: When Billy Doll hit Mary Doll, it hurt her, but instead of hitting Billy Doll back, do you know what Mary Doll did? She pretended that Billy Doll hadn't hurt her a bit. By not hitting back, she was showing that the blow didn't bother her at all. Otherwise, she might be hit again. [*The play therapist simultaneously plays such a scene out with the Mary doll.*]
> or
> THERAPIST: When Mommy Doll paid more attention to Sister Doll and made Mary jealous of Sister Doll and angry at Mommy Doll, instead of hitting Sister Doll, Mary pretends that another doll is her sister and makes believe that all kinds of awful things happened to her. Sometimes she also pretends that she really likes Sister Doll and does nice things for her when Mommy Doll is around so Mommy Doll will notice her being good and praise her for it. [*Therapist simultaneously plays out scene.*]

ENCOURAGING SUBLIMATION AND REACTION FORMATION

A large portion of play therapy time is spent in helping children learn to sublimate impulses and substitute acceptable impulses for unacceptable ones. Therapists often attempt to use verbal therapy techniques with the latency-age child, but the latency-age child who has never developed his or her imagination can also profit from play therapy. Instead of being disorganized and messy in the uninhibited expression of impulses, the child is encouraged to be orderly. The normal child in latency is a collector and organizer of collections. Stamps, coins, or baseball cards are organized and reorganized. These obsessive-compulsive activities, or reaction formations, keep the child from experiencing and acting on destructive impulses.

Sarnoff (1987) grouped the defenses of reaction formation, undoing, sublimation, and rationalization as "mechanisms of restraint," all activities that assist in repression and symbol and fantasy formation. Without mechanisms of restraint, children have little energy to meet developmental challenges. They cannot move to the stage of development in which a relatively calm, impulse-free state is needed to initiate and complete the tasks required to become industrious children.

The play therapist can encourage children to collect rocks, baseball cards, coins, or stamps and to play repetitive, meaningless games, such as organizing dominoes so that they fall down in sequence. Children can collect lollipop sticks to glue onto cardboard, pictures of athletic figures, and so forth. They can draw and color geometric forms, with all the forms of one shape colored black, those of another shape colored red, and so on. Children also can be encouraged to sublimate their unacceptable impulses through engaging in activities that are symbolic equivalents of their wishes. The play therapist can encourage aggressive children to collect miniature war toys or war pictures or to make war scrapbooks, the purpose being to develop intellectualization as a defense, with the hope that the child will feel less anxious when more is known about war and defense.

Games also can be used to develop mechanisms of restraint. The games should be simple, repetitive ones like Candy Land, Chutes and Ladders, and occasionally, checkers. Games help to develop a sense of organization and adherence to regulations in a manner that can be pleasurable (Sarnoff 1987). As with other play activities, the children can engage in a calming activity while the therapist is helping them verbalize feelings aroused during problematic situations that have occurred during the week. Even better than games are the partially absorbing miniature "puzzles" that many children play, such as getting all the little balls in the holes in plastic-enclosed frames. Pick-up-Sticks and other "nonsense" games engage the child just enough to provide sufficient distance to handle anxiety generated by the therapist's interpretative statements, the next step in the ongoing therapy of the child.

CALMING ACTIVITIES

Some years ago, Dr. Mordock administered the Thematic Apperception Test to an anxious, disruptive boy and found that almost all of the stories he told to the pictures were of violent, hostile interchanges between the figures depicted. In an effort to tap other feelings, Dr. Mordock asked the boy to tell new stories to each of the cards, but the "new rule" was that he could not tell violent or aggressive ones. To the author's surprise, the boy proceeded to do so. At the end of the day, his special class teacher asked what the author had done to him during testing because he returned to class calm and worked better than he had all week. Pondering over what had taken place, the staff concluded that the boy's telling of nonviolent stories must have changed his mood. He had to look into his memory and find images to project onto the cards that were not violent ones. The process of searching for and finding these images calmed him. Perhaps the images were of positive times he had spent with caregivers and thereby served to strengthen his positive feelings about himself, or perhaps the images distracted him from the violent images that excited him. Whatever the reason, this serendipitous finding altered our approach to working with aggressive children. We began to teach them strategies to change their mood and to calm themselves.

We were encouraged in this effort by Jerome Singer's research (1966, 1976). In contrast to the prevailing view that expression of aggression in fantasy helps reduce aggressive behavior (catharsis theory), Singer found that individuals who are practiced daydreamers handle aggressive feelings by daydreaming of pleasant and enjoyable states. They obtain relief from negative affect following frustrating experiences by emoting fantasies that change their mood. Individuals who are practiced daydreamers handle aggressive feelings by daydreaming of pleasant and enjoyable states. They obtain relief from negative affect following frustrating experiences by emoting fantasies that change their mood. Singer also discovered that individuals who rarely daydreamed tended to remain aggressive when frustrated.

The calming strategy we taught children who became overly upset when frustrated was to remember those activities they enjoyed and to perform them when upset and angry. For some children, it is thinking about going to a ball game with a relative. For others, it is coloring with brightly colored crayons. Each child is helped to find and to utilize his own calming, mood-changing procedures. For some, it is images; for others, actions. For those prone to actions, an effort is made to find a symbolic equivalent. The child who is calmed only by eating is encouraged to draw foods and to color his drawings. One drawing from the "Ego Supportive Drawing Series" (Garritt and Crenshaw 1997) is called the "Calming Scene Drawing." The child could be instructed as follows:

> THERAPIST: Close your eyes and think about the most calm and peaceful place you have ever been or could ever imagine. A place where you feel completely calm, relaxed, peaceful—without a care or worry of any kind. When you can picture yourself totally calm and peaceful in that place, I want you to open your eyes and draw it for me.

Whenever children become unduly upset, they are instructed to remember their picture of the calm place and to go there in their imagination. The actual picture can be given to the child to aid in calming, or the child can draw it again from memory. Other children are calmed by engaging in the activities used to develop the mechanisms of restraint discussed in the previous section.

This effort to help the child to learn how to change his mood when angered is not incompatible with the effort to get the child who harbors specific, retaliating, aggressive fantasies to relate them to the therapist in detail (see

Figure 9.2.   Grandparents' Farm: Calming Scene

chapter 7). The first effort is used when the child is upset and the goal is to help the child develop calming skills. The second effort is employed when the child is calm and is designed to generate guilt or anxiety that will result in the inhibition of direct aggression. It is not hard to tell if the second effort is working. If the child delights in relating his specific hostile fantasies and regularly repeats them unchanged with vengeful relish, the effort has failed.

REWARDING MATURE DEFENSES

When children start using more mature defenses, the play therapist, as well as other meaningful adults in the child's life, should actively comment on the child's improvement. Some troubled children can become extremely pessimistic about their ability to change. They need reassurance when others see change. Improvements come in steps so small that often neither the children nor other adults notice them. If the child has never progressed to flight before, praise should be given for the first use of flight with comments such as "It's more grown-up to leave the room instead of hitting me." When attempts to hit the therapist are displaced onto the dummy, the play therapist can remark, "Hitting the dummy is more grown-up than hitting me."

Sometimes improvement is viewed as regression rather than as progress. For example, when the pseudoautonomous child experiments with abandoning this behavior and giving in to unfulfilled dependency needs, the child can become clinging, revert to baby talk, and at times seem confused and disoriented. Similarly, a play therapist can confuse the development of a defense with resistance to therapy. A boy who used to get very anxious, agitated, and disruptive every time the therapist commented about the boy's mother now starts to play actively with some toys or even openly states, "I don't want to talk about it." The boy has initiated avoidance to handle his anxiety, a sign of progress rather than of resistance.

> THERAPIST: You feel really nervous talking about your mother right now.
> CHILD: I just don't want to!
> THERAPIST: So not talking, pulling back, helps you not to feel so anxious. Is there anything else you are doing right now to prevent you from feeling anxious?

Because the use of a more mature defense may not, at first, appear as progress, the play therapist needs to be familiar with concepts of developmental change (Chethik 1987; Ekstein 1966; Freud 1963; Klein and Mordock 1975; Rosenfeld, Frankel, and Esman 1969). It is important that progress notes include material on the child's defenses and that all the drawings and artwork the child produces be kept. Periodically referring to these materials also helps children develop a continuity of self and a past they can relate to their present. This way, the therapist can concretely demonstrate progress.

WHEN TO BEGIN TO INTERPRET DEFENSES

When the child has developed some mature defenses but periodically uses a less mature defense that is maladaptive (i.e., the defense effectively lowers anxiety, but its use gets the child into other difficulties), the play therapist can begin to interpret the defense to the child. For example, a girl plays out an aggressive theme with dolls. Her responses to the play therapist's reflections about this play suggest that other children gang up on the girl when she is inappropriate with them, but that she denies any wrongdoing against them. The girl's use of denial is a well-established defense, but she is capable of using more mature defenses. In play therapy, when she is neither actively engaged with peers nor in danger of regression, the defense can be gently confronted within the metaphor of play by the ignorant interrogative approach.

> THERAPIST: I wonder why the other dolls ganged up on Sally Doll like that? That must have made Sally Doll very upset.

In chapters 10 and 11, we discuss the role of interpretation in treatment and illustrate both the wording and the timing of such therapeutic actions.

CONCLUSION

Understanding the defenses a child employs is the first step in designing treatment that will support the child's ego development. The therapist can then direct his or her efforts toward helping children to use each defense more efficiently and to develop those defenses that will elicit more positive responses from caregivers. In many situations, the play therapist needs to actively select play materials and create play themes, to model defensive play behavior, to reinforce the child's developing play, and to accept and praise the child's use of defenses that are more mature than those the child previously employed. Many children who lack imaginative play can learn to play imaginatively.

When the play therapist actively models imaginative play and praises the child for playful behavior, the child will learn to play. When he or she does so, the play can reveal some of the experiences, particularly preverbal and presymbolization impressions, that produce disturbing impulses and activities. Play with toys can stimulate memories, and associations to these memories can result in more elaborate play. Considerable time is devoted to selecting toys that the therapist feels each child can eventually associate with his or her troubling experiences and to modeling imaginative ways to play with these toys.

The Role of Interpretation:
Elementary Concepts

Interpretations are divided into two categories: empathetic interpretations and dynamic interpreta-tions. Empathetic interpretations, such as reflections of feelings, are used by most play therapists. Dynamic interpretations are those that many child therapists are reluctant to employ, perhaps from lack of a model to follow. They include interpretations of defenses, of the transference, and of im-pulses and wishes and are appropriate only for children on the invitational track. A step-by-step model to follow when making interpretations in play therapy is presented, starting with prepara-tory statements, such as attention statements, reductive statements, and situational statements, and moving to interpretations within the metaphor. Examples are given of ways to word interpreta-tions so that they don't appear threatening.

$\mathcal{C}$onsiderable confusion surrounds the term *interpretation* and its role in play therapy. Many experienced therapists fail to appreciate the delayed and hidden influence of a well-timed interpretation, while others are not sure how to in-terpret, when to interpret, or even what to interpret. Kevin O'Connor (2002) cites three reasons child therapists refrain from explaining to children the pos-sible meanings of their verbal communications or their play. Some consider in-terpretations as overly directive, preferring to follow the child's lead and pace in sessions. We would ask therapists holding this view, "Where do you expect the child to go?" Without reflecting on the child's play, or attempting to clar-ify meanings, the play of the confused and conceptually disorganized child, reflecting screen memories and cognitive distortions, is not likely to lead to positive outcomes without some structure from the therapist. In fact, as we have emphasized in earlier chapters, the less the child plays, the more the ther-apist has to structure the sessions, even when following the child's lead. When doing play therapy with children in gorilla suits, the line between education, especially affective education, and therapy is a blurred one.

Perhaps client-centered therapists narrowly define interpretations as guesses about unconscious wishes and unexpressed impulses. If so, their reluctance to use them is warranted, particularly if they aren't knowledgeable about when and how to make them. O'Connor (2002) states that some child therapists may not appreciate how interpretation supports therapy. Nevertheless, O'Connor believes the chief reason therapists don't make interpretations is because they lack a well-organized, step-by-step model of interpretation formation and delivery. Such a model will be presented in this chapter.

Historically, the concept of interpretation came from psychoanalysis, where the task was to unmask the unconscious motives of the client; in short, to make the client aware of how symptomatic behavior was influenced by unconscious determinants. But simply discovering unconscious motivations and verbalizing them were not enough. First, the analyst had to create a special kind of relationship with the client. For interpretation to work, the client needed to reexperience earlier conflicts within this therapeutic relationship.

Trained play therapists know that children speak through fantasy and play. Instead of conveying meaning directly, they use illusion, analogy, displacement, condensation, and symbolic representation. The child in a gorilla suit, who feels unloved and abandoned, uses them, when he or she can, to avoid hurtful perceptions. It is as if the child is thinking, "I must not know what I know" or "I must not feel what I feel." The child defends against awareness to manage the overwhelming anxiety that the undeveloped self can experience. The child's purpose is to keep perceptions from the self and from threatening adults. The therapist's job is to explain the child to him or herself—to make the child more emotionally aware that his or her behavior, possibly adaptive at one time, now prevents the satisfaction of needs.

Gorilla-suit wearers typically become more self-aware in therapy when active efforts are made to clarify and interpret the transference relationship, a phenomenon some therapists don't attend to consciously. The child learns how angry and defiant behavior could lead to the therapist's rejection, but that it does not. This fact, and the therapist's guidance, slowly leads the child in another direction. In work toward the ultimate goal of changing the child's habitual ways of responding, interpretations have various intermediate aims. They include labeling feelings; fostering the therapeutic alliance; overcoming resistance; clarifying the child's relationship with the therapist or with others; facilitating remembering, particularly the remembering of complete experiences rather than the frightening and confusing screen memories the child typically experiences; and creating dynamic shifts in functioning.

We have subdivided interpretations into two major categories: those that the empathetic therapist employs to help a child to understand feelings better, which we have called empathetic interpretations, and those that address hidden motives, called dynamic interpretations. Empathetic interpretations are those that help the child to understand universal feelings, individual feelings, individual conflicts, and others' behavior, such as "Lots of kids would feel bad about that," "The puppet seems angry," "Hawk wants a friend, but he doesn't want to share with Eagle," or "Johnny got mad at you because he thought you bumped into him on purpose." Adults offer such explanations to children all the time. They're not just prerogatives of therapists! Dynamic interpretations are interpretations of defenses (including the contents of fantasies), transference and displacement, and drives or wishes (including the contents of dreams, fantasies, and bodily sensations). The most simple are comments such as "When Baby Doll gets anxious, she tries to hide it behind anger," "You make me the bad guy when I'm really not," or "Brown Bunny would like Gray Bunny to notice him." Dynamic interpretations are used only with children on the invitational track.

EMPATHETIC INTERPRETATIONS

A therapist interprets behavior when making efforts to anticipate the feelings of a child starting therapy. When the therapist says to a withdrawn, somewhat fearful-looking child, "Often children are upset when they first come to a new place and don't know what to expect," an empathetic interpretation has been made. Interpretations of universal feelings are those in which the therapist attempts to normalize the feelings a child might have about a situation such as beginning therapy. To make universal interpretations requires knowledge of how children feel who experience particular stresses. For example, unloved children, many of whom blame others for their problems, also blame themselves for past events over which they had no control. Interpretations of universal feelings are efforts to help the child realize that many children have similar feelings, to facilitate discussion of how things really are, and to correct the child's self-defeating misconceptions.

> THERAPIST: Most kids here spend lots of time thinking about what might be happening back home. It keeps them from concentrating on their schoolwork. Does this ever happen to you?

Interpretations of individual feelings are similar to interpretations of universal feelings because many children experience stresses similarly. An interpretation of an individual feeling might go like this:

> THERAPIST: I guess you're very disappointed at not winning "student of the week" [*an incentive system in a special education classroom*]. I knew you

were trying very hard, and when you try hard and don't make it, it sure can feel bad.

Interpretations of individual conflicts might follow these lines:

THERAPIST: Boy Doll would like to tell Father Doll that Father Doll hurt his feelings, but he is afraid Father Doll will get even more angry at him.
THERAPIST: It's hard to get angry at your mother when you visit home because you're afraid she won't want you to visit anymore.
THERAPIST: Part of Mary Doll would like to say she's sorry, but another part insists that it wasn't her fault.

Interpretations of others' behavior are simply explanations of how another might feel in response to the child's behavior or to the behavior of an important figure in the child's life.

THERAPIST: Mr. Wizard [*a wizard hand puppet the therapist uses to speak to playing children*] wonders if Bobby Doll understands that Mother Doll feels bad when he knocks over the food she just prepared for him.
THERAPIST: Did you ever think how awkward Mom must feel only being able to see you twice a month? She plans an activity, and if it doesn't work out or you get angry at her, she doesn't get to set it right for another two weeks.

Empathetic interpretations help children to understand and to accept themselves and to understand the feeling world, so confused and distorted in abused and rejected children.

DYNAMIC INTERPRETATIONS

Dynamic interpretations deal exclusively with unconscious material, such as defensive operations, repressed drives, distorted memories, or the hidden meanings of behavior patterns and their unconscious connections. Dynamic interpretations transcend the clinical data and are preceded by a prolonged preparatory process during which the child's misconceptions have been clarified through empathetic interpretations. Conflict always blurs reality, and anxiety distorts it. Clarifying comments change the nature of the child's play as the child integrates new knowledge. The play becomes more elaborate, less disguised, and more interpretable. Dynamic interpretations are made in a planned and supportive manner and only when the child's relationship with the therapist will support the child through the anxiety experienced each time an interpretation is made.

Therapists must be able to answer significant questions about a child's defensive behavior before interpretations of it are made. For example, a boy angrily rips up a drawing he made and switches to playing with toy soldiers—an avoidance behavior. Before a response can be made, the therapist must know the answer to many questions: Why is the boy so disappointed with failure? With whom is he identified? What are his self-perceptions? Whose admiration is he trying to win? What are his standards, and where did they come from? The thoughtful therapist will leave the child's defenses alone until some progress is made in answering these questions.

Dynamic interpretations have been subdivided into interpretations of defenses, interpretations of transferences and displacements, and interpretations of drives or wishes. The materials interpreted appear in behavior displayed, play and fantasy, bodily sensations, and dreams. The material relates to defenses used, wishes held, transferences experienced (feelings about the therapist that are actually feelings about parents), and displacements made (misdirected anger).

PREPARATION

Interpreting a defense is rarely done without preparatory work, particularly when treating children with brittle defenses. Preparation involves the use of attention statements, reductive statements, and situational statements.

Attention Statements

The aim of an attention statement is to direct the children's attention to facts that their actions or verbalizations might reveal. Attention statements are preliminary clarifications. Attention statements are directed at coincidences the child has not noticed or to paradoxes revealed. Often attention statements are made simply to highlight what the child is doing. The most elementary attention statements are running comments about the child's silent play.

> THERAPIST: The house is on fire . . . The man and woman escape to the roof . . . The fire engines come . . . The house collapses.

Running comments serve two purposes: First, children have difficulty reflecting on their actions. If their actions are impulse driven, reflection is even more difficult. One way children gain greater consciousness of themselves is by describing their own actions in words. Many children cannot put their actions into words. The therapist's running comments assist them in this process. Secondly, children may expand upon their play if they see a similarity between what the therapist is verbalizing and what they themselves have already been doing. Running comments focus on the result of the child's actions, not on the child's efforts. For example:

> CHILD: [*Engaged in making mounds of sand.*]
> THERAPIST: The sand is getting fatter.

The therapist should not comment that the child is "making mountains" simply because that is how they look to the therapist, nor should he or she comment, "Look how fat you're making it" because the very fragile child will interpret the comment as a criticism. In contrast, comments on the result help the child to shift his focus from small details to larger issues (They help the child to decenter and look at a broader picture). At other times the therapist, to clarify what the play might mean, offers a verbal or action counterpart to the action or feeling the child portrays.

> THERAPIST: Let's bring an ambulance to the fire so we can rush the victims to the hospital.
> CHILD: No, no ambulance. They all die.

A child repeatedly plays a scene where a car full of family members gets stuck in the mud and can go no farther. The parents and siblings get out of the car and sink over their heads in the mud. The therapist comments:

> THERAPIST: The little boy is left all alone in the car, unable to rescue his family.
> CHILD: He didn't try hard enough.

Melvin Lewis (1974) presents an example of an attention statement directed at the conspicuous absence of something from a child's play. He describes an eight-year-old phobic boy who repeatedly enacted a war scene in which the general was attacked and almost killed. Many fantasies were revealed in the play, but one prominent feature was the absence of any female. After attention was drawn to this "fact," the boy recognized his anger at his mother, his fear of her, his resentment that his absent father offered him no protection, and his displacement of his anger toward his mother onto his father, the safer target.

Reductive Statements

Reductive statements are made to reduce numerous disparate behavioral patterns to larger common behavioral patterns that the children have never noticed about themselves. A child may display similar forms of behavior whenever upset and be unaware of this fact. For example, every Monday on her return to her institutional home after a home visit, an eleven-year-old girl mocked, insulted, and degraded the therapist during her sessions. She was unable to respond to comments and questions about her anger. The therapist verbalized that she only seemed to get angry at him following a home visit. This reductive statement was accepted by the child. It was then followed by an interpretation of content: "Perhaps part of you hated coming back to the home and I'm the safest person toward whom you can express your anger." The child intensified these insults, but subsequently verbalized that her parents are able to care for her only on short visits and harshly punish any anger she expresses toward them.

Another example is seen in the treatment of an eight-year-old institutionalized boy who stole, was truant, and set fires. He behaved in a provocative manner, making it difficult for child-care workers to avoid manhandling him. While the workers learned to ignore his provocations, the larger children did not. This gave him justification for hitting and hurting them, but more often he was hurt by them. The therapist expressed wonder about this result, helping to clarify how his provocations actually led to punishments. Later, the child-care staff reported that after being beaten up by a boy, the child would attempt to engage the same boy in sex play. When the therapist focused on this sequence of behavior, the boy recognized that he needed help to stop it. The next step was to examine the "reasons" for his engaging in this seemingly masochistic behavior. Had he been beaten and then sexually abused by caregivers? Had he been beaten by a caregiver who, because of guilt, followed the beatings with hugs and kisses that eventually turned into sexual abuse? If the latter, the child's confusion about aggression, affection, and sexuality would be paramount issues to be addressed in the treatment. Dr. Mordock once worked with a child whose disturbed mother had used his head to masturbate with throughout his infancy and who paid him to masturbate her, both digitally and orally, when he was older.

Situational Statements

Situational statements naturally follow from attention statements and reductive statements. For example, when children are aware of their anger, the therapist can draw attention to frustrations that give rise to the anger and then try to clarify why the children are so easily frustrated in certain situations.

> THERAPIST: Every time you ask me for something that you know I can't give you, you can get angry at me for denying you.

When the child recognizes this pattern, then and only then can the therapist begin to show the child how this same tactic is employed to make another adult, such as a parent or a teacher, behave toward the child in a rejecting way. When the child recognizes that he or she employs this tactic with many adults, then and only then can the therapist help the child to look at how long the behavior has been going on and how it contributed to the development of problems with caregivers.

INTERPRETATION OF DEFENSES

Therapists, overwhelmed with a child's confusing play, often interpret the wrong things at the wrong time and with the wrong words. Often they interpret the child's wishes before they interpret the child's defense against expressing the wishes.

> GIRL: [*Playing aggressively with clay, mixing clay with water to make mud pies.*]
> THERAPIST: You're so angry with me today that you'd like to throw mud pies at me.

Following such a statement, the child is liable to become frightened by the therapist's knowledge of her angry feelings and will either run from therapy, because she fears retaliation, or throw the "mud pies" in order to strike the first blow. Such comments can be taken as "permission" to act out the impulses the child now "feels" more strongly. Before a therapist can interpret children's angry wishes, the children need to learn how they defend against expressing wishes. If children are unaware of their angry feelings toward the therapist, they first need to learn the mechanisms they use to avoid perceiving their anger and how to express it more directly. In addition, making mud pies is an acceptable way for a child to handle anger. No comment needs to be made about the pies. If a child is consumed with making mud pies and never appropriately expresses anger, then an interpretation may be in order.

> THERAPIST: I notice that whenever I have been late or have missed a session with you, you make mud pies instead of expressing your disappointment or anger at me for my letting you down. Have you noticed that?
> GIRL: [*More attentive to the therapist, less absorbed in play.*]
> THERAPIST: Most kids would be angry at me for missing a session or being late. Maybe making mud pies is safer than being angry at me. You think I'll get angry back?

The girl may have to "hear" such communications for some time before she will give up her defense of making mud pies, as well as the unspoken fantasies that accompany their making, and directly express her annoyance at the therapist. Only after the child acknowledges both her anger at the therapist and her manner of suppressing her awareness and expression of anger can she be guided to see that she behaves similarly with other adults in her life.

> BOY: [*Playing in sexual fashion with the mother doll.*]
> THERAPIST: Lots of children have sexual feelings toward their moms. Sometimes they even wish to marry their mom. Have you ever felt that way?

This example illustrates even worse errors. Not only was the wish interpreted before the defense against its expression, but the therapist failed to appreciate that feelings communicated in therapy are more often feelings held toward the therapist and created by the therapy situation. The child's sexualized play with the mother doll may be stimulated by the interpersonal closeness with the therapist, regardless of the therapist's sex. The child may have been sexually abused and is fearful of intimacy with the therapist. This interpretation about sexual feelings toward Mom is an example of "wild analysis" and is often the fantasy of clinicians familiar with psychoanalytic concepts of development but not with their therapeutic application. And last, but not least, if the child has been struggling for a time with sexual feelings for Mom, and the interpretation is not actually a wild one, then it should, at the least, be phrased tentatively, within the context of the child's play.

> THERAPIST: I wonder if Bobby Doll doesn't get exited when Mommy Doll rubs his back.

The boy who reveals his sexual curiosity or sexual interests in doll play should be encouraged to further develop and elaborate on such play, as we have illustrated in other chapters, before any comments are made about it. In fact, if the boy becomes increasingly agitated by his own play, the therapist should introduce another topic (e.g., "Here, play with these trucks.").

The request of a nine-year-old girl in a child-care institution illustrates the many choices that face a therapist. The girl wanted to take with her some drawings she and the therapist had made together and that she had been content to keep in her special cabinet in the therapy room. The therapist knew she was scheduled for a weekend visit home with her mother and her mother's latest boyfriend, a visit that caused noticeable agitation but which she would not admit worried her. The therapist could make any one of a number of responses. Attention could be drawn to her behavior with the comment, "I wonder why you might want these drawings now." The feeling could be reflected that, while she was home, she wanted something to remind her of positive times she had with the therapist, with a comment such as, "I wonder if you don't want these drawings now because their presence will help you handle your upcoming trip home." This interpretation of her defense, however, might force the girl to face abruptly her anxiety without the therapist's support. The therapist could make a more powerful interpretation of her wish for the therapist's protection, but such a move might leave her feeling stripped and defenseless and would violate the rule that defenses are interpreted before wishes. This wish could be linked with her reactions in other similar situations in which she had become anxious, but this could not be done without the previous steps. A connection could be made between this coming event and earlier events in her life, but this interpretation would be of no value because the girl did not have a clear idea of her feelings about this coming event. She could simply be given one of her drawings with nothing said. This last "response" supports the child's use of this defense (utilizing a soothing, transitional-type object).

Perhaps the best course of action would be to make a comment that would temporarily buttress the child and simultaneously support the defense and acknowledge the fear.

> THERAPIST: How nice it will be to take something home with you that you feel good about, especially if you're worried about the visit.

The therapist might decide to address the transference, but in a supportive way, and allow the girl to take the drawings and reserve for a later date further exploration of the act.

> THERAPIST: I think you would like to have something that's partially mine with you on your visit. When you come back, we can talk more about how you feel when you visit home.

STEP-BY-STEP PROGRESSION

Interpretations proceed in a step-by-step fashion. First the child learns that common elements exist in a series of events (attention statements); second, the child realizes that he or she displays specific behaviors in certain situations (reductive statements); third, the child learns that a specific behavior is manifested in a specific situation, for example, in competitive situations where rivalry is expected (situational statements); fourth, the child learns that his or her rivalrous feelings do not exist unconsciously but are replaced by a defensive behavior, such as avoiding competition (interpretation of the defense); fifth, the child learns how the defense (in this example, avoiding competition) helps to avoid perceived humiliation and loss of self-love; and sixth, the child learns how this behavior originated in response to certain events in early life and encompasses reactions and tendencies that could be grouped under the heading of, for example, rivalry with an intermittent and fitful father.

In all the stages just outlined, interpretation of the child's defense is emphasized rather than interpretation of content. Later the therapist may help the child understand the wishes that were defended against. A boy's rivalry with his father is not created just by the father, who may have ridiculed his child's immature rivalrous behavior, but was also initiated by the child. What was the wish that lay behind the desire to win out over Dad? Probably it was to have his mother all to himself. In rejected children, the wish is especially strong because the occasional presence of an otherwise absent dad usually results in the child getting even less attention from an inattentive mother. The rivalry is real, rather than a stage in human development, and rarely gets resolved because the child never identifies with any positive qualities of the father.

INTERPRETATION WITHIN THE METAPHOR

We have illustrated the use of attention, reduction, and situational statements directed at the child's behavior. Many children need intermediate steps, such as making these statements indirectly through some other hypothetical child or within the context of their play. Many dynamic interpretations should be made for the first time within the context of the play or fantasy the child expresses, called "interpretation within the metaphor." When a child is playing that a doll named Betty is attacked by a lion, the therapist can initially reflect that "lions are frightening." When the child elaborates that other dangerous creatures surround the doll, the therapist can respond with "Betty sure lives in a dangerous world." Both of these comments may set up reverberations that bring out the child's concealed perceptions of the real world, but they are comfortably contained within the fantasy. If the child responds with "Betty is brave," or even with "I'm brave," the proper distance from reality has been maintained. Questions put to the child to clarify issues also are asked within the metaphor. "Why was the lion so mean?" "Who let the lion escape from the circus?" "Was the lion always so mean?" No matter how transparent a child's fantasy appears, children are usually some distance away from being able to acknowledge directly even small parts of it.

Whenever a therapist violates the framework of the fantasy or the play and reaches into reality for the meaning of the symbols (e.g., "You must be scared of some grown-ups."), the child will terminate the fantasy and withdraw from the therapist. Dorothy Block (1968) relays a report from a colleague that dramatically illustrates the error in "describing the unconscious to the patient." When this analyst asked his client if he understood the meaning of the characters in his murderous fantasy, the client's immediate reply was, "If I understood what they meant, I'd kill myself."

Disturbed children are constantly engaged in defending themselves, whether in fantasy, play, or verbal communication, from experiencing forbidden and painful thoughts. Always remember that when a child's fantasy is of pleasant experiences, it is expressed unmodified. When the fantasy thought leads to fear of harm to self or others, it must be distorted, modified, and masked. The child is willing to examine emotional pain only in small doses and only in the presence of a supporting, trusted adult. The child's defensive efforts must be respected. Interpretations are not for the therapist's benefit.

Each time children achieve increased understanding of their fantasies, they can elaborate upon them in such a way that new fantasies appear and the therapist is assigned new roles. Those children that involve therapists in their play will often cue the therapists and give them their lines. The therapist elaborates on the directions only when a feeling the child displays can be expanded upon. In most cases, when the child directs the play and tells the therapist what to do or say, the therapist should follow along. When the play has served its purpose—to strengthen the child's self—the child typically abandons it and moves on to something else. There are occasions, however, when the therapist should refuse to play a certain part exactly as directed. For example, if asked to be a devouring or an abusive parent, the therapist should respond with the following clarification:

> THERAPIST: You want me to be a mean, scary, or hurtful person, but I don't hit or eat babies. I like to pet and feed animals and to take care of babies, but I will be Mr. [or Mrs.] Lion if you want to play with the puppets.

Later, the therapist can explore whether the child views adults as abusive or whether the child is the devouring lion, usually both sides of the same coin. To respond early on in treatment with "You have been hurt by grown-ups" or even with "The doll has been beaten by grown-ups" is untimely and leads to treatment setbacks. If the child orders Mr. Lion to eat the babies, then Mr. Lion can do so and comments can be made within the safety of the metaphor. If the child never moves past his or her obsession of the therapist being a devouring lion, the play should be redirected.

> THERAPIST: Mrs. Lion isn't very hungry today. Maybe she can just keep an eye on the children's whereabouts and think about eating them later.

WORDING THE INTERPRETATION

Considerable tact is required when interpreting the defenses of troubled children, even if the interpretation is made within the metaphor. Direct attempts to analyze defenses are experienced by most children as an attack on the self. Even sympathetic exploration is often taken as implied criticism. In addition, disturbed children have great difficulty tolerating ambivalence and find it difficult to accept their own hostile wishes or fantasies. Placing the anger in a fuller context may help ("It is very hard to be angry at someone you love."), but often it does not. Remember that interpretative statements should always be put tentatively, and in the form of a question that leaves room for doubt. The interpretation should always carry the implication that it is all right to have the feeling that is interpreted. Conveying this implication requires careful wording. Neither of the following interpretative statements accomplishes this goal.

> THERAPIST: I think you're feeling angry at me, but you hide it with silence.
> and
> THERAPIST: Behind your silence is lots of anger.

There is a subtle difference between these two statements and the following three:

> THERAPIST: Sometimes when people have nothing to say, they realize it's because they are actually angry.
> THERAPIST: I get the feeling that you're angry but may feel you're not supposed to be.
> THERAPIST: I wonder if you're staying silent because you feel you had better not say anything if what you are feeling is anger.

The last three statements do not emphasize hiding or denying feelings. Instead they emphasize the fear of expressing anger and suggest that the fear might be unwarranted. Skillful wording can bring forth a favorable response, even in aggressive children with brittle defenses.

> THERAPIST: I can understand your anger at me for not being available to you over the weekend when you were feeling alone. It is understandable because you've felt alone many times before, particularly when your mom was not around when you needed her.

This interpretation conveys empathetic understanding of the child's insatiable wish by focusing on the wish per se. Such interpretations result in children reexperiencing themselves in relation to others. They strengthen the children's feelings that emotions are understandable—that there are reasons for feelings, and that the "reason" resulted from past deprivations. In contrast, if the therapist remarks,

> THERAPIST: You are angry at me and perceive me as cold and uncaring because I was not available to you over the weekend when you

were feeling needy. You would like me to be available at all times and in all places,

Such a comment emphasizes that the child has insatiable needs that cannot be realistically gratified. This comment is not an interpretation; it is a confrontation that has no place in child therapy. A child will experience it as a reprimand and respond accordingly. Similarly, when the child displays hurtful or hostile behavior toward the therapist, limit setting can be accompanied by something like one of the following:

> THERAPIST: I think you want to hurt me today because somebody hurt you today. Who did something mean to you today?
> or
> THERAPIST: You need to treat me this way because you think I might do this to you today.
> or
> THERAPIST: I wonder if you don't worry that I might do things to you in here like others have done to you.
> or
> THERAPIST: You show me by your behavior how hard it is for you to control your excited, angry feelings. Sometimes, even when you talk to me, these feelings come out.

Contrast these supportive interpretations with the confrontations below:

> THERAPIST: Your effort to get me angry is an excuse for you to express your anger at me.
> THERAPIST: Do you do things elsewhere to get people angry so you can be angry back?
> THERAPIST: Whenever you get angry about something, your increased anger gets others more angry at you.

Poorly worded interpretations can convey to children that they have negative self-attributes. They communicate what they are rather than what they can be. For example:

> THERAPIST: You seem to have difficulty talking.

Contrast this remark with the following one:

> THERAPIST: Sometimes you talk more easily than at other times.

The second comment contributes to delineating whom the child talks to and why there is difficulty. All of us are better off facing difficult issues when we feel stronger than when we are fearfully hiding. Sometimes the therapist should wait until the child is very expressive and comment,

> THERAPIST: You are being quite expressive right now. I wonder why you can do this at this time.

CONCLUSION

Interpretations offered in a tentative and collaborative fashion can contribute significantly to the healing process. It can be comforting to children who are puzzled and baffled, like their parents, about their behavior or emotions. Part of the goal of therapy is to provide our child clients with an altered and more meaningful understanding of their behavior, feelings, motives, fantasies, and impulses. If interpretation is done in an unmasking way that leaves the child feeling exposed and dramatically uncovered, it poses the risk of great harm to the therapeutic relationship. Interpretations, particularly with extremely aggressive and especially with traumatized children, should be done only when children meet the criteria for the invitational track of therapy. It should also be noted that the extent of the threat and anxiety engendered by emotionally laden material may require the child therapist to cross over to the coping track when dealing with certain issues that the child is not ready to face, yet to be able to do interpretive work within the invitational track on less emotionally threatening issues. If a therapist's timing is off and an ill-considered interpretation is offered, the child will typically react in a manner that makes it clear the therapist is out of sync with the child's current emotional state and needs. When this occurs it can be helpful to admit the error in timing and say to the child, "I can see that I have upset you by making you look at something you are not ready to face. I am glad you can let me know when I make a mistake. I am very sorry, and I will try to be more sensitive to your feelings and needs. We will come back to this at a time that is more comfortable for you. Right now, why don't you pick a pleasant way we can be together for the rest of this session?" This acknowledgment makes the therapy a safer place for the child. The therapist is willing to acknowledge and take responsibility for errors in judgment and timing. The therapist is also willing to apologize, and the child is respected for the need to go slower and at a pace that is right for him or her.

· *11* ·

Making Interpretations:
Advanced Concepts

The stages in a child's acceptance of an interpretation of a defense are illustrated. The concepts of generalization, externalization, and projective identification are presented, and examples are provided showing how to respond to them. A discussion of transference interpretations, distinguishing transference behaviors from other phenomena, and interpretations of wishes closes the chapter.

SEVEN STAGES

There are seven stages in a child's acceptance and integration of an interpretation of a defense. Often the process is not observed until after the interpretation has been verbalized on many different occasions. These stages are as follows:

1. The child presents the material that prompts the interpretation.
2. The child assimilates the contents of the interpretation:
   a. The child perceives and registers the interpretation on a preconscious or unconscious level.
   b. The interpretation threatens the child's sense of well-being, and anxiety follows.
   c. The child represses the contents of the interpretation, and therefore the anxiety evoked by it diminishes.
3. The child emulates the power he or she perceives in the therapist's understanding the behavior. (The passive is turned into the active.)
4. The child denies in subsequent fantasies the painful aspects of the contents of the interpretation.

5. The child represses aggressive retaliatory impulses toward the therapist.

6. The child's successive symbolic representation, in fantasy and play, of the wish to give up the denial and to come to terms with reality reveals the considerable ambivalence the child holds about resolving this conflict. The child's play oscillates between accurate and distorted representations of reality.

7. The child displays insight, not in words, but in changed behaviors. If behaviors don't change, then the child's verbalizations of insights are meaningless and designed only to please the therapist.

The seven stages will be illustrated by examining clinical data from the therapy sessions of an aggressive latency-age boy. This youngster had responded favorably to limits set by the therapist and looked forward to therapy sessions. He identified with superhero figures, and his play behavior revealed his preoccupation with violence. The therapist had interpreted the boy's aggressive behavior as a counterreaction to his fears of being destroyed and vulnerable. Such interpretations had been conveyed both through the metaphor and directly. How the boy responded to these interpretations will be illustrated by looking at material from four sessions of his two-year stay in therapy.

Session 23: Interpretation and Response

CHILD: [*Goes immediately to building blocks and makes a moat surrounding a castle. A knight tries to cross the drawbridge to invade the castle, but sometimes the drawbridge is pulled up and the knight falls in the moat, to be eaten by crocodiles. On other occasions, he makes it across the drawbridge to the castle and defeats those inside.*]

This scene and similar ones have been repeated in a number of prior therapy sessions.

THERAPIST: [*Interpretation within the metaphor*] Maybe the knight needed to attack this fort before his enemies inside attacked him. Maybe he needs to strike the first blow to feel safe.

CHILD: But sometimes he falls into the moat.

THERAPIST: [*Elaboration*] Yes, but that's the price he has to pay for the fighting that makes him feel safe. He falls into the moat because of his fighting. His fighting causes him lots of troubles.

CHILD: [*Continues*]

THERAPIST: [*Direct interpretation*] I wonder if sometimes you don't feel a little like the knight—that you fight to feel safe and you get into trouble like the knight falling into the moat.

CHILD: [*Leaves the blocks, gets out a puzzle, and proceeds to put the pieces together.*] When I'm done, it will turn out to be a lion.

In Session 23, a major interpretation was made. The knight, like the boy, attacked the castle because of fear. The first interpretation was within the metaphor, and because the boy actively listened to this interpretation, the therapist related his interpretation directly to the boy's problem. The boy's aggressive behavior was his attempt to protect himself from helpless feelings, which were more frightening to him than the trouble his misbehavior got him into. The therapist had made similar interpretations before, but no noticeable changes had followed their communication. The therapist also chose not to interpret the boy's play in relation to the therapist (e.g., "You need to be strong to avoid some injury I might cause you"—a transference interpretation) but instead interpreted what he felt was the child's characteristic way of feeling and behaving.

Outwardly, the child seemingly ignored the interpretation by abandoning his play and initiating an unrelated activity. He assembled a puzzle (This behavior is not unlike the child who hears his mother's scoldings for not cleaning his room and yet goes outside to ride his bicycle). We know, however, that anxiety disrupts play. The child withdrew abruptly to a more remote and less disturbing activity. In addition, he exchanged a passive attitude of a child's listening to an adult with one in which he was active and the therapist passive. The activity was one in which he would be successful because he knew the outcome in advance. He bragged about this upcoming accomplishment to elevate his self-image.

The contents of the interpretation exposed the boy's inadequacy and elevated his anxiety. In response, he chose a new task in which he would be completely adequate. His successful feelings helped him to repress his anxiety. From this behavior, the therapist can infer that the boy unconsciously, at least, understood the message and chose to complete a puzzle to help dampen his anxiety. The puzzle pieces may be considered as the manifest phenomena and the lion as the hidden gestalt. Assembling the puzzle results in making manifest a latent content. The child turns from passively experiencing the interpretation to duplicating the feat of the therapist and making an "interpretation" of his own. This feat spares him from humiliation and allows him to "impress" the therapist. The child's active mastery reduces the anxiety stimulated by the interpretation and thereby facilitates its assimilation.

Sessions 24 and 25: Working Through

CHILD: [*Sets up the blocks, but this time he gives the knight wings that enable him to fly over the moat and successfully vanquish his foes. Following this play, he uncharacteristically puts away the blocks by himself without prompting by the ther-*

apist or without asking for the therapist's help. He then asks to play a game with the therapist.]

CHILD: [*Again plays knight with wings vanquishing foes.*]

THERAPIST: Now the knight has wings and doesn't have to worry that he will fall in the moat. He can attack his enemies and not get into trouble. It sounds like you'd like to have wings also, so you won't get hurt when you fight with classmates.

CHILD: Merwin, the magician, gave him them.

THERAPIST: Wouldn't it be nice if you also could find magic so you could fight and yet stay out of trouble? Do you make-believe you are the winged knight in class and that no child can hurt you?

CHILD: I don't daydream. The teachers are a pain in the ass.

THERAPIST: What do you think about in class that keeps you from doing your work so that no note goes home telling your mother how much you learned during the week?

CHILD: Lots of things, being a stunt-car driver. I have to do what's best for me!

The child attempts to deny the impact of the interpretation by intensifying the fantasy in Session 24. He gives the knight wings. The knight can now slay his enemies without fear of harm. He does not want to acknowledge his weakness and vulnerability. Nevertheless, his alteration of the fantasy signals that his fantasy life is negotiable—that, if he wishes, he can bring it into a closer adaptation to reality.

Following this play, he picks up his constructions. While he gave the knight wings, he eliminated the threat to his affectionate feelings for the therapist (The winged knight could destroy the therapist) by cleaning up to safeguard his relationship. He becomes a "good" client and picks up after himself. In Session 25, the wings sometimes fall off and the knight has to struggle without his magical powers.

Session 26: Insight

CHILD: [*Again he plays the winged knight, but occasionally the wings fall off and the knight falls into the moat. Nevertheless, he laughs at the knight's flapping efforts to remain aloft. He also reported that he had gotten into a fight in school, and while he had started it, he accepted his punishment. He then began to draw a cartoon of a dog who lived in the desert in a cactus. This dog was alone in the desert one day, and he met a zebra whom he befriended. He and the zebra went camping. The dog taught the zebra how to start fires from sticks, put up a tent, and hunt for food. The dog wanted to play with the zebra, but they didn't know what to play, so they went to sleep.*]

The boy talks about his functioning in school and admits for the first time that he started a fight. He then makes a cartoon of a lonely dog who tries to befriend a zebra, a theme suggesting that he wants to make friends, but the two do not know what to play, so they simply sleep. The child showed that the interpretation was effective by both admitting to starting fights and by developing a new fantasy, a less distant one, where friendships are sought.

During the process of working through, the child maintained his sense of well-being, a sense threatened by the interpretation, by fantasizing a state where he cannot accept or reject the reality situation revealed by the interpretation. The knight can fly or walk and can be in or out of the moat. Total denial can be maintained alongside an accurate representation of reality.

GENERALIZATION, EXTERNALIZATION, AND PROJECTIVE IDENTIFICATION

When treating children in gorilla suits, three phenomena are important to keep in mind. These are generalization, the defensive uses of externalization, and projective identification. Generalization occurs when a child, becoming aware of wishes about an adult, naturally assumes that the adult has similar wishes toward him or her (People in love often make similar assumptions). When angry at the therapist, the child assumes the therapist is angry also. Children arrested at this cognitive level of development need the therapist to serve as an auxiliary self. They need to realize that they cannot know the thoughts and feelings of others unless those thoughts and feelings are communicated to them, nor can others know theirs. Many people mistakenly believe they are loved only when their partner can intuitively recognize their unspoken needs. Disturbed children feel similarly. The children also need to learn that others are not like themselves and have thoughts and feelings different from theirs, an aim discussed in chapter 2.

The term *externalization* subsumes those processes that lead to the subjective allocation of inner phenomena to the outer world. Externalization is the opposite of internalization (introjection, incorporation, identification). Externalization is a way of dealing with unacceptable parts of oneself. When children attempt to integrate the various parts of their emerging selves, they have the most difficulty with the dissonant, unacceptable parts. As a transitory phenomenon, externalization is a normal defensive process. Its prolonged use results in a restricted personality, with important aspects of the self permanently split off and unavailable for integration. It is a defense not directed primarily against expressing unacceptable impulses or wishes, nor against experiencing love-linked anxieties. Rather, its aim is to avoid the pain that results from accepting devalued aspects of the self.

Children who berate the therapist as a "stupid, dumb, ugly person," as do many gorilla-suit wearers, are clearly denying the reality of the therapist and simply taking an opportunity to discard undesirable aspects of the self. Children who externalize also project anger onto the therapist. When children attribute hostile intent to the therapist, there is often a "degree of fit" between the projection and reality. The children may hang the projection on some real event, such as a canceled session.

But what if the child calls the therapist a messy person? Is it the messy, unacceptable aspect of the self-representation that is being externalized, or a drive derivative, such as the wish to mess upon the therapist? The therapist should note whether the child's statement leads to relief or to anxiety. If the child is projecting and, therefore, experiencing himself as an object of the therapist's wish to mess, the child will wish to flee from the situation. If an externalization, the child will perceive the externalization as unrelated to the self and as something to be ignored, derided, or treated with contempt. Often, however, it is difficult to make this distinction because the child may be displaying a projective identification with the therapist. Unacceptable parts of the self are externalized and unacceptable wishes projected onto the therapist, and then the child identifies with this "unreal" image of the therapist. As a result, the therapist may be feared because he has "been made into" an undesirable and autocratic tyrant.

If the differentiation can be made, it follows that interpretations of externalizations must focus on the need to defend against damaged self-love, whereas interpretations of projections must focus on the need to defend against the anxiety related to drive expression. Let's see how the two mechanisms occur in the same child:

Gloria was a thirteen-year-old girl in a special education class who rarely talked, kept her head bowed, and elicited much ridicule from male classmates whom she taunted and teased in retaliation. She continually belittled her female therapist. She included "stupid" and "ugly" among her various insults. Gloria's behaviors could be considered a direct expression of aggression or an attempt to ward off anticipated insults from the therapist. Gloria's affect and subsequent material clearly indicated that Gloria identified with her powerful, arrogant father, who felt humiliated by his daughter's special class placement and clearly made her aware of his disappointment in her. In response, Gloria externalized the "Little Gloria" who was laughed at, criticized, and often ignored.

Her therapist consistently responded to Gloria's outpourings of criticisms by verbalizing how she was being viewed by Gloria, how she was being seen and treated as a stupid little girl, and how it feels to be treated in this manner.

THERAPIST: You talk to me this way because you have been called "stupid" and "ugly," and it's very painful to be called these things. Sometimes I think you even believe these insults. It's hard being in a special class and not thinking you're dumb. Just because you take longer to learn things doesn't mean you're not a worthwhile, lovable person. I enjoy you when you're not insulting me.

Because Gloria frequently experienced insulting attacks from her father, she expected such attacks from her therapist. Following the principle of turning what is passively experienced into what is actively managed, she insulted others. Frequently, the therapist was the target of displaced anger. She was also the target of projected anger. Her anxiety about the therapist's "anger" was revealed in her nonverbal behavior. She would refuse to come to therapy sessions, walking way ahead or way behind the therapist. If she did come to therapy, she would sit far away from the therapist. She also shouted angry insults at her from a distance when she saw the therapist in the hallway between sessions.

Gloria would accuse the therapist of disliking her when her requests were denied or when sessions were canceled. The therapist did not deny Gloria's view of these events, accepting them as possible, but suggested that what she feared more than the therapist's dislike or inconsiderateness was that the therapist may wish to harm her in retaliation for all her earlier insults. In some sense, Gloria externalized her harsh and severe conscience onto the therapist, as well as projecting her own anger. After Gloria admitted to this fear, the therapist attempted to show her that her wish to harm the therapist, who stood for all adults who had hurt her, was actually her wish to retaliate for hurts inflicted upon her by others.

> THERAPIST: Simply because you wish to harm me doesn't mean that I wish to harm you. Often you think that your wishes will come true, but wishes are just wishes. I know that you are angry at me, and I'll never harm you, even if I get angry.

Often children incorporate the externalizations of a parent. Children who view themselves as "damaged goods" usually have accepted a parent's externalization of the parent's own self-image. The acceptance of the parent's externalization lies in the realization, at some level, that the parent needs such a devalued child and that abandonment would follow the failure to comply with this need. Treatment of such children is difficult because the externalizing parent becomes disorganized and disturbed in response to the child's improvement. Not only does the child feel guilty about depriving the parent of a needed vehicle for externalization, but as the parent struggles to find a new target, the child can feel rejected. Similarly, a child can be the victim of a parent's projections. The parent who harbors long-standing hostility may feel that her child harbors similar feelings toward him or her. The children are viewed as a "monster to be feared" whereas the murderous impulse actually resides within the parents themselves.

Most children in gorilla suits make extensive use of externalization and projection. Therapists are confronted with children who greet their helper with hostility. Understanding the dynamics behind this aggression will help therapists to keep some distance from this hostility and maintain objectivity.

TRANSFERENCE INTERPRETATIONS

Sigmund Freud initially felt that the strong feelings of love or hate that invariably developed toward the analyst were a hindrance to progress in treatment. Later, he learned that these feelings were those transferred from the client's childhood relationships within the family to the therapeutic relationship. Freud discovered that clients not only remembered earlier situations of conflict and anxiety from their childhood but always transferred them to the current analytic situation, where they reexperienced and relived them. He then discovered that improvement occurred only when this happened and when the analyst helped the client to understand the transferred feelings. The process involved a lengthy "working through" of childhood conflicts and feelings toward the analyst. The client needs to become fully aware of his or her conflicts and their origins and to gradually find new solutions to them.

In the early 1920s, Melanie Klein (1948) verified that children also transfer feelings for their parents onto the therapist. Children transfer and project unconscious images of parents or aspects of parents—images created by a fusion of their own impulses, feelings, fantasies, and external experiences.

Children need to realize that many of the feelings they have about the therapist are directed toward a fantasy person and not a real one. Each child needs help to contrast the fantasy of the therapist with the reality of the therapist. To achieve this task, the therapist must continually ask himself or herself, "What is the child doing to me at the moment?" and "What is the child feeling in relation to me now?" The therapist should follow these questions with the following: "Whom is the child trying to make me like?" "How is the child viewing me?" "Am I the angry, hostile father or the dominating, intrusive mother?" "Does the child have an image of me that is like himself or herself—a 'narcissistic transference,' where I am viewed as the self is viewed?" "Am I being made a past or a present person in the child's life?"

For example, a boy initiates a session by drawing a picture of a monster devouring a small animal. Is he the monster who can destroy his enemies? Is he the animal about to be devoured? He probably identifies with both creatures—he becomes the monster that he fears. But why does he draw this now—does he feel himself to be the helpless animal confronted by the therapist? Therapists can reflect this fear, but until the real monster is actually known, the child cannot be shown what behavior, either from the past or from current inner experience, has been transferred to the monster. When the fear is reflected and no attack from the therapist is forthcoming, the boy's anxiety will decrease, and in the safety of dramatic play, he will become the more complete monster and threaten to devour the therapist. These attacks will be followed by increased anxiety, no retaliation from the therapist, more play, and so on. Eventually, it may become clear who the monster really is. Another example follows.

> SALLY: [*Drawing*] This is Sherry. She lives all alone on the moon. She has no one to take care of her.

This story-drawing can be the communication of a wish (perhaps a wish to escape frustration—to live alone on the moon and take care of herself), a fear (My mom could abandon me and I would be all alone), or a reflection of actual feelings of rejection (I feel all alone). The rejection could be felt (overly sensitive child), actual (rejected child), or a combination of the two (child extremely sensitive to times of parental indifference). By knowing something about Sally's history and present life circumstances, the therapist can respond accordingly. Nevertheless, the best initial response follows from the knowledge that feelings communicated early in therapy are most often feelings held toward the therapist or elicited by the therapy situation.

> THERAPIST: When Sherry is in a new situation with a strange adult, she would like to get as far away as possible and take care of herself. Or perhaps Sherry hopes her new friend will help her not to feel so all alone.

If Sally has been in therapy for some time and a therapeutic alliance has developed, questions could be asked within the metaphor of the drawing.

> THERAPIST: What did Sherry take with her to the moon? Can you draw that?
> SALLY: I can't draw those things so well.
> THERAPIST: Would you like me to draw them for you? You tell me what they are and I'll add them to your drawing.
> SALLY: Yes. She took her puppy, her hamster, and all her storybooks.
> THERAPIST: Won't Sherry's parents miss her while she's on the moon?
> SALLY: No.
> THERAPIST: That must make Sherry sad.
> SALLY: They're glad she's gone.

The therapist must be careful because Sally may be "punishing" her parents for a perceived transgression on their part. Children can feel so revengeful toward parents that they will deprive themselves of a need in order to get back at them. Because Sally has a puppy, a hamster, and storybooks, her parents may have given her things that instill a sense of responsibility, and therefore the parents are not completely rejecting adults. (Of course, Sally may not actually have any of these things.) Therapy without some knowledge of a child's family life is a difficult task.

> THERAPIST: Did Sherry do something to make her parents so angry with her that they would send her to the moon? I wonder if Sherry isn't also mad at them and ran away to the moon.
> SALLY: [*Silence, draws stars around the moon.*]
> THERAPIST: I once knew a little girl who got so mad at her parents that she ran away so her parents would miss her so much that they would be sorry for the things they did that made her mad.
> SALLY: Who?
> THERAPIST: My cousin. [*Children are more impressed with such statements than they are with "another child I had in therapy."*]
> SALLY: She did that? Did they miss her a lot?
> THERAPIST: Yes, but they also worried that something would happen to her. My cousin was so mad that she risked getting hurt when she ran away, so she decided that running away wasn't such a good idea. The next time she got really angry at her parents, she decided to draw her angry feelings.

Children will often ask the therapist questions that reveal something about their lives. "Do you hit your kids?" "Do you drink?" Such questions often reveal the lives they live. The question "Do you hit your kids?" may also be an effort to find out how you will react to them when you get angry.

> THERAPIST: I wonder if the drawings you always make of smiling, neat little girls are your way of telling me that you want me to think of you as a nice girl who never gets into trouble.

When attempts are made to reflect possible feelings held, but not directly expressed, by the child, acknowledgment is rarely forthcoming. It takes many such communications before a child feels comfortable enough to express directly the feelings about the therapist. The child will wax and wane in becoming more direct, and indirect expressions will vary in style. Anger toward the therapist may be revealed in a violent drawing, knocking over blocks, punching a doll, hiding in a corner, displaying mock anger, or playing catch and throwing the ball poorly to the therapist. When feelings change to positive ones, things will be done or made for the therapist, or the therapist will be bragged about to others. Rarely will the child say, "I like you!"

Some therapists make a conscious effort to link the child's transferred feelings with the past or present feelings about the parents. Such efforts are rarely successful when tried directly. When a child is in therapy, parents and home are not in the child's immediate experience. Thinking about them in a detached and intellectual manner is difficult. The more important task is to interpret the current anxieties and conflicts the child has with the therapist, with the link to the past being implicit in the wordings. "You treat me like the mother you wished you had all to yourself." "You treat me like the father you often wanted to leave." "You're angry with me now, just as you were angry as a young girl with your mother when you thought she treated you unfairly."

The child's relationship to the therapist is a complicated mixture of a real relationship, a wished-for relationship, habitual ways of relating, an extension into therapy of current relationships, and a repetition or revival of past relationships. It is usually difficult to tease out children's transference manifestations from these other phenomena. Examining behavior outside of the therapy setting sometimes helps to make this distinction. Children who displace anger onto the therapist typically improve outside of sessions while those who transfer anger rarely show improvement. Only when transferred anger is interpreted and worked through will improvement be noted outside of sessions. When an entirely new behavior resulting from repressed infantile conflicts emerges in therapy, symptoms may diminish elsewhere. Here, the transferred feelings can result in improved behavior. For example, aggressive children who let themselves be babied by the therapist and who "mess" on the therapist often improve outside of sessions.

On other occasions, a child's behavior will deteriorate outside of therapy as a direct consequence of feelings aroused by the therapy experience and by efforts to resist the expression of these transferred feelings in treatment sessions. For example, a child with incest fantasies transfers these fantasies onto the therapist and then defends against their expression by becoming sexually involved with schoolmates.

Max Holder (1970) describes his treatment of a thirteen-year-old who always drew the curtains in the therapy room before beginning his sessions. The child never commented on this behavior, but from later material it was uncovered that the behavior occurred in response to the screen memories of witnessing the sexual activities of his parents. It contained the communication that he could only hear and not see because of the darkness. Holder labeled this behavior as "acting within the transference" because it was stimulated by the intimate relationship with the therapist within a confined space.

INTERPRETATION OF WISHES

After children understand the defenses they use to ward off the anxiety aroused by unacceptable or forbidden needs and desires, the therapist can begin to interpret the wishes that caused them to become anxious. Some of the transference interpretations cited earlier included those identifying wishes, such as "You treat me as the mother you wanted all to yourself." Other examples of interpretations of wishes follow:

> THERAPIST: Sometimes Bobby Doll wishes he could have Mommy Doll all to himself and that Brother Doll [*or Father Doll*] were gone.
> THERAPIST: Beneath that rough, tough part of Baby Lion is a part of him that would like to be taken care of. But that part becomes afraid of Mr. Lion's rejection if Baby Lion shows Mrs. Lion his loving feelings.
> THERAPIST: Sometimes you wish your dad was dead, but that thought makes you very anxious because part of you loves him.

Very angry children need help to manage unacceptable wishes toward parent figures. They need help to realize that while wishes are understandable, they will not come true and that some should not come true. A part of each gorilla-suit wearer does not want to act out the retaliatory fantasies held toward parents. Children need protection from such actions; they need to understand that wishes are only wishes and need not come true.

Children typically show their positive response to an interpretation of a wish by modifying future play or fantasy behavior. Henry Coppolillo's description (1969) of his treatment of a child with impulse control problems beautifully illustrates the gradual changes in a child's play in response to interpretation of wishes. The child would regularly leave the therapist's office and taunt the therapist to chase him and bring him back.

> COPPOLILLO: It appears that you like to be caught and held, but would like it to be all my idea.
> CHILD: [*Child giggles and takes therapist's hand, begins tugging and pulling it as if he had been caught and heads back toward the office. When back, he plays with boy and girl dolls. He makes them hug and kiss and chase each other around.*]
> COPPOLILLO: Why are they chasing each other?
> CHILD: They did lots of wrong things and that one chased the other to hold it so it would not do wrong.
> COPPOLILLO: Ah, now I understand, you want to be chased and to be held close, but you feel ashamed of this because it makes you feel like a little boy. So you play the pretend game of being naughty and having to be held.
> CHILD: Will you come to my house and play lots?

At the beginning of the next session, the therapist announced that he could no longer be the child's policeman. The child would have to be his own policeman and do those things he knew were good for him and avoid those things that were not. The child ran out of the office.

COPPOLILLO: I will not stop you or chase you anymore.

Five sessions later, the child brought a fifteen-foot length of cord with him to the session. He tied the cord to the therapist and then said that he was going to run away. He said he was pretending that the therapist would still like to chase him and hold him but could not because he was tied. He then tied one end of the cord to his waist. He left the room and went as far as the rope permitted him to go. He called out, "Pull me back," to which Coppolillo responded, "You want me to be your policeman because your own policeman inside your head is too mean." The boy gleefully returned and repeated the game several times.

In the next session, the child reported that he had learned two new poems. He told about Jack and Jill and Humpty-Dumpty. He gave a confused account of Jack only having broken his crown while Humpty-Dumpty broke "his whole self." He then added, "And that mean policeman inside his head got out". He sadly added that a king put Humpty together again because you need a policeman inside your head to be a good boy.

CONCLUSION

When a child responds to the interpretations of the therapist, the child repeats and relives conflicts in the therapy relationship rather than merely remembering them as matters from the past. Remembrances of the past that result in changes in present feelings are called insight. But in child therapy, the goal is rarely insight into the roots of a conflict. Rather, "insight" is revealed as a shift in the child's attitude of mind, a lessening of the need to project feelings and anxieties, which eventually leads to the increased capacity for self-understanding and which results from the internalization of an insightful or insight-seeking therapist. In essence, what the child requires is what Bertrand Russell calls "knowledge by experience," as opposed to "knowledge by description."

Windows into the Inner World: Spontaneous Drawings as a Bridge to Fantasy Play

In this chapter, we illustrate how the therapist can use spontaneous drawings to help children on the invitational track face unresolved fears and early traumas. Sometimes drawings serve as a bridge to other fantasy play, but often the drawing activities themselves are therapeutic.

*F*antasies revealed are less frightening than those bottled up. Children rarely express their fears directly. Many of their fears are only partially remembered. They are screen memories. Screen memories are bits and pieces of traumatic experiences that have been repressed but that enter consciousness in disguised forms when the mind lets down its guard, most often in unstructured play, at night just prior to sleep, in dreams, or in response to reminders in the environment. For example, a child who has repressed the memory, and along with it the connected pain, of being sexually molested by an alcoholic father may be extremely bothered by a screen memory (or flashback) when an adult with alcoholic breath leans over to pat her head. By quickly leaving the area, she avoids the event's happening again. Often, however, children do not connect their anxiety and partial memory of a dreaded event to their past experience. As one six-year-old boy from a violent family described it to Louise Silvern and Lynn Kaersvang (1989) after a year's therapy, "I used to think memories exploded you. It turns out that they do only when you don't really know what they were memories of."

The complete memory of the past experience can be so overwhelming that all experiences are avoided that could result in the memory's being revived. A girl's rapid departure from a friendly adult whose odor reminds her of an abuser is an example of acting out. When an emotion becomes unduly intense, and therefore in need of repression, remembering immediately gives way to action. The girl flees without knowing exactly why she does so; to know why is to remember, and to remember is to be overwhelmed. Many children distance themselves from remembrances of abuse and rejection by displacing the danger felt into an imaginary world. The fantasy of "creatures bent on destroying children" is much less agonizing than fear of an abusing parent. In fact, if they don't displace, it is the therapist's job to help them to do so, a topic we addressed in earlier chapters.

Unresolved fears continually cause children difficulty, often disrupting their development long after the reality of the situation has changed. The parent may no longer be abusive, or the child may be living in a foster home. Yet fantasies of destructive creatures still preoccupy the mind and prevent mastery of age-appropriate tasks. Young children will often play out aspects of their early abusive experiences, often in a confusing and disjointed manner. The confusion results from the play reflecting only screen memories of each experience rather than the compete experience itself. But older children, those between the ages of eight and thirteen, usually don't play in initial treatment sessions. These children are "too old to play, but too young to talk." So often, families and even therapists, especially young and inexperienced clinicians, view older children as resistant when they do not verbalize their private thoughts, feelings, and motives. Children in gorilla suits typically don't verbalize their feelings because they lack both the cognitive awareness and the language skills to express the details of their inner life. When they are judged recalcitrant, their developmental limitations are being ignored. If the therapist asks, "Why have you been so angry this past week?" or "You've been removed ten times this week from school—what is going on?" most often the children will look puzzled, shrug their shoulders, and wonder why the therapist keeps asking dumb questions. Children may be able to articulate some feelings or motives, but these occasions are the exception rather than the rule.

Children in normal latency have left behind the world of make-believe play in the microsphere for play acting in the macrosphere. As a result, when they come for therapy, they do not play with the toys toward which the younger children immediately gravitate. Yet they cannot sit and actively verbalize their difficulties either, so they tend to engage the therapist in table games, such as cards or checkers. The therapist can play these games occasionally, but an active effort should be made to get the children to return to earlier modes of play and to reveal their fantasies. The therapist should encourage them to draw, paint, or sculpt or to work with clay or engage in other creative, expressive activities that will allow a window into their inner life.

Most violent children referred for therapy missed the opportunity for mastering play at earlier periods. The therapist's active support for make-believe drawings may eventually result in the children's leaving the table and spending more and more time with the miniature-world toys left in the therapy room "for younger children" in spite of their initial reluctance to engage in such "baby" play. In fact, the more disturbed the child, the more he or she should be encouraged to play in the microsphere, and drawing is one way to do so. Almost all children will draw if the therapist is gently persistent. If the therapist gets out some paper, pencils, or crayons and begins to draw, most children will follow suit. The most reluctant or fearful will copy the therapist's drawings, but eventually they will draw their own creations. The therapist who constantly builds models or plays table games with the child is not likely to be of much help. The disturbed latency-age child should be viewed as a child who needs to engage in "playful talk" rather than as "too old to play, too young to talk," and drawing is a way to begin this process. In some rare exceptions, as was the case with Antonio, presented in chapter 2, a child can actively resist such play, and model building or table games may have to be played for long periods. But others quickly concretize their fears in their drawings.

Drawings are initiated by asking the child, "Is there a drawing or a picture you would like to make?" Most children seize the initiative and pick something they like to draw, typically enjoying the sense of control felt when they can make choices. Children should be encouraged to keep each drawing they make in a folder that remains in a locked file in the therapy room. Keeping the drawings enables comparison of earlier with later drawings in order to trace patterns and themes over time. Each therapy session is initiated by asking the child to draw something of his or her choosing. After the child has made a number of drawings, patterns and themes can be traced over time. Most children initially draw benign scenes of nature, flowers, animals, or favorite objects, like Play Station 2. If the child does draw something emotionally revealing, it takes on added significance.

It is especially striking when a child spontaneously draws a trauma event. Memories tend to be stored by intensity rather than by temporal sequence, so at times a child may reveal painful or scary material in early drawings. Such events, however, are not a good sign as they suggest inadequate development of defense mechanisms. Usually children inhibit such material in early drawings, revealing concerns only after formation of a strong therapeutic alliance. The child who is dominated by intrusive memories of past trauma and who expresses them in a spontaneous drawing early in treatment should be assisted to develop defensive strategies.

With such a child, the therapist should switch from evocative drawings to neutral tasks or ask the child to think about something pleasurable or about something the child likes to do. The therapist can ask, "If thinking about or remembering what happened to you becomes too upsetting or scary, what can you do to help yourself feel calmer, safer, or less afraid? Have you found ways before to make yourself less upset? If so, you can use them here."

A metaphor suggested by Mills and Crowley (1986) is a photograph album. The child is told, "Let's think what it's like for you when you look at a photograph album. You may come to a picture that makes you particularly sad or upset. If so, you can put the album back on the shelf or in a dresser and close the drawer. Then, later on, you may decide to take it out again and look at it at a time that is more comfortable for you. So in therapy, when you come to something that is just too upsetting to look at, we will put it away, put it on the shelf, until you are ready." This analogy models binding and compartmentalizing defenses and enables the child to "put away" material that is too painful to face at the moment. The analogy also gives the child permission to do so. Children can also use one of the calming techniques discussed in chapter 9.

Respecting and honoring each child's defenses and pace in therapy avoids or reduces crises, some of which can retraumatize the child. Young and inexperienced therapists, seeking validation of their skills, are prone to "push" children according to the therapists' needs rather than the children's.

Spontaneous drawings are a tool with which to gather data and to formulate tentative hypotheses about a child's inner life, thoughts, conflicts, fears, anger, dreams, and hopes. Our approach to understanding and interpreting drawings follows the guidelines proposed by Klorer (2000) for understanding artwork and Bonime (1962, 1989) for understanding dreams. The approach is a collaborative one, with the meaning of symbols kept within the context of the child and with no assumptions that universal meanings for symbols exist.

Betty, a nine-year-old, told the following story to her drawing of a pumpkin, a witch, and a girl, a spontaneous drawing she made in a therapy session several weeks before Halloween:

> BETTY: A girl and a cat pumpkin with a black light inside. She's got whiskery hands like cats do. The figure on the right is Grandma from the TV program *The Addams Family*. She's got pointy fingers. The pumpkin is their cousin, and they don't like her 'cause she's mean. The blood dripping is from her loose tooth that came out when she yelled. No, I'll make this red orange juice. She was sitting on a chair in the kitchen, and the pumpkin came in and scared her and she yelled and forgot about the glass of orange juice she had there, and it spilled. The pumpkin has points on his hands.

Over the course of several months, each of her spontaneous drawings contained threatening figures with "pointy fingers." Early drawings and stories to the drawings were quite chaotic but seemed more organized and recognizable as the therapist continued to reflect the feelings he thought lay behind each verbal and written expression. A later story to a drawing of a one-eyed monster is more revealing than earlier stories:

> BETTY: She has all red hair, her chin is blue, and she has one eye. Her hands are like witches' hands. They're no good either. And one day she was dripping blood out of them because she killed Wednesday. She scratched Wednesday and then killed her.
> THERAPIST: Why?
> BETTY: Because Wednesday was her daughter, but she didn't like Wednesday 'cause she played with the little boy in *The Addams Family* and she was supposed to play with Mama and not with anybody else. But she never did play with Mama 'cause Mama told her not to.

After a year in treatment, Betty realized that her initial preoccupation with pointy fingers, and later with long fingernails, was a screen memory of part of a sequence of abusive interactions with her mother when she was a toddler. Her mother, a prostitute who kept her fingernails long and polished red, scratched her when angered. She also would bend over the crib at night and threaten to scratch Betty if Betty bothered her during the night. Betty's drawings also reveal that, while children may draw characters and events from television shows or movies, they project their own feelings, fears, and thoughts onto the popular characters. After release of the movie *The Lion King*, in which loss was a featured theme, many children in therapy drew scenes from the movie but modified them in keeping with their own needs. Therapists familiar with the film had no trouble spotting these reconstructions.

Jennifer, an eight-year-old suspected of being sexually abused as a preschooler, told the following story to her drawings:

> JENNIFER: Mrs. Jones says, "My poor little Sara. She's been dead, but I can't help her 'cause she's dead." Mr. Jones came and said, "You killed Sara." Mrs. Jones laughed, "Ha, Ha, I killed her with my own bare hands because she lied."
> THERAPIST: What did she lie about?
> JENNIFER: She lied in bed. And I put my bare hands on her and she is dead. I touched her and she died. And Mama came and said, "You witch, you killed Sara." But Sara was not really dead; she was in the attic playing with her yo-yo. And she called Sara three times, and Sara reappeared and was walking toward her mother and said, "Yes, Mother." Sara was a bat. She didn't have no hands. She said "Yes, Mama." Sara has a big knife. She's going to kill her mother.
> THERAPIST: Sara wasn't really dead?
> JENNIFER: Nope. She put a dummy in her bed that looked like her and then went up into the attic. She killed her mother and is now the queen of the house.
> THERAPIST: Sara is glad her mother is dead?

JENNIFER: Yes, because her mother was wicked. And the husband is mad. He stays up in the attic all day long. And then Sara got married to Mr. Jones. [*Takes another sheet of paper and continues.*] Here's the wedding [*Draws a bridal couple.*].

THERAPIST: Sara married her father?

JENNIFER: Yup! Even though her father didn't want to get married, he married to her!

THERAPIST: How come he did what he didn't want to do?

JENNIFER: She forced him. He told nobody about it. Here's Sara's long black hair and some flowers, and here's Mr. Jones. He has long orange hair.

THERAPIST: Have you ever known anyone who has orange hair?

JENNIFER: I don't know. Here's the alligator that Mama plays with. She wrestles with an alligator and the alligator is in the wedding. He's holding the ring for them. He puts the diamond ring on her finger. Then you know what happened? When he put his hand around her, the alligator came over and opened his mouth wide, took his teeth, and bit her, and she died. Now Sara's dead, and Mr. Jones killed her, and now he has her crown.

THERAPIST: I thought the alligator killed Sara.

JENNIFER: But Mr. Jones sent the alligator to kill her.

Both Betty's and Jennifer's stories revealed the tremendous confusion each child experienced. Both try to comprehend their experiences, but they cannot because the experiences made no sense to them when they happened. The stories also reveal confusion about what each child did to get abused. The mother did not like Wednesday because she played with a boy rather than with her, but her mother also told Wednesday not to play with her either. Most likely, Betty was abused at the mother's whim rather than for her actual misbehavior. Children try to make sense out of parental behavior and would rather be "bad" children than have a bad mother.

Jennifer's stories reveal the anger that sexually abused children often feel toward their mother as well as their developing concepts of sexuality. Jennifer related sex with marriage. The abused must marry the abuser. She also reversed roles. She made the abuser marry her and "he told nobody about it." Also notice that when the therapist asked "Have you ever known anyone who has orange hair?" she stopped communicating within the metaphor. He should have asked her, "Who does Sara know who has orange hair?" Jennifer's answer of "I don't know," followed by the introduction of the orally aggressive alligator, suggests that the direct question raised her anxiety, and her fantasy productions regressed in response. Children's fantasy stories to drawings (and their play behaviors) are efforts to keep distance between themselves and the feared experiences. When they lose this distance, anxiety is aroused.

Both Betty's and Jennifer's stories also illustrate that related remembrances of the past are stories because they are created from the present. Jennifer's stories are quite different from those she might have told to drawings made at an earlier age. At each stage in Jennifer's development, she attempted to integrate into her personality the "unintegratable" experience of being sexually abused. With increasing knowledge about sexuality, she will attempt to reinterpret her earlier experience. Since this experience is partially repressed, her efforts are directed at handling the screen memories of this experience rather than the repressed experience itself. In some sense, Jennifer's personality is organized around a traumatic experience. But these organizational efforts are directed at only parts of the experience, and often these parts are kept separate. For this reason, we use the term *deviant mental organization* to label the functioning of abused clients. As Jennifer's thoughts become less disturbing in response to the therapist's interventions, she may actually reinterpret her experience in light of her developing relationship with the therapist. She may see traits in her past abuser that she didn't see formerly. She may remember him differently.

Both Betty's and Jennifer's drawings were made spontaneously. In fact, neither had to be encouraged to draw. Both went right to the drawing table immediately after entering the therapy room, often expanding on a theme they had begun in earlier sessions. But other children may need a little push to draw. While they can be asked to draw anything that comes into their minds, they can also be asked to draw specific situations that the therapist thinks will help them to approach a forbidden topic. Just as a therapist might select certain toys to stimulate trauma-related play, the therapist can ask a child to draw about a theme closely related to a past trauma, to actions that might be reenactments of trauma-related experiences (pieces of the trauma), to anxiety reactions to objects or events that might be reminders of the trauma, or to objects that might symbolize aspects of the traumatic experience.

Charles Sarnoff (1987) presents an example of a boy who felt compelled to look at smokestacks through binoculars. When asked to draw a picture of smokestacks, he indicated that there was something behind the smokestacks that he wished to see. Sarnoff then suggested that the child make clay figures of the smokestack. He made one with a hole in the base. The boy said that snakes went into the hole and he needed to watch them. He said that if his younger brother could see the stack, he would say it looked like a penis. Two years earlier, the child had penile surgery to correct a congenital deformity. Whatever residual memory he had of his response to the surgery was now part of his compulsion, or fear fantasy, involving smokestacks. First drawing and then modeling with clay helped the child deal more effectively with the feelings associated with this traumatic experience.

In the next chapter, we present some specific drawing techniques designed to uncover feelings whose expression is a step toward helping children to understand why their feelings dictate so much of their current behavior.

• *13* •

Windows into the Inner World: Specific Drawing Techniques

The specific drawing techniques introduced in this chapter are the Boat in the Storm, Family Doing Something Together, A Safe Place, Color Your Life, The Magic Key, Your Place, The Problem, and The Worst Experience of Your Life.

*I*n this chapter, we introduce a series of drawing techniques directed primarily at uncovering general attitudes about life. They can be used with children on the coping track. The drawings stimulate discussion of significant issues, but their chief purpose is not to stimulate trauma-related ideation. In selected cases, some can be used in the initial stages of uncovering work with children on the invitational track. The drawing and art techniques, called the Projective Drawing Series (Crenshaw and Foreacre 2001), help therapists to understand the child's internal world, much of which is outside the child's awareness. Again, we emphasize the importance of creating a safe place and a trusting relationship when exploring the child's inner life. Pursuit of the child's thoughts, feelings, and intentions can provoke significant anxiety, and any uncovering should be delayed until the child feels safe and cared about.

Drawing and artwork tend to reduce anxiety because they are usually enjoyable activities. Some children, however, are self-conscious about their artistic skills, and others are threatened after realizing they have unmasked their private thoughts, feelings, and impulses. The therapist can titrate the level of threat by selecting less threatening drawings in the early stages or by setting aside drawings and working on the therapeutic relationship while strengthening the child's defense mechanisms.

BOAT IN THE STORM

Violet Oaklander (1988), a Gestalt therapist, first described the strategy. The child is told a story about a boat caught in an ocean storm. Waves toss the boat about, and strong winds and lightning make the storm look intense. The storm finally subsides, and the boat makes it to a safe harbor. In an effort to get the child to identify with the boat, he or she is asked to "imagine what it must be like for the boat in the storm." This request is followed with questions such as these: If the boat could have feelings, what might it feel? If the boat could talk, what would it say? What does the boat do to take care of itself in the storm? Is the boat all alone, or does someone come along to help it? The child is then asked to draw a picture of a boat in a storm and, after its completion, is questioned about the drawing.

Many children ignore the ending of the story read to them. Instead of the boat reaching a safe harbor, it invariably sinks or breaks apart. Invariably the boat feels really scared and all alone. No one comes to help. A variation of this theme, reflecting the frequent experience of betrayal in their lives, is that another boat comes to help, but it turns out to be a trick. Often a child puts himself or herself in the boat before it sinks to the bottom. The drowning portrays the failure of distancing. Instead of staying within the metaphor, and allowing only the boat to sink, the child goes down with the boat. The drowning expresses hopelessness, vulnerability, impending doom, and a foreshortened future, feelings typical of many traumatized children. In one instance, a child depicted the boat surviving the storm, but then, from nowhere, a fighter jet arrived and blew the boat out of the water. Drawing can reflect not only a child's exposure to violence and trauma but also the poverty and deprivation suffered by the family in their uphill struggle against the odds. "Just when good things are expected, the car breaks down, Dad gets arrested, Mom loses her job, or you get blown right out of the water."

A child's "emotional pulse" at different stages in the treatment process can be assessed by examining drawings. The therapist can see how emotionally secure or, by contrast, how insecure, threatened, and vulnerable a child is at a given time. Three drawings by one child are reproduced in figures 13.1, 13.2, and 13.3.

The first drawing was completed early in treatment, the second at the midpoint of therapy, and the third near termination of therapy. The first two drawings picture a boat surviving but besieged and in turbulent waters, and the third vividly expresses a sense of calm and stability and the passing of the storm. Since children usually can't tell us directly about their inner emotional states, drawings help them to communicate their internal life. The drawing of another child appears in figure 13.4; when the drawing was complete, the following dialogue ensued.

Figure 13.1.   Boat in Storm Serial Drawings

Figure 13.2.   Boat in Storm Serial Drawings

Figure 13.3.   Boat in Storm Serial Drawings

Figure 13.4.   Boat in Storm Drawing

THERAPIST: Tell me about your picture.

JASON: Well, these are the storm clouds and the lightning up here and the waves down here. The water is about up to deck of the boat.

THERAPIST: Tell me about the boat.

JASON: It is made out of wood. This is the cabin [*pointing to the door and windows of the cabin*].

THERAPIST: Who are the people on the boat?

JASON: This is the captain steering the boat. The rest are crew.

THERAPIST: Are you on the boat?

JASON: Nope.

THERAPIST: Was the boat expecting the storm? Did it prepare for the storm, or was it taken by surprise?

JASON: It wasn't ready.

THERAPIST: The lightning looks very close to the boat. What is going to happen to the boat?

JASON: I don't know.

THERAPIST: Do you think the boat is well enough equipped to make it through the storm? Will it make it to the safe harbor?

JASON: I guess. I don't know.

THERAPIST: What do you imagine that boat must be feeling?

JASON: Pretty scared, I bet!

THERAPIST: I have a hunch you are right about that. It looks like a bad storm. That lightning looks fierce. It must be very scary not to know if you're going to make it through the storm and find that safe harbor [*empathetic interpretation within the metaphor*]. I wonder if the boat is stronger than it realizes [*an attention statement*]. The boat looks quite strong and well built to me. I notice that even with the crashing waves and the churned-up water, it still stands upright in the water. It doesn't tilt to the side. [*All three remarks are attention statements.*] I believe it may be a lot stronger and better prepared for this storm than it thought [*a reductive statement*]. What do you think about that?

JASON: Could be.

The therapist honored the hidden strengths of Jason. His drawing symbolizes strength because the boat is well built and steady in the water in spite of the storm. The lightning is severe and close, but it does not hit the boat. A captain and his crew skillfully pilot the boat. The drawing, and Jason's responses to the therapist's inquiries, reveal an interplay of healthy and unhealthy elements. The story is told within the metaphor of the boat, and the questions remained framed within the metaphor. Jason's insertion of the captain and crew could be his failure to distance, but the defense doesn't fail completely because he didn't put himself on the boat.

Children who feel vulnerable and threatened often put themselves on the boat. Jason's boat is well constructed and reflects inner strength and stability in the face of the storm, although Jason is not consciously aware of these personal resources. The captain and crew of the boat may represent attachments that can be potentially helpful to him. Nevertheless, his inability to decide the boat's fate and his disregard of the story's ending (the boat makes it to a safe harbor) imply a shaky and uncertain trust in these attachment figures. His depiction of a strong boat and helpful crew, but an uncertain outcome, may reflect ambivalence about his future.

Hardy (2003) stresses that the survival orientation of many low-income families precludes a long-term view of life. They are unwilling to adopt a hopeful outlook because it makes them vulnerable to further disappointment. For Jason, rocked by multiple losses, economic hardship, oppression, and violence, hope can be dangerous. Jason's early dreams and aspirations have already been shattered.

The therapist remained within the metaphor of the boat when validating Jason's feelings: "It must be very scary not to know if you're going to make it through the storm and find that safe harbor." Likewise, by highlighting the strengths outside of Jason's awareness, the therapist also communicated, through the metaphor of the boat, "I believe it may be a lot stronger and better prepared for this storm than it thought." Jason's response of "Could be" reflected his insecurity. The therapist stayed within the metaphor because Jason's anxiety level was high (as implied by how fierce and close to the boat the lightning was). The therapist knew that Jason could only hear and incorporate interpretative comments when they were offered within the context of the symbolism. Jason could then respond regarding the boat's fate rather than his own fate when faced with the turbulence in his own life.

Spontaneous drawings can sometimes lead to the same information. Cohen (1980, 1990) presents the case of Andrew, who spontaneously drew a large boat waiting to sail at a dock. The boat was named after his mother, who actually left him and went overseas, never to return. Nevertheless, the boat stayed at the dock, and a child on a raft drifted out to sea, where he was repeatedly threatened by sharks and enemy submarines, from which he was saved only on occasion.

FAMILY DOING SOMETHING TOGETHER

The child is asked to draw his or her "whole family doing something together." The authors follow the guidelines of Hobday and Ollier (1999) who suggest writing a caption on the picture or on another sheet of paper. They also suggest some inquiries, such as "Who in your family is the strongest?"

Children in gorilla suits often experience difficulty drawing family members engaged in activities together, frequently drawing the mother cooking, the father in the yard, and themselves watching television. People who are not family members are also depicted, and the drawing quickly becomes dominated by other themes. Because of the potent issues of abandonment, disconnection, and sometimes abuse, this particular drawing task can trigger intrusive memories from the child's traumatic past. Larry's drawing in figure 13.5 illustrates his inner turmoil.

> THERAPIST: Can you tell me about your drawing?
>
> LARRY: Whew! Well. [*long pause*] That's my dad yelling "Come back here!" My mom is trying to stop him because he is going for his belt [*the object lying at bottom center of the picture*], and she is saying "Oh no!" That's me, trying to run away, and I'm yelling "Oh no!"
>
> THERAPIST: Your mother was trying to protect you.
>
> LARRY: Yeah, but she couldn't. He just pushed her down and came after me.
>
> THERAPIST: That must have been really scary, but that was a long time ago [*empathetic reflection and clarification*]. Do you feel safe now?
>
> LARRY: Yes, except when I think of Dad getting out of jail. Then I get really scared.
>
> THERAPIST: When you think of Dad getting out of jail, what can you do then to help yourself feel calmer and safer [*facilitation of self-calming*].
>
> LARRY: I try to get my mind off of it, but it doesn't work most times.
>
> THERAPIST: Of the different things you've tried, what seems to work the best to help you feel calmer and safer when you are really scared.
>
> LARRY: I guess going out to shoot hoops with my [*foster*] dad.
>
> THERAPIST: Good! So you feel safe when you are with your foster dad?
>
> LARRY: Yeah!
>
> THERAPIST: I'm so glad that you feel safe when your foster dad is with you. Okay, so that would be your first choice. Now let's say your foster dad is not home. What could you do that would help you feel safe when you get really scared?
>
> LARRY: I [*long pause*] don't know. I can't think of anything.
>
> THERAPIST: Let's see if we can come up with something. We can practice it here in the session. Then you can practice it at home and have more options for making yourself calm and feeling safe. Is there any music you especially enjoy and that helps you to feel relaxed and comfortable?
>
> LARRY: I'm not sure. [*long pause*] I guess mostly I like country music, but the song "Tears from Heaven" is my favorite.
>
> THERAPIST: Do you know the words to the song?
>
> LARRY: I sure do.
>
> THERAPIST: When you listen to "Tears from Heaven," does it relax you and make you feel comfortable and safe?
>
> LARRY: Not really. It makes me sad.
>
> THERAPIST: Let's see if you can come up with something, if not mu-

Figure 13.5.   Family Doing Something Drawing

sic, maybe a movie, a TV show that makes you relaxed, calm, and safe, or maybe a place that you can go to in your mind that makes you feel really peaceful, calm, and safe.

LARRY: There is a place where my [*foster*] dad and I went hiking once, and it was so peaceful and calm.

THERAPIST: Try to get a clear picture in your mind of that peaceful place. Then go there in your mind and describe to me what you see. Maybe it would help if we could do some "wave breathing" together just to relax and to get comfortable. Let's do it together. We will take three deep breaths together. Let's fill our lungs up with air and then let it out, and as you do, just feel your whole body completely relax. The tension just flows right out of your body from your head down to your toes. [*Therapist and Larry take a deep breath.*] Let's do it again. And once more. There, do you notice just how much more relaxed you feel?

LARRY: Yup! I think I'll just go to sleep.

THERAPIST: Don't go to sleep. I need your help to find ways for you to feel safe and comfortable, but not quite that comfortable. Now go to the place that makes you feel so peaceful. When you have it clearly in mind, as if you were really there, tell me about it.

LARRY: We were hiking up this mountain, and we were bone tired. I didn't think I could go much farther. Then we came to this flat place and a bunch of pine trees. We sat on a big rock under the shade of those trees. It was so quiet. I felt really safe.

THERAPIST: Just stay there for a while, under the shade of those pine trees. Enjoy the warm, pleasant feelings of being there with Joe [*Larry's foster father*]. Enjoy feeling safe, peaceful, and calm. Notice how you feel, and hold on to those nice, calm, peaceful feelings. I'm going to just be quiet and relax with you. In a few minutes we will stop for the day, but for now let's just picture being on top of that mountain, calm and peaceful.

Larry, who had been repeatedly abused, both physically and sexually, by his biological father, immediately drew a traumatic event. Furthermore, he was quite anxious, even trembling at times. As a result, Larry's therapy was switched to the coping track. His ego resources and coping strategies were severely compromised, not only by the past trauma, but by the current threat that his dad was soon to be released from prison. Pelcovitz's (1999) comment is worth repeating. Treating children of domestic violence who remain in the violent family is akin to "treating [post-traumatic stress disorder] in the midst of a hurricane." As a result, the therapist focused persistently on how to counteract the threat and anxiety by focusing on ways to self-calm and to promote a sense of safety.

While it may be tempting to explore Larry's choice of "Tears from Heaven" as his favorite song, it would have been inappropriate to do so and perhaps even damaging, as Larry was feeling vulnerable, unsafe, and anxious. Larry might be drawn to this song, a sad one indeed, because Eric Clapton wrote it as a tribute to his own young son who died tragically—a highly moving expression of profound loss and longing for reunion. Larry's attraction to the song might reflect his longed-for closeness with a father he never had, a longing that can be filled only in an afterlife. The tragic death of Clapton's son might have captured Larry's imagination and his emotional investment because of his own unsafe feelings. Does his ability to feel sad suggest a capacity for empathy with the pain of others? All of these are interesting speculations, but therapy is about the needs of the client, not the curiosity of the therapist. Larry needed to develop coping skills to calm and soothe himself in order to counteract the intense fear and anxiety that accompanied thoughts about his father.

Children's drawings of their family doing something together often yield some surprising information not obvious from the drawings themselves. Dr. Mordock once saw a troubled six-year-old who drew a picture of her mother in the kitchen and her father and herself playing together in the living room. As a father active in his two daughters' lives, Dr. Mordock saw nothing revealing in this particular picture. But after the daughter showed it to her mother, who queried her about the session, the irate mother called and wanted her own appointment. She complained bitterly that ever since her daughter's birth, her husband spent more time with the girl than with her and that she bitterly resented her daughter, whom she depicted as "a little flirt." Further evaluation revealed the mother's immaturity and strong dependency needs and also revealed the father-daughter relationship to be a healthy one. The mother saw her daughter as a "flirt" so she could blame her and not her husband for the situation.

A SAFE PLACE

Children are asked to either draw or describe a "safe place" for them. Since many children in gorilla suits have not experienced a protected childhood, and their sense of safety and security in the world has been shattered, many of them are unable to describe or draw a "safe place." Nor can they even imagine one. They can't visualize any place in the world where they would feel safe. Others start to draw their vision of a safe place, but the place is invaded by some threatening, scary, or evil force that decimates what was intended to be a place of refuge for the child. We discuss the use of this drawing when presenting calming techniques in chapter 9.

Make a picture of a safe place you can go when you need to be calm, safe, and peaceful. It could be a place you've been or a place you make up. Most important . . . It's your safe place.

. . . you can go there when you need to.

Figure 13.6.   Safe Place Drawing

In figure 13.6, Willie, a seven-year-old boy who witnessed a severe assault on his mother by his father, drew a shed that houses the stray cats he likes to take care of. It also provides him refuge from parental conflict that is too much for him to bear.

> THERAPIST: When do you go to your safe place?
>
> WILLIE: I go there every day after school to see if any more cats have shown up. Mom gives me dry food to put out for them.
>
> THERAPIST: Do you go any other time?
>
> WILLIE: I go there when the fights between Mom and Dad are really bad.
>
> THERAPIST: Do your parents know that you go there in order to feel safe?
>
> WILLIE: I don't know. Mom knows I go there. When they're fighting, I don't think they pay too much attention. Sometimes they tell me to stay out of it, go outside, or go to my room.
>
> THERAPIST: Do you feel completely safe when you are in your shed with your cats?
>
> WILLIE: Most of the time, but sometimes they scream really loud and I'm afraid he will hurt Mom if he has been drinking lots.
>
> THERAPIST: What would you do if you thought your mom was being hurt?
>
> WILLIE: I would run to our neighbor and call my uncle. He came over last week and took Mom to the hospital.
>
> THERAPIST: That must have been very scary for you. Were you afraid that your mother was badly hurt?
>
> WILLIE: Oh yeah! She had a bloody nose and there was blood all over the place.
>
> THERAPIST: Have you talked over with anybody what to do if you couldn't reach your uncle?
>
> WILLIE: No, I don't want to call 911. I don't want Dad to go to jail. He is always sorry after they calm down. He doesn't mean to hurt anybody.
>
> THERAPIST: You are in a tough spot, Willie. I don't think a seven-year-old boy should be carrying such a heavy load [*empathetic interpretation*]. These are hard decisions for a little boy like you to have to make about how to deal with an emergency. Whom do I call? Do I call the police? If I do, will my father be arrested? How about I meet with your parents to talk about a safety plan that they can agree to, and then we will have a session with you and tell you what the plan is, but I think this is something for the grown-ups to work out.
>
> WILLIE: Okay.

COLOR YOUR LIFE

This projective drawing, developed by Kevin O'Connor (1983), requires children to pair feelings with colors that, in our culture, are frequently associated with a specific affect, such as red for anger, blue for sad, and yellow for happy. Then they are told, "Imagine that this blank sheet of paper represents your whole life up to this point. Color the page according to how much you have felt each of the feelings." This technique allows children to share inner feelings they find difficult, if not impossible, to share directly. The technique enables young children to express pain, sorrow, and rage since no words are required. It can help the therapist get a reading on the child's current emotional state.

The manner in which the child's artwork is processed depends on the therapist's judgment as to what the child can handle at a given point in treatment. If the goal is to confront traumatic events or painful affect and to address the deeper emotional roots of the aggression, the feelings manifested in the Color Your Life drawing would be pursued intensively. Interpretation, if appropriate, would follow the guidelines proposed in chapter 10. The interpretative techniques discussed in chapter 11, however, must await further strides in development. In the initial stages of therapy, gorilla-suit wearers usually misperceive interpretations as massive criticism or even rejection. If the child is on the coping track, efforts are directed at improving coping skills and strengthening defenses to help the child keep in check the strong feelings that are displayed in artistic productions.

Richard was an eleven-year-old whose Color Your Life drawing (figure 13.7) demonstrated he had sufficient ego strengths to undertake extensive exploration of the feelings revealed.

Richard's father left Richard's inept mother and two younger siblings when Richard was three. The father was a violent man, and when Richard made this picture, the father hadn't seen his children in more than five years. The one person who represented a stable attachment figure in Richard's life, his grandfather, died when Richard was nine. The boy's aggression escalated, and he was suspended from school for hitting a teacher shortly after his grandfather's death.

> THERAPIST: I see quite a mix of feelings in your picture. I see quite a lot of yellow for happy and about the same amount, although slightly more, red for worried. Can you tell me more about that? When you think about your life, were happy and worried each felt for about the same amount of time?
> RICHARD: I guess so. I don't know what to say about it.
> THERAPIST: Tell me about the happy times. It looks like [*points to the yellow colored area of the page*] the happy feelings are something you have experienced more than any other feeling except worried. Tell me about a time that stands out as a really happy time in your life.
> RICHARD: Maybe before my grandfather died. He used to take me fishing a lot. We also liked watching football and baseball games together on TV. He would come to all of my games. My grandmother would make us popcorn.

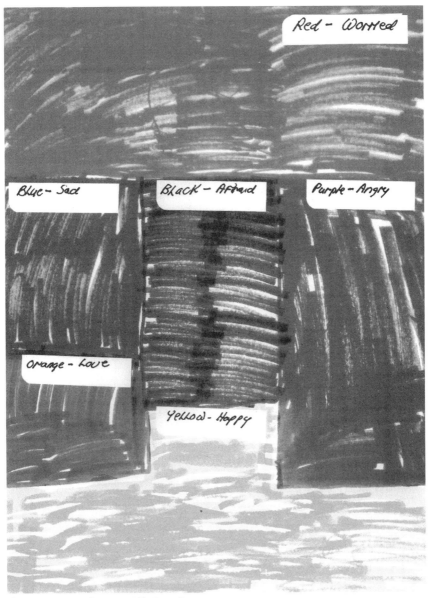

Figure 13.7.   Color Your Life Drawing

THERAPIST: Your grandfather's death was a huge loss for you [*empathetic interpretation*]. It sounds like you spent a lot of time together and he was very special to you and you to him. I bet you really miss him [*empathetic interpretation*]. I see quite a bit of blue for sad, black for afraid, and purple for anger. Is that the sadness and anger that you feel about losing your grandfather?

RICHARD: Nothing has been the same since that happened. My grandmother is always in a bad mood, doesn't want to keep living. My mom can't handle things. Grandpa was the one that stepped in and took care of things. I wouldn't be getting into so much trouble if he were still around.

THERAPIST: How about black for afraid?

RICHARD: Mom and grandma are falling apart. I don't know what's going to happen!

THERAPIST: I bet that's scary [*an empathetic interpretation*]. Grandpa kind of held everything together [*a reductive statement*]. Is there any way that you feel your grandfather is still around? Some kids tell me that after a loved one dies with whom they were close, even though the actual, physical person no longer exists, they still feel the closeness, the attachment, the connection with the loved person [*a refection of a universal feeling*]. Does that make any sense to you?

RICHARD: Sounds kind of weird. I don't know.

THERAPIST: Since your grandpa died, have there been any times when you have said to yourself, "I wonder what grandpa would say or what he would want me to do in this situation?"

RICHARD: Yeah, lots of times. I kinda talk to him every day.

THERAPIST: Since you knew him so well and you were so close, can you pretty much imagine what he would say or advise you to do in a difficult situation?

RICHARD: Sure can.

THERAPIST: When someone we love dies, we no longer have that physical person in our life that we can touch and hold and hug, but the attachment is timeless. It goes on. We don't have to let that go. Your grandpa's influence can be kept very much alive in you because your connection with him is something you can keep and treasure forever [*clarification of a feeling*].

RICHARD: Yeah, I guess you're right. I never thought about it that way.

THERAPIST: What do you think your grandpa would say to you about the situation you are in right now?

RICHARD: Oh wow! He would probably say, "Richard, what the hell were you thinking when you hit the teacher. You're smarter than that. Use your head."

THERAPIST: It seems to me that although you miss him terribly, in some very important ways you still have your grandpa here with you in your heart and mind!

This therapeutic exchange was the result of exploring some of the paired colors and emotions in the Color Your Life drawing. Richard's rage and anger were also depicted in the artistic representation by the significant amounts of purple, along with considerable worry represented by the color red. The feelings were also explored in depth in the therapeutic dialogue. The dialogue illustrates the usefulness of such tools and their value as a springboard to understanding and talking about the powerful affects that dominate the inner lives of children in gorilla suits.

What some therapists view as resistance is actually inadequate capacity to identify feelings, formulate them into words, and express them coherently. Cognitive limitations make this task especially difficult for young children. As children get older, their expressive skill increases, but emotions can still block verbal expression of feelings. From an early age, males receive cultural messages that invite binding and compartmentalization of feelings. Messages such as "Get over it!" "Be a man!" and "Pull yourself up by your bootstraps!" lead to disconnection from affective life. Girls, unless they act out like boys, are usually ignored if they are quiet and withdrawn; they are just being "good girls" (Hardy 2003). Children traumatized by violence and extreme poverty aren't likely to access feelings associated with the trauma because those feelings interfere with survival. Sometimes they are simply too painful. The self-anesthesia that occurs in older children and adolescents in self-cutting (which causes them to go numb) or in alcohol or drug abuse (which provides "novocaine" for the pain) reflects their underlying pain.

Consequently, the tools offered in this chapter not only allow therapists to understand what makes children in gorilla suits "tick"; more important, they create opportunities for meaningful connections with the children, as illustrated in Richard's dialogue about the life-changing impact of his grandpa's death. Undoubtedly, abandonment by his father, his unapproachable grandmother, and his inadequate and overwhelmed single mother made his grandfather's death all the more devastating. The therapist, through the use of the Color Your Life approach, was able not only to validate Richard's loss through empathetic listening, but also to initiate a process with which Richard could use his memories of his grandfather to help him chart a course through the rough seas of his current life.

THE MAGIC KEY

In this projective drawing, developed by Dr. Crenshaw, the child pretends that he or she has been given a magic key that will open just one door in "The Giant Castle." The castle has many rooms on each floor, and there are four floors in the castle. Children are asked to imagine going from door to door, trying the magic key in each, until they finally find the room that the magic key opens. Since the key is a magic one, the children are told that when they unlock the door and open it, they will see what they always thought would make them happy! Then the children are asked to draw what they see in the room.

Not surprisingly, in today's materialistic world, the children often draw video game consoles or big screen televisions, but some depict longed-for connections, such as a father who left the family years ago. One nine-year-old boy drew his mother, who died when he was three, and his picture is shown in figure 13.8. Most children in gorilla suits typically draw scenes that depict not only the trauma and horror of their lives but also the profound losses that define their emotional lives.

> THERAPIST: Can you tell me about your picture?
>
> JEREMY: It is a picture of my Mom.
>
> THERAPIST: Tell me more about why you chose to draw a picture of your mom. What specific thing did your mom do, above everything else, that you felt would always make you happy?
>
> JEREMY: I don't remember my mom. I wish I did. I have heard a lot of stories about her. I think my life would be happier if I had my mom.
>
> THERAPIST: I can imagine that it is very hard and sad to grow up without your mother [*empathetic interpretation*]. Tell me some of the stories you have been told about your mother.
>
> JEREMY: She was a nurse, and she was kind. She helped lots of people.
>
> THERAPIST: What else have you been told about your mom?
>
> JEREMY: She was funny and made other people laugh.
>
> THERAPIST: How do you think your life would be different if your mom had lived?
>
> JEREMY: I don't think I would've been such a bad kid. I wouldn't have gotten into so much trouble.
>
> THERAPIST: Could it be that what you consider to be a "bad kid" is really your anger about having to grow up without a mom [*dynamic interpretation*]?
>
> JEREMY: Yeah, I guess. I don't know.
>
> THERAPIST: If you are angry that you lost your mom when you were only three and now at nine you can't remember her at all, does that make you a bad kid [*an ignorant interrogator question*]?
>
> JEREMY: I get into a lot of fights and trouble at school.
>
> THERAPIST: What if that is your way of coping with the hurt inside? I have known a lot of kids who put on a gorilla suit to protect themselves from being hurt again [*a dynamic interpretation softened by reflection of a universal feeling*]. They don't want to let other people get too close to them because they might lose those people too, and that would be more hurt than they could bear [*dynamic interpretation*]. Do you think that makes them bad kids [*ignorant interrogator question*]?
>
> JEREMY: I think maybe I like putting the gorilla suit on.

Figure 13.8.   The Magic Key Drawing

THERAPIST: Sure, it protects you [*reductive statement*]. You don't want to be hurt anymore, and I don't blame you [*empathetic interpretation*]. I'm hoping that the day will come when you don't have to put the gorilla suit on so often or maybe not at all. Perhaps you will feel safe and strong enough that you won't need that protection. Or perhaps you will find other ways to protect and take care of yourself that won't get you into trouble. But there is no way that you can convince me that you are a bad kid. After all, you are your mom's kid [*empathetic clarification*].

JEREMY: [*Tears begin to roll down his cheek.*] Yeah, I'm my mom's kid.

Once again, the projective drawing led to both an understanding of the child's underlying emotions and to a potentially healing dialogue about them. More often than not, the children suffer from buried grief they have never talked about with a trusted adult. Their silence is the seed for their symptomatic behavior. Girls are more likely than boys to develop internalizing disorders, such as depression or mood and eating disorders, but as our society changes its notions about women, more girls are being referred for aggressive behaviors, and more are being arrested for violent crimes.

YOUR PLACE

Oaklander (1988) first described the technique of having children "draw your place." The therapist sets the scene by telling a story about a child "climbing a steep hill and upon reaching the top sees an opening to a cave." The child is asked to "pretend that while walking down the corridor of the cave, you see doors on each side of the cave, and each door has a name on it. When you come to a door with your name on it, visualize yourself standing in front of that door and try to picture what is on the other side of it." The child is then told, "It can be anything or anyplace you want it to be. It could contain people, animals, or nobody. It could be a place you have visited or a place you always dreamed of going." The child is then asked to open the door and draw what is inside.

When traumatized children complete this drawing, animals or nature scenes dominate more often than not, and people are in a secondary role or absent altogether. The children's shattered sense of trust makes it hard to include people in a picture of their ideal place. The absence or minimized role of people reflects the betrayal and deep wounds resulting from the children's experiences of abuse and trauma.

THERAPIST: Tell me about your picture.

SHAQUILLA: It is a lonely flower on top of a hill.

Figure 13.9.   Your Place Drawing

THERAPIST: Does anyone come to take care of the flower?

SHAQUILLA: No. I don't think so.

THERAPIST: What will happen to the flower? Will it survive?

SHAQUILLA: No, it is going to die.

THERAPIST: I'm curious. This drawing is "Your Place." It could be anything you want it to be. Yet, you chose to draw a lonely flower on top of the hill—a flower alone on a hill with no one to take care of it so it soon will die. I guess I'm worried that maybe you're feeling lonely and that nobody realizes it [*empathetic interpretation*]. So no one comes to help, and you're afraid you might die [*empathetic interpretation softened by being inflected as a question*]?

SHAQUILLA: I'm alone. No one really cares. I don't care if I live or die.

THERAPIST: Is that because you believe that no one could care about you, so you don't care about yourself? [*A clarification of a feeling, followed by a dynamic interpretation, framed as a question put by an ignorant interrogator.*]

SHAQUILLA: That's all I'm going to say.

THERAPIST: Like the lonely flower on top of the hill, you believe you're all alone [*a reductive statement*]. You don't feel it is safe to trust, so you don't want me to understand how you really feel [*a transference interpretation*]. But I really want to know. It matters to me because you matter to me. I find it very sad that you feel so lonely. It must be awful scary to think that you have no one to help you or anyone who cares about you [*an empathetic interpretation*].

SHAQUILLA: Shut the hell up! I told you I don't want to talk about it.

THERAPIST: I don't take it lightly when a nine-year-old says she doesn't care whether she lives or dies. I don't treat that lightly because to me it's important because you're important. I will not turn my back on you and leave you like that little lonely flower all alone on top of the hill.

SHAQUILLA: Is there something wrong with your hearing? Go to hell!

THERAPIST: You want me to see you as hopeless—as the dying flower—but I see you differently. It is only hopeless if you decide it is hopeless and stop working on making it better [*empathetic confrontation*]. You want me to believe you are just a bad kid. When I look at you, I see an angry kid, but you have good reasons to be angry [*empathetic statements*]. I also know there are times when you are kind to animals. You stick up for little kids and kids who are being picked on. And at times you can be very funny. You make people laugh [*highlighting strengths*]. I don't see a bad kid [*correction of a misconception*].

DRAW THE PROBLEM

When problems take on a specific shape on a piece of paper, they invariably are experienced as more manageable than when they are only in the mind. Asking a child to draw what the problem looks like or, alternatively, what worry, fear,

Figure 13.10.   Draw the Problem

pain, anger, or sadness looks like, can offer the child some relief. The child distances from these feelings by making them an image on a piece of paper. The drawing also promotes objectivity. A problem never looks quite as bad on paper as it does from within one's head. Making such drawings on repeated occasions allows for natural desensitization. The monsters within the child's head are gradually tamed. Mills and Crowley (1986) described a similar drawing procedure to help children deal with physical pain, such as from severe burns.

> THERAPIST: Tell me about your drawing.
> KENNY: Mom is crying and I'm scared.
> THERAPIST: What is happening that Mom is crying and you are scared?
> KENNY: Dad is really pissed!
> THERAPIST: What is going to happen?
> KENNY: He is going to come after me.
> THERAPIST: What will he do?
> KENNY: The belt will come off and he will beat me.
> THERAPIST: No wonder Mom is crying and you are looking scared
> [*empathetic interpretation*].

The exchange above led to a report to Child Protective Services, which investigated and mandated that the father go to a violence prevention/anger management group. In addition, the family was required to seek mental health treatment and training in parental skill. Whether Kenny would have told anyone about his beatings without the stimulus of this drawing is impossible to know, but, once again, when children are given the proper communication tools, they often relate painful, scary, and sensitive matters.

DRAW THE WORST EXPERIENCE OF YOUR LIFE

Careful judgment is called for when using this technique. If a child is ready to confront the most upsetting events of his or her life, then this drawing can be used. Its use should come after the use of other drawing techniques. It is used only with children on the invitational track whose therapeutic relationship has stood the test of time. It should not be used with children on the coping track. In addition, signs that the child is ready and has the inner strength to manage emotional pain should be evident. Variations of this technique include "Draw the scariest thing that ever happened to you" and "Draw the saddest thing that ever happened to you and your family." If a child shows signs of significant anxiety, the therapist should switch to a less threatening instruction, such as "Draw the funniest thing that ever happened to you or your family."

> THERAPIST: Tell me about your drawing.
> CHARLIE: My Dad is furious and is going to hurt me. Mom is running toward me to protect me. Dad just threw this knife at me [*points to bottom center of the picture*].
> THERAPIST: This sounds and looks terrifying [*an empathetic interpretation*]. Are you sure you want to talk about it now? We can put it away and talk about it at some other time if you wish [*inviting binding and compartmentalization*]. If not, I'm ready to listen.
> CHARLIE: Okay. I don't want to talk about it now!
> THERAPIST: I'm glad you related your fears, but now might not be the best time to focus on them [*redirection*].

Although Charlie wasn't ready to face this traumatic memory, he did allow the therapist to store the picture in his folder until he was ready to talk further about it. Charlie's frank depiction of a violent scene reinforces the need for caution when asking children to draw their worst experience. Children who possess sufficient ego strengths may profit from the drawing experience, but the opportunity should be weighed against the risk of activating trauma material before a child is ready to face it. The therapist needs to consider the risk of the child's being flooded by terrifying emotions rooted in the original

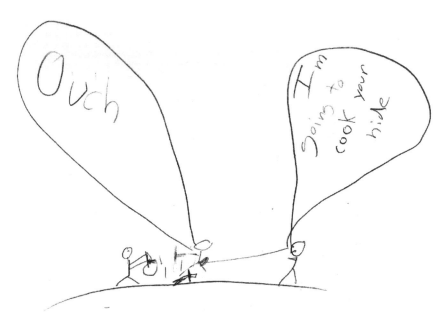

Figure 13.11.   Worst Experience Drawing

trauma events and the possibility of retraumatization if the child's ego resources are insufficient to cope with the activation of such powerful emotions and memories.

While we would never want to minimize the risk of insensitive or poorly conceived or timed interventions in trauma work, we also would not want to underestimate the potential benefits for the child in working through trauma events. When Dr. Crenshaw met with the late Walter Bonime for psychoanalytic supervision, Dr. Bonime would frequently challenge Dr. Crenshaw's concerns about the vulnerability of a particular child, saying that such cautions often amount to giving less to such children when, in fact, they need more. So when a therapist slows down and backs away, it is crucial that the demands of the therapeutic exploration and the pace are being reduced because the child's needs call for such an adjustment rather than because the therapist is becoming anxious or overwhelmed. Walter Bonime pointed out that the therapist's anxiety could result in pulling back at just the point when the child needs the therapist to be fully there. It is very painful and distressing for the therapist to accompany the child through the intense pain, rage, and sorrow that result from trauma exposure and invisible wounds to the child's spirit, but it is in addressing these wounds that healing becomes possible.

One of the most compelling arguments for undertaking the working through of trauma events with children who are able to cope with the emotionally taxing demands of invitational therapy was made by Daniel Siegel (2003), a psychiatrist at UCLA who has done pioneering work in delineating the implications of some of the new findings in neuroscience for therapy. In a presentation at the Psychotherapy Networker Symposium (2003), he discussed the distinction between implicit and explicit memory. Implicit memory consists of memories that are stored in the right hemisphere of the brain and have not been processed in a narrative or autobiographical form and derive from highly emotional and often traumatic experiences that could not be integrated at the time of the event. Implicit memories can be triggered by any reminder of the event, including sensory cues such as sounds, sights, or smells or situational cues, and when implicit memory is activated, there is no sense that one is remembering an event that happened in the past; rather the emotional experience is that it is happening now. Explicit memory processes and integrates memories in a narrative and autobiographical form that allows the person to remember the experience and also reduces the likelihood that its emotions will be triggered by reminders of the original events. If certain reminders trigger explicit memories, the person will have the experience of remembering something that happened in the past, not of reliving it in the present. Siegel (2003) believes that sharing the traumatic events in the context of a safe place and with a person the client has learned to trust allows for implicit memory to move to explicit memory, which is stored in a different part of the brain, the left hemisphere. Thus, the benefits can be enormous and must be considered along with the risks of undertaking exploration of documented trauma experiences in children.

• *14* •

Teaching and Modeling Pro-Social Skills with Special Emphasis on Empathy

Research has revealed that the path to youth violence can be altered by teaching, modeling, and rein-
forcing pro-social behavior and improving social competence. A compelling body of literature indicates
that positive social adjustment in childhood is one of the most powerful predictors of overall adjustment
and competence in adult life. Of all of the social skills, the ability to empathize with the feelings of
others is the most critical for breaking the cycle of violence. Techniques illustrated to teach empathetic
skills are the Empathy Picture and Story Series, the use of film clips, and role-playing.

*S*ocial skills training, when used in conjunction with other techniques, can enhance a child's prospects for successful adjustment. Resilient children have at least one trusting relationship that buffers them from stress-related mental health disorders. Children with better social skills have a greater chance of forming such a relationship. Pro-social skills, especially the ability to empathize, are crucial skills in preventing violence (Fraiberg, Adelson, and Shapiro 1965; Hardy and Laszloffy in press). A number of cognitive behavioral programs teach social skills (see chapter 5).

Social skills training programs should be culturally sensitive. It is a disservice to teach children social skills based on a white, middle-class value system and then send them back more vulnerable to neighborhood violence (Hardy and Laszloffy in press). Therapists must appreciate the survival orientation needed to function in violent communities. Gorilla-suit wearers typically know more about the rules of survival on the street than does the middle-class therapist who has lived a relatively sheltered life.

One valuable skill is discriminating between the times it is appropriate to be soft, tender, and vulnerable and the times it is not. In many situations, children will need protective armor to survive. But the armor cannot be their gorilla suit. A gorilla suit is never helpful because safety usually requires checking aggressive impulses or making a hasty retreat. Nor is it helpful to hide behind a brick wall of detachment. Children need options to aggressive behavior. They need to choose among a number of alternative actions; to learn when to be assertive, when to retreat, and when to disconnect; and to do so in flexible and discerning ways (Hardy and Laszloffy in press; Miller and Stiver 1997).

BECOMING MORE "LIKABLE"

Pro-social behaviors, such as "friendly behavior," should be practiced. The specifics are usually negotiated with the child, but normally the training consists of engaging in a ten-minute friendly conversation with the therapist about family pets, favorite music, or sports. Friendly greetings, such as making compliments and inquiring about others' welfare, are also practiced. Concrete expressions of interest in others can make others more interested in the child. And interest in the child can lead to more meaningful relationships.

APPROPRIATE SELF-ASSERTION

Fox (1994) described the unintended consequences of emphasizing compliance with adult directives in treatment programs for aggressive youth, a phenomenon she labeled "the catastrophe of compliance." Many aggressive children have been harmed by compliance with adult wishes and commands. As a result, children need to know when adults are trustworthy and when they are not. Fox reported that youngsters making the transition from group care to independent living were inept in asserting and protecting their legitimate needs and interests. In an effort to get children to comply with adult rules and program expectations, staff members forget that youngsters should defy the demands and expectations of adults who don't have their best interests at heart. Fox also reported that many youth were unable to assert themselves with peers. Skills need to be taught to enable children to decide when adults are trustworthy and safe and when peers are trying to take advantage of them.

Role-playing situations used for this purpose should begin with nonthreatening exercises in self-assertion and move to ones that provoke considerable anxiety. Examples of relatively nonthreatening role-playing exercises include the following:

- Saying no!—practice is offered in saying "no" to someone who keeps coming back to borrow pencils, clothes, or money;

- Returning a defective CD to a store;
- Refusing to sign on the dotted line with an aggressive salesperson;
- Correcting the waiter or waitress when the order for food is wrong.

In addition to helping children become self-assertive, role-playing exercises allow for practice at managing a variety of social interactions. Immediate feedback, coaching, encouragement, and reinforcement are given to facilitate skill development. If these skills are practiced in a group setting, other group members usually model various alternative actions.

The therapist titrates the level of challenge according to the child's assertive skills, but the level of difficulty remains in a range in which success is ensured. Following early successes, the therapist gradually increases the level of challenge and makes it harder for the child to say "no" in certain situations.

Another technique, learned from Barbara Seebourne, a talented psychodramatist, involves asking children to demonstrate the "wrong way" before attempting to perform the desired skill (Crenshaw 1976). This twist can be quite humorous and disarming, significantly reducing the performance anxiety associated with practicing new skills. Examples of later role-playing exercises include

- Being wrongly accused;
- Getting fired or expelled without being able to explain one's side of the story;
- Being "dumped" by a boyfriend or girlfriend;
- Having a best friend suddenly wanting nothing to do with you;
- Feeling pressured into sex or drugs.

Role-playing scenarios can provoke considerable anxiety when related to the powerful play themes described in chapter 6. Caution needs to be exercised since such themes, especially if a child is feeling vulnerable, can trigger a rage reaction.

When role-playing takes place in a group, two adults should share leadership, and the group should include only three or four members. Unfortunate reactions are more difficult to manage in groups because of group contagion. Dr. Crenshaw treated a child who was triggered into an extreme rage while relating a positive event. His mother and the therapist concluded that some internal stimulus led to the explosive episode since neither saw any lead-up to it.

Over the course of treatment, we discovered the boy's explosiveness was triggered by any kind of withdrawal from him, including people's turning their backs on him. His mother, trying to defuse his temper tantrums, had been walking away, but this action immediately triggered a strong reaction, and he became more agitated and often violent. In thinking back over the session in which he erupted, we realized that just shortly before the explosive episode, he had asked Dr. Crenshaw for a new set of magic markers for a drawing he was making. The author had briefly turned away to look in a cabinet in his desk for the new markers, momentarily turning his back toward the boy.

It is rare for children in individual sessions to lose self-control because the therapist monitors the level of stimulation. Nevertheless, the therapist has no control over internal stimuli, such as an abuse or trauma memory, that gets triggered by a sensory-motor reminder of the terrifying event.

THE IMPORTANCE OF EMPATHY

The capacity for empathy increases as the child develops the cognitive ability to take another's perspective and gains a greater appreciation, awareness, and understanding of the affective experience of self and others. Yet the capacity emerges early in childhood: preschool children often comfort each other on the playground when one is hurt, either physically or emotionally. Appreciating the pain of others first requires acknowledging and facing one's own pain. Children wearing gorilla suits are usually out of touch with their own internal suffering. To get in touch requires giving up the numbed, detached, anesthetized stance they have taken in regard to their own affective lives. With severely traumatized children, facing their own pain requires extraordinary courage and a readiness to face the full impact of the results. Children can be haunted by the questions, "Will the patient survive the operation?" and "Is the cure worse than the disease?" Giving up strategies of disconnection that have ensured survival requires enormous courage (Jordan 2003).

The Empathy Picture and Story Series

The Empathy Picture and Story Series, developed in collaboration with art therapist Pam Garritt, can be used to develop empathetic skills. The pictures are presented in a graduated sequence. The early pictures require the child to simply state or write in a cartoon bubble, placed next to the pictured animal, child, or adult, what they imagine, on the basis of facial expressions and contextual cues, the depicted animal or person is feeling. Children on the coping track may be asked only to identify the feelings of the pictured characters, no matter how many pictures are presented. In contrast, children on the invitational track are also asked to describe, write, or draw about a time when they experienced similar feelings. This task involves practice in taking the perspective of another, trying to imagine the person's feelings in light of the depicted situation, and sharing, in a way most comfortable for the child (describing, writing about, or drawing), an experience that produced similar feelings. Some examples of the Empathy Picture and Drawing Series are shown in figures 14.1, 14.2, and 14.3.

Figure 14.1.   Empathy Picture and Drawing Series

Figure 14.2.   Empathy Picture and Drawing Series

What is the snake feeling?

Write your answer in the bubble.

Please write about or draw a time when you felt the way the
snake does in the space below:

Figure 14.3. Empathy Picture and Drawing Series

In the first two pictures, figures 14.1 and 14.2, the child is asked only to identify the feelings of the baby and the child in the picture. In the third drawing, figure 14.3, however, because the child is on the invitational track, the child is asked to identify the feelings of the snake and then to recall and to draw or write about a time when the child felt the same as the snake.

Film Clips

Hardy and Laszloffy (in press) use emotionally evocative videotapes to assist aggressive and violent youth to access their feelings. Segments from *Ordinary People*, *The Stone Boy*, *The Lion King*, *Stand by Me*, and *Scared Silent* evoke strong affect and provide opportunities to experience and practice being empathetic. Children can be asked, when ready, whether anything like what they saw in the film clip ever happened to them. When not ready, children usually deny similar experiences or reject the invitation to talk more directly about such painful events. Nevertheless, groundwork has been laid.

Empathy Practice Scenarios

Teaching empathetic skills can be enhanced by practice and behavioral reversal. The child practices verbalizing the hurt, pain, sadness, fear, anger, and rage of the victim. Some scenarios for practicing empathy skills are reproduced below.

> Scenario 1: Larry saw his cherished cat get hit by a car just before he was to get on the school bus. He started to cry, and the kids on the bus, not realizing what had happened, were laughing at him. He ran to his cat and dragged the body off the road into his yard. His parents had already left for work, and he was adamant about not getting on the bus. His bus driver became rather stern and said to Larry, "Look, it's just a cat. You have to get on the bus—you are holding everyone up."

After the therapist reads the story aloud, the child is asked,

> THERAPIST: What are some of the feelings you imagine Larry is feeling? Remember, rarely do people have only one feeling. Usually they have a mixture or a blending of several different feelings. See how many feelings you can identify that Larry might be experiencing. Then either tell me about them, write about them, or draw about them.

After the child completes this task, he or she is asked to communicate, in the same manner, a time when he or she felt the same way.

Scenario 2: Michael's dad had a bad temper. His temper was really bad when he drank too many beers. One night Michael's father came home late after drinking with his pals. Michael had left his sneakers in the hall and had forgotten to put them away in his room. His father tripped over the sneakers and hit his head against the wall as he fell. Michael's father was extremely angry and went to Michael's room and woke him up. Michael's father yelled, calling Michael a "stupid ass" and telling Michael that if the sneakers were ever left in the hall again, he was going to "kick his ass."

THERAPIST: What do you imagine Michael must have felt when awakened by his dad yelling at him? Share with me his feelings by describing them to me, drawing them, or writing about them.

The child is than asked to communicate in the same manner a time when he or she felt the same way.

Scenario 3: Sharon found out from her friend Karen that Liz was having a birthday party and that all of Liz's friends were invited except Sharon. Sharon told Karen she didn't want to talk about it and just wanted to be left alone. Sharon had invited Liz to her party and considered Liz to be her friend.

THERAPIST: What are some of the feelings that you might imagine Sharon experiencing? Tell me, write, or draw about something that happened to you when you felt the same or similar feelings to what you imagine Sharon is feeling.

The child then relates, in whatever venue is most comfortable, his or her own experience of feeling similarly.

SALLY: I think that girl would really be pissed off! She invited this girl to her party and then she can't go to her party and her friends are all going— I bet she is really hurt.

THERAPIST: What else do you think she might be feeling?

SALLY: I guess lonely. All her friends are going to go without her.

THERAPIST: I think you have done a good job of describing the feelings that you can imagine Sharon would be feeling. Can you think of a time or a situation when you felt the same or similar feelings to Sharon?

SALLY: I don't know. I'm not sure.

THERAPIST: It's okay. Take your time. Just picture in your mind Sharon and the situation she was in and all the feelings that you did a good job describing to me and see if anything comes into your mind about a time, situation, or place when you felt something like that.

SALLY: I don't like to talk about it, but there was a time. The police and CPS [*Child Protective Services*] workers came to the house and took

Dad away after the nurse at school discovered the bruises. I didn't tell, but it felt like I had done something wrong. Mom was really mad at me. She said, "What kind of trouble are you making for this family now. Dad will lose his job. We won't be able to buy food or pay the rent. Don't you realize what you have done?" I felt like everyone hated me. I felt more alone than ever. My brothers wouldn't speak to me either and called me a cry-baby!

THERAPIST: No wonder that it was so hard to talk about that time—that sounds really tough. Everyone was mad at you and blaming you, but you were the one that had the bruises! It felt like you had done something wrong when the bruises were discovered, and even worse, there was no one you could turn to for help or support [*empathetic interpretation*]. I imagine you felt very alone in the world, and it must have hurt very much, probably far more than the bruises [*empathetic interpretation*].

Sally's efforts to empathize with Sharon were reinforced, and the feelings she expressed were validated, perhaps one reason this twelve-year-old girl was willing to risk sharing an even more painful situation in her own life. The dialogue also illustrates how Sally's feelings were first validated and then followed by expressions of empathy. Modeling empathy is a crucial component of therapy. But it can't be done in a mechanical or cookbook fashion. The empathy expressed must be heartfelt, or the child will quickly detect the insincerity. An adolescent boy once remarked that a psychiatrist who interviewed him after a suicide attempt was "overtrained." When asked what he meant, the boy said, "He has interviewed too many kids like me, and he no longer feels anything."

Therapeutic dialogues between the child and the therapist must involve matters of the heart. Remaining empathetic when repeatedly confronted with the dreadful life events of clients is a therapist's greatest challenge, yet empathy is necessary to heal the invisible wounds of children. We can't teach children to be empathetic unless we are truly empathetic. Healers lacking empathy for the pain of others will heal no one.

> Scenario 4: Sheila is a sixth grader and, although somewhat shy and quiet, has been able to get along well with other students up until this year. This school year, she has been bullied, teased, and harassed by three bigger girls in her class. She has been intimidated into giving her lunch money to the girls at least once a week and has been told that if she tells anyone, they will beat her up. They have also pushed, shoved, and tripped her and then made fun of her when she cried.
>
> THERAPIST: What do you sense Sheila is feeling? Draw, write about, or describe a time when you felt the same or similar feelings as you imagine that Sheila feels.

Scenario 5: Richard has had a rough time at school, and because he is somewhat slower in doing his work than other kids, he gets teased a lot. Once in awhile, the teasing will get to be too much, and he will lose his temper. Since Richard is very strong, when he loses his temper it is very bad news. One day Richard had taken all he could, and when a kid just kept teasing him, Richard hauled off and landed a punch to the mouth of the classmate. At that point a teacher jumped between them, but unfortunately Richard was so mad that he took another swing. This one hit the teacher in the back of the head, and she fell to the ground. She wasn't badly hurt, but she was a very popular teacher, and the other kids were furious with Richard. He was also suspended from school.

THERAPIST: What do you imagine that Richard is feeling? Try to think of a time when you felt the same way as Richard or a similar way. Tell about, write, or draw about that time.

The child then is encouraged to share his or her own experience.

KAREN: [*Takes out the following puppets: monkey, rabbit, turtle, frog, and owl, and sets up a classroom. Then she brings in the alligator puppet to sit behind them. She selects the bumblebee to be the teacher—a revealing selection. Alligator says*] I don't want to sit next to no smelly monkey, stupid rabbit, slimy frog, or dumb owl. Teacher, can I move away from these creepy, smelly dummies? [*Rabbit says*] I don't like it when Alligator calls me stupid or calls my friends bad names! [*Bumblebee says*] Well, Rabbit, if you studied your spelling words and didn't get half of them wrong, maybe Alligator wouldn't call you stupid! [*Rabbit starts to cry; her friends try to comfort her. Bumblebee says*] If there is one thing I can't stand, it's a crybaby! Can't we get through just one day of school this year, Rabbit, without you crying like a baby? [*Alligator laughs loudly and mocks rabbit.*] Poor Baby Rabbit! Poor thing!

The puppet play depicted the girl's humiliation by those who mocked and teased her, including her teacher, who embarrassed her twice in front of her classmates. Her ability to express through play her own sense of devaluation and humiliation demonstrated her ability to empathize with the shame and humiliation Richard experienced when taunted by peers and alienated from them after accidentally hitting a popular teacher. Until children can acknowledge and express their own pain, they cannot empathize with the pain of others. Bruce Perry's chilling story (1997) of a child murderer who inflicted pain on others without blinking an eye demonstrates that aggressive children who repress their own losses, shame, and humiliation never develop empathy.

EMPATHY FOR THE HEALER

Dr. Crenshaw once supervised a young, extremely bright, dedicated, and compassionate child psychologist who worked in a residential treatment center. After about six months, she expressed that she was disturbed by changes taking place within her. She related that, when new to the program, she was horrified in some cases, deeply moved in others, and at times deeply saddened and shaken by reading the social histories of the children and their families. She said she no longer felt so deeply. Now, when she read the life histories, she had a more muted reaction. She realized her current reaction was a self-protective one, necessary to survive in such work, but she felt guilty and worried about the impact of this change on the children. She feared being emotionally unavailable when the children related their stories to her, yet she realized that emotional availability was essential to the healing process. This very articulate young clinician captured beautifully the dilemma faced by staff who seek not just to contain, control, and correct children, but to attend to and heal their invisible wounds.

When working with children in gorilla suits, the staff has a need for empathy that is also critical. The work is demanding and difficult. Some talented and dedicated therapists, as well as direct-care staff, can engage in such work for only a relatively brief period in their career. *Understanding and Treating the Aggression of Children* is dedicated to clinicians who devoted their entire professional careers to healing deeply troubled children.

Empathy for staff must be supplied by the therapist, and we discuss this role in *Understanding and Treating the Aggression of Children*. But who empathizes with the struggles of the therapist? The need for a balanced life, one that includes satisfying personal relationships, family and friends, recreation, and a wide range of interests and hobbies, along with proper nutrition, exercise, and rest, can be met only by the clinician himself or herself. Therapists also need ways to distance themselves from grueling work while at work. One way is to be intellectually curious about the children and the treatment process. Both of us selected the Astor Home over other residential treatment centers because of its active research and training programs. Since we were trained in the scientist-practitioner model, we knew from our work at other residential centers that we would burn out quickly if we couldn't function within this model. The very act of writing this book creates distance between ourselves and our clients.

The therapist also needs the support of the agency by being provided with regular supervision and training (and neither of these can be overdone in this kind of work). In addition, adequate compensation and generous vacation, sick, and personal leave are needed to allow staff to regroup when drained and exhausted. But the most important need is to experience the unequivocal support of administrative and supervisory staff and their appreciation for how much clinicians give of themselves even though they are not direct-care staff. There is no adequate compensation for what is given from the heart, but knowing that clinical efforts are appreciated and valued is vital.

Unpopular administrative decisions have to be made, such as budget cuts that reduce staff, but the manner in which these decisions are handled is critical. When administrative decisions are handled in an open, honest, and sensitive manner, most dedicated people will rise to the occasion. Throughout these two volumes, we have repeatedly emphasized the great healing potential in dialogue. Dialogue is also critical when working with staff. Even the best agencies always face financial problems, but the manner in which these problems are handled can determine how much care is given, not only to children, but to healers as well. In order to teach, model, and facilitate the crucial skills of empathy, empathy for staff cannot be overlooked. Turnover is very high among those who work with angry clients. Yet it is stability and consistency of caring that result in children's removing their gorilla suits. Insensitive agency administrators contribute to staff turnover, and if the turnover is frequent, no meaningful changes will occur in clients.

· *15* ·

Teaching the Language of Feelings

Children experience difficulty differentiating one feeling state from another, let alone describing and expressing feelings to others. This deficiency results from developmental factors, such as cognitive and language limitations, but also from emotional factors that block access to, or disconnect the child's intellect from, his or her affect. Techniques presented to help children label feelings include the Basket of Feelings, the Gingerbread Person, the Feelings Map, Affect Recognition Pictures and Stories, and Feelings Charades.

*M*ax Talmadge introduced Dr. Mordock to the language problems of go-rilla-suit wearers. Max came to the Astor Home from the Bradley Psychiatric Hospital for Children in Providence, Rhode Island, a model residential treatment center at the time. George Mora, The Astor Home for Children's second medical director, who was also trained at Bradley, lured away several of Bradley's key staff to help him implement the Bradley model at the Astor Home. Max was hired to be the director of psychology. Max emphasized, in his supervision of interns, residents, and staff, spending lots of time preparing children for traditional therapy. He felt that most children in gorilla suits lacked a "language for feelings" and emphasized teaching them the words they would need to express the gamut of human feelings. His pioneering efforts were mentioned in Jerome Singer's 1966 work, *Daydreaming: An Introduction to the Experimental Study of Inner Experience,* as a promising direction in the treatment of seriously disturbed children. Since then the agency has implemented a language development program in its residential school and hired a speech therapist to work intensively with selected individual children.

Twenty years later, a formal study at the Astor Home, directed by Dr. Crenshaw, examined the relation of verbal ability to the display of aggression by children in the center (Burke, Crenshaw, Green, et al. 1989). Essentially, children were ranked on their display of aggression, and these ranks were correlated with their scores on selected indices of language development. The results indicated that children displaying higher levels of aggression scored lower on several measures of language skill. When results were controlled for intelligence, children whose reading levels were well below age level were more violent than those scoring closer to grade level. In addition, expressive language ability differentiated more aggressive from less aggressive children. Subjects who had been referred for speech therapy displayed more aggressive behavior than those not referred for such help.

The range of scores on measures of aggression and of language development were extremely narrow because most of the children in treatment were aggressive and most had language delays. The smaller the range of scores on measured variables, the less likely it is that correlations will be found. Yet the correlations found in Dr. Crenshaw's study were not just statistically significant; they were substantial. The results were consistent with earlier studies in which delinquent boys with reading deficiencies and language delays displayed more violent behavior than other delinquents (Green 1978; Lewis et al. 1979; Tartar et al. 1984).

These findings help to explain why some children frequently express anger in actions rather than words. Further, they underscore the need to develop the children's expressive language skills, including writing, and to teach them to express feelings verbally. Stern (1985) remarks,

> Words . . . separate out precisely those properties that anchor the experience to a single mode of sensation. By binding it to words, they isolate the experience from the amodal flux in which it was originally experienced. (p. 176)

Hardy (1998) describes "learned voicelessness" as a predictable consequence of trauma, violence, and cultural oppression. The strategies discussed in this chapter were designed to help children to regain their voices as well as to label their feelings.

BASKET OF FEELINGS

The Basket of Feelings technique is one used in the initial stages of language training. It helps children, particularly those in gorilla suits, to find a language to identify, label, and express their feelings (James 1989). Most children wearing gorilla suits experience anger as an "all or none" experience. They are unable to appreciate that irritation and annoyance can be stepping stones to anger and rage. In this exercise, children are asked to join the therapist in coming up with the names of as many different feelings as possible. The name of each feeling is written with magic markers in big letters on a separate 8.5 x 11-inch sheet of paper. The therapist usually goes first, modeling the effort, and names some feelings that children usually fail to recognize as distinct ones. For example, they often say they are angry when they are actually impatient, annoyed, disgusted, repulsed, or nauseated, and they need help to distinguish these feelings from anger. Similarly, they say they are sad when they are actually disappointed, dispirited, sorrowful, gloomy, downcast, or more important, when they are depressed, grieving, or mournful.

The therapist tells a story about an incident that aroused a wide range of emotions in himself or herself, such as,

> THERAPIST: Yesterday, I went to the store, and a man waiting in line became irate and started shouting at the clerk because the line was moving slowly and he was late for an appointment. The man became more and more angry, and finally the security guards were called, and he was escorted from the store, but only after a struggle.

The therapist then places poker chips on each of the pages on which a feeling has been written, with the number of chips placed according to how strongly he or she, witnessing the event, felt each of the stated feelings. Before this exercise, the therapist explains to the child that one chip will be used to express a mild feeling and ten chips to express a strong feeling. Chips can also be stacked in separate piles on each page to represent judgments about the feelings of other characters in the story. The therapist might say, for example,

> THERAPIST: At first, I was slightly annoyed [*one chip*] at the wait and was losing patience [*one chip*] myself, but then, when the impatient man [*three chips for his impatience*] became so annoyed [*four chips for his annoyance*] that he actually became angry [*seven chips for his anger*] and started yelling at the clerk, I felt sorry [*four chips*] for her. She was trying her best and feeling frustrated [*three chips for her frustration*]. It wasn't her fault that the store was short of clerks. I felt guilty [*four chips*] that I didn't say anything in support of the clerk.

With each identified feeling, the therapist puts the poker chips on the sheets of paper naming the designated emotion. The story continues:

> THERAPIST: At first I was annoyed [*two chips*] by the man's rudeness, but then I got a little anxious [*three chips*] wondering what he would do

next. Then my anxiety turned to fear [*five chips*], and I became scared [*six chips*] because the man was getting increasingly angry [*eight chips*] and I was worried that something was going to happen. Then, when the security guards arrived, I became concerned [*seven chips*] because a scuffle developed, and I was worried [*eight chips*] that someone would be hurt.

When the story ends, the distributed poker chips are sorted according to how prominent each of the emotions was in the story. The piles graphically depict the range of feelings that can be experienced in response to one event. The child is then encouraged to create his or her own story, also being asked to use one chip for the mildest feeling, but as many chips as desired for the strongest feelings, providing there are enough chips. Kids can use hundreds! Therapists shouldn't be surprised when children create stories identical to theirs because identifying and labeling feelings is new to them. Support whatever each child comes up with. As a passenger in a car, we rarely learn the specific routes to where we are headed. It is not until we drive the same routes ourselves that we learn to get around in a new neighborhood. Eventually, the child's stories will be more creative.

When children first begin the task, they are helped to select the feelings to write on the paper with their magic marker and to create stories in which the feelings are used, even if used incorrectly at first. Sometimes the therapist playacts a feeling, or displays it on his or her face, and then gets the child to mimic the actions. Learning theorists describe the process as "shaping behaviors by successive approximations," and the description is certainly appropriate to denote the effort that takes place. But once the children have learned some words for feelings, they can get "into it," as the following example illustrates.

THERAPIST: I see you have more chips on the Anger sheet than on any of the other feelings. So in this situation, you felt mostly anger?

CHILD: Yeah, I guess I was really pissed! I'm fed up with getting kicked out of class for stuff that other guys get away with!

THERAPIST: You feel that any time there is trouble, they come looking for you?

CHILD: Yup! Those teachers don't give a damn about me! They would love it if I dropped out and never came back.

THERAPIST: I see you have some chips on Surprise. What surprised you?

CHILD: Most of the kids don't care one way or the other, but Bill stopped me in the hall and said, "Don't let those bastards get to you." I didn't think he cared.

THERAPIST: This "surprise" must have felt good—to realize that at least one person cared. Do you think there are some teachers who care?

CHILD: Most don't give a shit. Mr. Reynolds, my shop teacher, he likes me and has gone out of the way to help me. I think he cares about kids. There should be more teachers like him.

The primary value of such tools is that they lead to dialogues that contribute to healing. Children find a voice with which to express themselves. The youngster above starts with the position that no one cares. He then identifies a student who stood by him, followed by the recognition that at least one teacher went out of his way to be helpful. This recognition enables the child, and perhaps the therapist as well, to avoid an overpowering sense of hopelessness. When pursuing affects, the therapist should accept simplistic responses, such as feelings described in gross terms, but the therapist should persist until the goal is achieved. Children usually say they were mad, sad, or happy, a very constricted range of feeling words, and need guidance in being more precise. Yet by the therapist's patient, persistent inquiry, stemming from a wish to understand, children learn to be more curious about their feeling life.

GINGERBREAD PERSON/FEELINGS MAP

The Gingerbread Person, also called the Feelings Map, is another tool (Drewes 2001b). This strategy requires the child to pair emotions, such as happy, sad, angry, worried, or scared, with colors the child selects. The child then colors in a drawing of the Gingerbread Person according to how much the child feels each of these feelings. Typically, children are asked to color the Gingerbread Person according to how they felt about an upsetting event that has been the focus of attention in therapy, such as when their dad left the house after a fight with their mom. Drewes recommends that children try to locate the region in their own bodies where they feel certain emotions and color the Gingerbread Person in that spot. An example of a colored Gingerbread Person appears in figure 15.1.

Not only does this technique facilitate identification, labeling, and expression of feelings in a drawing game that is enjoyable; it also opens a window into inner feelings. When a Gingerbread Person is completely colored, the therapist can pursue, in collaboration with the child, a more detailed understanding of the mixed and variously proportioned affects contained in Mr. or Miss Gingerbread. Interpretation of these figures should be approached carefully, if at all.

Some children get interested in the coloring process and the mix of colors and lose track of the feelings with which the colors are paired. When

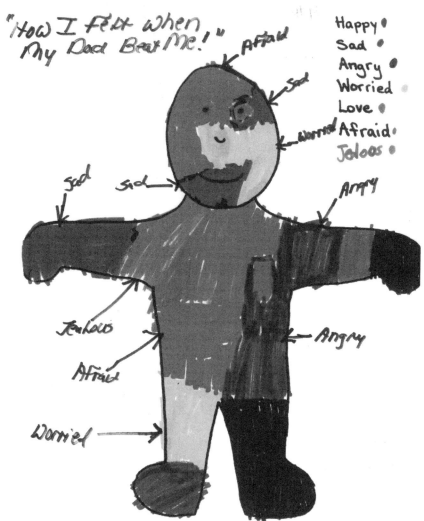

Figure 15.1. Gingerbread Person

children start to use a certain color, they can be reminded of the feeling represented by that color and asked "How much of that feeling should be shown in the Gingerbread Person," and then "Where in your body do you feel that feeling? Impulsive children and those with a poor sense of proportion may color a major portion of the Gingerbread Person with the first color they use and will need more guidance. The technique also helps children to learn that feelings can be mixed and conflicting, even totally opposite, in response to an upsetting situation. As part of the lead-in to this strategy, the therapist can say,

> THERAPIST: Usually, when something upsetting happens, children tell me they don't have just one feeling but a number of different feelings. They might feel sad and mad, but also worried, disappointed, or scared. They might also feel relieved or even happy about something good that came out of the very upsetting experience. It is possible to have all of these feelings in response to the same situation.

The therapist typically writes on the Gingerbread Person page the specific upsetting event and any spontaneous comments made by the child. An example is shown in figure 15.2.

In the above example, the child added a name for a feeling: "The feeling that it would never end." Drewes (2001) recommends asking children to "name a feeling" in an effort to expand the range of feelings that children can identify and label. In this case, the name revealed the hopelessness this youngster, who was surrounded by domestic violence, experienced. Another example appears in figure 15.3.

Through this strategy, a girl was able to express some sadness, considerable worry, fear, and a significant amount of anger. She communicated, in a colorful and vivid way, not feeling safe in the company of her dad when he is drinking. When asked directly how she felt about this issue, she became anxious and unable to voice her feelings.

Another example, called the Feelings Map, figure 15.4, shows a boy split down the middle between sadness and fear, reflecting the split in the boy's family following a devastating family trauma.

AFFECT RECOGNITION PICTURES AND STORIES

Dr. Crenshaw has developed an Affect Recognition and Story Series using clip art depicting people and animals expressing clearly identifiable emotions and, in some cases, ambiguous emotions. After being shown a picture, the

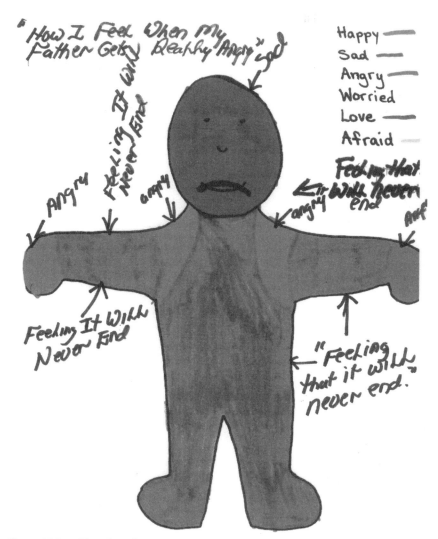

Figure 15.2.   Gingerbread Person

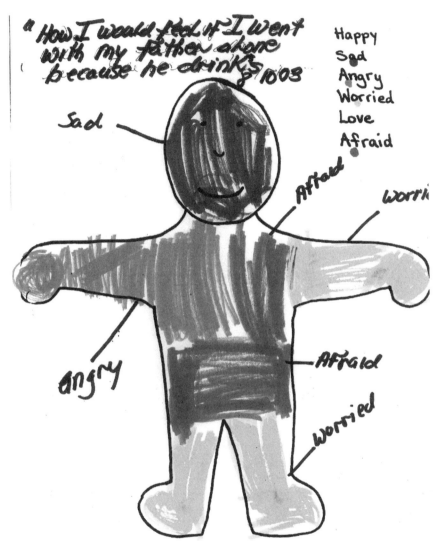

Figure 15.3.   Gingerbread Person [related to father's drinking]

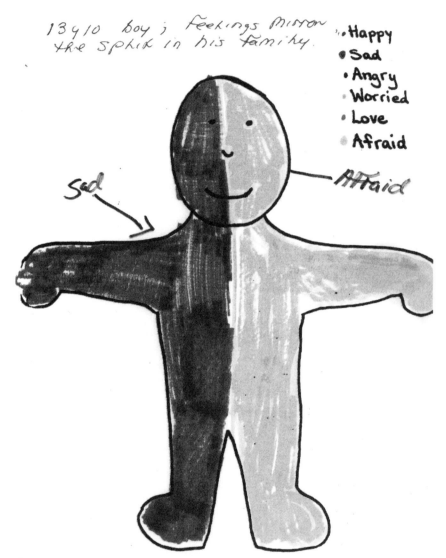

Figure 15.4. Feelings Map [reflecting split down middle]

What is the lion feeling? Write next to each face what feeling the lion is expressing.

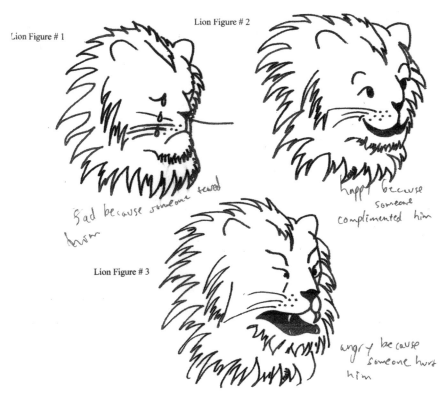

Lion Figure # 1

Lion Figure # 2

sad because someone teased him

happy because someone complimented him

Lion Figure # 3

angry because someone hurt him

Figure 15.5.   Affect Recognition and Story Series

What is this child feeling?

The Child is feeling unwanted and sad

Make up a story about what happened to cause this child to feel this way:

the Child had the first day of school. She was nervous about how she's day was going to be. She was left out of all the different friend groups. She was to lousely for the popular group, didn't have the technique for the chess group, and wasn't smart enough for the math olympics. When she got home she sobbed in the bathroom listening to the little voice in her head sayed your not good enough, you are unwanted.

Figure 15.6. Affect Recognition and Story Series

child is asked to elaborate on it by making up a story about the persons or animals depicted and what they are feeling. This task allows for practice in creating an appropriate context for the specific feelings perceived by the child. An example is shown in figures 15.5 and 15.6.

Most children enjoy the pictures and telling stories. The stories can reveal their inner struggles and predominant feelings as they identify with the central character depicted in each story. The therapist should avoid interpreting the stories, but tentative hypotheses can be made from the common themes and self-identifications. While the stories may yield rich clues to understanding the child's inner world, the primary purpose of these pictures and accompanying stories is to teach and develop a language for expression of and understanding of feelings.

FEELINGS CHARADES

Once the child has acquired words to label a range of feelings, more advanced techniques can be introduced. Children love games, and if the language of feelings can be taught in a playful context, better results can occur. A stack of cards, each one with a specific feeling written on it, is placed on the table, and the therapist and the child take turns drawing a card. Then the child, without words, acts out or mimics through bodily and facial gestures the emotion written on the card, with the therapist guessing what feeling is being depicted or acted out. An added step is asking the child if he or she could describe a time when he or she felt that specific feeling. This game offers an opportunity for a child to learn subtle variations of emotional states.

· *16* ·

Facilitating Affect
Expression and Modulation

Children in gorilla suits typically express a limited range of affects, and they express them in an all-or-none way. They need to learn to moderate the expression of affect and to express affects in ways that contribute to interpersonal relations. Several techniques to help them modulate affect are presented. They include empowerment play and psychodrama.

*B*everly James (1993) writes that traumatized children have a broken modulator. The children shut down their sensory awareness because a touch, a sound, or even a smell can evoke an abuse memory or flashback. Unwilling to relax and let go, they fear their pent-up anger will overwhelm them and others around them. To treat them effectively, the therapist must serve as a "container" (Bion 1959, 1962; Boston and Szur 1983), helping them to keep a lid on the powerful emotions that threaten to overwhelm them. They need to be taught that it is okay to feel (James 1993), but that the feelings need expression in a manner that doesn't alienate others. They need to modulate the behaviors that typically accompany expression of their strong feelings.

In addition to a broken modulator, gorilla-suit wearers have a broken "muffler." They can always be heard loud and clear, and so loud, in fact, that their anger interferes with solving the problem that led up to it. The children need to express a need in such a way that the need is attended to rather than its expression.

Those gorilla-suit wearers with some social conscience fear seriously hurting or even killing somebody when angry. Or they feel that their profound sadness will alienate listeners—getting in touch with their sadness would be too much to bear, not only for them but also for others. They approach their

230

emotions in an all-or-none fashion. The children need to hear reassurance such as the following:

> THERAPIST: It's okay to feel angry. There is nothing in this room that you could seriously hurt me with. It's okay to feel sad. I can hear it. Hopefully, you won't always feel that way.

Likewise, children may need to hear another direct message about their emotions:

> THERAPIST: It's okay to be happy sometimes, even if your mother is in a drug rehabilitation center. She is safe there and, hopefully, working on her own problems.

EMPOWERMENT PLAY

One way to help children modulate the expression of feelings is through empowerment play. Children typically love playing the role of powerful superheroes or even supervillains. Adopting such roles frequently gets some children into trouble because they bully when they get carried away. Others alienate their peers because they don't know when to quit and move on to other activities. Superman or Superwoman, Batman and Robin, Spiderman or Spiderwoman, GI Joe, Ninja Turtles, the Hulk, the Terminator, and many other comic book characters have sparked children's imaginations for many years.

Using their natural inclination to play being a superhero or vicious animal, therapists can help aggressive children to modulate the play. They can learn to have real power. The supervillain can change from an all-destroying creature to one that damages less and less during each treatment session and eventually turns into a superhero who, with his partner, the therapist, rescues and heals people. The children can roar like Lion Puppet or growl like Tiger Puppet. They can be asked to stand tall and proud like Giraffe Puppet. Then they can be asked to reduce their roars or growls. Such play appeals to most youngsters, and they enjoy exercising power. But they also need to temper it. The lion's roar can be reduced and practiced at different levels of ferociousness, depending on the degree of threat the lion feels. If the lion or tiger only wants his presence known, with no clear threat or danger present, a mild roar or growl will do the trick. This can be practiced until the appropriate level of mild intensity is reached.

The level of intensity is increased if a threat appears on the horizon so that potential intruders know that the lion is the king of the jungle. When a threat becomes imminent, the lion or tiger has to crank up to full throttle and let the invader know he or she is messing with the wrong creature. The therapist usually demonstrates. Such demonstrations can be fun for the therapist who is still young at heart. Of course, people in adjoining rooms may become alarmed because no amount of soundproofing can fully contain the ferocious roar of a lion.

When a child identifies threats to the lion's well-being, within the metaphor of power play, the therapist can uses these threats to clarify the degree of "potential damage." The child can learn that some of the threats require only a quiet roar while others require a louder one. Also emphasized is that no lion roars all the time and no tiger growls all the time. Strength and power can be demonstrated through restraint. Mr. Lion can exert a commanding and proud presence without roaring at all. The child can practice being quietly assertive without being aggressive and can display strength with a variety of nonaggressive postures. For example, the child can learn

> THERAPIST: If a child takes your pencil and does not give it back upon request, no roar is actually required. Without tattletaling, you can ask your teacher for one, and if she asks where yours went, you can say, "Carlos didn't have one, so I lent him mine."

As we have said repeatedly, most traumatized children display gross motor actions or, at best, action play, such as putting on a cape, pretending to be Superman, and running around the playroom. The play doesn't last long because the child can't think of things for Superman to do in the small playroom that don't result in limit setting. Consequently, the child usually moves to another theme if not encouraged to move the Superman play into another domain, such as drawing, puppet play, or dollhouse play. Moving the play into miniature-world characters helps the child to develop playacting skills in the microsphere. Such play contributes more to affect modulation than does action play without structure because play actions take place in the mind and not in behavior.

Some children, however, need explicit encouragement to play being a superhero if their traumatic experiences have left them frozen and unable to play freely (van der Kolk 2003).

Those feeling guilty may need permission to play. James (1993) tells such children that "it's still okay to play even if terrible things have happened to you or to members of your family. Play can help you in your struggles with feelings about these terrible things. Just because others are in pain doesn't mean you can't have fun sometimes."

PSYCHODRAMA

Another fun way to help children with affect regulation and modulation is through drama play. The therapist pretends to be a movie director audition- ing actors for different parts in a movie. The child is asked to try out for var- ious parts, depending on the specifics of the child's difficulties. If a child's self-assertions are inhibited, he or she may be asked to audition for a part as an assertive police person, an emotionally expressive coach, or a spirited pros- ecuting attorney. If the child's self-assertions are limited to angry outbursts and restraint is needed, the child might be asked to try out for the part of judge, forbearing physician, or wise old sage. Children love playing these parts, and once again the therapist can have a lot of fun with them as well. The audi- tions can be video- or audiotaped and played back so that both the child and the therapist can collaboratively critique a performance and decide ways to fine-tune it. Throughout this volume, we emphasize the importance of a col- laborative therapeutic relationship (Bonime 1989). Critiquing auditions with the child is an excellent way to achieve this end.

Psychodrama, as utilized in play therapy, involves rehearsing a desired level of affect expression, embedded in nonthreatening role-playing skits; modeling of divergent play by the therapist; and highlighting and reinforcing each step toward affect regulation. In this fashion, the child is helped to develop modulation. No longer at the mercy of the emotions, the child need no longer fear harmful or punitive consequences following emotional expression. Such a sense of personal control is vital to the positive mental health of any person.

GARBAGE BAG TECHNIQUE

In chapter 9 we discuss binding and compartmentalizing, referred to by Bev- erly James (1993) as the Scarlett O'Hara approach to mastering anxiety: "I'll think about that tomorrow." When facing strong emotions, children need cop- ing strategies to guard against being overwhelmed, as we have emphasized. James (1989) has utilized what she calls the "garbage bag" technique to teach children to use binding and compartmentalizing. The children are helped to identify all the worst, ugly, painful, and scary things that have happened to them and are helped to write them on 3 x 5-inch index cards. The cards are put into the "garbage bag," and the bag is tied shut. (A decorated shoe box will serve just as well, with the lid kept on except when the child reaches in to pull out one of the cards.)

In each session the child is encouraged to pull one of the topics out and to decide if he or she is ready to talk about it. Perhaps the child pulls out a card that says, "The time the police came to my house to arrest Daddy." If the child turns away or becomes anxious, he or she can be told, "We will put that one back in the bag (or the box), tie it closed (or put the lid on the shoe box), and come back to it at another time, when you are ready to talk about this."

The child is told it is okay to bind and compartmentalize the feelings associated with an issue because they are too upsetting to tackle at this time, but the expectation is planted that the issue will be dealt with later. Both messages are crucial. Nothing is gained by pushing a child to deal with issues prematurely. The child can become overwhelmed by frightening memories or even retraumatized. Nevertheless, we don't want the child to shy away from the "really hard and painful stuff," so a clear message is given that the issues will be revisited.

Most gorilla-suit wearers, however, are unable to recite the nightmarish events of their lives, so they or the therapist can write them on index cards. Such topics provoke dramatic reactions and acute anxiety and have to be approached in a gradual and titrated way. As a consequence, the Garbage Bag Technique must be modified. The child is asked to list problems he or she would like to solve or worries that trouble him or her. The therapist or child can write these down on index cards, and the child is invited to draw out the worry or problem he or she would like to work on in that session. We would advise caution when using the instructions James recommends, especially early in treatment, before a strong alliance has been established. To ask a child with shaky defenses to confront traumatic events directly, and in rapid succession, is risky because trauma memories can be activated before the child is sufficiently prepared to face them. These risks, along with preventive and corrective steps, are discussed below.

A CAUTIONARY NOTE ABOUT TIMING AND PACING

More important than specific techniques is the presence of a clear rationale and a consistent theoretical framework that guides therapeutic actions when selecting techniques. Techniques should be employed only when the therapist has a clear understanding of how each technique will meet the specific therapeutic needs of the child. Many unnecessary treatment crises, which can result in violent or self-destructive acts and often psychiatric hospitalization, can be avoided if coping and defense mechanisms are taught first and their use honored and respected. When mistakes are made that result in a crisis, they are often the result of therapists' pushing children in keeping with the therapist's agenda rather than the child's. Dr. Crenshaw once supervised a therapist in private practice whose clients experienced frequent crises followed by hospitalizations. The therapist strongly believed that it was his job to force clients to face the painful events in their lives, and the sooner they did so the better. By learning to be more patient and respectful of his client's resources, he dramatically reduced the number of client crises and hospitalizations. This therapist was treating adults. It is even more important to honor the defenses of children because, being less mature than adults, they have fewer coping resources to draw upon.

When the therapist errs in pushing a child too far, and the child becomes upset, usually masking the discomfort instantly with anger, the therapist quickly apologizes and instructs the child to close his or her eyes and visualize being in the safe place they have been trained to go to in earlier sessions. The child can then be asked to draw the safe place in order to become even calmer. The therapist then stresses that the child will become stronger in the future and will deal with this issue then.

At the same time, the impression should not be left that children, even those in gorilla suits, are so fragile that therapists must "walk on eggshells" to avoid major crises. At times, when traumatic memories are triggered or painful events uncovered before children are ready to face them, they may simply ignore the therapist or storm out of the room. At other times, the child responds constructively and moves therapy to a more challenging and productive level. We are not advocating a timid or hesitant approach, but rather one in which the therapist pays proper attention to the selection and use of therapeutic interventions. Children on the invitational track should have demonstrated to the therapist that they have sufficient ego strengths and defensive resources to undertake uncovering therapy. These children can and need to be pushed harder and further than children on the coping track. Timing and strength of the therapeutic alliance are crucial factors in influencing the outcome of any therapeutic intervention.

• *17* •

Facilitating Contained
Reenactment of Trauma

Children fear confronting repressed traumatic events. Nevertheless, they have an equally strong, if not more powerful, need to unburden their pain and have it witnessed by someone they trust. Establishing the level of trust required to enable a child to fully recall traumatic experiences takes considerable time. Working in the child's favor, however, are the healthy forces that seek the long-awaited opportunity to reveal life's secret horrors to someone who has become close to the child. We discuss helping children on the invitational track to face and reenact traumatic experiences and illustrate the process with a detailed case presentation.

*W*hen the body state is set in the alarm position, triggered by physiological hyperarousal, the higher-order cortical brain apparently goes "offline." Stimuli similar to or associated with traumatic events or screen memories of the events can immediately activate the child's physiological alarm state, leading to shutdown of the higher cortical centers. As we discuss in chapter 4 of our companion volume, this activation leaves the child on a "ship besieged by an affective storm and piloted by the midbrain and brain stem," the primitive control centers of the brain. Enabling the children to remain calm in the face of stormy events and to safely return to shore is the first priority of therapeutic interventions.

A number of clinicians addressed this issue long before the effects of trauma on the brain centers were first recognized. Numerous writers (Dolan 1985, 1991; James 1989; Terr 1990; Herman 1992) emphasize the need for safety when treating trauma victims, especially when therapy can activate the original terror associated with the trauma. Techniques need to be employed that enable trauma survivors to anchor in the present and experience traumatic memories without being flooded or overwhelmed with painful memories and affect.

WHY UNDERTAKE TRAUMA WORK?

Uncovering trauma memories is troubling to clients, if not overwhelming, even when approached sensitively. Consequently, some might ask, Why do it? Why not just leave the memories filed in a "locked drawer of the mind," where they won't cause upheaval in the client's emotional life? This decision would be reasonable if the client is relatively free of troubling symptoms. Many holocaust victims kept their horrifying experiences repressed and functioned reasonably well. They survived partly by keeping their focus on the future, particularly on the success of their children. Some experienced heightened anxiety when pulled over by a traffic cop, but the anxiety passed after the ticket was issued. If they had to work in a prison or in prison-like environments, however, they would find it difficult to keep their traumatic memories repressed. Of course, most would actively avoid such an occupation. When there is no compelling need to undertake emotionally grueling work, traumatic memories can remain buried in a client's unconscious.

Uncovering traumatic memories should also be avoided when clients need better coping skills just to face life's current challenges. Children who lack the needed ego defenses and coping resources to manage strong emotions should not be required to confront past traumas. But children who possess the requisite internal resources and have sufficient external supports should be helped to uncover traumatic memories when the memories intrude into their lives in disturbing and disruptive ways. Not only do repressed memories create symptomatic behavior, but they put clients at risk for future trauma due to the repetition compulsion, or the effort to master past trauma by placing oneself in similar situations. "See, I have walked down this dark passageway and I did not get raped!" Children who have been sexually abused are at high risk of being sexually abused again, even as adults (Arata 2002). These children need to undertake in-depth, emotionally focused work because the intrusive and disruptive effects of trauma have adversely influenced their lives.

Therapy with trauma victims is not merely a matter of unearthing past memories. These memories intrude while doing math in school or playing a game of tag on the school playground. If therapists don't pursue working through traumatic experiences and their associated affects, victims are left to struggle with these feelings and their inappropriate response to them and are likely to feel abandoned.

A number of clinicians emphasize that healing requires having trauma-associated pain witnessed by someone who is trusted. A strong need exists to unburden and share the plethora of intense and disturbing feelings accompanying a traumatic experience (Herman 1992; Miller 1997). Others emphasize how trauma leads to fragmented memories, fragmented affect, and even fragmented sensory experiences (James 1993). Treatment involves examining and reexperiencing all the pieces—the scared parts and the angry parts—differently. The client's inside horrors are pursued in such as way that they are gradually revealed, integrated into narrative memory, assigned meaning, given perspective, and stored as a memory of the past. When a traumatic experience is unprocessed, it waits inside the client, to be activated by reminders of the experience. And when these reminders occur, the massive anxiety associated with the trauma reappears, as if the trauma had just happened. James (1993) discusses a rape victim who smells a certain kind of cologne at work that activates her memory of the perpetrator. She becomes so anxious that she loses bladder control and escapes to her home for the rest of the day.

THE MEANING GIVEN TO THE EXPERIENCE

Unfortunately, neglectful or abusive acts by themselves are not what cause victims the most troublesome emotional pain. Rather it is the meaning victims, or those around victims, give to the actions, or to the victims' responses to the actions, that is the most troubling. For example, a young boy was pushed into an old, abandoned well by two other children, and he wasn't discovered for almost eight hours. Later, he felt compelled to push other children around and to corner them in tight places. Treatment revealed that while being in the well was terrifying, it wasn't the reason behind his bullying behavior. The behavior resulted from his father's chastising him and calling him "a wimp" for letting the other boys push him into it. Identifying with this self-concept, he felt compelled to prove his father, and himself, wrong. Terr's studies (1981) of children buried in a school bus revealed that not all children were traumatized by the event. Those who were traumatized undoubtedly gave the event meanings that the others didn't.

Sexually abused children often give meanings to their abuse that cause them emotional difficulties. They may blame themselves for enjoying parts of a gradual seduction or for relishing the initial attention. They may fault themselves for being duped by the perpetrator or for not resisting the abuse. Many relate their physical abuse to earlier experiences with the abuser and blame themselves for the abusive acts. "He never beat me before I went to school. If I was a better student, I wouldn't get hit." If the abuse is the child's fault, than the abusing parent is still a good parent and the child is still loved. A child once told Dr. Crenshaw that it was his fault that he had been burned when his angry father pushed him into a hot radiator: "If I had been wearing long pants instead of shorts, I wouldn't have burned my legs."

SECONDARY TRAUMA: THE SILENT BOND

The secrecy surrounding physical and sexual abuse often promotes a "silent bond" between the child and the perpetrator (Lister 1982), especially in cases of sexual abuse. The forced silence—the secret pact never to tell to avoid retribution—carries with it enormous power. Threats of further harm to the victim, or to the victim's family, if the abuse is revealed, accompanied by the burden of maintaining the secrecy, produce a secondary trauma, adding to the negative affects of the primary trauma. The frightening process of disclosing the secret is illustrated in the following vignette.

> Elizabeth, an eleven-year-old girl, had disclosed to her therapist extensive sexual abuse by an uncle. She shared this information with her parents in an emergency family session following the disclosure. Two days later, her mother placed a frantic call to Dr. Crenshaw, who then saw Elizabeth in an emergency session. Her pupils were dilated and she was shaking, crying, and speechless. Her mother held her hand and softly touched her on the shoulder. Dr. Crenshaw tried to calm her by speaking in a soft, soothing voice while telling her that, in order to help her, they needed to know what happened. Both her mother and Dr. Crenshaw emphasized that she was safe now. Her mother added that "your dad and I, and your big brothers, are never going to let anyone hurt you again." Because she was struggling to speak, Dr. Crenshaw added, "Take your time, we have all the time in the world to listen to you." When she regained her voice, she related that when coming home on the school bus, she saw a red Chevy following the bus. Her uncle drove a red Chevy. Even though her uncle had moved to a distant state, she had broken the "silent bond" by her disclosure and was certain that he had returned to retaliate. He had told her that if she ever told anyone, someone she loved would have to die.

As this vignette was being written, Dr. Crenshaw acutely felt the strong emotions that vibrated throughout the therapy room on that day, even though the event occurred more than twenty years ago. Another dramatic example occurred when Dr. Crenshaw was employed in a residential treatment center.

> A nine-year-old boy was disclosing the details of his abuse by his father to his favorite child-care worker when the phone rang in the living unit and the boy's father asked to speak to him. The boy was terrified and could not be consoled. Nor could he be convinced that it was impossible for his father to know what he had just revealed to his counselor. The boy was certain that his father was on his way to exact his revenge.

The behavior of both children illustrates the emotions experienced when a silent bond is broken. Both experienced a vivid sense of imminent retribution.

Lister (1982) has observed the same phenomenon in adult victims. Realizing that thinking can regress in fully mature adults helps one to appreciate how children can imagine all sorts of repercussions when they disclose their abuse. The fact that the abuser lives far away or has become too old to hurt anyone cannot be appreciated by the child.

The immediate goal in such situations is to reestablish the sense of safety. Reaching the goal can involve networking with the family, the school, and, at times, members of the larger community, such as the clergy or the police. Everyone working with the child should be alerted that a disclosure has occurred and encouraged to make unusual efforts to help the child to feel safe and secure. In residential treatment centers, it can be helpful, in the days immediately following disclosure, for the child to accompany the supervisor on duty to personally check that all the outside doors to the building are securely locked. Such assistance helps the child to feel less anxious, to get to sleep, and to have fewer nightmares.

A compelling reason to uncover memories of trauma is to relieve the additional burden of secrecy and forced silence. If the effort is successful, the child can separate past from present events and realize that he or she is now safe from further harm. Such efforts are feasible, however, only if the child has sufficient coping and psychological resources to undertake such work.

INTERVENING IN POSTTRAUMATIC PLAY

In line with the views of other clinicians (Gil 1991; Herman 1992; James 1989, 1994; and Terr 1990), we believe that interrupting the repetitive enactment of posttraumatic play is absolutely necessary. Responding to such play in a nondirective manner is not helpful. Nondirective responses can actually be harmful because they reinforce the sense of helplessness and powerlessness, a significant feature of the original terrifying experience. Initially, repetitions of scenes resembling the trauma are the child's attempts to master the situation. Yet the very fact that posttraumatic play is compulsively repeated indicates that the play does not relieve the child's anxiety (Terr 1983). Play in a nontraumatized child relieves anxiety. After an emotionally distressing scene is played out, such as one in which a teacher doll yells at a girl doll, the child's anxiety is relieved, and the scene is not repeated with the same intensity. Eventually, the scene is no longer played, and the child moves to another topic.

The traumatized child, however, can get stuck in endless repetitions of the same scenes, with little or no variation, because the mastery of the situation and the relief expected is not forthcoming. When Dr. Mordock's youngest daughter was five years old, she stopped playing with one of her friends because the child only wanted to play school. She was always the teacher, and Dr. Mordock's daughter always the student. Later, the girl developed a school phobia and refused to go to school.

When play themes are endlessly repeated, the therapist needs to become actively involved. Gil (1991) suggests a number of different interventions. One includes actively reflecting the feelings of one or more characters in the play. Another involves introducing other characters that allow for correction of the traumatic scenario. Terr (2003) describes three essential phases in healing trauma in children: (1) abreactions—speaking, writing, or playing out the emotions directly related to the trauma events; (2) creating context—putting the traumatic memories into some kind of meaningful perspective; and (3) correction—stating or playing out hoped-for solutions or modifications of actions to prevent future occurrences. Most interventions in posttraumatic play typically fall into the last category. Introducing a corrective action, such as having helpful neighbors, policemen, emergency medical technicians, or superheroes arrive on the scene, suggests that the trauma situation can be corrected and that things can be done and plans can be made to reduce the chance of the traumatic event's recurring in the future. Such interventions also address the victim's "frozen inaction" (van der Kolk 2003). Introducing a corrective action that modifies the original scene empowers the child to take action that mitigates the overpowering sense of helplessness.

CRUCIAL CUES FROM THE CHILD

Children who have adequate resources to undertake the invitational track are helped, little by little, to uncover and face the repressed memories associated with traumatic experiences. In many cases, therapists are not privy to what traumatized the child. But most gorilla-suit wearers have been repeatedly traumatized throughout their young lives, and their behavior often reveals their efforts to master some rather specific early experiences. Adults may suspect the child has been traumatized because of the symptoms displayed, although symptoms are not easily tied to the event. For example, we may not realize for some time that a boy's disruptive behavior on a school bus results from his having been beaten up on one. Knowing the general circumstances surrounding a child's abuse is different from treating clients whose trauma histories are unknown or clients in crisis following a newly disclosed trauma event.

When developing therapeutic strategies for children in gorilla suits, the plans must address the way the therapist will respond if the child's actions suggest a specific trauma has been experienced. When a child's traumatic experiences are documented in the child's medical or social history, the therapist can prepare the child to deal with these past events. Many mothers admit to their abusive behavior or remember times when a past paramour abused their child or when the child was injured and sent to the hospital. The need for a detailed history of the child's life should go without saying. Nevertheless, while a therapist may know that a child has been traumatized by an event, or a series of events, the details of each event, the circumstances surrounding it, and the meanings the child gave to it are rarely known.

Many gorilla-suit wearers spend a large part of their young lives in foster care, and much of their past is either forgotten or buried in county social service or hospital records never seen by the treating clinician. Records obtained from one hospital may state that a girl suffered head injuries when she was seven, but it may not mention that she visited the emergency room of another hospital on numerous occasions when younger, experiences that will affect the meaning she gives to her later head injury. In some cases, a thorough psychological evaluation often suggests the presence of attitudes and perceptions that may stem from early traumas, but in other cases, the therapist must wait and see what unfolds in therapy and then determine if the child needs a period of ego strengthening before approaching the topic.

When a trauma has been documented, the therapist should communicate to the child that he or she knows about the traumatic event(s). Therapy will proceed more smoothly when the child doesn't feel the need to start at square one. If the therapist waits for the child to bring up a past trauma, its revelation might not occur unless specific play materials are introduced that stimulate playing scenes associated with the trauma.

Dr. Crenshaw treated a child whose younger brother died in a fire in their home. At the first reference to fire in the child's play, Dr. Crenshaw said, "This must be hard for you because I know that your little bother died in a fire at your house." The therapist encouraged the child to continue his ongoing activity, but the scary secret was now out in the open, and the child knew it was not up to him alone to broach this painful topic. The child was not expected to tackle this topic at the time, but the seed had been planted that he would eventually do so. When a therapist is unclear about the exact trauma a child has experienced, the following can be communicated:

> THERAPIST: I'm aware that lots of terrible and scary things happened to you in your life, some of which your mother [*grandmother/foster parent/social worker/teacher*] told me. I also know that these bad things still trouble you—even though you try not to think about them. Sometimes you even dream about them and cannot sleep. And sometimes you resist going to bed, and when your mom finally makes you, you try to keep awake so you won't dream. Therapy is a place where we will deal, perhaps not right away, but definitely at some later time, with these past hurts and pains and

the troubles they have caused you over the years. In fact, I'll bet you don't know how your present troubles are related to your past hurts. We will work together on this task when you are ready.

CHILD: I have no troubles.

THERAPIST: But other people have troubles with you—otherwise you wouldn't be here. They have lots of trouble with your temper. Maybe you don't realize that you didn't always have a bad temper and that it started soon after some of your early hurts and pains.

CHILD: What did my mother tell you happened to me?

THERAPIST: That your father often beat you when he was drunk.

CHILD: He never did!

THERAPIST: And children never beat you up at school?

CHILD: Nope. I beat them up!

THERAPIST: Here, make me a drawing of you doing something on the playground.

CHILD: I don't want to.

THERAPIST: What would you like to draw?

This child needs to develop coping skills before being invited to work on uncovering emotions associated with early traumas. Others, however, when given tacit permissions by the therapist, move rather quickly into trauma-related play. In fact, as we emphasize in chapter 5, some move too quickly and will need the therapist's help to avoid the compulsion to repeat painful topics. The therapist can help by restructuring sessions around board games, drawings, and conversations about the child's current life. But, at the same time, the therapist must communicate the following message:

> THERAPIST: These painful topics will be talked about later in therapy when you and I know each other better and I have helped you learn to create certain play themes or make specific drawings without feeling uncomfortable or being upset immediately afterwards.

When conveying this message, the therapist must choose the words carefully. If the therapist should say, "These tropics will be dealt with later," the child may think that a reprimand or punishment will come later because children usually associate adult anger with the words "dealt with." But the message must be given. If not, the child will think his or her experiences are too horrible for even the therapist to witness, and the child will feel even more hopeless and rejected.

When play scenarios become less distant and more transparent—when they begin to resemble the actual trauma events—the child is communicating, "I'm getting close to being able to face what happened to me." Often the therapist agonizes over whether to remain in the metaphor of the play or to "bring it home" with a clarifying question, such as "Has anything like that happened to you?" The therapist has to judge whether the child can manage the strong emotions that follow direct confrontation of the trauma, such as reexperiencing the original terror or feeling overwhelming rage or profound sorrow. If the therapist decides the child cannot, because of inadequate ego and defensive resources, then a period of ego strengthening is offered. In chapter 5, we discuss some of the factors to consider when making such judgments.

Play therapists uncertain about how to proceed with specific cases should seek consultation in which they can discuss the child in depth and the child's readiness for exploratory work. Few negative consequences follow exercising caution and patience. Since the play dramas of children show considerable redundancy, the therapist will have a number of opportunities to focus the child on trauma experiences. Sometimes, when the therapist makes the wrong judgment, or the timing is off, the child may simply stop playing, want to leave the session early, or back off from trauma play scenarios for several subsequent sessions. The child communicates "You're pushing me too hard" or "I'm not ready to go there yet." Therapists can confirm the child's message.

> THERAPIST: I believe you want to leave early today because I'm pushing you too hard. I'm glad you can tell me when therapy has become too much. I was asking about something you are not ready to talk about just yet.

Sometimes the consequences of poor timing can be significant. Triggered by trauma memories, the child may become enraged, start breaking things, make sexual advances toward the therapist, or act out in a manner dangerous to the self or others. The first priority in handling a reactive episode is to reestablish safety, both within and outside of therapy. The therapist cannot responsibly act as the "Lone Ranger" in such crises. The family or caregivers need to be involved and made aware that the child is trying to face very "tough stuff" in the therapy, and extra measures must be taken to ensure the safety of the child and others during this period.

In some situations, an emergency assessment for inpatient hospitalization is required because around-the-clock structure may be needed to help the child to stabilize. Medications may also be used to facilitate stabilization. If the child is in residential treatment, sometimes extra measures can be taken to ensure the child's safety within the program and result in less disruption in the child's ongoing treatment. Such situations require careful monitoring. Suicidal impulses are often acted on without planning or forethought, reflecting children's action orientation and their impulsive, nonreflective responses to stress.

Reactions to the exploration of traumatic memories can range from momentary setbacks to major crises. Most of the time, the consequences of wrong judgments or of poor timing fall between these two extremes. Children can get angry but not lose control. They may refuse to come to the next appointment or may avoid issues in therapy for longer periods than seem warranted. When children pull back and remain detached from affective material for long periods, therapists typically become anxious, feeling they are failing in their job. Once again, reasoned judgments need to be made. Is the avoidance allowing a child to regroup and to reestablish safety, or does the child need a gentle push from the therapist to resume therapeutic exploration? If the former, the attuned therapist will recognize that the child is still testing to see if therapy remains a "safe place" for future exposure of "invisible wounds" (Hardy 1998). If the latter case, it is to be hoped that the therapist will "read" the child's need for direction and encourage approaching the scary material.

> THERAPIST: It has been a long time since you have played out the scene about the boy being chased by his angry stepdad.
> THERAPIST: I have the feeling that we need to do more work with that. I don't believe we are finished.
> THERAPIST: Perhaps we could interview that boy-doll and get his ideas of what needs to happen next.

By keeping the inquiry within the metaphor—within the safe haven of symbolic play—the child is less threatened by the therapist's efforts to refocus sessions on the really "scary stuff." If the child adamantly refuses, with comments such as "F— you! I'll decide what I want to play!" then it is important to convey, with clinical conviction, that the child's protest has been heard and honored. "I understand you don't want to go there now. We will go there later when you feel stronger!" If the therapist has determined that the child belongs on the invitational track and ongoing treatment efforts have confirmed that decision, then an expectation that the "hard stuff" will eventually be discussed is conveyed. It is not a matter of if but of when. The planting of this mind-set—the firm conviction that the child will eventually deal with the hard stuff and that the child has the strength and courage to do so—is necessary to progress in therapy.

REFLECTIONS OF AFFECT AND MOTIVES

As the play scenarios approximate more closely the actual traumatic events, the therapist reflects feelings of the play characters, particularly if no affect is communicated. Reflections are not simply parroting the child's verbalization. They must add greater complexity and convey a larger picture, much of which lies outside the child's awareness. The reflections relate to the affect suggested by the central characters but not verbalized by the child. For example, a child may create a scenario involving an out-of-control car careening down a mountain at high speed. The affect is unspoken but richly symbolized in the play action. The therapist reflects the affect.

> THERAPIST: Oh, the car is out of control and going down the mountain! The people in the car must be very scared.

If the reflections are off the mark, often children correct them. O'Connor (2002) mentions that sometimes the therapist is better off being wrong because the child, in the eagerness to correct, often reveals more about the actual affect. In the above example, it may turn out that the child is enraged with the passengers in the car. Perhaps his dad is in the car, and his dad beats him. The proper reflection in this case would be "Someone must be angry with the people in the car." This proper reflection, however, may not be learned until the child makes a revealing correction of the therapist's response. Reflections of motive can also be valuable (O'Connor, 2002). For example, when working with a child who must win every game, the therapist might point out that the child always quits the game after falling behind. The therapist might follow this comment with, "You try to win every time because you like to be in control," followed by, "If you were to lose the game, you would feel like you have lost control." Notice that no attempt is made to connect the child's rigid efforts at control with emotions related to past trauma, even though the need to control may stem from loss of control during the traumatic experience. The task is simply to help the child become aware of present feelings and motives, symbolized in the play, which are not explicitly expressed because, to a large extent, they are outside of the child's awareness.

AN ILLUSTRATIVE CASE

Max Sugar (1988) presents his treatment of a preschooler who witnessed a disaster. We have abridged the case here to illustrate how the disaster, in and of itself, did not produce Peter's symptoms. We have embellished some of the details, expanded on the case material, and added our own clinical thinking to make Peter's treatment more illustrative of the clinical thinking required to treat traumatized victims. We also use Peter's case as a "stepping-off place" to expand our discussion of the invitational approach to treating traumatized children. We chose to abridge this case rather than one of our own because the reader has the opportunity to study the complete treatment of this child by reading the original publication. Peter was referred for insomnia, night terrors, increased irritability, phobic reactions to noises and thunderstorms, and hostile behavior, such as bullying other children and provoking his mother. He experienced separation anxiety, resented his parents' absences, was fearful, and felt unsafe. He was preoccupied with airplanes and crashes, wished his house would burn down, marked the walls in his house, and was caught attempting to burn newspapers.

An airline plane crashed seventy-five feet from his home. On the way to its resting place a block away, it had destroyed the homes immediately adjacent to Peter's neighbor. Part of the flaming fuselage landed in the street near Peter's home, and part of a tree, which the plane hit, landed in the yard. After Peter's mother saw a wall of flames around the neighboring houses, she ran with Peter's younger brother in her arms and with Peter and another brother in pursuit, only to meet with a wall of fire about thirty-five feet away. Peter froze in panic and screamed for several minutes. This screaming occurred several times during their efforts to remain safe. The family stayed elsewhere for several days while city engineers assessed the safety of their home. Unusual traffic and heavy machinery and equipment were in their neighborhood for some time.

Peter lived with his parents and three siblings in their own home. Of his brothers, one older and one younger, neither displayed the symptoms that Peter displayed, nor did either engage in the incessant postcrash reenactment play that characterized Peter's behavior. Peter bullied both younger and older peers and provoked his mother with "yes-no thing" behavior (e.g., asking for water at bedtime and then refusing the water offered). This behavior was a recurrence, first having appeared about fifteen months before the crash and lasting for nine months.

Before the disaster, Peter did well in the preschool he was attending. His birth was several weeks premature but otherwise normal, as was his birth weight. He needed orthopedic shoes during his early development and had repeated ear infections, requiring ear tubes from age eighteen months to thirty months. About nine months before the crash, he had tried to set fires in the house when his parents were away.

When initially seen, Peter was oriented to time and place and seemed overly knowledgeable about his father's work. Peter reported no physical symptoms, but he admitted to the sleeping difficulties reported by others. He said that he ate well and had friends with whom he played. While he had destructive wishes (counterphobic efforts?), he had no suicidal ones. His strong reenactments of the crash made it difficult to assess for hallucinations and delusions. Because of his preoccupations, he experienced difficulty concentrating on other topics. Regarding the crash, Peter incorrectly perceived time, time sequences, and time duration, errors often reported by child victims of disaster.

Peter played throughout the initial interview while he verbalized experiences related to the crash, seemingly driven to express the details of this event through play followed by words. Yet, the compulsive retelling only served to heighten his anxiety. He also was preoccupied with his father's car and his work. His play suggested unusual anger at his parents, perhaps because they failed him as protectors. The therapist asked himself the following questions as he began treatment with Peter. Why did Peter react to the disaster differently than either of his brothers? Is his detailed knowledge of his father's business activities and his preoccupation with his father's car a dynamic to consider? What is the implication of his return to earlier regressed behaviors ("yes-no thing," fire setting, return of enuresis, bullying others)? Why did he wish his home destroyed? Is his intense reaction to noises merely the intrusion of stimuli reactivating the crash scene? Why did he display marked panic reactions after the crash?

Max Sugar made a psychodynamic formulation about the case. He said that at the time of the crash, Peter was at the height of his oedipal conflict. He had stopped fire setting and playing with matches. His interest in his father's activities was intense, and he knew many details of his father's business at age four. Yet his identification with his father was incomplete. The father was still experienced as a rival for Mother. His early interest in his father's activities predates the oedipal period and may reflect atypical rivalry with his father in response to the mother's possible dissatisfaction with the father or the father's passivity. The early fire setting and taunting of Mother supports the view that some marital friction was present. His oedipal conflict also was complicated by repressed hostility toward his brothers, who were rivals for his mother's affection.

Peter's intense reaction to noises, especially noises in the night, resulted from intrusive stimuli from the crash scene and from primal-scene material. Neither brother experienced similar reactions, nor did they fear, as Peter did, the house shifting or being destroyed. Perhaps Peter's early medical problems heightened his fears of bodily harm. Observations of the behavior of disaster victims reveal that many become angry. Peter directed his anger at the airplanes, the airline company, and his parents, weaving it in with oedipal issues and displacing it through rivalry with his father, brothers, and peers. His response to the disaster also involved his regression to earlier modes of functioning. Anal-sadistic behavior was displayed in torturing his mother with the "yes-no thing," marking the walls (possible reenactment of the city engineers' behavior?), his wish to mess (also the turning of passive into active—I'll create the mess as opposed to being the victim of a mess), and his defiance. The return of enuresis, fire setting, and bullying and the provoking of his mother and other children revealed regression from the marginally achieved phallic stage of

psychosexual development. Peter's reenactments included components of identification with the aggressor as well as efforts at mastery.

Preschool children expect perfection from their parents and believe them
to be omnipotent. The disaster temporarily shattered this belief, resulting in
anger at his parents, who failed him, which in turn threatened his own omnipotent feelings. The trauma increased his fears of his own aggressive feelings
and magical wishes. The crash prevented him from resolving the oedipal conflict and, at the time, added the additional threat that, if he was not "good" and
did not give up his claim on his mother, he would experience further destruction. He may have felt responsible for the crash and projected this responsibility onto his siblings. In summary, Peter felt helpless and guilty, feared
abandonment, was angry at his parents and others, and feared injury (not getting hurt equated with being "good"), all exaggerated by regression from resolution of the oedipal complex.

While helpful to the psychoanalytic therapist, Sugar's psychodynamic formulation would need to be carefully reworded when it is placed in the child's
clinical record as it is not a family-friendly formulation. The parents would not
understand much of it, and if they asked to read the record, it would alienate
them, and they might withdraw Peter from treatment. We would reword it as
follows: Peter's early medical problems heightened his fear of bodily harm. His
anger, and perhaps his fire setting, were efforts to master the frightening experience. Nevertheless, he had set a fire before the incident, and his subsequent
fire setting may represent regressive anger or may result from some association
he made between the fires he set and the fires on the airplane.

Children Peter's age view their parents as all-powerful, yet for some reason Peter didn't experience his mother as protective. She didn't stop the crash!
Perhaps this is why Peter was angry at her. Peter's immature behavior was an
attempt to retreat to a more comfortable stage in life when his coping efforts
were successful. Other behaviors were reenactments of the trauma or of elements of the experience surrounding the trauma. Children Peter's age also can
believe that their thoughts can cause things. Perhaps he was angry at a sibling
just before the crash and believed that these angry thoughts caused the plane
to crash. Perhaps his early fire setting was also sibling related and associated
with the plane crash.

In addition, we do not believe it necessary to explain Peter's troubles by
anchoring them in Sigmund Freud's psychosexual theories of development.
We would have attributed Peter's problems to the idiosyncratic meanings he
gave to the incident, meanings that may have stemmed from his earlier medical treatment and his specific family history. Perhaps his overly close relationship with his mother, which might have followed his early medical treatments,
gave him the covert message that he was more vulnerable to injury and needed

more care. His rivalrous feelings toward his siblings could also stem from his self-perception of being "damaged goods" and needing more care. The father's distant relationship with Peter could have resulted from a number of factors, including his wife's possible overprotection of his son. The father's role in a son's development is to remove him from the "sheltering mother" (the mother's normal role) and expose him to both the "dangers" and the exciting potentials of the outside world. For reasons yet to be discovered, Peter's father had failed him in this role. Still, we would have proceeded in play therapy in a manner similar to that of his psychoanalytic therapist, Max Sugar.

Because Peter's play revealed his efforts to master the stress to which he was exposed, play therapy for Peter and guidance of his parents was the treatment of choice. Abreactions are a necessary condition for therapeutic growth, and when they occur in the presence of a therapist, the child can be helped to reconstruct memories of the trauma and relate them to other memories while the therapist serves as an auxiliary ego when the memories evoke strong anxiety.

When developing a therapeutic plan for Peter, the therapist should attempt to answer the following questions: How can Peter be helped to move toward latency as well as to master this traumatic experience? What feelings will Peter displace in his transference relationship with the therapist? What defenses does Peter need to develop to replace those in current use? (He currently uses projection, denial, and splitting.) Are the mother and father responding appropriately to Peter's postdisaster behavior?

The goals of Peter's therapy are (1) a decrease or cessation of reenactments and an increase in periods of more normal play, (2) repeated abreactions in small doses until the trauma and its effects are linked and mastered, and (3) a decrease or cessation of symptomatic behaviors.

If therapy is working, observations of Peter's play during therapy will reveal more actual crash-related details and less reversal, magic, fantasy, denial, and displacement, and observations of play at home and school will reveal fewer crash-related themes and increased preoccupation with age-appropriate conflicts. Peter will also display relief through more connected and integrated play. His play themes will last for longer periods and be interrupted less by tangential associations. Peter's increased memory of the actual details of the crash will sometimes be accompanied by intense anxiety. Abreactions are not likely to occur until he is attached to the therapist and feels safe in the therapist's presence. Peter will report less awakening during the night and less time lying awake before falling asleep.

Therapy will focus on helping Peter to understand that his play reflects both distorted memories of the trauma and defense wishes related to the trauma. He needs to transform the feelings connected to the memories, and to the defensive wishes, into forms that can be verbally expressed. The task is not to uncover structured memories but to construct memories. The former task is an uncovering process, while the latter is a structuring one. Pathological forms of memory, which include both Peter's play and his incessant talk about the crash, need to be transformed into normal memories. The therapist has to pay close attention to the timing of clarifications and interpretations and to structuring efforts so that Peter's alliance with the therapist will help him withstand the anxiety that such work generates.

Peter's play therapy focused on the therapist's serving as an auxiliary ego and helping him withstand the onslaught of strong feelings and terror about both the facts and the fantasies he experienced before, during, and after the trauma, some of which he reexperienced in therapy. He was helped to organize, manage, and recall his actual experiences; to remember the details; and to separate the facts of his traumatic experience from those associated with his intrapsychic struggles to master developmental challenges.

Although Max Sugar doesn't focus on his work with parents, we would explore how family members were reacting to Peter's behaviors and would guide them in the appropriate direction. We might also see his mother individually to learn how she has coped with the disaster and how she views her husband's role as an aid in her own recovery. We would also suggest family activities to help Peter to resolve his rivalry with his father for his mother's attention.

Peter's insomnia and night terrors are symptoms of Type II Pavor Nocturnes. A persistent sleep disturbance and recurrent nightmares indicate that a child is struggling with overwhelming anxiety. Some children defend against the intrusion of traumatic memories or repressed impulses by trying to stay awake (avoid the loss of control that comes with increasing drowsiness), or they awaken fully with the help of anxiety dreams when repressed impulses threaten to overcome the sleeping ego. These children are considerably less troubled than children with Type I Pavor Nocturnes, who remain in a "dream" state upon awakening. Type II children have full recall of the events during the night when they get up. In contrast, those with Type I Pavor Nocturnes do not fully awaken, and their confused and delusional dream state continues, even though the child may be out of bed, walking, or talking, i.e., motorically awake. Sperling (1982) reports that the prognosis for children with Type I Pavor Nocturnes is guarded because these children typically develop more serious problems.

Peter's enuresis following the disaster served (as does the anxiety dream) to awaken him and protect him from being overwhelmed or from expressing forbidden impulses. Many children with enuresis keep themselves up deliberately in order to prevent themselves from nightmares and bed-wetting. As therapy helps Peter to master his fears, his enuresis and sleep problems will wane and eventually disappear.

During Peter's first dozen or so therapy sessions, his conflicts and efforts at resolution became more clear. He believed the crash to be his brother's fault because his brother wanted it to crash (projection of blame). He verbalized the wish to destroy his own home (viewed as a displacement from anger at Mother and passive surrender to Father). At this stage of his treatment, he was leaning toward identifying with his mother rather than his father—a situation now complicated by feelings that she both protected him (he was not hurt) and failed him (he was exposed).

Therapy goals now focused on these issues, and his play revealed fewer and fewer destructive fantasies about his house or about being in the plane and less effort at restitution (less undoing play). Outside of therapy, Peter spent more time with his father, and his parents reported less arguing and fighting with his siblings. After approximately thirty-five sessions, Peter's treatment game to an end. He showed marked increases in genuine playfulness, minimal crash-related play, and resumption of normal development.

ENACTMENT OF TRAUMA AS A RESULT OF UNPREDICTABLE TRIGGERING

Tommy, a nine-year-old boy, broke some office equipment in an impulsive rage triggered by his falling behind in a game he insisted on playing. The therapist, Dr. Crenshaw, failed to fully appreciate what losing meant to him. When his story gradually unfolded, he told Dr. Crenshaw that his grandfather, with whom he had a cherished relationship, had died within the past year. His grandfather was the one person who unequivocally loved him. His status in his nuclear family was very shaky. He was an impulsive and disruptive child, and both his mother and his father managed him with their own temper outbursts, blaming him for the constant disruptions and crises the family often experienced. When his grandfather died, Tommy was openly blamed for causing the death. It was Tommy's raucous behavior that caused the heart attack! In reality, Tommy was no more disruptive than his two brothers, who were also quite active and impulsive. For unknown reasons, Tommy became the family scapegoat, always the loser when competing for the meager resources available from his beleaguered parents.

Tommy reacted so powerfully to the thought of losing a game because of the very real loss of his grandfather, the one person who truly loved and spent meaningful time with him. In addition to the unmourned loss of this significant other, Tommy bore the devastating burden of feeling responsible for his grandfather's death. Tommy shared his profound loss during a moment of great anguish. The moment occurred after Tommy smashed the answering machine while running out of Dr. Crenshaw's office. Dr. Crenshaw followed him out to the street. He then ran to the entrance of the community hospital next to the medical building in which the office was located. He entered the hospital and ran down the main corridor with Dr. Crenshaw in hot pursuit. A security guard joined the chase when Tommy was about halfway down the long corridor. Tommy then ran out the back door of the hospital (with Dr. Crenshaw thinking that this scene was not going to enhance his reputation as a child therapist!), and Dr. Crenshaw finally caught up with him in a parking lot in back of the hospital. He was sobbing, and Dr. Crenshaw told the security guard that he would take it from there. The boy sat with Dr. Crenshaw on the lawn next to the parking lot and tearfully related his feelings. He was almost hysterical. "I didn't mean to smash your answering machine! I didn't mean to kill my grandfather. I just want to die!"

> THERAPIST: Tommy, I know you feel horrible pain that your grandfather died, but you didn't kill him. He died because his heart was worn out and wasn't working anymore. It had nothing to do with your running around the house or making a lot of noise with your brothers. Nothing at all! Your grandfather loved you and you loved him. I know you miss him terribly, but it's not your fault that he died. It is your fault that my answering machine is broken, but I know you feel bad about it and you did it when you were not in control of your anger, and that is something we can work on together.
>
> We can talk about that more later. Right now I want you to know that the love you had for your grandfather and the specialness of your relationship with him is something that you can hold as a treasured memory forever. Tommy, you have lost a lot that has been important to you, but your feelings for your grandfather can never be taken from you. That feeling of being so loved and so special to your grandfather—you can keep that, Tommy. You can take it with you always. And that is far more valuable than a thousand answering machines!
>
> TOMMY: [*A slight beginning of a smile appearing.*] More valuable than a million answering machines?
>
> THERAPIST: That's for sure! Now let's head back. We have quite a walk back to the office.

Tommy's treatment reveals how trauma material can be dramatically and unexpectedly triggered, as well as the power of accompanying affects. Dr. Crenshaw knew about the grandfather's death. He also suspected that Tommy felt excluded from his nuclear family. But he did not realize that, in addition to his unbearable loss, Tommy had been blamed for the grandfather's death. By impulsively breaking the answering machine and then running out of the building to the hospital and down the hospital corridors, Tommy recreated the disruptive scenario that his parents claimed had caused his grandfather's death. He assumed that the painful exclusion he had experienced in his family would now be repeated as a result of breaking the office machine. When he had fully processed this event, it became clear that he assumed Dr. Crenshaw would reject him and no longer be his therapist.

Tommy's case is typical of child therapy. No matter how well a therapist plans and prepares, children can go in unanticipated directions. When this happens, preconceived notions about the therapy process must be set aside and the child's needs considered rather than the needs of the therapist to be viewed as effective. We don't remember any graduate school textbook addressing what to do when an enraged child breaks your answering machine, leaves the building, and runs down the corridors of the hospital next door, alarming hospital personnel, who alert a security guard who joins you in the chase. Yet that experience was a turning point in Tommy's therapy. He learned that, even at his worst moments, something good and redeemable in him could be appreciated. He also learned that his therapist, like his grandfather, was not going to exclude him or give up on him. This was a pivotal corrective emotional experience for this troubled boy.

DYNAMIC FLEXIBILITY AND TITRATING THE APPROACH

In an ideal and perfect clinical world, an incident like the one experienced during Tommy's treatment would not occur, even though its occurrence yielded beneficial results. Normally, traumatic imagery is approached gradually, allowing for titrated amounts of affective release. The children are unburdened by telling their story in small, manageable segments to avoid being overwhelmed or flooded by strong emotions. Nevertheless, such smooth progression rarely occurs. The coping and invitational tracks, discussed in chapter 5, call for a fluid and dynamic approach within each track, as well as for shifting tracks when the child's functioning requires it. Temporary regressions, or pulling back from trauma-related material, may involve nothing more than accepting the child's need to slow the pace. If intense anxiety is activated, or increased acting out follows, either in therapy or elsewhere, or if a resurgence of symptoms occurs, then the therapist returns to the coping track until the child's functioning is stabilized.

The goal is to create ego strengths and coping skills that will enable the child to face repressed memories without the risk of retraumatization. Switching tracks when needed more adequately captures the complexity of trauma work than does the dichotomous decision that either the child can undertake trauma work or the child cannot.

· 18 ·

Helping Children to
Mourn Tangible Losses

In this chapter, we describe helping children to mourn tangible losses. The developmental limitations, as well as other obstacles, to undertaking the grieving process are discussed, especially with children in gorilla suits, whose lives are typically replete with loss. Structured activities to help children on the invitational track to deal with tangible losses include memory books or albums; poems, songs, and journal writing; "linking objects" and photographs; relived funeral or memorial services; and structured family therapy sessions.

*E*rna Furman reported the results of her study of children's grief reactions in her classic work, *A Child's Parent Dies* (1971). Nevertheless, fifteen years later, Furman (1986) reminds clinicians that, while a parent's death is always stressful, it is not necessarily traumatic. She emphasizes that, like all traumas, the idiosyncratic meanings the child gives to the death can make it traumatic. We would add that the care the child receives after the death can also adversely affect development. Following the loss of a parent, through either death or abandonment, toddlers require reassurance that their needs for love and safety will continue to be met. Affirming the caregiving relationship with the surviving parent and other family members is especially important. Maintaining discipline is also key because young children control their impulses in an effort to please cared-for adults; they develop control because they fear the parent will withdraw his or her love. When that parent dies, the child's controls break down. The surviving parent needs help to understand the child's need for clear and firm external controls. Consumed with their own grief, they may not administer discipline consistently. Nevertheless, easing up expectations for the child is not helpful. If a child's need for security and discipline is not met at this time, these unmet needs can be seeds for future problems. In addition, children often express anger at the

255

surviving parent, and an undisciplined environment can accelerate the process and set in motion an antagonistic parent-child relationship.

Young children (ages three to six) play games and answer questions about death in ways that indicate that they see it as reversible. When queried about whether dead things can be brought back to life, they respond, "Take them to the hospital" or "Let them rest up and sleep." During what Selma Fraiberg (1959) has called "the magic years," symbolism abounds. Anything can stand for anything. Children may resist certain activities because they symbolize loss. For example, number games may be avoided because they stimulate thoughts about changes in the number of family members. Because children think in concrete terms, they respond to stimuli associated with the lost person. They may chase red sports cars calling, "Daddy! Daddy!" because their father drove one. Although grieving adults make similar associations, to them it's just a reminder; to a young child, it's the real thing and can contribute to false hopes for the loved one's return.

As a result of their cognitive limitations (They don't realize the person is permanently gone) and their emotional instability (When they do miss the person, they can't cry for long), children are "reluctant grievers," rarely displaying behavior shown by grieving adults. Yet it should not be assumed, even in very young children, that mourning is unnecessary. Some mourn on their own while others need help from a facilitating environment (Kranzler et al. 1990). Generally, children under age three are incapable of understanding death. Yet while they may not understand it, they react to its effects, particularly when a parent dies.

Around the age of nine, children's views about the mysteries of death approach those of adults, and by adolescence, with the advent of abstract thought (the cognitive stage of formal operations), death is seen as (1) final and irreversible, (2) universal, and (3) inevitable. Nevertheless, many adolescents fail to truly comprehend the finality of death, as shown by their suicide fantasies, which include thoughts about the attention they will get from others after the suicide. Those involved in school shootings, whether they planned to shoot themselves or to be shot in a grand standoff, may have fantasized about the fame the shootings would bring them and the satisfaction they would feel at having sought revenge—"In death there would be life."

CHILDREN GRIEVE IN STEPS

Because of immature cognitive capacities, defenses, and coping resources, children express their grief in steps, able to tolerate the intensely painful, and often overwhelming, emotions of grief only for brief periods. As a result, for preschool and school-age children, mourning can last throughout childhood and adolescence. As the child matures, better understandings of the implications of a loss follow. The boy whose father died when he was four may experience new grief when he enters school and has no father to attend parents' night. He may grieve again when he plays Little League Baseball and he has no father to watch his game or to attend a father-son banquet. At adolescence, he may grieve again when fathers of his friends take pictures as their children, "dressed to kill," head off to the prom.

The natural protective instincts of adults lead them to shield children from the emotional impact of life's inevitable losses, not realizing that embracing and expressing grief is essential to the healing process. Many parents are reluctant to grieve in front of their children or to encourage children to express their own sadness. Hating to see their child in pain, they convince themselves that the child is too young to understand. Nevertheless, parents should share their grief as long as the display is accompanied by the reassurance that "we will make it through this, and one day it all won't hurt so much." Children most likely to mourn are those whose parents model the process (Kranzler et al. 1990). Such modeling allows the child to see that it is okay to have these feelings and to express them and, most of all, that strong feelings can be borne. Adults who actively encourage, facilitate, and support the child's grieving, even well after the actual loss, are the most helpful.

A preschool child who repeatedly puts a doll in a shoe box but who shows no outward signs of sadness may be viewed by the surviving parent as not dealing with the loss. "She never says 'I miss mommy' or sheds any tears." But at age four, that may be the best she can do. When older and able to better appreciate the significance of her loss, she may verbalize feelings about the loss and grieve more fully.

But if the surviving parent becomes uncomfortable with its expression, the child learns that grieving makes the pain of the parent greater. The child can shut down and repress affects to protect the parent. Later, the child's repressed feelings can reappear as a behavioral disturbance (Kranzler et al. 1990). Likewise, a tentative therapist, unsure about what is helpful, may not pursue the child's grief and, as a result, may unwittingly shut down the child's mourning process. Therapists who are convinced that mourning is helpful will explore, in a diligent but compassionate manner, feelings connected with unmourned losses.

TREATMENT OVER TIME

The therapy door should always be left open to enable the child and family to return for more grief work. Returning to treatment is not a failure. Instead, a

return means that, because of the child's age at the time of the loss, only partial mourning was achieved. The child had become symptom-free at the time,
but the mourning remained incomplete, and further mourning did not occur
naturally. The child, now older, begins to display signs of complicated grief.
The signs may include the onset of uncontrollable tears following sad movies,
exaggerated reactions to minor losses, intrusive thoughts about the lost one,
sleeplessness, or decreased academic functioning due to impaired concentration. Because the child is now more mature, however, he or she can, with help,
take further steps to mourn.

Children approaching adolescence may also need to mourn the loss of
the "parent figure" they never had but who might have been a major influence in their life: "If I had a father, I would have been a better ball player." "I
wouldn't have been called a "sissy" by other boys and gotten in so many
fights." "I would have achieved more in school."

ACKNOWLEDGED LOSSES

Young children who have lost a loved one may engage in fantasy play resembling funeral activities. They may repeatedly bury dolls or other objects in an
attempt to master their fears, guilt, anger, sadness, and other painful feelings.
Through play, situations that were passively experienced can be actively mastered. Young children may also express loss through drawings, artwork, and clay
productions.

> Michelle's play, also presented elsewhere (Crenshaw 1990a), illustrates the futile
> coping efforts of children traumatized by loss. Michelle was five when seen in in-
> dividual play therapy. She was referred for extreme anxiety that made it difficult for
> her to sit still and adjust to her kindergarten class. When Michelle was three and a
> half, her father was shot and killed in his office during a robbery.
>
> In Michelle's play, she repeatedly created scenes depicting one catastrophe after an-
> other. Typically, someone would die or be murdered. Sometimes tall buildings would
> come crashing down, and entire cities would be crushed. Sometimes Michelle
> would laugh in the midst of the catastrophic happenings, an obvious attempt to deny
> her anxiety. Sometimes the catastrophes were undone by powerful superheroes. Her
> sense of vulnerability and fear of making new attachments were vividly expressed in
> one session when, in the throes of an intense play drama, she abruptly turned to the
> therapist and asked, "Do you think someone could break in here and kill you?"
>
> Gradually, with the therapist clarifying and interpreting feelings within the
> metaphor of her play, Michelle worked through her fears about death and her anger
> at her father for abandoning her. The therapist explained, within the metaphor of
> her play, that sometimes horrible things happen, but these are rare events, and
> while evil people exist in the world and can harm others, the world contains many
> more people who are kind and caring.

When she was ten, new symptoms emerged, and Michelle returned to therapy. At this age, however, she talked about her loss as well as about feeling abandoned by her mother, whose complicated grief grew into a depression that lasted nearly four years. She felt deserted by both parents. Her father was absent physically and her mother emotionally. Her mother was encouraged to join a bereavement group in addition to entering into individual therapy, and she did so.

In adolescence, Michelle began to behave in ways that concerned her mother, and she was again referred for treatment. She drank heavily with friends and engaged in high-risk behaviors, the most significant of which resulted in a car accident. Fortunately, no serious injuries occurred, even though her car was packed with teenagers. [*She ran into a fence rather than a tree.*] At this time, she actively participated in therapy and also joined a bereavement group that assisted her to fully mourn. At this stage, witnessing her mother resuming a normal life motivated her to mourn herself. Michelle was able to move forward in life when convinced that her mother was also ready to give up her painful feelings. She felt she couldn't "desert" her mother by moving forward, and a protective attitude, characteristic of many children, inhibited her willingness to grieve. When Michelle's mother took steps to grieve, Michelle took similar steps, but only when convinced that her mother was okay.

Another example is four-year-old Jessie, seen in play therapy after his two-year-old sister died following a brief illness. Jessie had become oppositional and provocative and, when disciplined for these behaviors, became full of rage. His parents noted that he seemed much calmer for a period of time after these episodes subsided. In therapy, Jessie endlessly played with the ambulance and hospital toys. One person after another fell sick and needed a quick trip to the hospital [*signs of undoing harm?*]. Jessie's play suggested that he experienced guilt connected with his sister's death and actively sought punishment to alleviate these feelings.

THERAPIST: I wonder what is going on? One person after another falls sick or hurt and has to go to the hospital [*attention statement*]. I wonder why these things keep happening [*ignorant interrogator*]?

JESSIE: He is the bad guy.

THERAPIST: What do you mean?

JESSIE: [*Points to a boy doll hiding behind the house.*]

THERAPIST: Why is he the bad guy? What did he do?

JESSIE: He is bad.

THERAPIST: What did he do?

JESSIE: He made bad things happen.

THERAPIST: Wait a minute! He is just a little boy. How bad could he be? What bad things did he do?

JESSIE: He was mad at his sister and he wanted her to die!

THERAPIST: Oh, I get it. He was mad at his sister. In that moment when he was really mad, he had thoughts that he wished she was dead. Then his sister gets sick and dies and he thinks he is bad and all the bad things that happen are his fault [*reductive statement*].

JESSIE: Right.

THERAPIST: Let's talk to that boy. Lots of kids think things like that, but he is wrong. He just got mad at his sister. All brothers and sisters get mad at each other. But that doesn't cause them to die. He is not a bad kid. He is just a kid! Very serious illness and sickness or accidents cause people to die, but not being mad at someone. Look at that boy. He looks really scared [*modeling empathy*]. We need to help him understand that he didn't make all these bad things happen. He is just a little boy. How sad and alone he must feel [*empathetic clarification*].

Eventually, Jessie related times when he got so angry at his sister that he shouted at her, "I wish you were never born!" At that time, and over the course of therapy, the therapist repeatedly stated, "Angry words and thoughts don't cause people to die." His parents were asked to find opportunities to reinforce this fact at home, which they did repeatedly. Gradually, Jessie would repeat this statement to himself as he took injured people to the hospital in his play scenarios. Finally, the play with hospitals and ambulances stopped altogether.

Through the use of symbolic play, Jessie gave up the distorted notion that his angry wishes caused the death of his sister, and his guilt subsided, as did his acting-out behavior at home. Once again, his family played an active role in the therapy and in bringing about a positive resolution. Very few cases in the literature describe the treatment of children who have lost a sibling (Davids 1993). Evidently, few are referred for treatment following a sibling's death. Because the death of a sibling has stimulated the writing of novels and screen plays, we know the event is a profound one for many children.

Preschool children express their grief through drawings and play while school-age children more often cry, express sadness, and talk to others in an effort to organize and make sense of their experiences (Raphael 1983). Nevertheless, older gorilla-suit wearers, whose emotional development has been frozen by trauma at an age coinciding with the loss, will also need puppets, a dollhouse, drawings, work with clay, and dramatic play to provide them with the psychological distance needed to express their feelings and successfully mourn.

By playing out scenes in which Freddy the Frog is teased by Harry the Skunk or Billy the Turtle because he doesn't have a father or mother, children can gradually master feelings that would be overpowering if approached directly. Some children who use symbolic play to place distance between themselves and potentially overwhelming feelings can reach a point at which the feelings are directly expressed.

Children over the age of seven are usually more interested in board games and rule-governed games of all kinds. Their interest in rules and conventions is understood as one way to internalize the rules and regulations of authority so that the children are less dependent on the presence of authority figures to follow rules (Peller 1954). Those who have been traumatized by early losses may be functioning, both emotionally and socially, like much younger children. Many will need to develop coping skills first and then, with encouragement and modeling by the therapist, move from structured games to puppet play enacting dramatic events, expressing related feelings, and resolving related conflicts.

But even those on the coping track, who steadfastly remain with structured games or activities, can be helped by creative therapists to deal with loss. When they or the therapist loses a game, the larger meaning of the loss can be explored. Ablon (1990) has described his treatment of an eleven-year-old boy whose drawings and play with clay served as a springboard to a discussion of losses. Even when they played cards, Ablon and the boy talked about why some people were dealt good hands and others bad hands and what could be done to make the best of poor hands. Ablon also equated card playing with therapy, helping the boy to realize that the chief goal of therapy is like playing cards—remembering cards played in the past helps one to play better in the present.

DRAMATIC PLAY AND TANGIBLE LOSSES

Child therapists often find themselves playing a spirited game of hide-and-seek with school-age children who have experienced traumatic and/or multiple losses. This game, along with the more infantile version of "peek-a-boo," is played the world over by children trying to master the feelings of anxiety regarding separation and loss (Peller 1954). The high drama and tension experienced by the child when in the process of hiding and seeking attest to the psychological importance of mastering abandonment anxiety.

In dramatic play, children will hide puppets or stuffed animals and the therapist is asked to close his or her eyes and then, on signal, to seek and find the hidden object. As the therapist searches for it, the anxiety the child displays, as evidenced in worried looks, fidgety movements, or unnecessary clues, reveals the power of this theme. When the puppet is hidden and cannot immediately be found, anxiety can mount to such an intolerable level that the child refuses to play anymore. It can also play out in reverse, with the child searching for the puppet and, like Robert below, becoming more anxious as the search proceeds.

> ROBERT: I don't want to play anymore.
> THERAPIST: You were getting very close to finding Alligator. Do you think you would like to hang in there a little while longer? I think you are going to find him.
> ROBERT: No, I don't want to play anymore.

THERAPIST: Robert, I've noticed that this seems to be a pattern. When you have trouble finding one of the puppets, it seems to really upset you, and you stop playing. I have an idea. I hope you won't think this is silly, but I was thinking that maybe the game reminds you of not knowing when you are going to hear from your father again. He disappears for periods in your life. Then he comes back. Then he is gone again. I bet that can be very upsetting [*dynamic interpretation softened by empathy*].

ROBERT: Let's play the Talking, Doing, Feeling Game.

THERAPIST: [*Talking out loud to himself, but not directly to Robert.*] I guess Robert didn't hear my question. Or maybe he heard it and didn't want to answer it, and so he now wants to play a different game. Maybe thinking about his dad and not knowing when he will see his dad again is too difficult for Robert right now. We will talk about it at a later time, when he is ready.

ROBERT: Come on! I want to play this game!

The therapist didn't push the issue further, but the soliloquy (a common practice of many play therapists) laid the groundwork for Robert to tackle the difficult topic of his father's disappearances at a later time.

STRUCTURED ACTIVITIES TO HELP EXPRESS TANGIBLE LOSSES

Memory Book or Album

Structured drawings are a useful tool with school-age children suffering from traumatic losses. Children draw a picture of the deceased loved one and themselves doing something together. Then they are directed to add the drawing to a "memory book" or "album" that includes pictures of special and favorite things they did together, family trips and vacations, holidays, birthday parties, and funny things that happened along the way. Once an experience is concretized on paper, children talk more openly about the details of the experience. The task is to structure activities so that they stimulate specific feelings, bring them into awareness, and differentiate them from the mass of confused feelings the child has been experiencing. The child can then be encouraged to put these specific feelings into words or, if lacking language skill, to play out the feelings rather than continuing to experience them in confusing ways.

THERAPIST: I know it is hard to find words to express the sadness, the anger, the fear, or the other feelings you hold inside, but do the best you can. Go as far as you can.

If a girl's favorite memories are of a family trip to Disneyland or a picnic at a park or a lake, once she draws a picture of the experience, the blurred memory becomes sharply focused, making it much easier to engage in a give-and-take discussion about what made the experience so special. (To experience this phenomenon, the therapist can get out an old school yearbook, thumb through its pages, and get in touch with thoughts about people and incidents long forgotten.) At the same time, corresponding feelings can be explored. In this way, artistic productions can be cathartic for children who are verbally reticent, inhibited, or language delayed.

Poems, Songs, and Journal Writing

Some children express themselves freely through poems or songs that they write, although this behavior is more common during adolescence. Children can be encouraged to keep diaries or journals of their feelings and asked to share their entries unless they view them as too private. If so, their privacy needs to be respected unless they become suicide risks. In that case, their safety becomes an overriding concern. When privacy rights are respected, and the children are comfortable that they can keep their feelings and thoughts to themselves, they usually end up sharing them with the therapist. It should be emphasized that the respect for privacy must be authentic and not a ploy to disarm the child. Otherwise, the child will quickly see through the insincerity and become distrustful.

Memories can also be elicited by asking the child to remember childhood artifacts. Reiser (1994) uses childhood songs, family pictures, and childhood books to elicit memories. The child is asked to think of a song they sang when young and is then asked for associations to it. While most parents of gorilla-suit wearers failed to read or to sing songs to their children, many have lots of family photographs. When visiting apartments in Harlem, the Northeast Bronx, and the inner city of Poughkeepsie, where curtains are drawn during the daylight hours and doors securely locked, the walls are covered with family photos. Many attend church, and the child can be asked about songs sung in church with lost loved ones.

Photographs and "Linking Objects"

Children can bring to therapy favorite photographs to serve as springboards for sharing memories and associated feelings. School-age children can be asked to draw pictures of special items that link them to the lost loved one (Volkan 1972). Often the item drawn is one given to them just after divorce or just before death or abandonment. Other items include cherished possessions that everyone in the family associates with the lost member, such as a particular coffee mug, favorite chair, or old hat. Children can bring these "linking objects" to the sessions. These treasured objects can stimulate mourning in youngsters who have never mourned but whose repressed grief has led to symptoms of distress.

Reliving Funerals and Memorial Services

Children can be asked about the funeral of a deceased loved one. "What did you like and not like about it?" Inquiries can be made about the tributes and kind words said about the loved one. The details of the burial can be explored, visits to the cemetery made, and feelings cautiously explored that were aroused by these activities. Children who have never been to the cemetery can be encouraged to visit the actual grave. Others can be accompanied by the therapist to a local cemetery to stimulate thoughts about the death.

Children can be asked if they ever carry on one-way conversations with the deceased, either at the cemetery or at other times. They can be asked, "What do you put on the grave and who goes with you when you visit it?" "What does the headstone look like and what is written on it?" Such questions make the death and loss more real and can be especially useful for "reluctant grievers" (Crenshaw 1992), those showing "absence of grief" (Deutsch 1937), or those with a "short sadness span" (Wolfenstein 1966).

Dr. Mordock treated a nine-year-old girl, Shirley, who was referred to a residential treatment center for disruptive and sexualized behavior. Before placement, she dressed up in adult women's clothes, put on lipstick, and smoked cigarettes. Her young father related that she acted more like his girlfriend than his girlfriends did and that her jealously of them was one of her chief problems. He had given her more attention, but it made no difference. The more he gave, the more she demanded.

When first seen in therapy, she dressed up in costume clothing, including high heels, pranced around, and pretended to smoke a cigarette. Rather than exploring the reasons behind her need to act seductively, Dr. Mordock instructed her to act her age, and the costume clothing was locked in a cupboard to remove the stimulation to do otherwise. After many sessions of therapy and explorations of a number of issues, Dr. Mordock learned that several years before her placement, her father had instructed her to watch her baby brother while he backed his car out of the garage. She was distracted by something and forgot about her brother, and he was run over and killed by the father's car. For several sessions, Dr. Mordock and the girl walked to the local cemetery, where the girl found it easier to talk about the tremendous guilt she felt over her neglect. She considered herself to be a despicable human being and worthy of being only a slut or a whore [*perhaps one motive behind her dressing up and prancing around*].

Although the girl gave up her seductive behavior toward male staff in the residence and began to act and think like the little girl she was, her treatment was never considered a complete success. At no time did she cry or show real remorse for her mistake, only primitive guilt. Although Dr. Mordock stressed that her father should never have given a child her age such a weighty responsibility, she was never convinced. She had replaced her lost mother in her own eyes and felt capable of the task. In addition, the loss of her mother and her feelings about the loss remained a mystery. Dr. Mordock communicated his belief that she kept the image of her mother alive by adopting a womanly role, even fantasizing about being married to her father, but his interpretations fell on deaf ears. [*Looking back on this case, Dr. Mordock realizes that he should have asked her father whether she put on the clothes her mother left behind or his girlfriend's clothes. If they were the girlfriend's, his initial interpretations would have been different. Hindsight is always better than foresight!*] .

At discharge, she continued to act seductively with her father, although to a lesser degree than when first placed, her self-image had improved significantly, and the gap between her academic achievement and her expected grade level had decreased. Nevertheless, she was considered a high risk for future problems because of complicated grief and incomplete mourning.

Family Therapy Sessions

Individual sessions with children are helpful when the surviving parent is too grief stricken to encourage the child's mourning or when the child's protective stance toward the parent inhibits the mourning process: "I must take care of Mommy." Nevertheless, whenever possible, the family system should be involved for maximum impact. The surviving family unit's meeting together draws on the family's strengths and recognizes the reality of the remaining family composition. The mutual sharing of grief and the support for mourning can be more powerful than anything the therapist can offer to each individual. It builds a sense of togetherness, unity, and cohesion, so vital at a time of loss. By encouraging the open expression of grief, the therapist gives permission to all family members to mourn, reducing the inhibiting influence of protective responses.

Elisabeth Muir, Ann Speirs, and Ginny Todd (1988) have presented a detailed case illustration of the contribution of family intervention and parental involvement in facilitating mourning in a four-year-old boy whose father was killed by a falling tree. The boy, his mother, and the grandparents met together to share their grief and explore misunderstandings, including helping the grandparents to see that anger is part of grieving. The boy's aggressive and destructive play was observed unobtrusively by the mother, who had never expressed her own anger at being abandoned, and she was upset by the boy's anger. With the therapist's support and guidance, she accepted her own need to grieve, as well as her boy's. The case presentation is excellent and well worth reading.

Once parents understand how children express their sadness and longing, they can, sensitively and capably, facilitate their child's mourning. Much more can be accomplished by working through cooperative parents than by working with children alone. Because of the highly ambivalent relationships or the excessive guilt that complicates the grieving process, some children may need individual therapy sessions in addition to the support they receive from their families.

Other parents get upset because their children don't grieve as expected. They wonder if the child actually cared for their dead partner, and they begin to see the child as unfeeling, which sparks anger at the child for the seeming indifference. "For God's sake, my wife, his mother, just died, and my son is playing contentedly with his toys!" A rift is begun and widens with the passage of time. A self-fulfilling prophesy helps widen it as the parent begins to see the child as "not caring about anything," and the child reflects the parent's feelings by modifying his or her self-concept in keeping with that perception. Parents with this attitude rarely refer the child for treatment, however, because they don't see the child's indifference, or even "coldness," as a treatable mental health problem but as a newly discovered personality flaw that causes them discomfort and alienates them from the child. These feelings are discovered after the child has been referred for other problems and a thorough history reveals the past concerns about the child's "indifferent and unfeeling demeanor." In contrast, some parents refer their children for treatment when they don't mourn because the parents know it is unhealthy for them not to do so.

Unfortunately, the families of children in gorilla suits are rarely able to help their children grieve. Most children aren't referred for treatment until long after the loss. A father abandons his family, and the mother becomes caught up in meeting the family's need for food and shelter. At the same time, the child's needs to grieve the lost father are, at best, neglected or, at worst, actively punished. Continual crying over the loss of a man the mother resents for abandoning her is rarely tolerated. In addition, many gorilla-suit wearers have lost both parents, and perhaps even a series of foster parents when the children are moved from home to home for various reasons, some of which have to do with the children's misbehavior, which in turn helps to solidify negative self-images.

These children will have to be helped to grieve by their individual therapists.

· *19* ·

Helping Children to
Grieve Unacknowledged,
Intangible, and Invisible Losses

In this chapter, we discuss helping children on the invitational track to mourn losses that are not only unacknowledged but also intangible or invisible. Special techniques needed to help children overcome their reluctance to grieve and mourn are described. Those techniques dealing with intangible losses include structured drawings, Re-create the World, two memory books, selected film-clip and video viewing, and Color-Coded Time Lines. Therapists need to be careful to use the evocative techniques described in this chapter with children who are able to handle the emotional demands of the invitational therapy track.

DENIAL OF LOSS

*A*cknowledging a loss causes great pain. As long as losses are denied, pain is avoided. Ambiguity also aids and abets repression. Children without parents for long stretches of time because of drug addiction, prison sentences, or abandonment are unable to acknowledge losses because the children expect the parent to return. Unfortunately, when the parent does return, the child may experience loving concern for only a brief period because the parent relapses and disappears again, sometimes for months or even years. Dr. Crenshaw once treated a seven-year-old boy, Johnny, whose mother was kind and generous when not abusing drugs. At those times, she would show up at the residential treatment center and shower him with gifts. Johnny would be thrilled. She truly loved her son, and he loved her. Then she would be gone again. Denial of the loss would reappear, and Johnny would fantasize about her next visit. The visit never came, however, because Johnny's mother was brutally murdered in a drug-related incident.

Johnny finally had to acknowledge his overwhelming sense of loss and face the pain that even intermittent parenting was gone. During the intense grieving period that followed, Johnny made several attempts at suicide and had to be hospitalized twice. Even though his mother had been totally unreliable, he depended on those intense but sporadic meetings for his sense of worth. He wanted to track down the killer and seek revenge in the name of his mother. He became very combative with staff and other children, and the slightest frustration triggered extreme rages. Once he slammed the door to his room so hard it bent the door frame.

During this period, he experienced torturous nightmares of his mother's killer coming after him, often a fear of children whose parent with whom they are identified suffers a sudden or traumatic death. To address this and other post-traumatic stress disorder symptoms, a drawing technique, Party Hats on Monsters, developed by Dr. Crenshaw (Crenshaw 2001) to master fears related to trauma was initiated. Johnny was asked to draw the frightening parts of his dreams. By giving shape and form to the frightening images and putting them out on paper, he achieved a degree of distance and objectification that was not possible when these scary images were whirling around in his mind. Once a scary image is drawn, the therapist then initiates the next step. Johnny was asked to add to his picture any people or superheroes that might help him to feel safer. He drew his uncle, who was a policeman, and a favorite child-care worker, who was big and strong. He was then asked if he would like to add anything to his picture that would make him feel even safer. He drew his uncle putting handcuffs on the killer and taking him off to jail and the child-care worker standing next to Johnny and putting his arm on Johnny's shoulder. In the last step, based on techniques developed by Eriksonian hypnotherapists, especially Joyce Mills (Mills and Crowley 1986) and Yvonne Dolan (1985, 1991), who have worked extensively with trauma victims, the therapist calmly says something like the following:

> THERAPIST: I have used this strategy with lots and lots of kids who were scared of all kinds of things or who suffered very frightening dreams. Once they put the scary thing on paper, it no longer seems so scary. They also discover that when they change the scary pictures on paper, they can change the scary pictures in their head too! It seems like magic! You will discover that the scary people of your dreams aren't so scary anymore when you put them on paper and look at them in a new light.

The child is not put into a formal trance, but the soft and soothing voice of the therapist induces a state of greater calm and relaxation, making the child more receptive to the embedded suggestions contained in the message. The technique was first used by Dr. Crenshaw with a child who had frightening nightmares for years. To the surprise of his adoptive parents and the child, as well as Dr. Crenshaw, the nightmares stopped after this technique was used in just one session, and they never returned. Children can also put a drawing of the helpers on the door to their rooms to keep the bad monsters out.

The drawings were only one step in the complicated course of Johnny's treatment, but they were a very important one. Without concrete assistance, he was unable to access the comforting and soothing, loving memories of his mother because, when he thought of her, he was flooded with frightening images of the terrifying killer, both when awake and when dreaming. After much work, Johnny expressed some grief although, owing to developmental constraints, some grief remained unexpressed. Nevertheless, he was discharged to the care of his loving grandmother.

When a loss is sealed with the finality of death, the child grieves not only for the lost parent but also for the longed-for parent that "never was." Fortunately, Johnny had some happy memories which, after expression of his acute grief, he was able to access. When a child is unable to grieve, happy memories are difficult to retrieve because the child represses all memories to avoid pain. Pleasant memories will not be recalled because painful memories accompany them. Eventually, Johnny accompanied his grandmother to his mother's grave on home visits. He wrote letters and poems during therapy to leave at the grave when he visited—his way of giving gifts to his mother and reminiscent of her arrivals with bundles of presents for him. One of his letters is reproduced below.

> Mommy, I hope you will read this.
> I miss you much and I wish I could see you.
> I hope you are warm, and not hungry and are okay.
> I wish I could be there to help you.
> Love, Johnny

This moving note captured Johnny's love for his mother as well as his sense of responsibility for her well-being. He worried constantly about her when she was doing drugs, frequently verbalizing his fears about her status, especially that she might be cold and hungry. These worries were especially intense at night. Because of his major sleep problems, he arrived for school in the morning tired and lethargic. When told that Johnny couldn't sleep, the therapist devoted time to helping him evoke images of happy reunions with his mother, helping him to picture the warmth, love, caring, and giving that they both experienced at these times. When he recalled these images at bedtime, he became calm and better able to get to sleep. Immediately following his mother's death, he was unable to do so because all memories caused him too much pain.

Conflicted Relationships and Loss

When the relationship with a deceased family member is conflicted, it is especially hard to acknowledge loss. Giving up attachments, even painful ones, involves grieving (Ablon 1990). Even children traumatized by caregivers experience "traumatic bonding" (deYoung and Lowery 1992), and the child must grieve this loss as well. Children neglected or abused by fathers can declare that their father was never around anyway, so what is there to miss.

Kareem, an African American boy treated by Dr. Crenshaw, made this claim. Both his parents were crack addicted before his father was shot and killed by an off-duty policeman while committing an armed robbery at a convenience store. Kareem was initially placed, with his younger sister, in a foster home. At age five, he was placed with a preadoptive foster family, but he was not actually adopted by them until he was ten. His foster father died in an industrial accident two years after Kareem and his sister were placed in the preadoptive foster home. The following dialogue with Kareem, then eleven, took place after about six months of play therapy.

> THERAPIST: What was it like for you to have your dad die so suddenly and while committing a crime?
>
> KAREEM: I don't know. I don't really think of him as a dad. He was never around the way kids want their dad to be. I don't miss him. I really don't think about him.
>
> THERAPIST: What about the part that he died while doing a crime?
>
> KAREEM: The kids teased me a lot about it. How could he have been so stupid? He loved drugs more than me and my sister.
>
> THERAPIST: I imagine that must make you really angry when you think that he chose drugs over you and your little sister.
>
> KAREEM: If I had a chance to punch him out, I would. Same with Mom; they didn't give a damn about us!
>
> THERAPIST: You have very good reasons to feel the way you do. Only you can say what it is like for you. But sometimes, when kids first tell me that they don't think about their dad or mom who died and don't miss them, I find out later that they really do. They will tell me, "My dad was never a part of my life. Why would I miss him?" In a way they are right. How can you miss someone who was never around much? But I often discover that, in their quiet and alone moments, there is some sadness— they do feel a loss. Maybe it's for something they hoped or wished for from a dad that they now know will never happen [*reflection of a universal feeling*]. Do you ever, in your quiet and alone moments, have feelings like that?
>
> KAREEM: [*a long pause*] One night I woke up and started crying so hard I thought it was going to wake everybody. I didn't know what was going on. It was kind of weird. I just felt like crying.

THERAPIST: Have there been other times when you felt very sad and felt like crying but couldn't explain it?

KAREEM: I guess sometimes I'm mad at the whole world and I don't know why. That's when I get into trouble. My mom gets so fed up with me. She has all these kids, and I give her a hard time.

THERAPIST: Maybe you're angry, not just because your birth parents weren't there for you, but your adoptive mother has a lot of responsibilities and, while she tries hard and means well, perhaps you feel she can't be there for you either.

KAREEM: Maybe.

THERAPIST: How about the death of your foster father? What was he like and how did you cope with his tragic death [*crushed by a falling beam at a construction site*].

KAREEM: I don't like to talk about it. It really upsets Mom when she thinks about it. That was . . . I don't know. He was good to me and my sister. He laughed a lot, and he liked to do things with us. He was only my dad for, I don't know, not very long. I had two dads die.

THERAPIST: That has to be very hard. You were just getting used to having a dad who wanted to do things with you, and then he gets killed too!

The above dialogue was a tiny fraction of the healing dialogue that took place following a long struggle to establish a therapeutic alliance. When beginning treatment, Kareem made it abundantly clear that he wanted no part of therapy. One reason for his reluctance was that he had seen, for brief periods, a number of therapists during his foster home career. It was easy to anticipate another loss. In addition, he perceived the previous therapists as primarily interested in figuring out what was wrong with him. Bonime (1989), who supervised Dr. Crenshaw, emphasized that therapists should be just as interested in what is "right" with the child. An exclusive focus on pathology is an alienating and demoralizing experience. We believe strongly in personal therapy for the therapist, not only to increase the awareness and understanding of the self, but to experience what it is like to be a consumer of therapy. Most of us would not tolerate the process to which we subject others. The manner in which clients are greeted and welcomed, how missed appointments are followed up, and how arrangements are made to handle therapist absences all convey either respect or disrespect for clients.

If a child wearing a gorilla suit feels devalued by the therapy process itself, forget healing the wounded self-esteem, loss of dignity, and hopelessness that have resulted from other devaluations the child has experienced within the larger culture. Although the purpose of this handbook is to provide child therapists with practical tools to use in the therapy room, work on the therapist's self is equally important. Therapists need awareness of how insensitivity, even when unintentional, can devalue a child.

Children can be devalued by someone's failing to recognize the importance of even minor losses. This failure can activate a child's feelings about prior losses. Once, an otherwise capable and compassionate intern under Dr. Crenshaw's supervision made an inexcusable error. She had a meeting in the outpatient clinic that she needed to attend and that conflicted with her therapy appointment with a boy she treated in the residential treatment center. Knowing that the boy had a poor sense of time and frequently failed to keep track of his scheduled appointments, she decided to say nothing to him in advance and planned to see him upon her return in the afternoon. When it was time for his appointment and his therapist did not arrive, he became agitated. The teacher, alarmed by his behavior, called the front desk and had the therapist paged repeatedly. When the pages went unanswered, the boy, now distraught, was removed to the crisis room, where he spent the whole morning in a rage. The corrective emotional experience needed by gorilla-suit wearers includes the therapist's sensitivity to prior losses, which helps the children to rehumanize the losses. When losses take a personal and human face, the child regains the capacity to feel. If therapists remain insensitive, traumatized children will not engage in a process that requires trust, enormous courage, and a willingness to explore vulnerabilities. In addition to personal therapy, regular supervision for inexperienced therapists is a must, as is readily accessible consultation for experienced clinicians.

Insecure Attachments

Securely attached children more easily separate from loved ones, whether the separation is caused by distance or death. Winnicott (1948) observed this phenomenon during World War II, when children in London escaped bombings by moving to temporary homes in the surrounding countryside. Children securely attached to their parents more easily adjusted to their "surrogate parents" than did children less securely attached. The latter needed frequent concrete evidence and reassurance that they were loved. The insecurely attached constantly conjured up images of lost loved ones, which seriously interfered with their ability to concentrate on other pursuits. This pattern is frequently observed in children in residential treatment. Those regularly visiting homes on weekends and holidays, homes awaiting their discharge, adjusted to separations better than those making no home visits and those unclear about their discharge destinations. More securely attached children also managed more successfully the transition of home visits and returns to the agency. In contrast, visits home by the insecurely attached were accompanied by high manifest anxiety and disruptive behavior, reflecting their shaky connections with their families. Others have observed this same phenomenon in preschool children (Heinicke and Westheimer 1965).

Divorce and Loss

Another unacknowledged loss follows a bitter parental divorce and the accompanying uncertainty about the future roles of parent figures. Nearly one-half of the children enrolled in a residential treatment center return home to a significantly different family constellation when discharged (Mordock 1978). While some divorces are handled in a relatively amicable fashion, with the best interests of children clearly weighed, rarely do such divorces occur in the families of children wearing gorilla suits. The hostile interchanges between caregivers contribute to the children's difficulties. Except in rare cases of extreme abuse, neglect, violence, or serious psychiatric illness of a parent, children want continued contact with both parents. The loss of the intact family, even when both parents stay constructively involved with the child, can be very painful. Often the divorce involves other unacknowledged losses. The family relocates and suffers economic hardship, and the children lose friends and change schools. Children worry about the permanence of the noncustodial parent, and their anxiety is masked by aggressive behavior. In an acrimonious separation, custodial parents resent the grief children display for the absent parent, viewing missing or longing for the other parent as disloyalty. Children have to suppress these feelings or disconnect them so that they are no longer part of the self, no longer acknowledged. These unacknowledged losses can remain buried until some event, such as a subsequent loss or threat of loss, activates them, sometimes in dramatic or even destructive ways.

When a loss is unacknowledged, therapy becomes more complicated. The loss, and its associated pain, can be completely repressed. In other cases, cognitive awareness of the loss exists, but the affect is disconnected and unacknowledged. As stated earlier, it is common for boys to verbalize that father loss doesn't matter: "I didn't need him anyway!" In still other children, even cognitive awareness is lacking, but a persistent feeling of sadness, something missing, and mournful longing may cause them to flounder without direction.

The first step, and it can be a slow and painstaking one, is to facilitate both cognitive and affective acknowledgment of the loss. In the dialogue with Kareem presented above, he was helped to connect his unexplained feelings to the sudden deaths of his biological and foster fathers, one small step in the process of recovery.

If the therapist is aware of the unacknowledged loss, opportunities to broach the topic can be found in the child's play or drawings. After observing the redundant theme of loss and disappearance in the child's play, the therapist might, in a tentative and puzzled manner, make the following reductive remark:

> THERAPIST: I notice that in many of the play scenes, someone gets lost, dies, or disappears. I just had this thought that maybe this is something that

has happened in your life. I was just wondering if somewhere along the way, you have lost someone important to you—someone who died, someone important to you who is no longer around?

The child may or may not respond to the query, but it brings the issue to the surface. As the theme continues to appear, the therapist can push further.

> THERAPIST: I was just thinking about the scene you just played out— when the house caught on fire, and the firemen were unable to get all the people out. I expect that was a hard one for you because I know that your uncle died in a fire.

Children may not stop their ongoing activities when the remark is made, but the issue is now "on the table" and can be revisited at every opportunity. Even the popular therapeutic board game developed by Richard Gardner (1986), the Talking, Doing, Feeling Game, offers opportunities to further acknowledge losses. The therapist may take a card that asks "What was the worst thing that ever happened to you?" The therapist might pause and say "This is a tough one for me because I am thinking of what happened to your brother and how hard it must have been for you to witness the accident." The child might accuse the therapist of cheating because he was supposed to speak about the worst thing that happened to him and not to the child. In that case, the therapist quickly apologizes and explains that the death of his brother just popped into the therapist's mind because of thoughts that it must have been so hard for the child.

Such attempts at dialogue lay the groundwork for more extensive review of a loss and the expression of repressed feelings. With boys, the football metaphor, "to go up and down the turf," can be used to describe the effort required for the child to develop a realistic understanding of the loss, including correction of cognitive distortions, relief from excessive guilt and self-blame, and the expression of painful affects. If successful, the child will be able to construct a narrative memory and integrate the loss into his or her ongoing life.

Most gorilla-suit wearers have received little recognition for their invisible wounds. Consequently, the wounds must be approached with care, respect, and sensitivity. Repeated experiences with devaluation make children suspicious when their wounds are approached. Hardy (2003) emphasizes three important efforts when treating aggressive children: (1) attend to their invisible wounds, (2) counteract devaluation by conveying profound respect, and (3) highlight their strengths. We include these three factors when discussing the therapeutic alliance in chapter 1. They also need to be addressed throughout therapy because children who feel valued and respected by their therapist are more willing to unburden their grief. These factors are especially important in the terminal phases of treatment, when the focus is on shaping new meanings, enlarging perspectives, and creating a future orientation. Such work comes only after confronting traumatic events and painful losses.

Finding New Meaning and Shaping a Narrative Memory

Children in gorilla suits need to attribute new meanings to the horrific events that contributed to their sense of who they are. They need a meaningful narrative memory—a story that makes sense to them about what happened in their lives. Intense feelings of self-blame and self-condemnation, partially resulting from stigmatization by others, should be confronted, tested, and challenged in order to fashion a more positive and meaningful outlook. Efforts to change the child's outlook must be undertaken, but the losses must always be respected; otherwise, the child's horrific experiences are trivialized.

The children need to feel hopeful about their futures. They can dare to hope only after their invisible wounds have been shared with an empathetic listener—a listener who had been courageous enough to accompany them into their "deep pit of rage and sorrow" and to emerge from the pit "holding hands" with a healthier child. In *Understanding and Treating the Aggression of Children*, we discuss specific strategies to facilitate hope.

Shaping a New Perspective

After children have faced some of the traumatic issues that contributed to their problems, the Time Line, presented in chapter 13 of *Understanding and Treating the Aggression of Children*, can be used to assist children to develop a new life view. This graphic description of life events over time can help counteract the tendency of children to define themselves by their problems, the aggressive behaviors that caused them, or the traumatic blows contributing to problem development. The therapist can emphasize that the time frame of traumatic events actually encompassed a relatively brief period in each child's life span, helping children to learn that their selves are much richer than the problems others focus on. Seeing themselves in a more balanced way and appreciating their unique qualities and humanness help to shift their self-image to a more positive one.

STRUCTURED ACTIVITIES TO ACCESS FEELINGS ASSOCIATED WITH INTANGIBLE LOSSES

Structured Drawings

When working on intangible losses, such as the loss of respect, dignity, and hope, children can draw or make two collages. The first is "How I Would Like

My Life to Be," and the second is "How My Life Actually Is." These two draw-ings bring into focus losses, both tangible and intangible, that are difficult to verbalize or even to acknowledge.

Jorge was a nine-year-old Hispanic child treated by Dr. Crenshaw during Jorge's stay in residential treatment. Jorge's natural parents were crack addicted, and he and his older brother were frequently left to roam the streets or enter abandoned buildings until authorities were called by concerned neighbors. The boys were removed from home when Jorge was four and his brother was six. They lived with a series of foster families, but Jorge's escalating aggression and explosive behavior made him unmanageable. On one occasion, he seri-ously injured a younger foster child and had to be separated from his brother and placed in residential treatment. The younger child had disrespected his mother, or "dissed" her, as they say on the inner-city streets. Jorge broke the boy's nose and two of his ribs.

Separation from his brother was one of the many tangible and intangible losses Jorge experienced before residential placement. The loss of his parents to drug addiction was his greatest loss and had both tangible and intangible com-ponents. His longing for them remained, and he could not tolerate even a younger child (the boy Jorge injured was only four years old) making dis-paraging remarks about his mother. The devaluation he experienced because of his ethnicity, parentlessness, rootlessness, and homelessness (he and his brother had been moved to five different homes in five years) resulted in loss of dignity, hope, and self-respect. His explosions at even hints of disrespect masked his own self-contempt.

Even carefully and sensitively stated suggestions sent Jorge into fits of rage. In the living group and the classroom, he often attacked children he thought looked at him "funny." Nor could he "hear" affirmation. One particular child-care worker overextended himself in an effort to establish a relationship with Jorge, but Jorge wanted no part of him. One day, while shooting hoops, the child-care worker said, "Jorge, that was a terrific jump shot!" Jorge flew into a rage and said, "F— you!" He then stormed off the court and refused to rejoin the game. Jorge greeted even well-intended compliments with suspicion. In his confused mind, all self-references were equated with disrespect.

Many children have trouble forming a therapeutic alliance, but Jorge stands out from all the rest. Jorge was determined not to let anyone "get to him" because, in his mind, that would result in a serious breach of his protec-tive armor. His need to keep distance was honored, and the adaptive value of his strategies of disconnection accepted.

JORGE: [*Looking sullen, angry, and bored, slumped in a chair, looking away from the therapist.*] I have nothing to say to you.

THERAPIST: You have no reason to trust me.

JORGE: I don't wanna listen to this crap! Take me back to class.

THERAPIST: You think that, like so many other people who have tried to get to know you in the past, I just want to figure out what is wrong with you.

JORGE: F— you! I have heard enough of this s—! [*He storms out the door.*]

At times, Jorge refused to come to therapy. The author persisted, telling him that the time was set aside just for him and that his slot wasn't going to be given to anyone else. After coming to the classroom door and hearing Jorge's loud refusal, the therapist told him, "I will be in the therapy room, and when you're ready to come, let Mrs. Brown know, and she will call me, and I will return and get you." If nothing happened in ten minutes, the therapist returned to the classroom and said, "Jorge, my time with you is very important, and I would very much like you to accompany me to the therapy room." At times Jorge would reluctantly come along, mostly to get the therapist off his back, or he would blast out in rage, "What the hell is the matter with you? Are you stupid or something? I told you I'm not coming!" The teacher did not appreciate the disruption, a fact that gratified Jorge because it not only humiliated the therapist but also gave Jorge a sense of power over him.

After several months of active resistance, followed by inconsistent and passive resistance, Jorge routinely came to the therapy room. Because he was unable to verbalize his inner world, various structured drawing activities were used, especially projective drawings completed in sequence, with those aimed at emotional awareness of losses, and the strong affects associated with them coming later in the sequence. His wounds came into sharp focus when he drew "How I Would Like My Life to Be" and "How My Life Actually Is." His first drawing portrayed him and his dad fishing together. The second drawing depicted himself alone on the street.

Re-Create the World

Children are asked the following question, a variation of the drawing technique described above: "If you had the power to change the world, what things would you add to it to make it a better place to live? What things would you take away?" The list is kept in a safe place, and the child is asked to expand on both lists as therapy progresses.

Two Memory Books

In a technique developed by Samuels (1995), each child is asked to create two memory books early in treatment. In the first book, the child is asked to list all the good and bad times he or she can remember. The child entitles the first book, "My Memories: Volume One." The second book remains empty, and the child entitles it, "My Book of Forgotten Memories." The child is then told that over the course of therapy, he or she will complete the second book, but it won't be easy because many forgotten memories are memories that are very painful to remember. The therapist tells the child that the therapist will help the child to complete the second book in ways that will keep the child from being completely overwhelmed by the memories. At the end of therapy, the title of the second book is changed to read, "My Memories: Volume Two."

Evocative Aids: Color-Coded Time Line

Kenneth Hardy (2003) discusses using evocative aids to access the emotional life of children who are "reluctant grievers" and who avoid situations in which they might feel a loss. He describes using a Color-Coded Time Line that diagrams in a clear and evocative way the tangible and intangible losses experienced by children and their families. The Color-Coded Time Line was developed to differentiate tangible from intangible losses. The Color-Coded Time Line is especially useful with older children and adolescents who can grasp the distinction between tangible and intangible losses. This technique is only appropriate for children on the invitational track because it focuses on cumulative losses. Remember, however, that the name *invitational* was chosen to emphasize that clients are *invited* to approach threatening material and to go only as far as they can at any point in time.

The invitational approach respects the child's need to pull back or refuse to approach such material when invited at any given time. If the child consistently feels threatened by emotionally evocative material, the therapist should reassess the approach. The child may need to return to the coping track before proceeding. This exercise can be employed in the coping track by using the time line to record only positive events. There is always the risk, however, that children in gorilla suits cannot remember any. In that case, the therapist has unwittingly focused them directly on the emptiness of their lives. A safer approach is to highlight positive life events which have already been mentioned, as only happy memories are brought into focus. In this way, children are not hit between the eyes with the holes in their lives, a confrontation that many are unprepared to face. Kareem, the boy discussed above, suffered numerous losses in both categories.

> THERAPIST: Kareem, let's work on something together that may make it easier to talk about some of the important things that have happened to you along the way—the things you somehow managed to get through, although I'm sure getting through them must have been very hard. I call this a "Time Line." [*The therapist puts down on the drawing table a diagram of the time line, as illustrated in the example below.*]

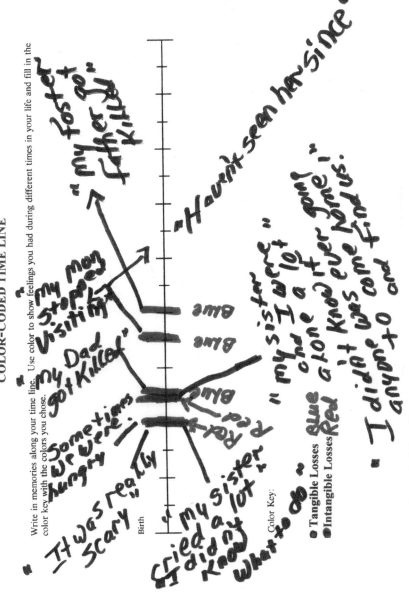

Figure 19.1. Color-Coded Time Line

THERAPIST: Now I want you to pick a color to go with tangible losses and a color to go with intangible losses. Tangible losses are like the death of your father and foster father. Intangible losses are like changing schools, moving to a new apartment and neighborhood and not knowing anyone, feeling disrespect from other kids, or losing hope for a good future. Other intangible losses could include having one's dreams come crashing down, often called "invisible losses" because no one sees them. Tangible losses are the ones that are easily recognized, and intangible losses are not always recognized, especially the invisible ones—like loss of respect or hope, but they can be very hard for a child, perhaps even harder because no one notices that the child hurts inside.

KAREEM: [*Picks blue for tangible losses and red for intangible—an interesting choice since these two colors are commonly paired in our society with two distinct emotions—blue with sadness and red with anger.*]

THERAPIST: Now I want you to look at the time line. Each vertical line represents a year in your life. I want you to write whatever you remember about the losses you have had during your life. Write those memories next to each year on the graph, and then pick either blue or red to show whether it was a tangible or intangible loss.

KAREEM: Will you write the things that happened? I don't write that good.

THERAPIST: Sure, you tell me what to write and then decide on what color should be used to show whether it was a tangible or intangible loss.

KAREEM: Well, my dad got killed when I was only five, and my mom stopped visiting when I was seven. I haven't seen her since. My foster father died when I was eight.

THERAPIST: So what color would you pick for these important losses? Blue for tangible or red for intangible?

KAREEM: I say blue.

THERAPIST: Good. How about the intangible losses, especially the invisible ones. These are harder to recognize. Can you remember times when you lost hope? Or times when you suffered a lack of respect from others or felt all alone in the world with no one to turn to?

KAREEM: I can remember about here [*ages four and five*], when my sister and I were left alone and I was really scared. My sister was crying a lot and I didn't know what to do. Sometimes we were hungry. I didn't know if anyone was ever going to come home or find us. It was really scary.

THERAPIST: You were very young to be looking out for yourself, let alone your baby sister. I'm sure that was very scary. So these were intangible losses, loss of safety, loss of being cared for, having to fend for yourself and look after your sister. So these intangible losses we will mark with red. Are there any other losses, tangible or intangible?

KAREEM: I don't think so.

THERAPIST: When you look at the Time Line and see the blue and red colors, each one representing a tangible or intangible loss, what comes to your mind, or what feelings do you have?

KAREEM: No wonder I wake up crying some nights!
THERAPIST: You have a lot of tears inside because you have been through a lot of loss. I'm glad you're starting to let some of them out.

The Color-Coded Time Line of losses is intended only for children on the invitational track. In fact, all the evocative aids described in this chapter should be used only with children on the invitational track.

Evocative Aids: Selected Video Clips

The therapist can assemble a library of evocative videotapes that help children gain access to affects associated with profound loss. With younger children, *The Lion King* powerfully portrays loss. When this compelling story of loss and the search to find a psychological home was first released, children in settings where both of us worked reenacted the story in countless play scenarios. Other useful videos that evoke affect around issues of loss include *Stand by Me*, *The Stone Boy*, *Ordinary People*, and *Hard Ball*. Often emotionally evocative clips from these films can be shown in group sessions, followed by discussion. Dr. Crenshaw initially used brief film clips to develop empathy. The child is asked how he or she would describe the feelings expressed or implied in each scene. An additional step is taken with children on the invitational track. They are asked to remember a time when they felt similarly.

Evocative emotional aids are useful when children are ready to undertake uncovering work. External events in the children's lives, such as the birth of siblings, changes in housing, loss of employment, or heightened neighborhood violence, may require a temporary reduction in taxing demands and a switch to the coping track. When a child becomes overwhelmed by taxing events in everyday life, the invitational approach is not warranted. Therapists must not get so caught up in therapeutic narcissism that they ignore the other twenty-three hours of the child's life. Therapists must adapt their technique to the shifting needs of the child.

If used properly, media are a powerful tool because they capture children's interest. The scenes selected are deeply moving and provide "grist for the mill" over multiple sessions. All but the most "hardened" children will be saddened by the films, and efforts to relate the sadness to their own losses should proceed cautiously. If the children seem reluctant to confront their own sadness, their reluctance should be respected. Signs of reluctance can include failure to bring linking objects, photographs, or mementos to the therapy session or an unwillingness to draw such objects or associated memories. In that case, the therapist can plant the expectation, "We will wait until a time that is more comfortable for you." Some "reluctant grievers" may require work in the coping track before tackling the more demanding and challenging tasks on the invitational track.

CONCLUSION

Strategies to counter devaluation include using dialogues about respect, accentuating the capacity for giving, highlighting strengths, searching for "islands of competence," finding meaning and perspective, and facilitating hope. The specific techniques described above are helpful only when introduced within this framework. Searching for strengths and competencies, finding new meanings, using explicit dialogues about respect, accentuating the capacity for giving, and creating hope are discussed in considerable detail in *Understanding and Treating the Aggression of Children*.

· 20 ·

The Process

The first stage in the therapy of gorilla-suit wearers includes defining the nature of therapy, set-ting limits, allaying anxiety, and forming a relationship, not necessarily in that order. The second stage usually includes helping the child to develop more appropriate defenses against anxiety, to develop calming skills, to move from diffuse fears to specific fears, and to render specific fears less disturbing. In the third stage, the child moves from the coping to the invitational track. "Explain-ing the problems" to the child becomes the major task of the third stage. Constant interpretations of the child's feelings, including those of low self-worth, and of the defenses used to avoid these feelings are the "explanations of the problem." Reenactments of trauma may occur during the third stage, followed by working through of the strong emotions that accompany them. At the same time, the therapist has implemented a formula for change by employing strategies to promote the child's development. The major task of the fourth stage is to encourage the child's entry into latency-age functioning and to aid progress with the developmental tasks of latency. During this stage, the child brings up everyday issues with which he or she is struggling, and the therapist attempts to relate them to earlier or ongoing explanations of problems and to the formula outlined for change. Top-ics like peer relationships, school functioning, or future plans are openly discussed as the child plays or draws with the therapist. Interpretations within the metaphor are no longer needed; interpreta-tions can be made directly.

*W*hen a child first enters therapy, the therapist's empathetic focusing results in predictable gradual changes. The initial feelings the child expresses are dif-fuse and undifferentiated. They are global responses to anxiety. The child has lost contact with the experiences and the conflicts that aroused negative feel-ings. Anxieties have become pervasive and are no longer tied to the reality sit-uations that produced them. As these pervasive feelings are accepted, the child begins to focus on specific sources of negative feelings. The depressed, with-drawn, and isolated child will become more aggressive while the aggressive

283

child will concentrate less on playing "Breaking Everything Games" and more on pounding the baby doll or manipulating, in fanciful ways, the miniature people. As these more specific feelings are accepted, some positive feelings are expressed, and ambivalence is recognized. Feelings become more related to reality situations of the moment.

THE FIRST STAGE: ANXIETY MANAGEMENT

By discovering both their suppressed needs and the specific reasons for their anxiety, children recapture those phases of earlier development that were not assimilated fully. The child's increasing activities in therapy are manifestations of the different stages of development that were poorly assimilated. When therapy has progressed to the point that pressing concerns have lost their compelling power, the child will begin to play and respond to the therapist's modeling of play. As Erik Erikson remarks, the play will outline the "inner maze in which he is caught." If the child is capable of symbolic play, the play will evolve from disorganized regressed play to more complex play. Remember that the child's play is shaped by the presence of the therapist. Typically, children about five years old avoid adult observation of their play, making play in therapy a unique experience for the child.

The progression from diffuse, undifferentiated expressions of anxiety early in therapy to more focused anxiety later in therapy is illustrated by the behavior of Carol, a seven-year-old child whose first treatment session we present in an earlier chapter. Because Carol was referred before she put on a gorilla suit, her progress was more rapid than that of longtime suit wearers. Carol's progress was evident by the fourth session. We repeat her first session below:

Session 1

CAROL: I never do anything fun. I'm not happy. [*She looked sad and scooped sand endlessly to no apparent purpose. She then noticed the stuffed bears.*] The bear is unhappy, too. This is Winnie Gentle Pooh, Small Bear, Honey Bear, and I am "Carol Sunshine" because I like that name better than mine. Your name is "Bracelet Mouth" [*The therapist wore braces.*] or "Mousie." [*She then gave Pooh Bear a spanking.*] He should "Ssh." He was a naughty bear. [*She built a house out of blocks and put Pooh Bear in a room with no way out.*] He had to stay there 'cause he said naughty words—the "f" words. His parents could say them, but he couldn't. I don't like Small Bear. Pooh Bear swore at Small Bear and needs to go to bed.

[*She then made a "tea party" and brought some friends.*] There's only Raggedy
Ann, Andy, and me. Pooh Bear, Pooh Bear, Pooh Bear. There is the quiet
box. He's got to go in the quiet box. Pooh—you're too fat. Too much
honey. You take the slide and squish him, squish him, squish him. Nobody
can look in, and he's not going to look. Pooh would be screaming if they
came in and didn't let him out of there. [*She then stacked four big blocks to block
Pooh Bear in there.*] I don't care—somebody cares, but not me. I don't care.

In this first session, Carol, almost parrotlike, reports that she is unhappy.
We speculated about reasons for her play earlier but added that her feelings,
like those of most children beginning therapy, were blurred and confusing.

Sessions 2 and 3

CAROL: [*She shows curiosity about the large "bean" bags in the room. She
opens zippers and keeps plunging her arms in and out of each bag.*] I love the soft
feel of the stuff [*styrofoam*] inside. [*She then tells a story about a girl who touched
her mother's glasses and broke them—the therapist wears glasse*s.] The girl got
caught. She never wanted to touch anything again. But then she got this
friend who told her what to touch and what not to touch. Then she could
touch things again. But Pooh Bear doesn't remember her. [*The therapist
replies that "Pooh Bear doesn't forget his friends." Carol continues.*] I like to do
things that scare me—Pooh Bear is scared, but I don't like it if people scare
me.

In these two sessions, Carol expresses her need for affection and for a new
friend (the therapist?) to help her. She admits to doing things that scare herself
and that she doesn't like being scared. (One of her presenting symptoms was
playing mean tricks on others—are they counterphobic behaviors?)

Session 4

CAROL: I can be mean. I was mean to you last week. Maybe I'll be mean
again. I locked my brother in the bedroom and told him he'd better shut up.
I'd like to, but I won't. I'd like to make a sand pile and go "potty." Then
you'd have to clean it up. I'd like to, but I won't. [*She hugged Pooh Bear, and
then jumped on him, slammed him on the floor, and made him sit in a corner. She
then went to the easel.*] I hope you had fun when you were away. We went to
the beach. I made you a present.

By session four, Carol expressed some aggressive feelings more openly, especially her hostility toward her brother, whom her mother had said she
adored. She is uncomfortable with doing so, however, even when feeling ac-

cepted by the therapist. To make up for her aggressive feelings (to undo them), she makes the therapist a gift. The therapist reflects these ambivalent feelings in subsequent sessions. "It's hard to be angry at people you like because you can feel guilty, but sometimes we need to get angry at others instead of being angry at ourselves."

Later Sessions

In later sessions, she added two friends to the guests at her tea party and talked about her father.

> CAROL: My daddy doesn't know how to do things. He never went to school; he "quitted"—it bothers him. I never could quit. If I could quit, I would quit right now. [*She then talked about a little girl she knew whose mother enrolled her in the wrong class.*] She was put in the first grade for the second time—no one talked to her at recess—not even second graders like her. This little girl hurts inside be cause "no one likes her."
>
> [*She then talked more directly about herself.*] I think it's really funny that when you're out of school, you play school, and when school starts, you wish you could play something else. [*She also reported a possible visual problem that should be investigated.*] I have to lay my head sideways to see correct numbers on the page; then I get sleepy. The teacher told my mother I needed more sleep.

Revelations in the First Session

In the initial sessions, children often play out or draw a symbolic map of where their therapy needs to go. We urge clinicians with videotaping capabilities to videotape the first therapy session with clients, not just for supervision purposes, but to retain the tape and view it at later points in each child's therapy. Frequently, the issues that emerge later in the therapy are hinted at, if not explicitly laid out, by children in their very first session. Children, with very few exceptions, rarely verbalize troubling issues in the first session, not only because they lack the ability to formulate issues into words, but also because the issues are outside of their awareness. We never cease to be amazed by how unconscious material is so naturally expressed in the symbolization of the child's play. Play is truly children's primary language to communicate the emotional truths of their inner world.

Jesus was an embittered six-year-old who had been acting out aggressively and refusing to do schoolwork. In addition, he interacted with his teacher in a sullen, withdrawn, and uncommunicative manner. Evidence suggested that his spirit had been crushed by hostility between his estranged parents. Their refusal to cooperate and communicate with each other was replicated in the boy's relationship with his teacher. Witness his play in the first session.

> JESUS: [*Jesus enters the playroom, gathers up all the jungle animals, and carefully places them around the room. On top of each one, he puts a much larger animal, in some cases a giant dinosaur, and has the large animal literally and figuratively crush the smaller creatures.*]

Even without knowledge of a child's background, one often finds that dramatic play reveals all one really needs to know.

> ANITA: [*Anita enters the playroom for her first session, selects a baby doll and mother doll, goes behind the puppet theater, and creates a scene in which the mother doll beats the baby doll for wetting her bed. She then anxiously flees the therapy room.*]

Most children enjoy puppet play or play with miniature figures provided they don't become overwhelmed with anxiety following their own productions, as Anita was when her first dramatic production came too close to her own problems. Imaginative children love to create their own stories and may want the therapist to just watch and listen. Their play becomes a safe, natural, and playful vehicle for expressing their fears and conflicts and for mastering painful early life events. Other children need considerable modeling of puppet play by the therapist because they are frozen in fear, unable to symbolize, riddled with primitive guilt and/or shame, or find it too scary to engage in spontaneous and emotionally expressive play. In such cases, the therapist models a play scenario and encourages the child to be one of the characters in the therapist's dramatic play. The therapist starts by first modeling a fantasy scene far removed from the scary issues of the child and then works gradually toward painful material as the child gathers strength over the course of therapy. Some children for long periods just sit and watch the therapist put on puppet shows. Other children prefer playing in collaboration with the therapist. Each has a part that is played out through one or more of the puppet characters or the miniature family dolls.

Violent Play and Identification with the Aggressor

Children with trauma histories, or repeated exposure to violence, can display extremely violent or sadistic behavior immediately after entering the playroom. A child might, for example, pick up a doll, lift it by its legs, and smash its head with great force into the table. Regardless of whom the child identifies with in this scenario, the aggressor or the victim, the therapist must intervene rather than passively stand by and observe. Mere reflection of angry feelings is inappropriate in this situation. Therapists should verbally protest the abusive treatment of the babies and try to redirect the child to a healing and helping role, such as calling an ambulance, police, or rescue worker, thereby helping the child to feel empowered in response to aiding injured babies and by the neighborhood onlookers' expressing gratitude for this brave and heroic assistance. We emphasized earlier that children in gorilla suits have had little opportunity to give to others. They often adopt an aggressive posture because it is the only avenue they know to both express their crushed spirit and imprint their presence. Bruce Perry (2003) states, "Ironically, many violent behaviors are the result of a defensive response to perceived aggression" (p. 1). When therapists successfully address both the overt and the underlying fears of children, their violence and aggression usually wane.

Sublimation of aggressive drives and impulses through play takes many forms. In puppet play, children are encouraged to pick puppets symbolizing primitive (oral) aggression, like Alligator, Crocodile, or T. rex. Typically, they will dominate, decimate, and devour the weaker and more defenseless puppets and dolls, broadcasting their power and strength—compensating fantasies because they actually feel small and vulnerable. Once the child can displace aggression onto play materials—once masking symbols have been developed—then therapy can move forward.

Children must move past violent play because the play not only masks helpless feelings but also helps the child to identify with an aggressor, a gratifying identification. Powerful themes in children's play tend to be redundant. If unsure about the purpose of the play, the therapist can track it until its meaning becomes clear. If the play merely reflects unhealthy identifications, new alternatives and new play characters should be introduced by the therapist. The child is encouraged to try out different roles, with the therapist also playing different parts, introducing different outcomes, and reflecting the feelings of the play characters, all in an effort to free the child from unhealthy identifications.

As we stress in *Understanding and Treating the Aggression of Children*, evidence suggests a neurobiological basis for destructive patterns. Aggression is accompanied by the release of neurotransmitters that reinforce the aggression and, in turn, increase the likelihood that it will be repeated. In addition, each time the child adopts an aggressor role, anxiety related to the state of helplessness and powerlessness is reduced—reinforcing, again and again, an aggressive posture. Not redirecting repetitive play (referred to earlier as a repetition compulsion) that suggests identification with the aggressor is akin to allowing the child to engage in endless repetitions of posttraumatic play—play that reinforces the child's sense of powerlessness (Terr 1990; Gil 1991).

THE SECOND STAGE: CONFLICT RESOLUTION

After children in gorilla suits have responded to limit setting and have begun to work on meaningful issues, they experience considerable identity conflicts. Many will not engage in the kind of reenactment play needed to work through traumas until they have resolved these conflicts. Therapy progresses only when children begin to relinquish the pathological identities they believe they need to survive and to maintain a relationship with their parents. The children actively struggle with feelings generated by the conflict between their earlier identifications and their developing identity with the therapist and other positive caregivers.

The therapist meets the child's emotional and maturational requirements during each phase of the child's unfolding and developing fantasy play until the real child emerges. The therapist fulfills the child's needs by taking direction from the child and praising, punishing, scolding, caring for, or loving the fantasized characters. By introjecting the empathetic qualities displayed by the therapist, the gorilla-suit wearer gets in touch with passive longings and denied dependency needs. The urge to be taken care of, even babied, becomes strong. The stage is set for the emergence of these conflicts when the child begins to ask questions about the permanence of the therapist: How long will you be my therapist? Will I change therapists when I change classes next year? Can I stay longer? Can I have more sessions? The child wants to give things to, or do things for, the therapist. The child might report that "I beat up other children because they said mean things about my mom (dad)," a thinly disguised effort to befriend the therapist. One child with a female therapist remarked that "I don't hate little girls or women, only girls my age who pester and bother me." The therapist who experiences such behavior should be forewarned that an affective storm is coming and should brace for it.

Most gorilla-suit wearers respond to their growing dependency needs with massive denial. They continue to come to therapy but complain about the "dumb and boring" sessions. Many are the suit wearers who use thrill seeking to avoid depression. Escape from intimacy is a prime motivator. The child who actively struggles with this conflict is a healthier child. Less disturbed, but more disturbing! Those willing to struggle often become interested in baby books or may wrap up in blankets. Many begin to talk "baby talk." Others want to wear articles of the therapist's clothing.

> One eleven-year-old, a streetwise, inner-city girl, who initially entered therapy looking like a "little hooker," later would suck on a baby bottle and threatened to kill her therapist if he ever told anybody. During this period, she also drew pictures of pregnant-looking women with giant suction-cup stomachs that sucked in and spewed out babies. Because the fear of passive dependency increased, she temporarily resolved this conflict by killing the "babies within her."

INCREASED NEGATIVISM

As their massive denial of intimacy wanes when faced with an empathetic adult, children often refuse to come to therapy, and there is very little that can be done about it. Gorilla-suit wearers initially defend against expressing their passive longings by increasing their negativism. They also negate these feelings: "This is not me." And when the children do come, they refuse to leave. At this stage, therapists must work through their own feelings of being devalued, bored, and restless; otherwise, countertransference reactions can hamper treatment. Therapists can be encouraged by Abrams's statement (1990):

> The experience of being solaced, accepted, even forgiven can have a mutative effect in many treatments even when it is not actively offered by the analyst. (p. 415)

As the intensity of their need to be taken care of grows stronger, children begin to lose their identity as "tough guy" and some of their willpower, both frightening experiences. Therapists still in touch with how they felt when they first fell in love—how they lost their will—will be better able to empathize with these feelings. And those who have lost a loved one will remember that they temporarily lost their "reason to be." The children experience both sets of feelings in their struggles. But even more powerful can be an unconscious feeling that change will result in the loss of the little parental love that is available to them. Part of the child "knows" that he or she is an externalization of the parents' negative self-images. By accepting these negative self-images, the child keeps the parents healthy and ensures his or her fragile place in the family.

When suit wearers finally yield to their dependency longings, they both overidealize the therapist and increase their unreasonable demands. They will then feel betrayed. When the therapist cannot meet their insatiable demands, they temporarily revert to their old ways: "Since I can't get enough, what's the use in trying?" In addition, the therapist's empathy awakens a sense of loss that precipitates depressed and angry feelings: "How come my mother never treated me like this?"

This problem can be confounded by sexual feelings associated with passivity, especially in those who have been sexually abused. A boy with a male therapist may experience homosexual panic, while the child with a therapist of the opposite sex may become seductive. A boy may often do things for his female therapist that are symbolic preludes to sexual invasions. He will show her things from his pockets, offer to clean out her desk drawer, or organize things in her purse. This will be followed by snatching her purse and rifling through it. He will want the therapist to show her new clothes to his father. He will want to draw marks on both his hands and the therapist's hands. He will save his marks and look to see if the therapist saved hers over the week. (Experienced therapists will not allow children to mark their arms.)

All these factors—passive longings, identity confusion, loyalty conflicts, survival fears, betrayal feelings, and sexual stirring—combine to create a period of resistance to change. The therapist needs to convey steadfastly that he or she recognizes the existence of these struggles, a task made difficult by the therapist's being constantly bombarded with renewed hostility. The task is particularly difficult in school settings because the child's conflicts with the therapist spill over into the larger school environment and subject the therapist to unjust criticism by educational staff. The therapist needs to remember that the child is reliving old conflicts (feelings of passive helplessness in response to angry parents).

The successful resolution of these conflicts within the therapy situation brings about progressive changes. Insight for a child is a shift in the child's attitude, a lessening of a need to project feelings and anxieties. The therapist needs to communicate that emotions are manageable and need not run wild. And the child must be helped to distinguish dependency on the therapist, from which the child rebels, from necessary dependency on others. The passive-active conflict must be actively verbalized.

CHILD: I'm not leaving.

THERAPIST: Sometimes it's hard to separate from someone you're beginning to like.

CHILD: Not me.

THERAPIST: And at other times you refuse to come. The need to be close to me really bothers you. You think I'll reject you.

CHILD: Don't be stupid.

THERAPIST: I wonder if there isn't a part of you that likes coming here and another part that doesn't. The part that likes it is the part that needs to be taken care of—like all of us need. The other part is the tough guy that feels he needs nobody and can take care of himself.

CHILD: Therapists sure are screwy!

THERAPIST: And the tough-guy part fights with the other part. Just because you sometimes fight this inner battle doesn't mean being taken care of a little makes you a helpless baby. You can't allow yourself to feel soft feelings because soft means weak and weak means "girlish" or whatever you say to yourself about soft feelings. I'll bet you've never seen men hug before, and when your mother hugs you, you squirm.

CHILD: My mom doesn't hug me.

THERAPIST: Did she ever hug you?

CHILD: I can't remember.

THERAPIST: Can you remember anyone ever hugging you? How about when you were a baby? Somebody must have held and fed you when you were a baby. Otherwise, you'd have starved to death. Perhaps your grandmother? [*The therapist uses the opportunity to get the child in touch with some early positive care.*]

CHILD: I don't remember.

THERAPIST: Do you ever give anybody a hug?

CHILD: Ugh!

THERAPIST: That's sad that you've never been hugged—no wonder we're having such a struggle. Don't worry, I won't hug you, but someday maybe you and maybe your mother or grandmother will hug each other again.

The female therapist may have to address any sexual issues confounding this conflict.

THERAPIST: One way to avoid having to experience soft or warm and tender feelings is to make me into a girlfriend instead of an adult. Then you don't have to deal with these feelings.

CHILD: You have a dirty mind.

THERAPIST: I think of you as a therapy student, not as a boyfriend, but the way you treat me tells me that this "dirty mind" you speak about is your own sexual feeling. But sexual thoughts are not "dirty." All people have them. They're normal. But you confuse tenderness with these thoughts, and that is a problem we need to work on even though it will make you very uncomfortable.

These comments are typically made as the child stands in front of the door, turns the lights on and off, and insults the therapist. As the child works these feelings through, they continue to be discussed, but in a more calm and relaxed manner while the child engages in play or games. Often, the child has to be challenged to make progress at this stage.

THERAPIST: Now you only know how to hit or kick or yell at me. You don't seem to remember that you once played quietly alongside me and then talked with me. When you decide to talk or to play again, I'll be here for you, but right now, if you can't play or talk, I'll have to have you escorted back to class.

The distrustful gorilla-suit wearer maintains pseudoautonomy because no other means of survival is readily available. The energy expended to maintain this pseudoautonomy blocks the development of true initiative. With a therapist's help, the injured sense of trust is repaired and the pseudoindependence wanes, but not without considerable conflict. When the child surrenders to dependency needs, the vulnerability felt in this position causes periodic flights into independence, followed by anxiety relief, but also by depression because the child now experiences a weakening of the developing attachment to the therapist or to other caregivers.

This oscillating behavior occurs for a long period. When the child finally allows himself or herself to be dependent, and to please preferred adults, movement toward true autonomy begins. But such progress occurs with regular setbacks. Sometimes the child will want help on a task, and other times he or she will want to do the same task without help, a normal behavior but exaggerated in the child shedding the gorilla suit. Resistance to help will be strong, and the response to failure, when on one's own, even stronger.

Depression will again follow failure to achieve age-appropriate autonomous actions. And when the child takes the initiative, self-judgment of achievements will be unfavorable in comparison to others, and with competition, the child will be anxiety ridden. Again, each time the child judges an effort unfavorably, depression and anxiety follow, accompanied by retreat to the safety of earlier behavior. Pseudoautonomy will be reasserted. Considerable patience is required by those working with children shedding their gorilla suits. Their "one step forward, two steps back" behavior frustrates and creates despair in those trying to help them. The therapist's role is to serve "humbly" as the captain of the "team," working with the child as well as with the child's caregivers, supporting, encouraging, and praising their efforts.

THE THIRD STAGE: PRODUCTIVE PLAY

We have repeatedly emphasized that traumatized children are too scared or too frozen to spontaneously play out their life dramas. In the midst of abject terror, the child becomes immobilized and unable to resist the assailant. This helpless and powerless moment becomes frozen in time and etched deeply in the psyche. It becomes a significant barrier to progress. Nevertheless, to move forward in therapy, and in life, it must be surpassed. The moment of inaction is stored within the body and cannot be resolved by verbal processing alone. "The body keeps the score" (van der Kolk 2003). Corrective action is required, not verbalization. Turning experiences passively responded to into experiences actively mastered, a core feature of play therapy, is helpful.

Many abused and traumatized children enact rape scenes, stabbings, and shootings they witnessed. A number have witnessed the murder of a family member, terrifying to remember even years after the event. Some have narrowly escaped their own death. When children on the invitational track are emotionally prepared to reenact their traumas in play, the enactments, if kept under control, much like the control inherent in the behavior therapist's simultaneous use of progressive muscle relaxation and systematic desensitization, allow for the rehearsal of corrective action. Through play, the children can use their strength to ward off the attacker and reclaim their power. Others, through play characters, scream loud and long, alerting a neighbor or a policeman who intervenes. These actions, impossible to take at the time because of the overwhelming fear experienced, help the child to process the event. The knowledge that such actions at the time may have resulted in more harm or even death is irrelevant.

When traumas are reenacted, the affective tone in the room is serious and somber. The scenes created lack the imaginative and playful characteristics of nontraumatized play. The therapist may also experience, along with the child, some of the terror associated with a trauma. By creating a safe, consistent, reliable, and trusting relationship with the child, the therapist helps free the child from the crippling anxiety associated with the original trauma. By playing out a corrective action, the child moves forward emotionally and then developmentally.

Clinical progress is illustrated in the treatment of Anthony, a Caribbean American child adopted by a loving older couple who had no other children. Anthony was first seen when he was five years old. In addition to unabashed assertiveness, he suffered from intense multiple fears and phobias, especially the fear of abandonment and loss (the flip side of anger and aggression is often fear). Through the use of hand puppets, Frog and Turtle, Anthony confronted his fears in gradual steps.

Initially, Anthony, through Frog, became a frightened, weak, and helpless creature, a role that paralleled his own fears. Turtle [the puppet assigned to the therapist] became the helper, teacher, guide, and coach and assisted Frog to face each of his fears one by one. This play, however, probably raised Anthony's anxiety since the masking symbols he selected were not distant enough from his own situation to keep anxiety at a minimum—the play was too close to home and left him feeling too vulnerable, so several weeks later he reversed the roles. Frog became strong, brave, and heroic, and Turtle became timid, fearful, and reluctant to take risks and to try new things. Anthony loved this role reversal, and he and Dr. Crenshaw embarked on a series of dramatic journeys known as "The Frog and Turtle Adventures." The common theme of these escapades was that Frog was fearless and adventurous while Turtle was reluctant, hesitant, protesting, and fearful.

One of Anthony's favorite episodes, played out in numerous variations, entailed Frog convincing reluctant Turtle to take a hot-air-balloon ride. Each time Frog and Turtle embarked, some disaster would befall them, reflecting Anthony's view, projected onto Turtle, that the world is a dangerous place. Invariably a storm would appear and blow the hot air balloon off its course. During such events, Turtle was directed to complain bitterly, "We should have never come!" or "I will never let you, Frog, talk me into doing such a thing again!" Frog would get impatient and tell him, "Oh shut up! Everything is going to be okay. I'll handle it. Don't be such a wimp!"

Then Frog and Turtle would typically land on some deserted island [*abandonment fear*]. At that point, the author would reflect, through his role as Turtle, fears of separation and abandonment and lament: "We are so far away from home! We're lost. We'll never get back home! We're all alone out here!" Frog would, in turn, express confidence and reassure Turtle that they would find a way to deal with the disaster. The situation usually deteriorated, however, as Frog and Turtle were captured by island natives who tied them up, strung them up by their feet, and hung them over an open fire. Or they would be attacked by jungle animals or, in some cases, by vicious dinosaurs. During these hostilities, Turtle would yell at Frog, "Now look at the mess you got us into! We are going to be barbequed or eaten by a Tiger! Are you happy now?" Frog, however, always managed to escape and rescue Turtle, who portrayed the helpless, immobilized side of Anthony—bound not by ropes but by his fears.

Frog and Turtle always found their way back home [*this had surplus meaning for Anthony in light of his adoption*] and on returning cried out, "How good it is to be back home!" Turtle would exclaim, "I'm never going to travel again!" Turtle emphatically told Frog that he could forget about getting into a hot air balloon again! The next time, of course, Frog persuades Turtle, in his confident manner, that when they go up in the balloon, nothing bad will happen. Turtle protests vigorously and reminds Frog of previous disasters, but Frog counters that they survived the last disaster. Eventually, Turtle yields to Frog's pressure and off they go, only to face another catastrophe, reminiscent of Charles Schulz's nefarious cartoon character Lucy. Lucy always promises to hold the ball for Charlie Brown, but each time Charlie runs up to kick the ball, Lucy snatches it away.

A later scenario, with many variations, was Frog playing tricks on Turtle, a less frightening experience for Turtle than being lost and eaten by vicious animals, suggesting that Anthony was making progress. His parents also reported his willingness to go to bed without argument, suggesting greater willingness to confront nighttime fears. Anthony enjoyed the control and power of this role because in real life he still struggled with myriad fears and a sense of helplessness. One scenario he repeated often involved Frog talking Turtle into going to the movies. Turtle was willing to go as long as the movie wasn't scary. Frog would say, "Oh, No! I would never do that to you! The movie is Bambi. You'll love it!" Of course, when Frog and Turtle sat down in the theater, it turned out that the short feature was a gruesome depiction of how to make turtle soup and the main feature was *Godzilla*!

Frog loved turning the tables on Turtle and terrorizing him in a multitude of ways. This play was gratifying because he was the terrorist instead of the victim. To master anxiety, normal children turn passively experienced events into active attempts at mastery—often attempting to change the outcome. Play offers numerous opportunities to master fears of abandonment, a fear of all children but a catastrophe that Anthony had actually experienced. He was separated, not only from his birth parents, but from his native country and culture, and he feared subsequent separation from his adoptive parents.

After Anthony's symbolic play diminished his fears of abandonment, he lost interest in the theme and moved on to other issues. At the end of his adventures, after close to three years of weekly treatment, Frog and Turtle parted company. Turtle was now strong enough to face dangers that might come his way without Frog's help. But before they said good-bye, Frog and Turtle revisited, in a condensed version, every previous adventure, one by one, and played them out with affect and intensity similar to that displayed in each original drama. And then they said good-bye. The author felt a significant loss and sadness [*they had been through so much together*] but was glad that Anthony felt ready to face life relying on his own resources.

   One rather humorous twist in their journeys together followed a natural disaster. The Medical Office Building, where Dr. Crenshaw's office was located, caught on fire on a Saturday night. One end of the building was partially destroyed, but fortunately Dr. Crenshaw's office was located in the opposite end, which suffered only smoke and water damage. The building could not be occupied, and fortunately other office space was quickly procured. The fire was pictured on the front page of the Sunday newspaper. The following Monday morning, the author received a call from Anthony. He asked, "Dr. Crenshaw, are Frog and Turtle all right?" He was assured that they were, although both reeked of smoke, and that they would be washed and ready when he came for his next appointment. He was greatly relieved.

Anthony has been seen intermittently over the years as he has faced new issues and crises in his life. He is now eighteen years old and enthusiastically endorsed our inclusion of the Frog and Turtle adventures in this handbook. When reminding Anthony about his phone call after the fire, Dr. Crenshaw pointed out that he could have been burned to a crisp, but because Frog and Turtle were saved, Anthony was relieved. He and Dr. Crenshaw laughed heartily.

Readers desirous of achieving greater understanding of the therapy process are referred to the case presentations of Cohen, (1980), Gavshon (1995), Goldberger (1995), and Kaufman (1990).

The Reemergence of Anger and Chaos

Anger at the therapist can reemerge later in treatment when the therapist cannot live up to the child's idealized image of the good parent. The idealization quickly plummets, replaced by devaluation of, and anger at, the therapist, who now becomes another uncaring adult in an endless string of uncaring adults. Chaos and confusion reemerge, and the child regresses to earlier behavior. Limit setting becomes important again, particularly when the therapist is threatened or the child becomes dangerously reckless or starts destroying play materials. A permissive attitude will not convey safety, nor will it lead the child to feel confidence in the strength and capability of the therapist. An example follows.

   Just before a boy's mother was supposed to pick him up from the residential treatment center for a visit home, she called and canceled the visit. When he met with his female therapist later that afternoon, he was enraged and looking to do battle. His extremely provocative and verbally abusive behavior was his effort to bait the therapist. Every time a limit was stated in a calm but firm way, he would yell at the top of his lungs, "Shut up!" Observers watching through a one-way mirror were concerned for her safety. To her credit, she remained calm and in control of her own emotions. On one occasion, he actually swung his fist toward her as if he were going to hit her, but he didn't.

His therapist firmly and calmly told him he could not hit her. Nor could he talk to her that way. At no time, however, did she comment that his behavior reflected his anger at his mother, considering such a connection as too threatening: he was not yet ready to acknowledge his rage toward his mother because he felt on such shaky ground with her. He felt as if one false move might drive his mother from his life. The therapist, who had set firm limits when therapy began over a year before, trusted that she could help him to contain his anger and not hold it against him. She also had confidence that, as enraged as he was, he would not hurt her. She was able to constantly convey firm limits, along with a kind, accepting attitude, all transmitting sensitivity to his present pain. If she had slipped even once and responded harshly to his verbal abuse, the situation could have spiraled quickly and become dangerous.

The Struggle with Confusing Parental Ties

The therapist needs to help each child realize that the "good" and "bad" images that have been projected onto the child's family are not reality. Many parents of children in gorilla suits possess some positive qualities, but because they are locked in power struggles with their child, just as the child is with the therapist, these positive qualities are unavailable. The child needs to know the parents' positive attributes. Unfortunately, when some troubled children make developmental advancements, their parents develop symptoms. Children need to know that their parents also can seek help. A child's improvement is not harming parents; they have problems and need help for themselves.

THE FOURTH PHASE: COUNSELING ABOUT PRESENT CONCERNS

In outpatient settings, children are usually discharged before this stage is reached. Children in day and residential treatment settings, who have successfully completed treatment and are awaiting a discharge placement, often reach this stage. The therapy delivered is akin to counseling as the child discusses anxieties about the upcoming decisions in his or her life, concern about making friends in new settings, concerns about family matters, and other worries that characterize the child's age stage. The therapy differs from conventional counseling, however, because the therapist can relate some of the child's current worries to past struggles worked on earlier in treatment.

THE LAST PHASE: TERMINATION

All children need preparation for the ending of therapy. When Anthony and his therapist decided he had made as much progress as he could at this stage in his life, an end date for therapy was discussed. When the date was set, Anthony, as already described, repeated in encapsulated form all the travels Frog and Turtle had made over the course of treatment. Other children display similar needs to review their therapy, and the therapist needs to supply no other structure. Still others, however, need help when ending treatment. In the final chapter, we discuss the termination process.

Stages in therapy are very much like stages in growth. Jean Piaget describes growth as transitions from one stage to another, resulting from a "set" or attitude that comes from within. What is learned at any given point is determined by what has gone before, not merely by what the child has experienced but more by the elements to which the child has paid attention. "Every instruction from without presupposes a construction from within."

Ending Therapy

With progress in therapy, a child will begin to express the conflicts associated with the next stage of psychosocial development. The child may become more competitive or exhibitionistic or may increase sexual misbehavior outside of treatment. The child should be periodically reassessed to determine if new symptoms are signs of "higher level" conflicts. If so, then it is time to terminate therapy. Making attachments is very difficult for children in gorilla suits, and when finally made, those attachments are equally difficult to give up. This chapter focuses on the key aims of a therapeutic termination with children whose lives have been replete with loss. Several structured activities are illustrated to help the child through the termination process. They are the Talk Show Interview, the Year Book, and the story "Jose and Pete on the Mountain."

$\mathcal{D}$eciding when to terminate therapy isn't always easy. With children in gorilla suits, treatment can last for years. If the child is in a residential setting, termination of individual therapy usually coincides with discharge from the center. Most children are discharged from residential treatment centers with key issues left unresolved, sometimes because additional isolation from the larger community will produce diminishing returns, but other times because funding sources become exhausted. If the child is discharged to a day treatment center, a new therapist is usually assigned, but if the child is discharged to the natural parent or a foster family, outpatient follow-up rarely occurs unless the child's condition deteriorates. Although most clinicians want therapy to end when the child's behavior suggests that age-appropriate challenges are being mastered, rarely are their wants realized. The child is usually still symptomatic but seems to be on the road to recovery. Rarely do the child and the therapist decide together that therapy is no longer needed (Mordock 1996). More often the child's parents or foster parents terminate the sessions.

Garcia and Weisz (2002) reported that premature terminations of therapy were largely accounted for by "therapeutic relationship problems." Under this heading they included the following concerns:

> The therapist did not seem to be doing the right things, talking about the right problems, talking enough with family members, or helping the child; that the therapist did not seem to understand or failed to explain the child's treatment clearly to the parents; and that the child or parent simply did not like the therapist. (p. 442)

A second, but less important, factor contributing to premature endings was "money issues."

These findings suggest that dropping out of treatment sometimes has more to do with concerns about money than with the child's improvement. Garcia and Weisz also highlight that a strong therapeutic alliance can prevent premature treatment endings. Diane Hailparn and Michael Hailparn (2000) suggest that a parent's problems, such as envy, jealousy, competition, and narcissism, can be activated by the child's therapy, and the parent may either sabotage or terminate the therapy even though the child's need for treatment is well established. We discuss working with parents in chapter 9 of our companion volume, *Understanding and Treating the Aggression of Children.*

Children also can be reluctant to continue treatment. With behavior under better control, the children no longer want to be identified as "needing help." During treatment, they may talk about a future time when the therapist is no longer seeing them. The comments will differ from earlier refusals to come because they will be expressed in a more realistic, and often sad, tone. The child may talk about new friends made and new activities undertaken that conflict with therapy times. The tone of the comments suggests the child is exploring separation and reworking issues of separation and loss. Part of the child wants to leave, another part wants to stay, and the ambivalence is expressed in wanting reassurances that return is possible. Controlling behaviors may recur in response to fears of letting go.

Ambivalence about ending therapy may also be expressed in metaphors. The child may draw scenes of far-off places, picture himself or herself in a plane or boat, draw a picture of a new house, rearrange the dollhouse furniture in new ways, or reenact funerals. Julia Fabricius and Viviane Green (1995) present the case of a young girl who suddenly asked her therapist if she knew about Super Glue, telling her that it would stick them together forever. After the therapist suggested that the girl half wished that they could be stuck together like that, the girl played that they were glued, laughing at the joke, but then said seriously that she wanted to end her therapy on her upcoming birthday.

Nevertheless, the focus of this chapter is on those children who have become attached to the therapist, usually after major testing and struggle, and then have to break the tie because therapy is ending. We discuss those situations in which the child and the therapist decide together when therapy is no longer needed. Deciding when to terminate therapy isn't always easy. With children in gorilla suits, treatment may continue for some time. Therapy ends when the child's behavior suggests that age-appropriate challenges are being mastered. The child may still be symptomatic, but he or she is on the road to recovery. Carolyn Gruber (1987) suggests evaluating a child's functioning in three areas to assess improvement: (1) control of drive activity, (2) reality testing, and (3) identifications.

The child with better control over drive activity is one who can accept substitutes for gratification, who shows a longer time delay between frustration and response, who uses words instead of actions, who displays self-soothing behavior, and who reveals less disorganized thinking.

The child with improved reality testing is one who looks and verbalizes before acting, verbalizes the difference between reality and fantasy ("This is only pretend"), and reveals the ability to verbalize anticipated changes and feelings about them.

The child who has begun to identify with healthy individuals is one who displays concern for others, plays cooperatively with others instead of imitating them or omnipotently controlling their play, and responds in the socially accepted manner for his or her age.

A number of years ago, Dr. Mordock and a colleague, Beatrice Klein, developed a guide to help therapists evaluate change in five basic areas: main focus of satisfaction, relationships, socialization, nature and source of disturbances that interfere with adaptation and development, and ego development (Klein and Mordock 1975). For example, a child who formerly showed pleasure in buttock flaunting, nose picking, making messes, and "dirty talk" and who now shows competitiveness, envy, exhibitionism, and sexual curiosity has moved from the pleasures of a two-year-old to those of a four-year-old. While the child's chronological age may be eight, these new pleasures, while still not age-appropriate, may reveal that the child is on the road to recovery. Similarly, the child who moves from intense interest in a preferred adult to friendships with peers shows developmental advancement in relationships. A formerly aggressive boy who begins to show guilt when he transgresses, who shows less self-esteem when he does not live up to his ideals, and who has developed affectionate feelings for peers is a child who has improved in the area of socialization.

An article by Rosenfeld, Frankel, and Esman (1969), written more than thirty years ago, is still the best journal article we have read on the topic of assessing change. We recommend it to all child therapists. Before therapy is terminated, the therapist needs to be clear that the child displays behaviors indicative of developmental advancement. Generally speaking, children who have shed their gorilla suits will reveal the following behaviors (A former colleague, Chris Brown, contributed to the formation of this list):

1. The child displays decreased power struggles with adults and is more compliant. He or she may be verbally defiant, but the child's actions are generally compliant ones.
2. The child holds fewer unrealistic expectations of others.
3. The child can tolerate emotional conflict. While rebelling at the thought of tender feelings, the child has made several friends.
4. The child is playful. Fantasy play is no longer constrictive and stereotyped.
5. The child begins to accomplish things at school and at home.
6. The child demonstrates interests and hobbies.
7. The child can see beyond his or her own needs and appreciate the needs of others as different from his or her own.
8. The child can finish tasks initiated.
9. The child has positive expectations for his or her efforts.

The therapist should not be surprised, however, if regression occurs when the subject of termination is broached. Often the child has come to rely on the therapist, and the anxiety experienced by thoughts about ending can cause temporary setbacks. The child should be informed that setbacks are expected and that he or she will bounce back after realizing that the improvements demonstrated will remain following termination.

THE PROCESS OF ENDING THERAPY

The termination process needs to incorporate some procedures to deal with separation and loss. Termination from therapy allows a child the opportunity to rework, in the present, the unfinished business of past separations. The process is a growth experience in and of itself. For those who experienced a series of disrupted attachments, termination holds a special significance—the painful memories of past losses are relived. Children can react to the loss of the therapist with depression, feelings of rejection, fear, anger, panic, and the return of original symptoms. Termination is such an emotionally charged process that it can be difficult for both the child and the therapist. Yet successful termination increases the child's chances of making meaningful future attachments.

Therapists should realize that the child's attachment to the therapist, although necessary for growth, is usually not the attachment that most children remember after terminating therapy. It is the attachments they made after progressing in treatment. For example, children who leave residential treatment centers rarely call or write their former therapists. Most often, they contact their favorite teachers or child-care workers. And this is the way it should be. Children who have improved should take credit for their improvements, and one way of doing so is not to forget the therapist but to diminish his or her importance over time.

Our entire lives can be viewed as a series of beginnings and endings, of making attachments and letting them go. Attachments include birth and death, graduations, leaving home, marriage and remarriage, and even our numerous "good-byes," some of which are harder than others. It is the most vexing problem of human existence. Development is a process of attachment, individuation, and separation. The people who are most important to us, those whom we love the most, we eventually have to separate from. Separations from those who have made major contributions to our lives are the most difficult, no matter how long they have been in our lives. All of us remember people who briefly entered our lives but who assisted us greatly. We remember teachers, football coaches, camp counselors, and others whose influence marks us. The marks are part of who we are. One woman, who was very deprived as a child, remembers fondly a cook in her father's fledgling restaurant who made sure she ate some food before she went home and who sang songs to her while she ate. She conjures up this memory when she feels depressed.

Children in gorilla suits—children who have suffered ruptured bonds with many significant adults—who now feel bonded to a therapist are faced with having to sever this bond.

Because the bond with the therapist is usually forged after relentless struggles, the separation process can be painful for the therapist as well, especially for young and inexperienced therapists who can be tormented by excessive guilt.

PRIOR LOSSES REVISITED

The termination process can be agonizing because it brings into focus previous endings that ended poorly. For those who have experienced a series of disrupted attachments, termination can be especially troublesome because painful memories associated with past losses are revived. The emotions attached to these losses intensify feelings about termination. While these emotions can complicate termination, they also provide an opportunity for growth. All endings can arouse deep-seated anxieties and can be experienced as a loss, akin to weaning and other relinquishments throughout life (Wittenberg and Nemeny 1999), but each ending also provideds opportunities for growth. While the termination process is painful, it too can be a growth experience. It can also be a corrective emotional experience. As termination approaches, often the therapist gains entry into the child's previous losses and can help the child explore unfinished business. Foremost, however, is that the ending of therapy can be different from the child's previous endings. One way the ending is different is that its planning is done in collaboration with the child. The child and the therapist face the ending together.

REHEARSALS FOR ENDING

All interruptions in therapy, including missed appointments, whether planned or unplanned, such as planned vacations and unplanned illness, can be viewed as rehearsals for therapy termination. With planned interruptions, the child and therapist can prepare for the upcoming separation and anticipate possible reactions. The child is given the therapist's vacation schedules and asked whom he or she might like to see in the therapist's absence. The child and the child's parents can be made aware of actions to take should an emergency arise while the therapist is away. Therapy sessions are devoted to exploring feelings the child might have in the therapist's absence. On the therapist's return, sessions are devoted to discussing the child's feelings and experiences during the therapist's absence. Such attention to the child's feelings and to the issue of separation and its meaning lay the groundwork for the final separation, when therapy ends.

Therapists shouldn't be surprised when brief separations don't go well. In fact, if they go too well, the child probably isn't very attached. Shirley Samuels (1995) presents her treatment of two foster children, Frances and Larry. Frances was deserted by her father and emotionally abandoned by her mother. At age five, Frances, her mother, and her two younger siblings were found in a dirty, cockroach-infested house. Her mother was catatonic, and Frances was caring for her two siblings. After about a year in therapy, Frances's therapist was scheduled for a vacation. Samuels describes Frances's reaction to learning about the upcoming separation.

> Frances talked about food, tried to feed the therapist, and attempted to control her every mood. Two days before the separation, she wet the floor, tore up a calendar the therapist had used to count off the days before the vacation, and scattered the pieces all over the room. The interpretations during that time focused on her feeling that she was bad, dirty, and lonely, as she had felt when her mother left her. She regressed perceptively in her adop-

tive home during the separation and tore up the post cards the therapist sent
to her. (p. 312)

After Frances's second year of treatment, she verbalized that she would
miss the therapist during her vacation and admitted to fearing she wouldn't return. She followed this revelation by first demanding food and then drawing a
picture showing both sadness and anger. Being more firmly attached to the
therapist, she could better tolerate the thought of separation.

Larry, the second case presented by Samuels, was released for adoption at
age two. His mother had a history of drug addiction, and his father had been
in prison for most of Larry's life. Larry was referred for treatment when he was
three years old. After about a year in therapy, he reacted to the therapist's
month-long annual vacation as follows.

Larry reacted to the bad news by first hitting the therapist and saying she
was bad. He said that he was Superman and that nothing hurt him. He then
demanded to end the session immediately. The therapist related this behavior to his past abandonment and his anger and pain about it. She added that
he was telling her that he was going to be in charge and was leaving her before she left him. (p. 316)

During her absence, Larry regressed at his day camp. He soiled, disobeyed
his teachers, and sucked his thumb constantly. At home, he had frequent temper tantrums, withdrew to his room, and slept a lot. On the therapist's return,
Larry verbalized that he felt sad during her absence and in subsequent sessions
tried to control her every move. He also screamed at her and called her a "poo-
poo." The therapist reflected Larry's anger at being left and linked the anger
and sadness with feelings that accompanied earlier losses. She also emphasized
how these earlier feelings were reactivated when separated from the therapist.

One key component of termination is making children aware of their
gains and helping them own the gains and take credit for them. If the changes
are seen as permanent and not dependent on continuing involvement with the
therapist, children will face termination with more confidence.

SPECIFIC TECHNIQUES FOR PREPARING
THE CHILD FOR TERMINATION

Three specific techniques to help children work through the termination
phase of therapy (Crenshaw, Holden, Kittredge, and McGuirk 1983) will be
described. They are "The Talk Show Interview," "The Year Book," and "Jose
and Pete on the Mountain."

The Talk Show Interview

The Talk Show Interview introduces the idea of termination approximately one month before the end of therapy. This particular activity asks the child to reflect on the therapy experience in primarily a cognitive rather than an affective way. The Talk Show runs about ten to thirty minutes, about fifteen minutes on average. The text of the show, which is audiotaped, follows:

Talk Show, Kids in Therapy, Introduction: "Our guest today is (child's name) who has been seen weekly (or twice weekly) in therapy for the past year. Since there are lots of kids listening to our show who have been in therapy or will be someday, this topic is of great interest."

Part I: (Therapist, as Talk-Show Host, interviews child)

1. Who is your therapist?
2. What do you like most about going to therapy?
3. What don't you like (or what is the hardest) about going to therapy?
4. Was there anything that your therapist said or did that was not helpful to you?
5. Was there anything that your therapist said or did that was just right— just what you needed?
6. What changes, if any, do you see in yourself since going to therapy?

Part II: (Child, as Talk-Show Host, interviews the therapist. Children who are not good readers can be coached to learn the questions by repeating them after the therapist.)

1. Who did you see in therapy this year? (therapist gives child's name)
2. What did you like most about working with (child's name) this year?
3. Was there anything you found difficult about working with (child's name) in therapy?
4. Is there anything you wish had been different?
5. What changes do you see in (child's name) since starting therapy?
6. Is there anything about (child's name) that stands out in your mind and will help you to remember (child's name) in some specific way?

This therapeutic strategy is useful in highlighting the child's gains, and doing the interviews on audiotape allows for further consolidation of the gains in the child's mind. At the last session, the child is offered a copy of the tape to keep.

The Year Book

A second technique, the Year Book, is used throughout the termination phase of therapy. The child is given a photograph album that contains twenty blank pages and is told that the child and therapist will put together a therapy Year Book to help remember their time together. Each page is covered with clear removable plastic that holds the pictures or other materials in place. The child is asked to recall significant events in treatment, such as a favorite activity or a particular turning point in the therapeutic relationship, and then to take photographs that are reminders of these things. The therapist's role is to help the child focus on such events. The child can also cut out pictures from magazines to supplement the drawings or photographs. Captions are added to the pictures. The child is given the Year Book to keep when therapy ends.

For this activity to be maximally useful in eliciting the child's feelings about termination, a moderate to high level of structure is needed over a period of several weeks. The Year Book is intended to elicit both cognitive and affective experiences. The child may also contribute drawings or artwork to the Year Book. The last page should include a letter written to the child by the therapist that highlights the child's strengths, the gains made during therapy, and the things the therapist found enjoyable about working with the child. Something positive that the therapist will always remember about the child should conclude the letter.

Jose and Pete on the Mountain

The story of "Jose and Pete on the Mountain" was written as a metaphor for the experience of therapy. This technique helps children to face the affective experience of termination. Each difficulty encountered by the characters in the story, Jose and Pete, conveys some of the emotional struggles in the process of therapy. For example, the child's developing trust in the therapist is symbolized by the experience of Jose and Pete facing a storm together.

The therapist reads the story out loud to the child. This takes about ten minutes. The child is then asked to complete the story by adding a new chapter. After the child completes this task, the therapist finishes the story by reading either Ending A, for the child leaving therapy, or Ending B, for the child transferring to a new therapist. The text of the story and the two different endings are reproduced at the end of this chapter.

EXPANDING THE CIRCLE OF TRUST

Proskauer (1969) emphasizes that children should not be left feeling that goodbyes have been said to their only trustworthy confidant. During the weeks leading up to termination, therapy should focus on identifying other individuals who can be trusted to help the child in times of trouble. A "Helping

Hand" exercise helps identify resources the child can seek. On each finger, the child writes the name of someone trusted who could be turned to for help. The child is encouraged, and perhaps even helped, to enroll in activities such as sports, scouts, and community center–sponsored events, which can expand the child's circle of adult and peer friendships.

THE COUNTDOWN TO TERMINATION

Since children have a poor sense of time, the therapist marks on a calendar the remaining sessions to termination. This collaborative countdown of remaining sessions brings feelings about endings into focus as termination becomes more real and imminent. The therapist introduces the issue at each session during the countdown.

> THERAPIST: Let's count together how many sessions we have left together. [*The child counts them out loud.*] So we have four more sessions together. I was wondering what feelings come up for you about our having only four more sessions together?
> CHILD: I don't know. I don't want to think about it.
> THERAPIST: That's okay. But if you were to take a few minutes right now to think about it, what would some of your feelings be?
> CHILD: [*Ignores the question and starts to pull a game off the shelf.*]
> THERAPIST: We can plan together how to use our time these last few visits, but before we play that game, how about using the "Gingerbread Person" to help you share your feelings about our ending therapy?
> CHILD: Okay. Then can we play Connect Four?

The above interchange illustrates how difficult it is for children to share feelings, even those that arise when thinking about ending therapy. Clearly this child preferred to avoid discussing the topic. Children should be given ample opportunity to express all feelings about termination, especially negative ones. Most children are ambivalent about termination but have great difficulty verbalizing conflict. The expression of negative feelings should be encouraged because hidden negatives can taint the child's memory of what should have been a positive therapeutic experience (Proskauer 1969). When both negative and positive feelings are fully expressed, through words, drawings, artwork, a Year Book, a talk show, or other structured techniques, the child gains a greater perspective on the therapy experience. The structured and directive techniques discussed in this chapter help the child to share feelings that might remain unspoken or outside of conscious awareness.

PLANNING TOGETHER THE FINAL SESSIONS

Termination should be planned in collaboration with the child. Children often choose to include in the final three or four sessions some favorite therapy activities. Or they plan a celebration for the last session. Unlike many of the child's previous losses, the child exercises some control—the child has a say in how the ending takes place. Planning together helps counteract the feelings of helplessness and powerlessness that children often experience when facing loss. It also brings into focus the finality of therapy and helps to surface unexpressed feelings. We have repeatedly emphasized the healing potential in dialogue. The child's previous losses were marked by things left unsaid and unfinished. As Allen (1942) pointed out, in one of the first books devoted exclusively to child therapy, termination from therapy allows a child the opportunity to rework, in the present, unfinished business of past separations and differentiation.

ONE FINAL CONVERSATION ABOUT WORDS UNSPOKEN

To provide maximal opportunities for working through complicated feelings about endings, a therapist can ask a child to pretend, as the car pulls away after the last day in treatment, to make one final call, on a cell phone, to the therapist. In this last conversation, anything can be said that has been left unsaid. This structured exercise focuses precisely on the finality of termination and may bring to the surface anything left unsaid.

SOME CONCLUDING REMARKS

These structured activities focus the child's attention on the termination phase of therapy. They also encourage the child, with the assistance of the therapist, to draw on inner resources to face the challenge of ending a meaningful experience. The opportunities for growth and for further work on prior losses is an integral part of the termination phase. Sadly, in today's world of brief and abbreviated treatment, often dictated by managed care companies, a therapist may find an alliance forming just as treatment must end. In such rapid-fire treatment, the uncovering work described in this chapter does not occur because a meaningful attachment with the therapist has no time to develop. The therapy process loses its meaning, and the opportunity to do further work on prior losses is lost.

Jose and Pete on the Mountain

Once there was a boy named Jose. He was scared about climbing mountains, yet he wanted to climb one special, very steep mountain. He was introduced to a guide named Pete. Pete had climbed many mountains before but had not climbed this one. That meant that they had to work together closely to get up the mountain. Jose had tried to climb the mountain before and had fallen and gotten hurt.

During the course of a year, Jose and his guide Pete made many attempts to scale the mountain. At first, the trail was not very steep. They found a waterfall and a swimming hole with some pretty flowers. Later, the trail became very steep, and they encountered many obstacles.

In the fall of that year, Jose and Pete decided they would attempt an especially steep and tricky climb on the west side of the mountain. They were roped together and feeling very confident. Jose was starting to feel a little tired when suddenly his foot slipped on some loose rock. He fell about five feet and landed on a narrow ledge. He became very angry with Pete because he felt Pete had made him climb too hard and too fast.

"It's your fault that I'm hurt!" he yelled.

His ankle was twisted and so sore that he could hardly stand up. Pete reached down to him and with his hand tightly gripped around Jose's wrist, he pulled Jose gradually off the ledge to safe ground. Jose was very scared that Pete might be pulled down in the struggle and felt like crying when the two of them sat together and rested on the side of the mountain.

For a week or so after the fall, Jose didn't want to go near the mountain, and he was still a little angry with Pete for making him climb so hard.

A week later, Pete asked, "How about it, Jose? Are you ready to climb again?" Although still scared and angry, Jose knew that he really wanted to do it, and besides, Pete wasn't going to let him give up so easily. So they started off again.

Pete and Jose were walking up the mountain, and everything was going well. All of a sudden, they both spotted a group of dark storm clouds in the distance coming quickly towards them. Pete, trying calmly to alert Jose, stated matter-of-factly, "There is a big storm coming. When it gets here, we will have to find cover." Jose did not respond as they continued their journey up the mountain.

As the two walked up the mountain watching the clouds get closer and closer, Jose became scared. He wondered to himself if Pete had ever encountered a storm before. Also, Jose wondered if he would be able to handle the dangerous situation that was certain to reach them soon. Pete was also silent as they walked. Instead of being scared, he was thinking about how Jose would react. Pete knew the storm was very scary. Pete also wondered if Jose would be able to let Pete help him. Pete knew that for the two of them to survive, Jose would need to let Pete lead him without any questions.

All of a sudden, quicker than either thought possible, the storm was upon them. The winds blew strongly, and the rain fell hard. Without a moment's hesitation, Pete grabbed Jose by the arm and walked off the trail. As they headed for a cave that could be seen from the path, Pete picked up wood for a fire, telling Jose to do the same. Pete also gave Jose many orders on the way to the cave, as well as when they were inside. Although Jose was somewhat angry at Pete for being bossy, he did feel safe. Jose found himself making suggestions about what to do. Pete agreed with many of them. Jose did not feel as scared anymore.

The storm passed as quickly as it had come. When it was gone, Pete and Jose said in unison, "I'm glad it's over." They started walking. As they continued their journey up the mountain, they walked in silence. There was a new closeness between them, however, brought about by their experience of fighting the storm together.

One day, Jose and Pete were carefully working their way along a ledge. They were quite a way up the mountain when suddenly they heard a threatening growl from behind them.

"Wildcat!" yelled Pete. "I knew there were quite a few of them on this mountain, but I'd hoped we could get farther along our climb before we ran into one."

The cat loomed behind and above Jose on a ledge. It bared its fangs and tensed its muscles menacingly. Unfortunately, Jose, who did not have much experience taming wild animals, was on the ledge closest to the mountain lion. Pete was a distance away and could not get past him to take charge. Jose realized this all of a sudden and felt panicky. He felt very afraid and helpless in the face of the large and powerful animal.

Pete said quietly, "I can't get over to you, Jose, so you're going to have to handle it. We don't have enough weapons, and we're not strong enough to kill it, and I don't think we want to, anyway. They're beautiful animals and there aren't enough of them as it is. We just want to continue climbing higher up the mountain and not get hurt. So the idea is to just be cool and slowly take some of the food we were carrying for dinner out of your knapsack. Lay it right where you're standing."

Jose did as Pete suggested. "Now," Pete whispered, "just start inching away, higher and higher up the trail. Slowly . . . slowly . . ." Jose inched along with his heart pounding in his chest. The cat seemed to grow quieter as Jose moved away and began eyeing the meat with interest. When Jose had moved about twenty feet away, Pete whispered, "Good job. Now, let's walk quietly." When they had walked away, Jose sighed with relief and said, "Whew! I'm glad that's over!"

Pete laughed heartily and replied, "Don't worry. You'll run into animals all the time as you go higher. But I think now you've got an idea about how to handle them better." Jose thought to himself that he'd think about that before he started up the mountain again. For now, he was just very glad that the mountain lion was gone.

Pete and Jose had gone through some difficult times together and were again starting to make progress up the mountain. Jose was feeling as if he could really trust Pete to help him. They climbed higher. Jose had learned a lot from Pete about mountain climbing. As Pete and Jose climbed higher, Jose began to notice that it was getting cloudy on the mountain. He couldn't see things as far away as before. He couldn't see other mountains or even the bottom of the mountain he was climbing. Suddenly the clouds seemed real close.

"Hey, Pete—what's going on?" Jose said a little louder than he expected to.

"It's just one of those mountain fogs," Pete answered. "They happen all of a sudden. Sometimes they last a while and sometimes not."

Jose felt glad that Pete knew what it was and did not sound worried. They kept climbing higher, but the fog got worse. Jose was thinking maybe they should go back, but he did not want Pete to know he was scared. He decided to ask sort of casually, "Should we keep going up in this fog?"

"Oh sure," replied Pete. "No problem." Jose was watching his feet so he could climb carefully up the rocks. The next time Jose looked up, he could not see Pete. "Pete," he cried, but Pete didn't answer. Jose saw fog on every side of him and nothing else. He was completely lost. He did not know which way to go, and he was alone. There was an awful feeling in his stomach. He sat down. He could feel tears coming into his eyes. He was really scared when something dark came toward him. All of a sudden, it turned into Pete. Jose was so glad to see him!

"I got lost," he tried to say calmly. "I didn't know what to do." Jose did not sound so calm.

"I realized you weren't right behind me," Pete explained. "I called you but you didn't answer."

"Me too," Jose replied.

"Sound doesn't carry very far in the fog, so I guess we couldn't hear each other."

"Oh."

Pete looked at Jose. "Did you get a little worried?"

"Yeah," admitted Jose.

Pete and Jose decided to climb the mountain one last time before parting. They started off together and [*Ask child to complete this part of the story.*]. . .

After the last climb, Pete said to Jose, "I am going to miss you, but I have enjoyed teaching you to climb mountains."

Ending A: "I think you are now ready to climb the mountain yourself. You have learned a lot about mountain climbing in the past year. Don't be afraid to make use of what you have learned." Jose felt really sad saying good-bye to Pete. He had lots of different feelings as Pete walked away. He knew he was really going to miss Pete, but he also felt like he could climb new mountains.

Ending B: "I think you have learned a lot about climbing mountains this past year. Don't be afraid to use what you have learned. There is another mountain I think you would like to climb, and I will introduce you to a new guide who will help you with the new mountain." Jose felt really sad saying good-bye to Pete. He had lots of different feelings as Pete walked away. He knew he was going to miss Pete, but he felt like he could climb new mountains.

It is often useful for the therapist to follow up the story with questions of the child like the ones below:

What is the moral of this story?
What do you think we can learn from it?
Do you think anything was left out of the story that should be there?
How do you think Jose's life turned out over the long run?

Bibliography

Ablon, S. L. 1990. Developmental aspects of self-esteem in the analysis of an 11-year-old boy. *Psychoanalytic Study of the Child* 45:337–56.

——— and J. E. Mack. 1980. Children's dreams reconsidered. *Psychoanalytic Study of the Child* 35:179–218.

Abrams, S. 1990. Orientating perspectives on shame and self-esteem. *Psychoanalytic Study of the Child* 45:411–36.

Ackerman, S. J. and M. J. Hilsenroth. 2003. A review of therapist characteristics and techniques positively impacting the therapeutic alliance. *Clinical Psychology Review* 23:1–33.

Adams-Tucker, C. 1985. Defense mechanisms used by sexually abused children. *Children Today* 14:9–12.

Allen, F. H. 1942. *Psychotherapy with children*. New York: Norton.

Altman, N. 1995. *The analyst and the inner city: Race, class, and culture through a psychoanalytic lens*. Hillsdale, NJ: Analytic Press.

American Psychiatric Association. 1994. *Diagnostic and statistical manual of mental disorders*. 4th ed. Washington, DC: Author.

Applestein, C. D. 1993. Peer helping peer: Duo therapy with children in residential care. *Residential Treatment for Children and Youth* 10:33–53.

Arata, C. M. 2002. Child sexual abuse and sexual revictimization. *Clinical Psychology: Science and Practice* 9:135–64.

Bar, D. L., M. J. Karcher, and R. L. Selman. 1998. Pair therapy. In J. D. Noshpitz, N. E. Alessi, J. T. Coyle, et al. (eds.), *Handbook of child and adolescent psychiatry*. Vol 6, *Basic psychiatric science and treatment*, 423–31. New York: Wiley.

Benjamin, J. A. 1994. What angel would hear me? The erotics of transference. *Psychoanalytic Inquiry* 14:535–57.

Bennett, M. J. 2001. *The empathic healer: An endangered species*. San Diego, CA: Academic Press.

Bion, W. R. 1959. Attacks on linking. *International Journal of Psychoanalysis* 40:102–5.

———. 1962. *Learning from experience*. London: Heinemann.

315

Blatt, S. J., and R. B. Blass, 1990. Attachment and separateness: A dialectic model of the products and processes of developmental throughout the life cycle. *Psychoanalytic Study of the Child* 45:107–28.

Block, D. 1968. The use of interpretation in the psychoanalytic treatment of children. In E. F. Hammer (ed.), *The use of interpretation in treatment*, 300–20. New York: Grune and Stratton.

Bonime, W. 1962. *The clinical use of dreams*. New York: Basic Books. Reprinted 1982, New York: Da Capo Press.

———. 1982. Private supervision session with David A. Crenshaw.

———. 1983. Private supervision session with David A. Crenshaw.

———. 1985. Private supervision session with David A. Crenshaw.

———. 1989. *Collaborative psychoanalysis: Anxiety, depression, dreams, and personality change.* Rutherford, NJ: Fairleigh Dickinson Press.

Bonovitz, C. 2003. Treating children who do not talk or play: Finding a pathway to intersubjective relatedness. *Psychoanalytic Psychology* 30:3215–328.

Boston, M., and R. Szur, eds.1983. *Psychotherapy with severely deprived children*. London: Routledge, Keegan, Paul.

Bowlby, J. 1969–1973. *Attachment and loss*. 2 vols. New York: Basic Books.

Bowman, E. S., S. Blix, and P. M. Coons. 1985. Multiple personality in adolescence: Relationship to incestual experiences. *Journal of the American Academy of Child and Adolescent Psychiatry* 24:109–14.

Boyd-Webb, N. 2001. The draw-your-bad-dream technique. In H. Kaduson and C. E. Schaefer (eds.), *101 more favorite play therapy techniques*, 159–62. Northvale, NJ: Jason Aronson.

Brooks, B. 1983. Preoedipal issues in a postincest daughter. *American Journal of Psychotherapy* 37:129–36.

Brooks, R. 1993. The search for islands of competence. Presentation at the fifth annual conference of CHADD, San Diego, CA.

Burke, A., D. A. Crenshaw, J. Green, M. A. Schlosser, and L. Strocchia-Rivera. 1989. The influence of verbal ability on the expression of aggression in physically abused children. *Journal of the American Academy of Child and Adolescent Psychiatry* 28:215–18.

Chethik, M. 1987. The defiant ones: A common form of character pathology in children. *Clinical Social Work Journal 15*, 35–42.

———. 2000. *Techniques of child therapy: Psychodynamic strategies*. 2nd. ed. New York: Guilford.

Clum, G. A., P. Nishith, and P. A. Resick. 2001. Trauma-related sleep disturbances and self reported physical health symptoms in treatment-seeking female rape victims. *Journal of Nervous and Mental Disease* 189:618–22.

Cohen, D. J. 1980. Constructive and reconstructive activities in the analysis of a depressed child. *Psychoanalytic Study of the Child* 35:327–66.

———. 1990. Enduring sadness: Early loss, vulnerability, and the shaping of character. *Psychoanalytic Study of the Child* 45:157–78.

Cohen, J. A. 1981. Theories of narcissism and trauma. *American Journal of Psychotherapy* 35:93–100.

Cohen, Y. 1988. The "golden fantasy" and countertransference: residential treatment of the abused child. *Psychoanalytic Study of the Child* 43:337–50.

Coppolillo, H. 1969. A technical consideration in child analysis and child therapy. *Journal of the American Academy of Child Psychiatry* 8:411–35.

Crenshaw, D. A. 1976. Teaching adaptive interpersonal behavior: Group techniques in residential treatment. *Child Care Quarterly* 5:211–20.

———. 1990a. *Bereavement: Counseling the grieving throughout the life cycle.* New York: Continuum. Reprinted 1995, New York: Crossroads, and 2002, Eugene, OR: Wipf and Stock Publishers.

———. 1990b. An ego-supportive approach to children in residential treatment. *Perceptions*, 26:5–7.

———. 1992. Reluctant grievers: Children of multiple loss and trauma. *Forum* 18:6–7.

———. 2001. Party hats on monsters: Drawing strategies to enable children to master their fears. In H. Kaduson and C. E. Schaefer (eds.), *101 more favorite play therapy techniques*, 124–27. Northvale, NJ: Jason Aronson.

———. 2004. *A guidebook for engaging resistant children in therapy: A projective drawing and storytelling series.* Rhinebeck, NY: Rhinebeck Child and Family Center Publications.

——— and C. Foreacre. 2001. Play therapy in a residential treatment center. In A. A. Drewes, L. J. Carey, and C. E. Schaefer (eds.), *School-based play therapy*, 139–62. New York: Wiley and Sons.

——— and K. V. Hardy. In press. Fawns in gorilla suits: Understanding and treating the aggression of children in foster care. In N. Boyd-Webb (ed.), *Traumatized youths in child welfare: Collaboration of mental health and children's service providers.* New York: Guilford.

———, A. Holden, J. Kittredge, and J. McGuirk. 1983. Therapeutic techniques to facilitate termination in child psychotherapy. Unpublished manuscript, Astor Home for Children, Rhinebeck, New York.

Davids, J. 1993. The reaction of an early latency boy to the sudden death of his baby brother. *Psychoanalytic Study of the Child* 48:277–92.

Davidson, P. 1997. The mad game. In H. Kaduson and C. Schaefer (eds.), *101 favorite play therapy techniques*, 224–25. Northvale, NJ: Jason Aronson.

Demos, E. V. 1983. A perspective from infant research on affect and self-esteem. In J. E. Mack and S. L. Ablon (eds.), *The development and sustaining of self-esteem in childhood.* New York: International Universities Press.

Deutsch, H. 1937. The absence of grief. *The Psychoanalytic Quarterly* 6:12–22.

de Young, M. 1982. Self-injurious behavior in incest victims: A research note. *Child Welfare*, 61:577–84.

——— and J. A. Lowery. 1992. Traumatic bonding: Clinical implications in incest. *Child Welfare* 71:165–74.

Dolan, Y. M. 1985. *A path with a heart: Ericksonian utilization with resistant and chronic clients.* New York: Brunner/Mazel.

———. 1991. *Resolving sexual abuse: Solution-focused therapy and Ericksonian hypnosis for adult survivors.* New York: Norton.

Drell, M. J., C. H. Siegel, and T. J. Gaensbauer. 1993. Post-traumatic stress disorder. In C. H. Zeanah (ed.), *Handbook of infant mental health,* 291–304. New York: Guilford.

Drewes, A. 2001a. Helping children deal with aggression. *Association for Play Therapy Newsletter* 20:3.

———. 2001b. The Gingerbread person/feelings map. In H. Kaduson and C. Schaefer (eds.), *101 more favorite play therapy techniques*, 92–97. New York: Aronson.

Ekstein, R. 1966. *Children of time and space of action and impulse*. New York: Appleton Century Crofts.

Epstein, R. 2003. Alice's loss of wonderland. *Residential Treatment for Children and Youth* 20:53–72.

Erikson, E. 1940. Studies in the interpretation of play: Clinical observations of play disruption in young children. *Genetic Psychology Monographs* 22:577–671.

———. 1963. *Childhood and society*. 2nd ed. New York: W. W. Norton.

Fabricius, J., and V. Green. 1995. Termination in child analysis: A child-led process? *Psychoanalytic Study of the Child* 50:205–26.

Fairbairn, W. D. R. 1963. Synopsis of an object relations theory of personality. *Journal of Personality* 53:224–56.

Feldman, R. C., and J. B. Mordock. 1969. A cognitive process approach to evaluating vocational potential in the retarded and emotionally disturbed. Part II. *Rehabilitation Counseling Bulletin* 12:195–203.

Femina, D. D., C. A. Yeager, and D. O. Lewis. 1990. Child abuse: Adolescent records versus adult recall. *Child Abuse and Neglect* 14:237–41.

Fenichel, O. 1953. Concerning the theory of psychoanalytic technique. In H. Finical and D. Rapaport (eds.), *The collected papers of Otto Fenichel*. New York: W. W. Norton.

Fineman, J. A. 1962. Observations in the development of imaginative play in early childhood. *Journal of the American Academy of Child Psychiatry* 1:167–81.

Fischer, K. W., and S. L. Pipp. 1984. Development of structure of unconscious thought. In K. S. Bowers and D. Meichenbaum (eds.), *The unconscious reconsidered*, 88–147. New York: Wiley.

Fox, L. 1994. The catastrophe of compliance. *The Journal of Child and Youth Care* 9:1–16.

Fraiberg, S. 1959. *The magic years—understanding and handling the problems of early childhood*. New York: Charles Scribner.

———. E. Adelson, and V. Shapiro. 1965. Ghosts in the nursery. *Journal of the American Academy of Child Psychiatry* 14:387–424.

Freud, A. 1936. *The ego and the mechanisms of defense*. New York: International Universities Press.

———. 1963. The concept of developmental lines. *Psychoanalytic Study of the Child* 18:245–65.

———. and J. Sandler. 1985. *The analysis of defense: The ego and the mechanism of defense revisited*. New York: International Universities Press.

Furman, E. 1956. An ego disturbance in a young child. *Psychoanalytic Study of the Child* 11:312–35.

———. 1971. *A child's parent dies*. New York: Yale University Press.

———. 1986. On trauma: When is the death of a parent traumatic? *Psychoanalytic Study of the Child* 41:191–208.

Gaensbauer, T. J. 1994. Therapeutic work with a traumatized toddler. *Psychoanalytic Study of the Child* 49:412–33.

———. 1995. Trauma in the preverbal period: Symptoms, memories, and developmental impact. *Psychoanalytic Study of the Child* 50:122–49.

Garcia, J. A., and J. R. Weisz. 2002. When youth mental health care stops: Therapeutic relationship problems and other reasons for ending youth outpatient treatment. *Journal of Consulting and Clinical Psychology* 70:439–43.

Gardner, R. A. 1971. *Therapeutic communications with children: The mutual storytelling technique.* New York. Jason Aronson.

———. 1986. *The psychotherapeutic techniques of Richard A. Gardner.* Cresskill, NJ: Creative Therapeutics.

Garritt, P., and D. A. Crenshaw. 1997. Ego-supportive drawing series. Rhinebeck, NY: Astor Home for Children.

Gavshon, A. 1995. The analysis of an overstimulated child. *Psychoanalytic Study of the Child* 50:227–51.

Gil, E. 1991. *The healing power of play.* New York: Guilford.

Gilligan, C. 1991. Women's psychological development: Implications for psychotherapy. In C. Gilligan, A. Rogers, and D. L. Tolman (eds.), *Women, girls and psychotherapy: Reframing resistance,* 5–51. New York: Haworth.

Gitelson, M. 1973. *Psychoanalysis: Science and profession.* New York: International Universities Press.

Goldberger, M. 1995. Enactment and play following medical trauma: An analytic study. *Psychoanalytic Study of the Child* 50:227–51.

Goldstein, A. P. 1989. *The prepare curriculum: Teaching prosocial competencies.* Champaign, IL: Research Press.

———, B. Glick, S. Reiner, D. Zimmerman, and T. M. Coultry. 1987. *Aggression replacement training: A comprehensive approach for aggressive youth.* Champaign, IL: Research Press.

Goodwin, J., M. Simma, and R. Bergman. 1979. Hysterical seizures: A sequel to incest. *American Journal of Orthopsychiatry* 49:698–703.

Gould, R. 1972. *Child studies through fantasy.* New York: Quadrangle Books.

Green, A. H. 1978. Psychopathology of abused children. *Journal of the American Academy of Child Psychiatry* 17:92–103.

Greene, R. 1998. *The explosive child.* New York: Harper-Collins.

Gruber, C. 1987. Repairing ego deficits in children with developmental diagnosis with a case demonstrating its use. *Child and Adolescent Social Work* 4:50–63.

Hailparn, D. F., and M. Hailparn. 2000. Parent as saboteur in the therapeutic treatment of children. *Journal of Contemporary Psychotherapy* 30:341–51.

Hall, T. M., H. G. Kaduson, and C. E. Schaefer. 2002. Fifteen effective play therapy techniques. *Professional Psychology: Research and Practice* 33:515–22.

Hardy, K. V. 1998. Overcoming "learned voicelessness." Washington, DC: Family Therapy Network Symposium.

———. 2003. *Working with aggressive and violent youth.* Presentation at the Psychotherapy Networker Symposium, Washington, DC.

——— and T. Laszloffy. In press. *Hurting teens: Strategies for working with adolescents' violence.* New York: Guilford Press.

Havens, L. 1989. *A safe place.* Cambridge, MA: Harvard University Press.

Hayes, J. A., and C. J. Gelso. 2001. Clinical implications of research on countertransference: Science informing practice. *Journal of Clinical Psychology* 57:1041–51.

Heinicke, C. M., and I. J. Westheimer. 1965. *Brief separations*. New York: International Universities Press.

Herman, J. 1992. *Trauma and recovery: The aftermath of violence from domestic abuse to political terror*. New York: Basic Books.

Hobday, A., and K. Ollier. 1999. *Creative therapy with children and adolescents: A British Psychological Society book*. Atascadero, CA: Impact Publishers.

Holder, M. 1970. Conceptual problems of acting out in children. *Journal of Child Psychotherapy* 2:5–22.

Horn, T. 1997. Balloons of anger. In H. Kaduson and C. Schaefer (eds.), *101 favorite play therapy techniques*, 250–53. Northvale, NJ: Jason Aronson.

Hubble, M. A., B. L. Duncan, and S. D. Miller, eds. 1999. *The heart and soul of change: What works in therapy*. Washington, DC: American Psychological Association.

Hudak, D. 2000. The therapeutic use of ball play in psychotherapy with children. *International Journal of Play Therapy* 9:1–10.

James, B. J. 1989. *Treating traumatized children: New insights and creative interventions*. Lexington, MA: Lexington Books.

———. 1993. *Treating traumatized children in play therapy*. Presentation at the First Annual Play Therapy Conference, cosponsored by the Astor Home for Children and Dutchess Community College, Poughkeepsie, NY.

———. 1994. *Handbook for treatment of attachment-trauma problems in children*. Lexington, Mass: Lexington Books.

Jernberg, A. M. 1979. *Theraplay*. San Francisco: Jossey-Bass.

Jordan, J. 2003. *The courage to connect*. A workshop presented at the 2003 Psychotherapy Networker Conference, Washington, DC.

Kaduson, H. 2001. The feeling word game. In H. Kaduson and C. Schaefer (eds.), *101 more favorite play therapy techniques*, 19–21. Northvale, NJ: Jason Aronson.

Kaufman, A. F. 1990. The role of fantasy in the treatment of a severely disturbed child. *Psychoanlaytic Study of the Child* 45:235–56.

Kendall, P. C. 2002. *Child and adolescent therapy: Cognitive-behavioral procedures*. 2nd ed. New York: Guilford Press.

———, K. R. Ronan, and J. Epps. 1991. Aggression in children/adolescents: Cognitive-behavioral treatment perspectives. In D. Popler and K. Rubin (eds.), *Development and treatment of childhood aggression,* 341–60. Hillsdale, NJ: Earlbaum.

Kernberg, O. F. 1975. *Borderline conditions and pathological narcissism*. New York: Science House.

Kiesler, D. L. 2001. Therapist countertransference: In search of common themes and empirical referents. *Journal of Clinical Psychology* 57:1953–63.

King, C. H. 1975. The ego and the integration of violence in homicidal youth. *American Journal of Orthopsychiatry* 45:34–145.

Klein, B., and J. B. Mordock. 1975. A guide to differentiated developmental diagnosis with a case demonstrating its use. *Child Psychiatry and Human Development* 5:242–53.

Klein, M. 1932. *The psychoanalysis of children*. New York: Hogarth Press.

———. 1948 [1927]. *Contributions to Psychoanalysis, 1921–1945*. London: Hogarth Press.

Klorer, P. G. 2000. *Expressive therapy with troubled children*. Northvale, NJ: Jason Aronson.

Kranzler, E. M., D. Schaffer, G. Wasserman, and M. Davies. 1990. Early childhood bereavement. *American Academy of Child and Adolescent Psychiatry* 29:513–20.

Krystal, H. 1978. Trauma and affects. *Psychoanalytic Study of the Child* 33:81–116.

Landreth, G. L. 2002. Therapeutic limit setting in the play therapy relationship. *Professional Psychology: Research and Practice* 33:529–35.

Larson, J., and J. E. Lochman. 2002. *Helping schoolchildren cope with anger: A cognitive-behavioral intervention*. New York: Guilford Press.

Levy, D. 1937. *Studies in sibling rivalry: Research monographs no 2*. New York: American Orthopsychiatric Association.

———. 1939. Trends in psychiatry: III. Release Therapy. *American Journal of Orthopsychiatry* 9:713–36.

Lewis, D. O., S. S. Shanok, J. H. Pinus, and G. H. Glaser. 1979. Violent juvenile delinquents. *Journal of the American Academy of Child Psychiatry* 18:307–19.

Lewis, M. 1974. Interpretation in child analysis: Developmental considerations. *Journal of the American Academy of Child Psychiatry* 13:32–53.

Lieberman, S. N., and L. B. Smith. 1991. Duo therapy: A bridge to the world of peers for the ego-impaired child. *Journal of Child and Adolescent Group Therapy* 1:243–52.

Lister, E. D. 1982. Forced silence: A neglected dimension of trauma. *American Journal of Psychiatry* 7:872–76.

Masterson, J. F. 1972. *Psychotherapy with the borderline child: A developmental approach*. New York: Wiley.

Masterson, J. S. 1975. *Narcissistic and borderline disorders*. New York: Bruner/Mazel.

Mayes, L. C., and D. J. Cohen. 1993. The social matrix of aggression: Enactments and representations of loving and hating in the first years of life. *Psychoanalytic Study of the Child* 48:145–69.

Miller, A. 1997. *The drama of the gifted child: The search for the true self*. New York: Basic Books.

Miller, J. B., and I. P. Stiver. 1997. *The healing connection: How women form relationships in therapy and life*. Boston: Beacon Press.

Mills, J. C., and R. J. Crowley. 1986. *Therapeutic metaphors for children and the child within*. New York: Brunner/Mazel.

Minuchin, S., B. Montalvo, B. J. Guerney, Jr., et al. 1967. *Families of the slums: An exploration of their structure and treatment*. New York: Basic Books.

Mitchel, S. A. 1993. *Hope and dread in psychoanalysis*. New York: Basic Books.

Mitchell, C. A. and B. Levine. 1982. Duo therapy in a residential program. *Residential Group Care and Treatment* 1:31–49.

Moore, T. 1964. Realism and fantasy in children's play. *Journal of Child Psychology and Psychiatry* 5:15–36.

Mordock, J. B. 1978. *Ego-impaired children grow up: Post-discharge adjustment of children in residential treatment*. Monograph celebrating the 25th Anniversary of the Astor Home for Children. Rhinebeck, NY: The Astor Home for Children.

———. 1988. Evaluating treatment effectiveness. In C. E. Schaefer and A. J. Swanson (eds.), *Children in residential care: Critical issues in treatment*, 219–50. New York: Van Nostrand Reinhold.

———. 1994. *Counseling the defiant child: A basic guide to helping troubled and aggressive youth.* New York: Crossroads. Reprinted 1998, Northvale, NJ: Jason Aronson.

———. 1996. The real world of the child guidance clinic. *Administration and Policy in Mental Health* 23:231–40.

———. 1997. Ego-supportive play therapy for children who lack imaginative play: Building defenses. *International Journal of Play Therapy* 6:23–40.

———. 1998. Some risk factors in the psychotherapy of children and families: Well-established techniques that can put some clients at risk. *Child Psychology and Human Development* 29:229–44.

———. 1999a. *Selecting treatment interventions: A casebook for clinical practice in child and adolescent managed mental health.* 2nd ed. Providence, RI: Manisses Communications Group.

———. 1999b. The life-space interview revisited: Stages in one professional's struggle to develop calming techniques for children in crisis and problems encountered in their utilization. *Residential Treatment for Children and Youth* 16:1–14.

——— and R. C. Feldman. 1969. A cognitive process approach to evaluating the vocational potential in the retarded and emotionally disturbed. Part I, *Rehabilitation Counseling Bulletin* 12:136–43.

Muir, E., A. Speirs, and G. Todd. 1988. Family intervention and parental involvement in the facilitation of mourning in a four-year-old boy. *Psychoanalytic Study of the Child* 43:367–83.

Nilsson, M. 2000. The dollhouse: Dream or reality? A borderline girl's psychotherapy. *Journal of Child Psychotherapy* 26:79–96.

Oaklander, V. 1988. *Windows to our children.* Highland, NY: Gestalt Journal Press.

O'Connor, K. J. 1983. The color-your-life technique. In C. E. Schaefer and K. J. O'Connor (eds.), *Handbook of Play Therapy*, 251–58. New York: John Wiley.

———. 1995. *Workshop on abused and traumatized children.* Fairleigh Dickinson Summer Play Therapy Workshops, New Hackensack, NJ.

———. 2002. The value and use of interpretation in play therapy. *Professional Psychology: Research and Practice* 33:523–28.

Parsons, M. 1990. Some issues affecting termination: The treatment of a high-risk adolescent. *Psychoanalytic Study of the Child* 45:437–57.

Pelcovitz, D. 1999. *Child witnesses to domestic violence.* Presentation sponsored by Four Winds Hospital, Astor Home for Children, and Ulster County Mental Health, Kingston, NY.

Peller, L. 1954. Libidinal phases, ego development, and play. *Psychoanalytic Study of the Child* 9:178–97.

Perry, B. D. 1997. Incubated in terror: Neurodevelopmental factors in the "cycle of violence." In J. D. Osofsky (ed.), *Children in a violent society*, 124–49. New York: Guilford Press.

———, 2003. *Aggression and violence: The neurobiology of experience.* The World Wide Web: http://teacher.scholastic.com/professional/bruceperry/aggression-violence .htm, 1.

Proskauer, S. 1969. Some technical issues in time-limited psychotherapy with children. *Journal of the American Academy of Child Psychiatry* 8:154–69.

Pynoos, R. S., and K. Nader. 1989. Children's memory and proximity to violence. *Journal of the American Academy of Child and Adolescent Psychiatry* 28:236–41.

Raphael, B. 1983. *The anatomy of bereavement.* New York: Basic Books.

Rapier, B. 2000. More about bop-bags. *Association for Play Therapy Newsletter* 19:24.

Reiser, L. W. 1994. Remembered childhood artifacts: Windows to the past. *Psychoanalytic Study of the Child* 49:241–62.

Roseby, V., and J. R. Johnston. 1995. Clinical interventions with latency-aged children of high conflict and violence. *American Journal of Orthopsychiatry* 65:48–59.

Rosenfeld, E., N. R. Frankel, and A. H. Esman. 1969. A model of criteria for evaluating progress in children undergoing psychotherapy. *Journal of the American Academy of Child Psychiatry* 8:193–228.

Rosenthal, K. 1987. Ritual of undoing in abused and neglected children. *Child and Adolescent Social Work* 4:226–37.

Samuels, S. 1995. Helping foster children to mourn past relationships. *Psychoanalytic Study of the Child* 50: 308–26.

Sarnoff, C. A. 1987. *Psychotherapeutic strategies in the latency years.* Northvale, NJ: Aronson.

Saunders, S. M. 2001. Pretreatment correlates of the therapeutic bond. *Journal of Clinical Psychology* 57:1339–52.

Schredl, M., G. Kronenberg, P. Nonnell, and I. Heuser, 2001. Dream recall, nightmare frequency, and nocturnal panic attacks in patients with panic disorder. *Journal of Nervous and Mental Disease* 189:559–62.

Schwartz, E. D., and T. M. Kowalski. 1991. Malignant memories: PTSD in children and adults after a school shooting. *Journal of the American Academy of Child and Adolescent Psychiatry* 30:936–44.

Sharp, T. J., and A. G. Harvey. 2001. Chronic pain and post-traumatic stress disorder: Mutual maintenance? *Clinical Psychology Review* 21:8576–77.

Shengold, L. 1979. Child abuse and deprivation: Soul murder. *Journal of the American Psychoanalytic Association* 27:533–59.

———. 1989. *Soul murder: The effects of childhood abuse and deprivation.* New Haven: Yale University Press.

Shenken, L. I. 1964. The implications of ego psychology for a motiveless murder. *Journal of American Academy of Child Psychiatry* 3:741–51.

Shure, M. 1996. *I can problem-solve: An interpersonal cognitive-problem-solving program.* Champaign, IL: Research Press.

Siegel, D. 2003. Brain-savvy therapy: Lessons of the neuroscience revolution. Presentation at the Psychotherapy Networker Symposium, Washington, DC.

Silvern, L., and L. Kaersvang. 1989. The traumatized children of violent marriages. *Child Welfare* 68:421–36.

Singer, J. 1966. *Daydreaming: An introduction to the experimental study of inner experience.* New York: Random House.

———. 1976. *Daydreaming and fantasy.* London: Allen and Unwin.

Smilansky, S. 1968. *The effects of sociodramatic play on disadvantaged preschool children.* New York: John Wiley and Sons.

Sperling, M. 1982. *The major neuroses and behavior disorders in children.* Northvale, NJ: Jason Aronson.

Stern, D. 1985. *The interpersonal world of the infant.* New York: Basic Books.

Stern, M. B. 2002. Child-friendly therapy: Biopsychosocial innovations for children and families. New York: Norton.

Stoeffler, V. 1960. The separation phenomenon in residential treatment. *Social Casework* 41:523–30.

Stone, B. 2000. Bop bags: To use or not to use. *Association for Play Therapy Newsletter* 19:3.

Strauss, M. 1999. *No-talk therapy for children and adolescents.* New York: Norton.

Sugar, M. 1988. A preschooler in a disaster. *American Journal of Psychotherapy* 42:619–29.

Tangney, J. P. and R. L. Dearing. 2002. *Shame and guilt.* New York: Guilford Press.

Tartar, R. E., A. M. Hegedus, N. E. Wiastein, and A. I. Alderman. 1984. Neuropsychological, personality, and familial characteristics of physically abused delinquents. *Journal of the American Academy of Child Psychiatry* 243:668–74.

Terr, L. 2003. Play therapy with victims of trauma: What has been learned from 9/11 and Columbine? Presentation at the New York Association of Play Therapy annual conference, Melville, Long Island, NY.

———. 1979. Children of Chowchilla: Study of psychic trauma. *Psychoanalytic Study of the Child* 34:547–623.

———. 1981. Forbidden games: Posttraumatic child's play. *Journal of the American Academy of Child and Adolescent Psychiatry* 20:741–60.

———. 1983. Play therapy and psychic trauma: A preliminary report. In C. Schaefer and K. O'Connor (eds.), *Handbook of play therapy*, 308–19. New York: John Wiley.

———. 1988. What happens to early memories of trauma: A study of twenty children under age five at the time of documented traumatic events. *Journal of the American Academy of Child and Adolescent Psychiatry* 27:96–104.

———. 1990. *Too scared to cry: Psychic trauma of childhood.* New York: Basic Books.

Tessman, L., and I. Kaufman. 1967. Treatment techniques, the primary process, and ego development in schizophrenic children. *Journal of the American Academy of Child Psychiatry* 6:98–115.

Trotter, K., D. Eshelman, and G. Landreth. 2003. A place for Bobo in play therapy. *International Journal of Play Therapy* 12:117–39.

van der Kolk, B. A. 2003. The frontiers of trauma treatment. Presentation at the Psychotherapy Networker Symposium, Washington, DC.

———, D. Pelcovitz, S. Roth, F. S. Mandel, et al. 1996. Dissociation, somatization, and affect regulation: The complexity of adaptation to trauma. *American Journal of Psychiatry* 153:83–93.

Van Ornum, W., and J. B. Mordock. 1990. *Crisis counseling of children and adolescents: A guide for the nonprofessional.* Expanded edition. New York: Continuum. Reprinted 2002, Eugene, OR: Wipf and Stock Publishers.

Volkan, V. 1972. The linking objects of pathological mourners. *Archives of General Psychiatry* 27:215–21.

Wallerstein, R. S. 1994. Psychotherapy research and its implications for a theory of therapeutic change: A forty-year overview. *Psychoanalytic Study of the Child* 49:120–41.

Weil, J. L. 1989. *Instinctual stimulation of children: Volume I. From common practice to child abuse.* Guilford, CT: International Universities Press.

Weis, J., J. Sampson, and the Mount Zion Psychotherapy Research Group. 1986. *The psychoanalytic process: Theory, clinical observation and empirical research*. New York: Guilford Press.

Westen, D. 1990. Toward a revised theory of borderline object relationships: Contributions of empirical research. *International Journal of Psychoanalysis* 71:661–93.

Whited, C. 2000. More about bop-bags! *Association for Play Therapy Newsletter* 19:23–24.

Wilkinson, S., and G. Hough. 1996. Lies as narrative truth in abused adopted adolescents. *Psychoanalytic Study of the Child* 51:580–96.

Winnicott, D. W. 1948. Children's hostels in war and peace. *British Journal of Medical Psychology* 21:175–80.

———. 1958. *The maturational process and the facilitating environment*. London: Hogarth Press.

Wittenberg, I., and E. Nemeny. 1999. Ending therapy. *Journal of Child Psychotherapy* 25:339–56.

Wolfenstein, M. 1966. How is mourning possible? *Psychoanalytic Study of the Child* 21:93–123.

York, C., et al. 1990. The development and functioning of the sense of shame. *Psychoanalytic Study of the Child* 45:377–410.

Index

Note: Page numbers in *italic* type indicate figures.

abandonment, as play theme, 82–84
Ablon, S. L., 37, 261
abuse: disclosure of, 239–40; meaning given to, 238; shame as by-product of, 30, 67–69
accidents, interpretation of, 26–27
action: displacement of anger through play, 91–110; play versus, 4, 36–37, 91–92, 114
administration, conduct of clinic, 216
adoption fantasies, 60–61
affect: expression and modulation of, 230–35; recognition of, 223, *227*, *228*, 229; therapist's reflection of, 245–46
aggressive behavior: calming activities for, 135–38; depth of, 20; expression through play of, 91–110; gratification from, 124–25, 287–88; language ability and, 217–18; loss of feelings through, 125; neurobiological basis for, 288; physical punishment and, 14; purpose of, 1. *See also* anger
alienation, child development and, 7–8
Allen, F. H., 309
anal-sadistic stage, 93
anger: anger balloon, 97–98; anger bucket, 96–97; anger thermometer,

105–7; displacement of, steps to, 118–19; displacement of, through drawing, 98–107; displacement of, through play, 91–98; range of, 218–19; reemergence of, 296–97; strategies for defusing, 107. *See also* aggressive behavior; rage
anger balloon, 97–98
anger bucket, 96–97
anger management training, 71, 77, 110
anger thermometer, 105–7
angry unwillingness, 60
antisocial behavior: outside therapy, 53–55; purpose of, 12. *See also* aggressive behavior
anxiety: autism and, 84; displacement and, 92; management of, 284–88; posttraumatic play and, 240; transformation of, 22
art: Empathy Picture and Story Series, 207–11; films, 211, 281. *See also* drawing
assertive training, 71, 205–7
attachment, 303
attention statements, 11, 145–46
autism, 84

autonomy, child development and, 7
autosphere, 86, 92, 126

babies, unattended, 114
Basket of Feelings, 218–21
battle play, 122–24
bed wetting, 6
behavior: controlling, limits on, 42–45;
    destructive, limits on, 37–42; feelings
    versus, 31
binding, as defense, 129, 172, 193,
    233–34
Bion, W. R., 34
Blass, R. B., 7
Blatt, S. J., 7
Block, Dorothy, 16–17, 117, 151
board games, 135, 260
"boat in the storm" drawing, 177–83,
    178–81
Bobo (punching bag), 122
body. *See* autosphere; self-injurious
    behavior
Bonime, Walter, 3, 20, 32, 34, 35, 60,
    172, 202, 271
Bonovitz, Christopher, 44–45
Bowlby, J., 7
boxes, 96
boys, expression of feelings by, 193
brain injuries, 14, 56
brain responses to trauma, 236
bricks, cardboard, 95–96
brief therapy, 309
broken things, as play theme, 89–90
Brooks, B., 16
Brown, Chris, 302

calming activities, 135–38
"calming scene" drawing, 136, *137*
charades, about feelings, 229
child as client: aims of therapy for,
    21–35; characteristics of, in normal
    latency period, 170–71; characteristics
    of well-adjusted, 302; dependency of,
    289–93; evaluation of, 301–2;
    expectations of, 2–4; fragmented

personality of, 71–72; highlighting
    strengths of, 15–16; knowledge of, 15,
    51, 164–65, 241–42, 286–87; and peer
    partners for therapy, 52–53; positive
    qualities of, 16; psychodynamics of,
    6–10; relationship with therapist of,
    11–16, 52–53, 163–66, 271–72,
    289–91, 296–97, 300; remaining in
    abusive situation, 186; respect for, 15;
    revelations from, 286–87; termination
    initiated by, 300; and termination of
    therapy, 298–313; therapeutic alliance
    formation with, 11–16; therapy stages
    for, 283–98
child development: Erikson on, 7–8;
    shortcomings in, 6–7
choices, child's understanding of, 32–33
Clapton, Eric, 187
clay, 93–94
clients. *See* child as client
Cohen, D. J., 26, 183
Cohen, Jonathan, 115
collections, 134–35
"color your life" drawing, 189–93, *191*
Color-Coded Time Line, 278–81, *279*
compartmentalization, as defense, 129,
    172, 193, 233–34
compliance with adults, 205
compromise, teaching, 99
compulsion: child's feelings about,
    14–15; and repetitive play, 51–52,
    240–41, 288
concrete skill building, 71
conflict resolution, 288–89
conflicts, child's perception of source of,
    2–4
conscience, development of, 120
consequences, child's understanding of,
    32–33
control, as play theme, 79–80
controlling behaviors, 42–45
coping approach, 70–75; goals of, 71;
    invitational approach versus, 62–64,
    64
Coppolillo, Henry, 167–68

counseling, 297–98
countertransference, 34–35, 61
Crenshaw, D. A., 77, 193
crisis counselors, 47
Crowley, R. J., 172, 199
cultural sensitivity, 204

Davidson, P., 96
daydreaming, aggression and, 136
death: funerals and memorial services,
    264–65; of parent, 255–56; of sibling,
    260. *See also* mourning
decision grid for therapeutic approaches,
    64, 74
defenses, 126–40; adjustment of, 33;
    approaches to developing, 127;
    binding, 129, 172, 193, 233–34;
    compartmentalization, 129, 172, 193,
    233–34; development of, 132–34,
    139–40; displacement, 91–125;
    dissociation, 31, 72, 128–29, 131;
    distancing, 91–125; externalization,
    160; grandiosity, 27–28, 131;
    identification with the aggressor, 81,
    287–88; inadequate, 126, 171;
    interpretation of, 139, 148–50,
    152–55; mature versus primitive, 127,
    128, 132–34, 138–39; negativism,
    131–32, 289–93; rationalization, 134;
    reaction formation, 82, 134–35;
    rewarding mature, 138–39; splitting,
    72, 120, 128–29; sublimation, 134–35;
    undoing, 132–33
defiance, 59–60
Demos, E. V., 8
denial of loss, 267–75
dependency, 289–93
depression, 32
deprivation, as play theme, 86–88
destructive behaviors, 37–42
deviant mental organization, 115, 175
Diamond, Neil, 33
discipline, after parent's death, 255
displacement: action-oriented approach
    to, 109–10; through drawing, 98–107;

in early treatment, 81; through play,
    91–98; steps to, 118–19; techniques
    for development of, 111–25; violent
    fantasies and, 107–9
dissociation, 31, 72, 128–29, 131
distancing: action-oriented approach
    to, 109–10; through drawing,
    98–107; excessive, 120; through
    play, 91–98; techniques for
    development of, 111–25; violent
    fantasies and, 107–9
distortion of reality, 22–23, 69
divorce, 273
Dolan, Yvonne, 268
dominance, as play theme, 79–80
doubt, child development and, 7
dragons, 103, 105, *106*
dramatic play, loss and, 261–62
"draw the problem," 198–99, *199*
drawing, 169–203; anger thermometer,
    105–7; "boat in the storm," 177–83,
    178–81; as bridge to play, 171; child
    reaction to, 176; "color your life,"
    189–93, *191*; dragons, 103, 105, *106*;
    "draw the problem," 198–99, *199*;
    encouragement of, 171, 175; "family
    doing something together," 183–87,
    185; interpretation of, 172; "magic
    key," 193–96, *195*; mourning
    through, 262–63, 275–77; Party Hats
    on Monsters, 268–69; "safe place,"
    187–89, *188*; spontaneous, 171–75;
    storms, 103, *104*; strategies for
    displacement of anger through,
    98–107; techniques for revealing,
    176–203; volcanoes, 99–103, *100*,
    102; "worst experience," 199–202,
    201; "your place," 196–98, *197*
dreams, children's relation of, 12
Drewes, A., 122, 221, 223
drives, control of, 301
duo therapy, 52
dynamic interpretations, 142–45
economic hardship, 87, 124, 183
ego resources, for facing trauma, 71

Ekstein, Rudolph, 30, 132
elective mutism, 45
emotions. *See* feelings
empathetic interpretations, 142–44
empathy: development of, 123, 207;
   empathetic interpretations, 142–44;
   Empathy Picture and Story Series,
   207–11; film clips, 211; in play
   situations, 123; practice for, 211–14;
   significance of, 11, 125, 207–14
Empathy Picture and Story Series,
   207–11, *208, 209, 210*
empowerment play, 231–32
entitlement, feelings of, 32, 54–55
Epstein, Richard, 44
Erikson, Erik, 7, 86, 126, 284
Esman, A. H., 301
expectations of clients, 2–4
explanation, excessive, 43
externalization, 160–63

Fabricius, Julia, 300
"fair trial" exercise, 123
"family doing something together"
   drawing, 183–87, *185*
family therapy for mourning, 265–66
fantasy: communication through, 142;
   reality and, in play, 112–13; as response
   to play materials, 23; steps to, 4, 51;
   violent fantasies, 107–9. *See also* play
feelings: Affect Recognition and Story
   Series, 223, *227, 228*, 229; Basket of
   Feelings, 218–21; charades involving,
   229; child's understanding of, 31–32;
   drawings as revealing, 177; empathetic
   interpretations and, 142–44;
   expression and modulation of,
   230–35; failure to express, 193;
   Gingerbread Person/Feelings Map,
   221, *222, 224–25*; identification of,
   218–29; incapacity for, 125; language
   and, 217–29; limits on expression of,
   5; range of, 231–32; therapist on
   client's, 11, 245–46
Feelings Map, 221, 223, *226*

Fenichel, O., 127
films: empathy exercises using, 211; loss
   addressed with, 281
Fineman, Jo Ann, 114
Fischer, K. W., 72
flashbacks, 169
food: play involving, 86–89; requesting,
   from therapist, 43
Fox, L., 205
fractionation, 72
Fraiberg, Selma, 256
Frankel, N. R., 301
Freud, Anna, 34, 127
Freud, Sigmund, 163, 249
friendship, 52, 205
frozen inaction, 68, 94, 110, 241, 293
funerals, 264–65
Furman, Erna, 255

Gaensbauer, T. J., 65–67, 69–70
games: as defense against anxiety, 135;
   and loss, 261; rule-governed, 260
Garbage Bag Technique for feeling
   modulation, 233–34
Garcia, J. A., 300
Gardner, Richard, 51, 119, 274
Garritt, Pam, 77, 207
generalization, 160
Gil, E., 131, 241
Gilligan, C., 72
Gingerbread Person, 221, *222, 224–25*
girls, expression of feelings by, 193, 196
Gitelson, Maxwell, 107
gorilla suits: protective armor versus,
   204–5; psychodynamics connected
   with, 6–10; purpose of, 1; symptoms
   associated with, 14–15. *See also* child
   as client
grandiosity, 27–28, 131
Green, Viviane, 300
grief. *See* mourning
Gruber, Carolyn, 301
guilt: child development and, 7;
   definition of, 123; play indications of,
   123; as play theme, 85–86

Hailparn, Diane, 300
Hailparn, Michael, 300
hallucinations, babies', 114
Hard Ball (film), 281
Hardy, Kenneth, 13, 20, 183, 211, 218, 274, 278
Havens, L., 73
healing, play symbols of, 89–90
helping: encouragement of play, 124; resistance of child to, 10
hide-and-seek, 261
Hobday, A., 183
Holder, Max, 166
holocaust victims, 237
hope: after loss, 275; development of, 34, 78; food as symbol of, 89; healing as symbol of, 89–90; therapeutic signs of, 89
Horn, T., 98
hospitalization, during trauma treatment, 244
Hudak, D., 119
humor: displacement of anger through, 95; limit-setting with, 41–42

identification: with the aggressor, 81, 287–88; progress in, 301
ignorant interrogator, 51
illness, as play theme, 89–90
impulse control, stages of, 132
industry, child development and, 7–8
inferiority, child development and, 7–8
initiative, child development and, 7
insight, 168
intentions, clarification of, 26–27
interpretation, 141–68; advanced concepts in, 156–68; aims of, 142; anxiety-producing, 126–27; child's acceptance of, 156–60, 167; confusing play and, 8–10, 24–25; of defenses, 139, 148–50, 152–55; of drawings, 172; dynamic, 142–45; elementary concepts in, 141–55; empathetic, 142–44; within the metaphor, 151–52; premature, 11, 234–35;

preparation for, 145–48; process of, 150–51; in psychoanalysis, 142; reluctance to use, 141–42; role of, 141–55; of transference, 163–66; of wishes, 166–68; wording of, 152–55, 249
introspection, 2–4. *See also* self-reflection
invisible wounds, attention to, 13–15
invitational approach, 65–70; coping approach versus, 62–64, *64*; guiding principle of, 65; preparation for, 65; working-through stage of, 65

James, Beverly, 64, 70, 77, 230, 232, 233–34, 238
Jernberg, A. M., 113
"Jose and Pete on the Mountain," 307, 310–13
journal writing, mourning through, 263
judgment: capacity for, 22–26; choices and, 32–33

Kaersvang, Lynn, 169
Kaufman, Irving, 29
King, C. H., 14
Klein, Beatrice, 301
Klein, Melanie, 85–86, 107, 163
Klorer, P. G., 172

labeling of feelings, 54
Landreth, Gary, 39, 93, 121–22
language: aggressive behavior and, 217–18; and expression of feelings, 217–29. *See also* verbalization
Laszloffy, T., 211
learning disabilities, 56
Leon, John, 107
Leonetti, Jennifer, 95
Levy, D., 119
Lewis, Melvin, 146
likability, 205
limits: on adoption fantasies, 60–61; on behavior outside therapy, 53–55; on comparing therapists, 55–56; on controlling behaviors, 42–45; on

defiance, 59–60; on destructive behaviors, 37–42; on dilution of therapy relationship, 52–53; on distracting institutional practices, 57–58; on efforts to anger, 49–50; on emotional expression, 5; firmness in setting, 39–40; humorous, 41–42; in later therapy phases, 59–61; necessity in play therapy for, 36; on perseveration, 56–57; on physical involvement, 45–48; on projections, 51; purpose of, 40, 48, 58–59; on seductiveness, 50–51; silent, 41; on therapy settings, 36–37; on unproductive play, 51–52

limit-testing, 38

The Lion King (film), 173, 211, 281

Lister, E. D., 240

loss: conflicted relationships and, 270–72; denial of, 267–75; divorce and, 273; finding meaning after, 275; insecure attachments and, 272; intangible, 267–82; mourning, 255–82; perspective on, 275; play concerning, 84–85, 258–62; structured activities to address, 262–66, 275–82; tangible, 255–66; termination of therapy and, 302–4

lying, 55

mad game, 96

"magic key" drawing, 193–96, *195*

magic markers, 97

masking symbols: mechanism of, 112; purpose of, 111

mastery approach. *See* invitational approach

Mayes, L. C., 26

McGrory, Virginia, 95, 97

meaning: abuse and, 238; after loss, 275; need for, 33–34

mechanisms of restraint, 134–35

medication, during trauma treatment, 244

memorial services, 264–65

memory: Color-Coded Time Line, 278–81, *279*; distortion of, 23; implicit versus explicit, 202–3; loss and, 275; memory books, 262–63, 277–78; play and, 116; screen memories, 169–70; thought in relation to, 23; trauma and, 115–17

memory books, 262–63, 277–78

Miller, Alice, 125

Mills, Joyce, 172, 199, 268

Minuchin, Salvador, 32

Mitchel, S. A., 3

monsters, psychic role of, 30

Moore, Terence, 112

Mora, George, 217

moral development, 120

motivations: clarification of, 26–27; therapist's reflections of, 246

mourning, 255–82; family therapy and, 265–66; intangible losses, 267–82; play and, 258–62; process of, 256–57; structured activities to aid, 262–66, 275–82; tangible losses, 255–66; time factor in, 257–58

Muir, Elisabeth, 265

multiple personality disorder, 131

mutism, 45

mutuality, child development and, 7–8

negativism, as defense, 131–32, 289–93

negotiation, teaching, 99

neurobiology, and aggression, 288

newspapers, tearing up, 94

nightmares, 251

Nilsson, May, 125

nurturance: child's need for, 88–89; parents' need for, 81

Oaklander, Violet, 177–83, 196

objects, requesting or taking of, 42–43

O'Connor, Kevin, 124, 141–42, 189, 246

Ollier, K., 183

Ordinary People (film), 211, 281

parents: child's moral image of, 120, 297; control by children of, 2; death of, 255–56; divorce of, 273; and mourning, 265–66; needy, 81, 162; role in therapy of, 2; single, 2; termination of therapy by, 300
Parsons, Marianne, 61
Party Hats on Monsters, 268–69
patients. *See* child as client
Pavor Nocturnes, 251
peek-a-boo, 261
peer therapy, 52
Pelcovitz, D., 94, 186
Perry, Bruce, 214, 288
perseveration, 56–57
perspective: development of, 30–31; on traumatic events, 275
photograph album metaphor for therapy, 172
photographs, mourning and, 263–64
physical problems, 14
physical punishment, 14
physical restraint of child, 45–48
physiological response to trauma, 236
Piaget, Jean, 298
Pipp, S. L., 72
play: action versus, 4, 36–37, 91–92, 114; battles in, 122–24; benefits of, 114; communication through, 142; development mirrored in, 8; displacement and distancing through, 91–125; emotional range of, 112–13; fantasy and reality in, 112–13; hallucinations of babies and, 114; and memory, 116; obstacles to, 113–14, 126, 232; posttraumatic, 240–41; productive, 293–97; therapeutic relationship shown through, 16–18; underdevelopment of, 4; unproductive, 51–52, 240–41, 288; violent, 287–88. *See also* fantasy; play themes; play therapy
play materials: aggression-releasing, 121–23; clay, 93–94; destructible, 93; fantasy as response to, 23. *See also* games; puppet play

play themes, 79–90; abandonment and rejection, 82–84; control, dominance, and power, 79–80; deprivation, 86–88; guilt and shame, 85–86; healing symbols in, 89–90; need for nurturance, 88–89; separation and loss, 84–85; threat, 81–82
play therapy: aims of, 21–35; approaches in, 62–78; case example of, 18–20; child's expectations of, 2–4; confusion in, 8–9; decision grid for approaches in, *64*, 74; first sessions of, 286–87; invitational approach to trauma and, 65; role of, 2, 4–5, 17; setting for, 36–37; timing and pacing of, 234–35; verbalization in, 5–6; winding-down activities for, 94. *See also* play; play themes; process of play therapy; termination of therapy; therapeutic alliance
poems, mourning through, 263
post-traumatic stress disorder (PTSD), 14
power, as play theme, 79–80
preverbal concepts, 115
problem solving: drawing used for, 99, 103, 105; teaching, 99
problems, drawing, 198–99
process of play therapy, 283–98; anxiety management, 284–88; beginning of, 283–84; conflict resolution, 288–89; counseling about present concerns, 297–98; productive play, 293–97
projections of clients, 51
projective communication, 87
Projective Drawing Series, 176–203
projective identification, 161–63
Proskauer, S., 307
pro-social skills. *See* social skills training
psychoanalysis, 142
psychodrama, as play, 233
psychodynamics of aggressive children, 6–10
punching bags, 122
punishment: child's need for, 85–86; child's sense of, 112; physical, 14

puppet play, 287
puzzles, 135

rage, 124–25. *See also* anger
rationalization, as defense, 134
reaction formation, 82, 134–35
reality testing, 301
Re-Create the World, 277
reductive statements, 146–47
regression: destructive behaviors and, 37–38; inadequate defenses and, 126; progress disguised as, 138; termination of therapy and, 302; trauma confrontation and, 62–63
Reiser, L. W., 263
rejection, as play theme, 82–84
relationships: with caregivers, 33; child's understanding of, 160; conflicted, and loss, 270–72. *See also* social skills training; therapeutic alliance
repetition compulsion in play, 51–52, 240–41, 288
repression, 63, 128
rescue behaviors, 124
rescue fantasies, 44, 61
respect, for child by therapist, 15
restraint of child, 45–48
risk-taking, professional, 19
ritualistic behavior, 14–15
role-playing, 206
Rosenfeld, E., 301
rules, 260. *See also* limits
Russell, Bertrand, 168

sadism: anal-sadistic stage, 93; fantasies involving, 107; in play therapy, 287–88
"safe place" drawing, 187–89, *188*
safety. *See* security
Samuels, Shirley, 304–5
Sarnoff, C. A., 134, 175
Scared Silent (film), 211
scheduling play therapy, 57–58
school: therapy problems in, 46–47; therapy scheduling in, 57–58

screen memories, 169–70
secondary trauma, 239–40
security: after parent's death, 255; of attachment, and separation, 272; child's testing to determine, 1–2; client's lack of, 84–85; therapeutic creation of, 73; trauma treatment and, 236, 240
seductive behavior of clients, 50–51, 290–92
Seebourne, Barbara, 206
selective mutism, 45
self: fragmented, 71–72, 120; high ideals for, 27–28; as organizing structure, 8. *See also* emotions; *terms beginning with* self-
self-assertion, 71, 205–7
self-blame, 28, 68
self-concept, 67
self-image, 29, 31
self-injurious behavior, 14, 86
self-love, 28
self-reflection, 11. *See also* introspection
self-understanding, 27–30
separation: as play theme, 84–85; significance of, 303
sexual abuse. *See* abuse
sexuality, and behavior of clients, 50–51, 290–92
shame: as by-product of abuse, 30, 67–69; child development and, 7; definition of, 123; play indications of, 123; as play theme, 85–86
Shenken, Leon, 107
siblings, death of, 260
sickness, as play theme, 89–90
Siegel, Daniel, 202–3
silence: as controlling behavior, 44–45; limit-setting with, 41
silent bond, 239–40
Silvern, Louise, 169
Singer, Jerome, 136, 217
situational statements, 147–48
sleep disturbances, 14, 251
Smilansky, S., 113

social competence. *See* social skills training
social skills training, 71, 76–77, 204–16;
    cultural sensitivity in, 204; for
    empathy, 207–14; likability, 205; self-
    assertion, 71, 205–7
socioeconomic hardship, 87, 124, 183
soliloquy technique, 262
songs, mourning through, 263
spanking, 14
Speirs, Ann, 265
Sperling, M., 251
splitting, as defense, 72, 120, 128–29
staff, therapist relations with, 215–16
Stand by Me (film), 211, 281
Stern, D., 218
Stern, Marcia, 77
The Stone Boy (film), 211, 281
storm pictures, 103, *104*
Strauss, Martha, 77
strengths, personality, 15–16, 131
stress balls, 94
"strong container" drawing, 129, *130*
sublimation, 134–35, 288
Sugar, Max, 246–51
suicidal impulses, 244
superheroes/villains, 231–32
symbols. *See* masking symbols
symptoms: of aggressive children, 14–15;
    trauma uncovering and worsening of,
    65–67

Talk Show Interview, 306
Talking, Doing, Feeling Game, 274
Talmadge, Max, 217
Tavistock Clinic, 34
termination of therapy, 298–313;
    circumstances of, 299–300;
    countdown to, 308; evaluation
    regarding, 301–2; final conversation
    before, 309; and loss, 302–4; planning
    sessions before, 309; process of,
    302–3; regression prior to, 302;
    rehearsals for, 304–5; repression from
    early, 63; techniques for, 305–7
Terr, L., 125, 238, 241

Tessman, Lora, 29
therapeutic alliance: countertransference
    and, 34–35; formation of, 11–16;
    problems in formation of, 12–13;
    significance of, 10–11; signs of
    developing, 16–18; termination of
    therapy and, 300
therapeutic holds, 47–48
therapists: adoption fantasies involving,
    60–61; aims of, 21–35; and anxiety
    over treatment, 202; attempts to
    control, 42–45; child-directed play
    involving, 152; client comparisons of,
    55–56; client expectations of, 3; client
    relations, 6–18, 52–53, 271–72,
    289–91, 296–97, 300; and
    countertransference, 34–35, 61; efforts
    to anger, 49–50; empathy of, 213,
    215–16; ideal behavior of, 5, 49;
    ineffective, 77–78, 213, 234–35, 300;
    inexperienced, 46, 52, 170, 172, 272,
    303; limit-setting by, 36–61; physical
    restraint by, 45–48; risk-taking by, 19;
    seductive behavior toward, 50–51; and
    silent clients, 44–45, 53; soliloquy
    technique of, 262; and staff relations,
    215–16; support for, 215–16; therapy
    for, 271; and transference, 163–66;
    trauma of child experienced by, 125.
    See also interpretation
threat, as play theme, 81–82
time lines, 275, 278–81
Todd, Ginny, 265
toys. *See* play materials
transference, 163–66; and
    countertransference, 34–35, 61
trauma: cues concerning, 241–45;
    disclosure of cause of, 239–40; frozen
    inaction and, 68, 94, 110, 241, 293;
    and loss of ideal parent, 19; meaning
    given to, 238; memory and, 115–16;
    physiological response to, 236; and
    posttraumatic play, 240–41; purpose
    of facing, 237–38, 240; reenactment
    of, 125, 236–54, 293–97; secondary,

239–40; symptoms of, 14; therapeutic approaches to, 62–78, 234–35; triggering of, 252–54; working through, 65, 202–3
trust: child development and, 7; developing, 307–8; healing role of, 20
Types I and II Pavor Nocturnes, 251

undoing, as defense, 132–33

van der Kolk, B. A., 68
verbalization: of anger, 105, 107; and excessive explanation, 43; facilitating, 5–6; during limit-setting, 40–41; overreliance on, 41; of violent fantasies, 107–9. *See also* language
victims, child's rage at, 124–25. *See also* empathy
videotapes: empathy exercises using, 211; feeling modulation using, 233; loss addressed with, 281

violence: fantasies involving, 107–9; in play therapy, 287–88
voices, hearing, 109
volcano pictures, 99–103, *100, 102*
vulnerability, aggressive behavior and, 1

wall, knocking down, 95–96
wastebasket, yelling into, 95
Weisz, J. R., 300
wild analysis, 149
Winnicott, D. W., 34, 272
wishes, 166–68
working through trauma, 65, 202–3
"worst experience" drawing, 199–202, *201*
wounds: attention to, 13–15; as play theme, 89–90

Year Book, 306–7
"your place" drawing, 196–98, *197*

About the Authors

David A. Crenshaw, Ph.D., ABPP, RPT-S, is currently in private practice in Rhinebeck, New York, and is director of the Rhinebeck Child and Family Center, LLC, www.rhinebeckcfc.com. He was formerly clinical director at the Rhinebeck Country School and the Astor Home for Children, both residential treatment centers for emotionally disturbed children located in Rhinebeck. For close to twenty years, he was also director of the Astor Home's doctoral-level psychology internship program, which is accredited by the American Psychological Association. He has authored numerous professional publications and book chapters on issues related to grief, abuse, and trauma in children and is the author of *Bereavement: Counseling the Grieving throughout the Life Cycle* and *A Guidebook for Engaging Resistant Children in Therapy: A Projective Drawing and Storytelling Series.* He is registered by the Association of Play Therapy as a play therapist–supervisor and is currently president of the New York Association of Play Therapy.

John B. Mordock, Ph.D., ABPP, was employed by the Astor Home for Children for twenty-eight years. In his last position, he directed the agency's community mental health programs, helping to develop a full continuum of services for emotionally disturbed children and their families. Before that time, he was coordinator of research at the Devereux Foundation in Devon, Pennsylvania. He is the author of twelve books, including a textbook on exceptional children, and has a chapter in *The Handbook of Child and Adolescent Psychiatry.* Dr. Mordock is a fellow of the American Psychological Association. His numerous writings on topics of play therapy and abused and traumatized children have appeared over the past forty years in many highly respected journals.

Both authors are board certified by the American Board of Professional Psychology.